The Rose

The Rose

A TRUE HISTORY

Jennifer Potter

Atlantic Books
London

First published in hardback in Great Britain in 2010 by Callisto and Atlantic Books, imprints of Atlantic Books Ltd.

This reissued hardback edition published in Great Britain in 2011.

Lines from *Anacreontea* reprinted by permission of the publishers and Trustees of the Loeb Classical Library from *Greek Lyric: Volume II*, Loeb Classical Library Volume 143, edited and translated by David A. Campbell, p.107, Cambridge, Mass.: Harvard University Press, Copyright © 1988 by the President and Fellows of Harvard College. Loeb Classical Library ® is a registered trademark of the President and Fellows of Harvard College; lines reprinted by permission of the publishers and Trustees of the Loeb Classical Library from *On Agriculture: Volume III* (*De Re Rustica*) by Columella, Loeb Classical Library Volume 408, translated by E. S. Forster and Edward H. Heffner, Cambridge, Mass.: Harvard University Press, Copyright © 1955 by the President and Fellows of Harvard College. Loeb Classical Library ® is a registered trademark of the President and Fellows of Harvard College; lines from 'Burnt Norton' in *Four Quartets* by T. S. Eliot, T. S. Eliot © 1944 reproduced by permission of Faber & Faber for the author; 'Red Rose' by Forough Farrokhzad reproduced with permission from *Modern Persian Poetry*, edited and translated by Mahmud Kianush (Rockingham Press, 1996); lines quoted from *The Hafez Poems of Gertrude Bell* by Shirazi Hafez (Author), Gertrude Bell (Translator), courtesy of Ibex Publishers; Rainer Maria Rilke, excerpt from 'The Roses', translated by A. Poulin, Jr., from *The Complete French Poems of Rainer Maria Rilke*. Copyright © 1979, 1982, 1984, 1986 by A. Poulin, Jr. Reprinted with the permission of Graywolf Press, Minneapolis, Minnesota, www.graywolfpress.org; lines quoted from *The Mystical Poems of Rumi* by Jalal al-Din Rumi translated from the Persian by A. J. Arberry, annotated and prepared by Hasan Javadi, general editor: Ehsan Yarshater. Poems 1–200 and notes © 1968 by A. J. Arberry. Poems 201–400 and notes © 1979 by Ehsan Yarshater. Combined and corrected edition © 2009 by the University of Chicago. Reproduced with permission from the University of Chicago Press; lines quoted from *If Not Winter: Fragments of Sappho* edited by Anne Carson, reprinted with permission from Virago, an imprint of Little, Brown Book Group; lines from 'Rosa sancta' in *Tender Taxes* by Jo Shapcott, Jo Shapcott © 2001 reproduced by permission of Faber & Faber for the author; lines quoted from *Hortulus* by Walahfrid Strabo and translated by Raef Payne, reprinted with permission from the Hunt Institute for Botanical Documentation, Carnegie Mellon University, Pittsburgh, PA; lines from *Death and Burial in the Roman World* by J. M. C. Toynbee. © 1971 J. M. C. Toynbee. Reprinted by kind permission of Thames & Hudson Ltd., London.

The author and publisher wish to thank the following for permission to quote from manuscripts in their collections: Board of Trustees of the Royal Botanic Gardens, Kew; British Library; Dumbarton Oaks Research Library and Collection; Linnean Society of London.

Every effort has been made to trace or contact all copyright holders. The publishers will be pleased to make good any omissions or rectify any mistakes brought to their attention at the earliest opportunity.

1 3 5 7 9 10 8 6 4 2

A CIP catalogue record for this book is available from the British Library.

ISBN: 978 184887 8341

Set in 11/14.5pt Esta
Designed by Nicky Barneby @ Barneby Ltd
Picture research by Charlotte Lippmann
Map and family tree by Martin Lubikowski and Nicky Barneby
Printed in China

Atlantic Books
An imprint of Atlantic Books Ltd
Ormond House
26–27 Boswell Street
London
WC1N 3JZ

www.atlantic-books.co.uk

In memory of Pat Kavanagh

I ask the rose, 'From whom did you steal that beauty?'
The rose laughs softly out of shame, but how should she tell?

JALAL-AL-DIN RUMI

Contents

Roses of East and West

The Useful Rose

Modern Times

List of Illustrations

Preface

I remember the day I first lost my heart to a rose. A British magazine had asked me to write a brief history of antique roses, and so I found myself one blisteringly hot day in early June travelling to Norfolk to interview Peter Beales, one of Britain's best-loved rose-growers. Then in his late sixties, he met me courteously in the café at his nursery wearing an old-fashioned straw boater and bright red braces, every bit the English gentleman.

Our talk ranged over flowers and history, and at the end I asked him to name his ten favourite roses. Virtually all have found their way into this book, their names redolent of blushing maidens and rambling rectors, of long-dead painters whose fame lingers on in the naming of a rose, of mysteries and romance.* Armed with my host's helpful introductions, I wandered the nursery on my own, looking each rose straight in the eye to make its proper acquaintance.

One in particular intrigued me: the pure white Damask 'Madame Hardy', which had something I had never noticed before: a fresh green eye surrounded by petals that fold inwards, as if deliberately exposing itself to your gaze. Alexandre Hardy, I recalled (falsely, it turned out), had gardened for Napoleon's first wife, the Empress Josephine, reputedly

*The ten roses are: the candy-striped *Rosa gallica* 'Versicolor' (Rosa Mundi); the blush-pink Alba 'Great Maiden's Blush'; the pure white Damask 'Madame Hardy'; the velvety Gallica 'Tuscany Superb'; the climbing Tea rose 'Gloire de Dijon'; the bright crimson Moss rose 'Henri Martin'; the vigorous Noisette 'Madame Alfred Carrière'; the highly fragrant Bourbon 'Madame Isaac Pereire'; the musk-scented Multiflora Rambler 'Rambling Rector'; and the luscious Centifolia 'Fantin-Latour'.

*Heinrich Arnz's 1838 lithograph of the Damask rose 'Madame Hardy'
attests to its immediate popularity. The breeder in 1832 was Alexandre Hardy of the
Luxembourg Gardens in Paris, who named it after his wife.*

one of the world's great rose-lovers. As well as its beauty, the rose he named after his wife had a heady Damask scent and came with a history I wanted to explore.

When the idea of a book about the rose was first suggested, I hesitated nonetheless, aware even then of the enormity of the task. So many words had already been dedicated to this 'Queen of Flowers' – did we really need a whole lot more? The rose is loved by so many and has rooted itself so deeply in our culture that I knew I would be treading dangerous ground. For a time I prevaricated, but 'Madame Hardy' had inspired my curiosity: what was it about this pure white rose that I found so beguiling? Was it beauty or culture? Was it her direct appeal to the senses, or was it the stories that lay behind that unblinking green eye?

The challenge was too great to resist, yet the more I looked into the rose, the less I felt I knew and the more I needed to unravel. While I was simply wrong about Hardy's imperial connections (he took over the Luxembourg's rose garden a little after Josephine's time), the Empress Josephine was not quite the rose-lover conventional history would have us believe. The rose has a knack of engendering myths that pass like a virus from one writer to the next until they are accepted as fact. Josephine's desire to plant at Malmaison every known variety of rose is one such myth that infects virtually every account of the rose. Another is the credit given to the West's crusading knights for bringing back the rose from the Holy Land (the Gallica rose by some accounts, the Damask by others). The truth is both more complicated and more interesting, and while such embellishments form part of the story, it is necessary – as far as it is possible – to separate myth from reality.

And so I threw away the book I had been planning and embarked instead on a work of detection. You will find here two interlinked stories: on the one hand, the development of the garden rose from its origins as a wild briar of the northern hemisphere, and on the other the rose's wider cultural resonances. Both stories concern transformations: physical transformations as the rose came in from the wild, and cultural transformations as its meanings subtly shifted. Representing at once the blood of Christ's passion and the sweat of Muhammad's brow, the rose succeeded in transforming itself from the venal rose of Roman pagans to the Marian rose of Christian iconography and the legitimizing emblem of the Tudor monarchs of England and Wales; and it remains today a symbol of both purity and passion. How it achieved such metamorphoses became my field of enquiry, without losing sight of the botanical rose which has experienced some equally startling transitions of its own.

My aim has been to uncover why the rose exerts such a powerful fascination for so many people in so many parts of the world. No other flower comes close. The popularity of one flower or another may flare more brightly for a time – think of tulip mania in the seventeenth century and the dahlia's rapid ascendancy in the nineteenth – but no other flower has insinuated itself quite so tenaciously into the consciousness – and the gardens – of so many ages and so many cultures.

While the story of the rose provides a strong narrative, this is a book you can enter at will, taking the chapters in any order you choose. The book is organized into five main sections. 'Origins' looks at where the rose came from, and the ancient cultures that first gave it prominence. 'The Symbolic Rose' takes its story from the flower's absorption into Christian iconography, its sexualization in the *Roman de la Rose,* and its adoption by the strange brotherhood of the Rosicrucians. 'Europe's Old Roses' presents vignettes of the developing rose in the gardens of Shakespeare's florist, John Gerard, and his contemporaries, and in the canvases of the Dutch Old Masters, and it hunts for roses in Josephine's garden at Malmaison. 'Roses of East and West' traces the rose's progress in three distinct regions: China, the Middle East and North America, revealing how the rose (and its influences) travelled between them. 'The Useful Rose' tells the story of the rose in medicine and perfumery, while 'Modern Times' brings the story up to date, exploring the 'rose mania' years of frantic rose-breeding in the nineteenth and early twentieth centuries, changing fashions in the rose garden, and the 'meaning' of the rose in contemporary art and culture. 'Why the Rose?' tries to answer my original question: what is it that makes the rose so *special*?

Most chapters follow a broad chronology, but some naturally stretch backwards and forwards in time. Endnotes set out my main sources and inspiration, and indicate other lines of enquiry. The map on p. 456 tracks the rose's more important journeys, and the family tree on p. 458 attempts to make simple sense of its complicated interbreedings. You will not find here everything that has ever been discovered or written about the rose;

sometimes I simply had to draw the line, or the centre would fall apart. And inevitably this 'true' history will contain a few unreliable facts, despite my best efforts to go back to source wherever possible.

For five years now, the rose has been my life. It has been a strange experience to look at life through such a particular focus, at times exasperating but more often exhilarating. I visit an art gallery and have eyes only for the roses. I travel to a city and look first for its rose gardens. I listen to music and hear only the rose songs. I journey to a country and find roses everywhere.

Of all the places this book has taken me, I especially enjoyed my visit to the White House Rose Garden in the final months of the Bush administration, and a journey to Iran a month or so before the presidential elections of June 2009 cast the country into turmoil. The rose, as I discovered, is both inescapably political and transcends politics. I have also travelled in search of the rose to New York, Washington, Los Angeles, Paris, Malmaison, Sangerhausen in Germany, and to countless rose gardens at home and abroad. As a book like this is never properly finished, I promise myself further visits – to Professor Gianfranco Fineschi's extraordinary rose collection at Cavriglia, Italy, for instance, and to China, which began to hybridize the rose very much earlier than the West.

The roses in my own garden attest to the rose's insidious powers of seduction. When I began this book, I had only one inherited rose: the Hybrid Tea rose 'Peace', whose story is told in Chapter 17. (There was also a violently orange rose, of a type and colour I particularly dislike. While I have no memory of uprooting it, this rose has conveniently disappeared.) Successive introductions plot my growing obsession: 'Madame Hardy', of course, and the fragrant Damask rose most commonly planted in the Bulgarian rose fields, 'Kazanlik' as it is usually known. I also have Albas, Hybrid Musks, Rugosas, a solitary Hybrid Perpetual, wild roses from western China, central Asia and Iran, and am currently finding space for Gallicas and my favourite Portland. It is in truth a fairly ordinary collection and will, I know, continue to grow. And the rose in all its guises will continue to surprise me, which is why it has held my interest for so long.

London, 14 April 2010

Origins

Chapter One
A Wild Youth

G EOLOGY and geography hint at when the rose tribe first appeared. Native to the northern hemisphere only, roses grow wild between latitudes 20° and 70°, from the Tropic of Cancer right up to the Arctic Circle. As the same rose species are found dotted around the frozen north, the genus *Rosa* must have arisen after the northern and southern continental landmasses split away from each other, some 200 million years ago, but before North America separated from Eurasia, 70 million years or so later. So roses appeared on earth after the dinosaurs but long before man.

The wild rose's apparent delicacy is part of its survival strategy. Flowers are single and generally five-petalled in muted shades of white, pink and cream (exceptions include the four-petalled Himalayan *Rosa sericea,* the flaming orange-reds of the Chinese *R. moyesii* and the vibrant yellow of *R. persica*). Flowers and sometimes foliage may be faintly scented to attract pollinating insects, and stems bear sharp prickles that have aided the genus's survival, as has its ability to mate and mutate in the wild.

The rose's natural reach extends from China, Korea and Japan, up into Siberia, across much of northern and central Asia, dipping south into India, then westwards into the Caucasus, Arabia, Europe, North Africa and on to North America, from Alaska in the north down to Mexico in the south. Of the world's estimated 150 species of wild roses (botanists cannot agree on the exact number), China is home to more than half and has more endemic species than anywhere else, which partly supports its claim to be the 'distribution centre' of the entire genus. But genetic testing is beginning to unravel a different story that is much more revealing.

A true native of the northern hemisphere only, this wild Chinese rose from an unbound collection at the Royal Botanic Gardens, Kew, points to China's importance in the story of the rose.

So-called rose fossils offer further clues about the origins of the rose, although they cannot pinpoint exactly when the rose first bloomed. Fossils survive best in wet marshy areas – just the sort of conditions roses detest – and botanists need more than a few bits of plant material to identify the species or even the genus of a plant with absolute certainty. But palaeontologists in China and North America claim to have unearthed rose fossils dating back to the Eocene epoch, some 35 to 40 million years ago. Both discoveries come from the far north: China's from Fushun in Liaoning Province, 415 miles or so (668 kilometres) to the north-east of Beijing, and America's from Alaska. Later fossils show a southwards drift: to Colorado, Montana, California and Oregon in

4

North America, and the Shanwang basin of China's Shandong Province, considered one of the birthplaces of Chinese civilization, where fossils of two wild roses were discovered in 1940. Dated at 25 million years old, they were named *Rosa shanwangensis* Hu and Chaney. Rose fossils have also been found in Japan and a growing number of sites across Europe, including Hungary, Germany, Austria, Bulgaria, Bohemia, Japan, and Poland.

Unsurprisingly, the story then goes quiet for millions of years, until man learned to record and represent the world in which he lived, and the way he was moulding the environment to suit his purpose. Here again, the Chinese claim the cultivated rose as their own, pointing to China's long history of plant cultivation and hybridization, which would revolutionize European rose-breeding from the end of the eighteenth century, when cultivated China roses made their startling appearance in the West. Archaeology has certainly produced some tantalizing horticultural finds, such as 7,000-year-old potsherds engraved with designs of pot plants, excavated in subtropical Zhejiang Province bordering the East China Sea; and colourful pots and elongated basins dating from 3500 BC painted with five- and eight-petalled lotus-like flowers, unearthed in nearby Jiangsu Province, home to China's garden city of Suzhou. But Chinese evidence relating specifically to roses dates from much later; and as no early plant records or botanical texts survive, the best we can say is that China's efforts to tame the wild rose can be traced back more than 2,000 years to Wu Ti's reign (141–87 BC) in the Han Dynasty, when wild roses appeared everywhere in the gardens of the imperial palace near the ancient city of Chang'an (modern Xi'an) in central China.

For the first recorded roses we must look further west, discounting the many stylized rosettes that are more likely to represent the lotus or even the chrysanthemum. As the earliest gardens appeared in urban civilizations, it is natural to look to the Sumerians and Akkadians of ancient Mesopotamia (now southern Iraq) for the first 'gardened' roses, but again the evidence relating specifically to roses is slight. By 3300 BC, a square mile of orchards (probably date-palm groves) graced the Sumerian metropolis of Uruk, where shade mattered more than flowers and no one talks of any roses.

The rose may have appeared in cuneiform script recorded on clay tablets and buried in the royal tombs at Ur near the mouth of the Euphrates (modern Tell el-Mukayyar in Iraq), familiar from the Old Testament as the birthplace of Abraham. The excavator was the English archaeologist Sir Leonard Woolley, who introduced the British crime-writer Agatha Christie to the romance of ruins (and to her much younger second husband, Woolley's assistant Max Mallowan). The tablet mentions the rose only in connection with rosewater, and we cannot be sure that 'rose' is the correct translation. The same is true of another of Woolley's exquisite finds in the royal tombs at Ur: two near-identical gilded and bejewelled statuettes of a horned animal rearing up into a bush with golden flowers, which some have likened to roses. 'Ram in a thicket' was Woolley's name for them, alluding to the ram in Genesis 22:13 which Abraham sacrificed in place of his son Isaac. But the 'ram' is more properly a goat, and the gilded 'roses' could be any eight-petalled flower, or none in particular.

Other sightings are equally inconclusive. According to some but not all transcriptions, roses occur with the figs, vines and other plants taken as booty from the Hittites by the Akkadian overlord, Sargon I, some time after 2350 BC, and brought back to his palace at Akkad on the Euphrates.[1] Later kings also planted their parks and gardens with trees and rare plants uprooted from subdued peoples; and as roses appear in a respected work on Assyrian botany, it is tempting to slip them into the empty root-pits excavated at the temple of the New Year Festival built by the Assyrian King Sennacherib outside the walls of Ashur, Assyria's traditional capital on the Tigris. This would be wishful history, however.

For the oldest undisputed image of a rose we must travel to Crete, where roses grew wild at least 3,500 years ago, their brief flowering captured in the celebrated 'Blue Bird fresco' discovered in the 1920s by the British archaeologist Sir Arthur Evans among a stack of painted stucco fragments in the closet of a Minoan town house at Knossos. All take wild nature as their subject: birds and monkeys stalking a landscape of rocks overgrown with wild peas or vetches and what appear to be dwarf Cretan irises, blue fringed with orange and pink edged with a deep purplish green.

Painted some 3,500 years ago, the 'Blue Bird fresco' from Minoan Knossos contains the oldest undisputed image of a botanical rose, now usually identified as Rosa pulverulenta.

You can hear the frisson in Evans's voice as he explains that there among the Cretan rocks,

for the first time in Ancient Art, appears a wild rose bush, partly against a deep red and partly against a white background, and other coiling sprays of the same plant hang down from a rock-work arch above. The flowers are of a golden rose colour with orange centres dotted with deep red.

As Knossos was destroyed some time between 1470 and 1400 BC,[2] we have at last a real rose – located and dated – which should have introduced a note of certainty into the story of the rose. Yet like so much else, Evans's Cretan rose served only to compound the confusion because, instead of leaving the frescos as he found them, Evans hired a pair of Swiss artists, Émile Gilliéron *père et fils,* to 'restore' his precious findings. While Evans himself was above reproach, the Gilliérons dabbled in the murkier trade of forged Cretan antiquities. Clearly no botanist, Gilliéron *fils* added a spurious sixth petal to the roses and painted them a flat yellowish pink, thereby provoking a rash of misidentifications from the yellow-flowered *R. persica* to the Holy Rose, *R. × richardii,* and the simple dog rose, *R. canina.*

Either through carelessness or design, the Gilliérons left one corner of the fresco untouched and here, towards the lower left-hand side, you can just make out the ghost of an original rose which has escaped the restorer's brush. Twisting slightly, this rose has five overlapping petals faded to a pale pink, slightly yellowed with age and now identified as *R. pulverulenta,* a native of the eastern Mediterranean which today still flowers amid the chalky rocks of western and central Crete, fêted for its pine-scented leaves and its fine crop of hips.

One final sighting of the rose in pre-classical Greece shows its steady rise as a plant with economic value. By the end of the thirteenth century BC, when fire destroyed the palace at Pylos in the south-western Peloponnese, the rose was cultivated for its fragrance and used to scent oils for anointment or perfume. We know this from the most mundane of sources: a palace storekeeper's records of the trade in perfumed oils found amid the debris of a perfume workshop – storage jars, dippers and scoops, basins and bowls and a surprising amount of broken pottery.

The so-called 'olive oil tablets of Pylos' listed two different sorts of scented oil – rose and sage – and an astringent herb, cyperus, added at an earlier stage to make the oil receptive to their fragrance. From these bare facts – baked hard in the fire that destroyed the palace while ironically aiding their preservation – we learn a little of the elegant lives of the palace elite, who oiled their clothing with perfumed unguents to make it shiny and supple, even after washing, and who used the perfumed oils for ritual offerings and as grave goods for the dead. But of the flowers grown and harvested for such purposes we learn nothing, perhaps because the palace burnt down before the rose harvest had begun. Flowers for perfume are needed fresh and in vast quantities, so we can only imagine the rose fields of Pylos stretching far into the sun-baked landscape.

To read of roses growing in a garden we must wait until the ancient Greeks of the fifth century BC and the *Histories* of the ever-curious Herodotus, who reported roses growing wild in 'the place called the Gardens of Midas, the son of Gordias ... wonderful blooms, with sixty petals apiece, and sweeter smelling than any others in the world'.[3] Above the gardens rose Mount Bermium, 'the heights of which are so cold that none can climb them'. This detail plainly situates the gardens of the legendary King Midas in the fertile and beautiful valley surrounding Aegae in western Macedonia, home to the first Macedonian kings.

King Midas's sweet-smelling roses have travelled a long way from the simple wild rose of five single petals and the barest of scents, but in his *Histories* Herodotus cheerfully mixed fact and fabrication, so we cannot assume that he saw them for himself. To the English patient in the novel of the same name by Michael Ondaatje, Herodotus appeared like 'one of those spare men of the desert who travel from oasis to oasis, trading legends as if it is the exchange of seeds, consuming everything without suspicion, piercing together a mirage'.

The honour of first differentiating wild from cultivated roses goes to another Greek, Theophrastus, whose two great works on plants have survived virtually intact. Born in Eressos on the island of Lesbos *c*.371 BC, Theophrastus travelled and worked with Aristotle, taking over his school when Aristotle fled Athens after the death of Alexander the Great, another of Aristotle's pupils. Aristotle died of a stomach complaint a few months later, leaving Theophrastus his books and his garden in the Lyceum. It was here that the first systematic botanist of the western world made many of his observations, supplemented by reports from the scientifically trained observers who had followed Alexander's conquest eastwards to the Punjab and the end of the known world.

Theophrastus was by all accounts a livelier lecturer than he was a writer; his observations on plants read like the notes he might have put together for his lectures. Displaying the habits of a born taxonomist, he was especially concerned to establish similarities and difference – between wild and tamed roses, for instance, and between roses and the other sorts of wild shrubs he examined (buckthorn, withy, Christ's thorn, bramble, sumach, ivy and the spindle tree). What is a plant's essential nature? What distinguishes this plant from another? These are the questions he debated as he paced his garden with a chosen few, inspecting, probing and revising his notes until he was satisfied.

In his *Enquiry into Plants,* wild roses appear in Book Three with several kinds of bramble, one 'erect and tall', the other running along the ground and rooting where it touched the earth. The 'dog's bramble' (wild rose) has a reddish fruit like that of the pomegranate, said Theophrastus; and like the pomegranate, 'it is intermediate between a shrub and a tree; but the leaf is spinous'. So the rose we know as the common dog rose (in Latin, *Rosa canina*) already had its canine link, attributed to the belief that its roots would cure the bite of a mad dog.

Theophrastus' more extensive descriptions of cultivated roses appear in a different book altogether, discussed under the general heading of 'coronary plants' – plants grown primarily for crowns and garlands, which in springtime included the gilliflower, wild wallflower, pheasant's eye, polyanthus, narcissus, mountain anemone, purse-tassels, dropwort violet, gold flower, meadow anemone, corn-flag, 'and pretty well all the mountain flowers that are used'.

The rose was the last of the spring flowers to bloom, according to Theophrastus, and the first to finish flowering. His description begins carefully:

Among roses there are many differences, in the number of petals, in roughness, in beauty of colour, and in sweetness of scent. Most have five petals, but some have twelve or twenty, and some a great many more than these; for there are some, they say, which are even called 'hundred petalled'.

The echo of these last with Herodotus' roses is unmistakable, and while his informant may have been one of Alexander's observers ('they say'), Theophrastus is altogether a more probing and cautious reporter than Herodotus. These roses are not apparently scented (or rather, he says nothing of their fragrance), but he explains precisely where they come from: most grew in eastern Macedonia near Philippi, a garrison city founded by Alexander's father, Philip II, to control the neighbouring

Rose Canina
Class Icosandria.

Common Dog Rose.
Order Polygynia.

*Named after the ancient belief that its roots could cure the bite of mad dogs, the
dog rose (R. canina) grows wild over much of northern Europe and western Asia. From a
nineteenth-century album of wild flowers from Devon by Lydia Penrose.*

gold mines, 'for the people of that place get them on Mount Pangaeus, where they are abundant, and plant them. However the inner petals are very small (the way in which they are produced being such that some are outside, some inside).'

This tells us two things: first, that out in the wild, the naturally promiscuous rose is mutating, intermixed perhaps with naturalized strains from elsewhere; and second, that people are transplanting wild roses into cultivation, thus beginning their slow transformation into the rose we know today. Although deliberate plant-breeding comes later, open pollination between varieties inevitably produces new crosses and skilled cultivators would have noticed and nurtured spontaneous mutations displaying different characteristics – deeper colours, more petals, headier scents or neater habits of growth. As Bartholomæus Anglicus warned his medieval readers: neglect a garden rose and it will quickly turn back into a wild rose, but 'by ofte chaungynge and tilyeng ye wilde rose torneth and chaungeth into a verray rose'.

Theophrastus' other roses all run into each other, so it is impossible to count how many cultivated varieties he recognized: not all were fragrant, and not all had large flowers. Among the larger-flowered roses, those with a rougher calyx were more fragrant, he declared (could he possibly have meant Moss roses, popularized only in Victorian times?), further suggesting that good colour and fragrance depended on where a rose was planted, 'for even bushes which are growing in the same soil shcw some variation in the presence or absence of a sweet scent'. In his opinion, the sweetest roses of all came from Cyrene on the North African coast, a Greek city – in modern-day Cyrenaica in Libya – founded in the seventh century BC by settlers from Thera, 'wherefore the perfume made from these is the sweetest'.

Writing as a botanist rather than a gardener, Theophrastus nonetheless hints at how the rose was being tamed and domesticated. As roses grow slowly from seed, he noted, cultivators preferred to take stem cuttings, which they would then plant out. They would also prune or 'burn' the woody stems to encourage better flowers, adding that the bushes had 'to be often transplanted; for then, they say, the roses are improved.[4] The wild kinds are rougher both in stem and in leaf, and have also smaller flowers of a duller colour.'

Born on the Greek island of Lesbos and Aristotle's appointed successor, natural philosopher Theophrastus takes credit as the first westerner to submit wild and cultivated roses to botanical enquiry.

In the Greece of Theophrastus, roses flowered only once, in springtime, unlike some Asiatic roses such as *R. chinensis* which flowered later in the year, often continuously. So no 'eastern' genes had yet entered the blood-stock. It is inconceivable that such a meticulous cataloguer would have missed a repeat-flowering rose, and Theophrastus anyway put the rose with the flowers of spring – the first to appear and the first to disappear, 'for its time of blooming is short'. Roses in Egypt, by contrast, appeared as much as two months ahead of those in Greece and lasted longer 'or at least not a shorter, time than those of our country'. And although Egypt's myrtles were marvellously fragrant, all her other flowers and sweet herbs were scentless, among which he presumably included the rose.

From Greek into Roman times, the rose continued to adapt and develop, propelled by a frenzy that turned it into the pagan flower par excellence. How and why this happened is the subject of Chapter 2, but let us stay with the flower itself for a moment. Tradition has it that the first repeat-flowering rose in the West appears in Virgil's *Georgics,* the Latin poet's discursive treatise on farming which he read over four successive days to the future Augustus, Rome's first emperor, in 29 BC. Virgil devoted the final book of *Georgics* to bee-keeping. 'Let there be gardens to amuse them, with the scent of brightly coloured flowers,' he wrote of the bees, slipping in a reference to *biferi rosaria Paesti*, the twice-bearing rose gardens of Paestum, to the south of Naples. Some 500 years later, an editor of Virgil's works described Paestum in Campania as a city where roses bloom twice in the year, thereby linking Paestum's roses with the twice-flowering Autumn Damask. The suggestion soon stuck; when the popular travel writer Henry Swinburne visited Paestum in the late 1770s, the inhabitants had long since succumbed to barbarian invasion and bad drains, but its roses still bloomed among the ruins, 'the small single Damask kind, with a very high perfume; as a farmer assured me on the spot, it flowers both in spring and autumn'.

Go back to the original Latin and you will see that it is not the *roses* of Paestum that flower twice but its rose *beds*, and Virgil was in all likelihood praising Paestum as a centre where roses were forced into flower early in the season, producing a first crop to rival that of the Egyptians. Spring roses would follow at the usual time, from different roses.

Certainly no twice-blooming Italian roses appear in the thirty-seven volumes of Pliny the Elder's *Natural History*, a vast compendium of all that was known of the natural and sometimes supernatural world, completed just before Pliny's death in the eruption that destroyed Pompeii in AD 79. Pliny was not the most reliable of witnesses, it should be said, often garbling his information through haste and faulty sources, but he is unlikely to have overlooked the economic marvel of a twice-blooming rose. Blessed with 'a keen intelligence, astonishing concentration, and little need for sleep', he was proud to have crammed into his great work more than 20,000 facts drawn from 2,000 books – figures now considered serious underestimates. 'Nature, which is to say Life, is my subject,' he explained in his preface, and among nature's great divisions he naturally had much to say about the rose.

From Pliny, we learn how the garden rose was continuing to develop, still considered primarily as a garland flower for wreaths and chaplets, and together with the violet, one of the very few garland flowers found in Roman gardens, grown on a thorn rather than a shrub, and sometimes even on a bramble (he meant the wild rose or Eglantine).

Pliny the garden-lover describes a bud opening into a fine garden rose:

The flower in all roses is originally enclosed in a bud, with a grained surface within, which gradually swells, and assumes the form of a green pointed cone, similar to our alabaster unguent boxes in shape. Gradually acquiring a ruddy tint, this bud opens little by little, until at last it comes into full blow [flower], developing the calyx, and embracing the yellow-pointed filaments which stand erect in the centre of it.

He gives us a dozen or so roses (among which he mixed in a mallow and the rose campion, *Lychnis coronaria*), which he arranged first according to place and then to smell, noting that 'the genuine rose, for the most part, is indebted for its qualities to the nature of the soil'. The most esteemed roses came from Praeneste (the last to come into flower) and Campania (which included Paestum's roses), to which some rose-lovers added the bright red roses of Miletus on the western coast of Anatolia, which never had more than twelve petals. Next came the pinker rose of Trachyn (possibly Heraclea Trachis or Trachinia, north of Delphi) and the whitish rose of Alabanda (also in Anatolia), which was 'not so highly esteemed'. The least esteemed of all was the many-petalled thorny rose.

Pliny then followed Theophrastus in referring to the hundred-petalled rose, 'thence known as the "Centifolia"' – a rose found in Campania and also in Greece, in the vicinity of Philippi, 'though this last is not the place of its natural growth. Mount Pangæus, in the same vicinity, produces a rose with numerous petals of diminutive size; the people of those parts are in the habit of transplanting it, a method which greatly tends to improve its growth.' It was never used for chaplets, however, as it was neither particularly beautiful nor scented.

And like Theophrastus, he praised North Africa's Cyrenaic roses as 'the most odiferous of all', dropping the barest of hints that 'at Carthage, again, in Spain, there are early roses throughout the winter'. Were the roses early because the climate was more benign or because the roses were forced, like Paestum's? Or might the winter-flowering roses already have contained repeat-flowering genes that can only have come from Asiatic bloodstock? While climate and forcing techniques

EQV
ac flor
frutice
fe tanr
tione:
flores:
earum
num g
omniu
totum
operif
intus
parent

urgemuf culpamœ noftram illi imi

*By Roman times, a dozen or so cultivated roses were grown and both
horticulture and agriculture were advancing. From a fifteenth-century illumination
to Pliny the Elder's* Natural History, *completed* AD 79.

provide the more likely answer, we must once again reserve the question
for a later chapter.

Pliny's instructions on growing roses show how horticultural knowledge was advancing, although he continued to defer to earlier authorities, and to planetary influences. For the rose, he said, the ground should
be dug to greater depth than it was for corn, but not so deep as for the
vine. As new roses grow very slowly from seed, grafting or propagating
'from the eyes of the root' were preferable. All roses benefited from
pruning and cauterization, he said, echoing Theophrastus, and grew

more quickly after they had been transplanted. 'The slips are cut some four fingers in length or more, and are planted immediately after the setting of the Vergiliae [another name for the Pleiades]; then, while the west winds are prevalent, they are transplanted at intervals of a foot, the earth being frequently turned up about them.' And he had this advice for those who wanted to force their roses to flower early: 'make a hole a foot in width about the root, and pour warm water into it, at the period when the buds are beginning to put forth'.

Nurtured and manipulated by such means, the rose was developing into a flower of great beauty and economic significance. It was also acquiring cultural meanings that would turn it into the world's favourite flower in virtually all parts of the world, except – ironically – its Chinese heartlands, where the lotus, the chrysanthemum and the peony take precedence.

Chapter Two

Aphrodite's Flower

THE Greeks were not the world's greatest gardeners, and no one can claim that they 'invented' the garden rose. But through their other arts they gave us a flower to celebrate the rites of love, drinking and death. The rose came to embody other meanings as well – and the Romans with their flair for excess would take the flower to the very limits of debauchery – but with its links to these three very human activities, its story properly begins.

The connection to death came first, as the rose makes its brief and sombre literary debut in the oldest work of western literature, Homer's *Iliad,* written in the eighth century BC[1] and considered by some the work of several hands. Indirectly responsible for the death of his friend Patroclus, the Greek hero Achilles has turned his rage on the Trojans and slain heroic Hector, knowing from prophecy that his own death will shortly follow. Still raging, he threatens to throw Hector's body to the dogs instead of committing it to the funeral pyre as custom demanded. But the goddess Aphrodite intervenes, keeping the dogs at bay and anointing Hector with an embalming oil – 'rose-sweet, ambrosial' – so that Achilles may not tear him as he drags his body through the dust.

So the rose is present as an oil but not yet as a flower, for although Homer has absorbed roses into his poetic vocabulary ('rosy-fingered' is his standard epithet for dawn, in contrast to the orangey-red skies he coloured with saffron), neither the *Iliad* nor the *Odyssey* includes a real rose among the fifty or so trees and plants mentioned by name. And we should be wary of reading too many roses into Homer's text, as later translators often chose to see roses in place of merely 'flowers' – in the double purple cloth that Hector's wife Andromache is weaving when she hears of his death, for instance, and on Achilles' great shield, which contained the Greek world in microcosm. The 'fair chaplets' or garlands worn by its dancing youths and maidens may conceivably have contained roses (they often did), but Homer did not specifically put them there.

Greek roses next come alive with the poetess Sappho, who was born on the Greek island of Lesbos in the second half of the seventh century BC and brought a distinctly feminine intelligence to Greek poetry after Homer's essentially male epics of war and friendship. Her songs of passionate, often lesbian love were sung at male drinking parties, their inner dramas drifting into fantasy, myth and memory. As the geographer Strabo wrote in the first century AD, 'Sappho [is] an amazing thing. For we know in all of recorded history not one woman who can even come close to rivalling her in the grace of her poetry.'

Only one poem has survived intact, addressed to 'Deathless Aphrodite of the spangled mind'; three more are nearly complete, among them a remarkable portrayal of the fires and torments of love as the poet watches a man watching her beloved. The rest survive as odd words or phrases on pottery shards and crumbling papyri, or as citations in ancient authors. Roses slip easily into the gaps, taking their place in a flora that includes the laurel tree, anise, the reddening sweet apple, the mountain hyacinth, golden chickpeas and violets in the lap of the bride. 'And the beautiful dew is poured out / and roses bloom and frail / chervil and flowering sweetclover.'

For Sappho, the moon rather than the dawn is 'rosy-fingered', and she brings roses into her magnificently offensive snub to a wealthy woman whom she judged indifferent to the 'roses of Pieria', an allusion to the Muses whose birthplace was believed to lie in the mountains of Pieria, close to Mount Bermium and the famous roses in the Gardens of Midas.

Dead you will lie and never memory of you
will there be nor desire into the aftertime – for you do not share in the roses
of Pieria, but invisible too in Hades' house
you will go your way among dim shapes. Having been breathed out.

Roses resonate in surviving fragments of verse by Greek lyric poet Sappho, who planted the flowers among apples trees in the sanctuary of Aphrodite. Detail from a Greek vase painting, c.440 BC.

Sappho's roses became so potent that you will often read that she crowned the rose the King (or Queen) of Flowers. She never did – that was Achilles Tatius in his love story, *Leucippe and Clitophon* – but people think she did, and poets continued to 'translate' this poem falsely attributed to her. Elizabeth Barrett Browning wrote one of its many versions, 'Song of the Rose', turning Sappho's Mediterranean lightness into something altogether more solid.

> For the Rose, ho, the Rose! is the grace of the earth,
> Is the light of the plants that are growing upon it:
> For the Rose, ho, the Rose! is the eye of the flowers,
> Is the blush of the meadows that feel themselves fair . . .[2]

And critically for the story of the rose, Sappho planted roses in the sanctuary of Aphrodite, goddess of love and human sexuality, invoking the goddess to appear in her 'graceful grove of apple trees' amid 'altars smoking with frankincense':

> And in it cold water makes a clear sound through
> apple branches and with roses the whole place
> is shadowed and down from radiant-shaking leaves
> sleep comes dropping.

... *And with roses the whole place is shadowed*: here for me lies the true beginning of the story of the rose: a flower that casts its shadow at the heart of love's inner sanctuary, one that later cultures will try to capture for themselves.

As the natural world was evidently numinous to the ancient Greeks, we must assume that roses – along with the apple, myrtle and many other plants and animals – were already sacred to Aphrodite, whose origins go back to the Sumerian goddess of love and procreation, Inanna, and to Babylonian Ishtar and the Semitic goddess Astarte, just as she would later metamorphose into the Roman Venus. The Greeks gave her two conflicting genealogies, one light, one dark, just as they gave her two manifestations as celestial Aphrodite (*Aphrodite Ourania*) and common Aphrodite (*Aphrodite Pandemos*).

Homer makes her one of the younger divinities, born from the union of Zeus with the Titan goddess Dione, while near-contemporary Hesiod elevates her to the earliest pantheon of Olympian gods, born from the severed genitals of Uranus (heaven) after scheming son Kronos had cut them off with a sickle provided by his mother Gaia (the earth), tossing them backwards into the surging sea.

About them a white foam grew from the immortal flesh, and in it a girl formed. First she approached holy Cythera; then from there she came to sea-girt Cyprus. And out stepped a modest and beautiful goddess, and the grass began to grow all round beneath her slender feet. Gods and men called her Aphrodite, because she was formed in foam, and Cytherea, because she approached Cythera, and

Aphrodite's sacred grove survived in Roman wall paintings, seen here in a Pompeian fresco of Eros punished by Venus, the Roman incarnation of the goddess of love.

Cyprus-born, because she was born in wave-washed Cyprus, and 'genial', because she appeared out of genitals.

The roses at Aphrodite's birth were added later, by one of the imitators of the Greek lyric poet Anacreon, who wrote of Venus-Aphrodite emerging from the sea 'in flushing hues', mellowed by the ocean's 'briny dews', while the earth produced 'an infant flower, / Which sprung, with blushing tinctures drest, / And wanton'd o'er it's [*sic*] parent's breast'. Hesiod's creation myth and Anacreon's roses come together in Florentine artist Sandro Botticelli's celebrated *Birth of Venus*, in which the goddess wafts gently shorewards on a scallop shell under a shower of blush-pink roses. Waiting to greet her on land is the Hour of Spring, adorned with plants sacred to the goddess: a myrtle wreath around her neck and roses for a girdle.

Florentine artist Sandro Botticelli added roses to his Birth of Venus, *c.1485, which shows the goddess wafting shorewards in the gentlest of seas.*

The double tradition of Aphrodite's birth shows how the Greeks thought of her as both native-born Greek and foreign, worshipped as the goddess of sexuality and reproduction, and essential for the community's survival. At Corinth and Mantinea in eastern Arcadia, 'black Aphrodite' wielded her power over the fertility of 'black earth'. In Athens, she was linked to a mysterious nocturnal ritual concerned with sexuality and impregnation, involving Athena's temple maidens, the *arrhephoroi*;[3] and prostitutes traditionally worshipped the earthier Aphrodite, although the precise links between prostitution, the goddess, and the cult of roses are uncertain. The historian Herodotus describes a form of ritual prostitution at the temple of Aphrodite in Babylonian Assyria, and similar customs in parts of Cyprus. And while some claim the rose as the compulsory badge of prostitutes, worn as a mark of disgrace, the Greek law-maker and poet Solon (640–560 BC) maintained that girls who had lost their virtue were prohibited from wearing rose wreaths.[4]

A little easier to track are the rose's associations with drinking, which are plainly and uproariously celebrated in songs attributed to Anacreon, who came from the Ionian city of Teos on the coast of Asia Minor, a city renowned for its cult of Dionysus, the Greek God of wine, intoxication and ritual madness. Born around 575 or 570 BC, Anacreon was a dedicated pleasure-seeker who wrote songs of love and revelry for his patrons at rich Greek courts; we think of him now as 'the archetypal merry old soul . . . tottering home from the party with garland askew and with a pretty boy to guide him'. But here, too, the story becomes confused as the body of Anacreon's work is swollen by that of later imitators, some writing as late as the fifth and sixth centuries AD, who produced a rash of rose-garlanded songs of love, wine, women, pretty girls and boys, now identified separately as the Anacreontea.

Many garlands survive in fragments and echoes of the real Anacreon – of lotus, celery and Naucratis (said variously to contain marjoram, papyrus, myrtle or lime); of coriander, willow and anise; but only a solitary reference to roses is quoted in Athenaeus' *Scholars at Dinner* where, according to Anacreon, 'each man had three garlands, two of roses and the other a garland of Naucratis'. And although roses abound in the later Anacreontea, they often suffer from ponderous translations

into English in the eighteenth and early nineteenth centuries, such as
John Addison's celebration of roses, wine and love:

> The Rose, Love's fav'rite Flow'r, let's join
> To red-cheek'd Bacchus, God of Wine.
> Then round our Temples let the Rose
> Its silken-bloomy Leaves disclose;
> Whilst gaily-laughing all the while,
> We like the Wine and Roses smile.

But here is one of my favourites, from a more recent translation of the
Anacreontea:

Once when I was weaving a garland I found Love among the roses. I held him by
his wings and plunged him in my wine, then I took it and drank him down; and
now inside my body he tickles me with his wings.

*The rose garland worn by Dionysus
(Roman Bacchus), god of wine and
ritual intoxication, illustrates the
antique world's connection between
roses and drinking. From a fresco
c.55–79 AD at Herculaneum.*

As well as growing roses for garlands, the Greeks continued to use them in perfumed oils (see Chapter 16), which were naturally becoming much more sophisticated than the simple rose and sage oils of Pylos. As the lightest perfume, roses were best suited to men, said Theophrastus, along with *kypros* and lily. Women, by contrast, favoured myrrh oil, *megaleion,* sweet marjoram, and spikenard, 'for these owing to their strength and substantial character do not easily evaporate and are not easily made to disperse, and a lasting perfume is what women require'.

Roses were also used in medicines, to flavour wine, to make perfume powders, and as fresh rose petals to enhance and refresh compound perfumes. As Theophrastus explained, these were used 'to impart pleasant odour to clothes, while the powders are used for bedding, so that they may come in contact with the skin: for this kind of preparation gets a better hold and is more lasting, so that men use it thus instead of scenting their bodies directly'. The bedding could also be soaked in fragrant wine before powdering; or you could moisten the powder with mead or mead mixed with wine.[5]

To satisfy the flower's many commercial uses, Greek cities must have been awash with roses – grown not in the cities themselves, which were simply too crowded for individual gardens, and the houses too close together – but cultivated in small, accessible plots around the outskirts in a shady belt of orchards, vegetable gardens and vineyards, much like the Garden of Alkinoos in Homer's *Odyssey.* For all their economic and utilitarian focus, such garden plots were undoubtedly pleasant places, where people grew roses and other favourite garland flowers; the poet Pindar described how the sweet scent of violets pervaded Athens 'and roses crown the brow'. Those with no garden space at all could grow their roses in pots, as villagers still do around their homesteads.

Philosophers, too, set up their schools on the outskirts of Athens in wooded parks or gymnasia set aside for physical exercise, such as Plato's Academy and Aristotle's Lyceum. A third park was Kynosarges; all three were established in ancient sacred groves planted with plane, elm, poplar and olive trees. We know that the philosopher Epicurus paid 8,000 drachmas for a garden in the same city – an enormous sum compared to the average daily wage of one drachma. Tradition plants the garden of Epicurus with roses, but the evidence is slight.

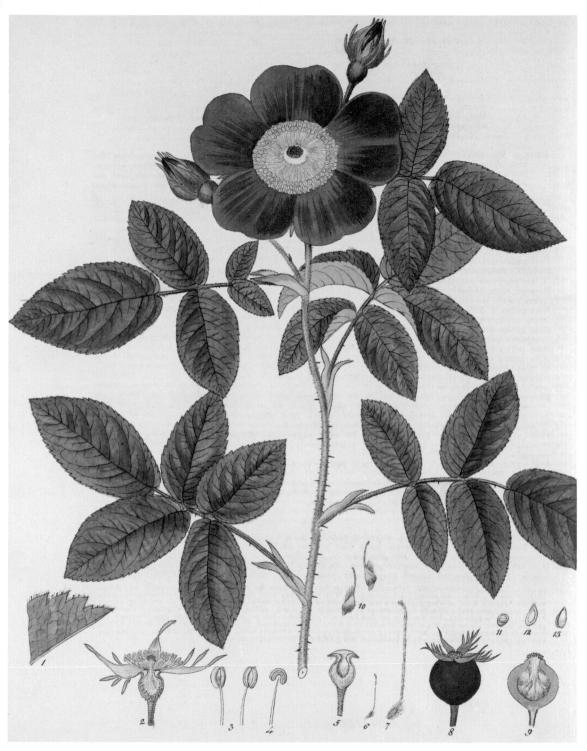

The single-petalled wild Rosa gallica *is the foundation species for many
of Europe's early cultivated roses, taken here from a German medicinal herbal
by Friedrich Gottlob Hayne (Berlin, 1830).*

We must wait for the Romans to domesticate the rose, welcoming it into their homes and extended gardens, while at the same time indulging in an orgy of rose worship that came close to insanity. For the Romans, roses were not merely tributes to the honoured dead, they could also be a cause itself of dying.

Chapter Three
Rome's Frenzy

G REEK roses have left only the faintest traces, strongest in their poets and especially in Sappho's rose-shadowed groves of the goddess Aphrodite. Roman roses, by contrast, linger everywhere – in art, architecture and gardens; at battles and banquets; in rituals of life and death; in the hearts and minds of men, and of women.

Already at the time of Emperor Augustus, roses aroused conflicting emotions. For Virgil, they slipped easily into his vision of the simple life, maintaining a fruitful balance between the cultivated and the wild. Although the poet's *Georgics* do not treat of gardening per se, he celebrated the garden of an old Cilician smallholder from the southern coast of Anatolia, who grew his cabbages among brambles, white lilies, vervain and fine-seeded poppies and whose happiness equalled the wealth of kings. 'First he was in spring to gather roses,' Virgil tells us, and apples in the autumn; and so he was always first to welcome the swarming bees who made for him the precious honey that was the Romans' only sweetener.

But for Virgil's contemporary Horace, the rose had become an emblem of impermanence and decay. 'What slender youth sprinkled with fragrant perfumes / now makes love to you, Pyrrha, on a bed of roses / in some pleasant cave?' begins Horace's famous 'Ode to Pyrrha', in which the older poet reflects on the fickle nature of women, and of youthful love. In another ode, here translated as 'Persian Fopperies' by the Christian evangelist and poet William Cowper, Horace defiantly rejected the decadent rose in favour of the plainer myrtle.

Boy, I hate their empty shows,
  Persian garlands I detest;
Bring not me the late-blown rose
  Lingering after all the rest:

Plainer myrtle pleases me
  Thus outstretched beneath my vine,
Myrtle more becoming thee,
  Waiting with thy master's wine.[1]

Yet for all Horace's distaste of ostentation and garlands played a leading role in the Romans' domestic, religious and ceremonial lives, marking the rites of passage of birth, marriage and death. Growing roses for garlands fitted better with Virgil's pastoral mood than with Horace's asceticism, and early writers on agriculture encouraged farmers to grow roses and other flowers expressly for this purpose.

The elder Cato's *De Agricultura*, written around 160 BC, had proposed that a typical farm of sixty-six acres should have an irrigated garden as well as a vineyard, osier bed, olive yard, meadow, cornfield, wood and cultivated orchard. 'Near the house lay out also a garden with garland flowers,' he advised, 'and vegetables of all kinds, and set it about with myrtle hedges, both white and black, as well as Delphic and Cyprian laurel.' According to Cato, responsibility for hanging garlands over the hearth at the three main stages of the lunar month belonged to the housekeeper, often the farmer's wife, who was also required to offer fervent prayers to the household gods.

A century or more later, the Roman scholar and encyclopedist Marcus Terentius Varro (116–27 BC) recognized the commercial potential of roses for suburban farmers, proposing that 'in the suburbs of a city, it is fitting to cultivate gardens on a large scale, and to grow violets and roses and many other such things which a city consumes, while it would be folly to undertake this on a distant farm with no facilities for reaching the market'. And while Varro believed that profit should come before pleasure, in an agricultural treatise he dedicated to his wife after she had acquired a farm he nonetheless encouraged farmers to cultivate 'what yields you profit in mere pleasure, like arbours and flower gardens',

A Latin writer on agriculture and animal husbandry from Cadiz in Spain, Columella celebrated the riches and pleasures growing roses might bring. From a fifteenth-century manuscript of De re rustica.

noting that violets and garden flowers should be set out in the open, where they could flourish in the sun.

Contemporaries of Pliny wanting more advice on rose-growing could turn to Columella, a native of Cadiz in southern Spain on the western margins of the Roman Empire and later the owner of several properties around imperial Rome. A cultivated and highly practical writer on agricultural management, Columella set out to fill the horticultural gap in Virgil's *Georgics* by writing a fine poem on gardening, which he claimed 'the husbandman of old [had] carried out in a half-hearted and negligent fashion but which is now quite a popular pursuit'. Just like Pliny, Columella treasured the beauty, colour and scent of a rose for its votive and commemorative roles. By the time of the flower harvest, he said,

> Roses, with modest blush suffused, reveal
> Their maiden eyes and offer homage due
> In temples of the gods, their odours sweet
> Commingling with Sabaean incense-smoke.

From Columella, we learn more about the rhythm of the farmer's year. February was the time 'to plant new rose-beds and attend to the old ones', while March was the time 'to have finished digging and preparing your late rose bed'. He gave precise planting instructions, noting that 'The rose-tree should be planted at the same time as the violet in furrows one foot deep in the form of shrubs or cuttings; but it must be dug round every year before March 1st and pruned here and there. If cultivated in this way it lasts for many years.' Like Virgil, Columella included roses as one of the flowering shrubs favoured by bees, although in his opinion thyme yielded the best flavours. If all his recommendations were followed, the Roman flower garden must have been colourful indeed:

White lilies sown between the furrows in the garden make a brilliant show and the gilliflowers have no less pure a colour; then there are red and yellow roses and purple violets and sky-blue larkspur; also the Corycian and Silician saffron-bulbs are planted to give colour and scent to the honey.

*

Of all the economic uses of roses, raising flowers for garlands was undoubtedly the most lucrative. A frieze in Pompeii's House of the Vettii illustrates the making and selling of garlands, beginning with the gardener delivering flowers on the back of a goat and ending with a psyche buying a garland from a winged cupid who holds up two fingers to indicate the price. No wonder Columella wrote of the farmer piling his baskets high with roses and marigolds and staggering home from market, 'well soaked with wine . . . and pockets full of cash'.[2]

According to Pliny, the earliest chaplets were made from evergreens and used to crown the victors of sacred contests. Flowers came later, developing out of a contest between art and nature, when a female garland-maker challenged her male artist admirer to a test of skill. Later still, the rose chaplet came into fashion, and sewn chaplets of leaves. 'More recently again, they have been imported from India, or from nations beyond the countries of India. But it is looked upon as the most refined of all, to present chaplets made of nard leaves [Indian spikenard, used in luxury perfumes], or else of silk of many colours steeped in unguents. Such is the pitch to which the luxuriousness of our women has at last arrived!'

Torn between his desire to inform and his moral disapproval of excess, Pliny spared the rose his condemnation of more extravagant perfumes. Although the most ancient unguents were deemed the most popular (those made from the oils of myrtle, calamus, cypress, mastich and pomegranate rind), he preferred to give the honour to the rose, 'a flower that grows everywhere; and hence for a long time the composition of oil of roses was of the most simple nature, though more recently there have been added omphacium, rose blossoms, cinnabar, calamus, honey, sweet-rush, flour of salt or else alkanet, and wine'. Fashions in perfumes depended, says Pliny, not on the quality of the ingredients used but on the relative popularity of the town that produced them. Just as Corinth's perfume of iris was eclipsed by that of Cyzicus, so the perfume of roses from Phaselis had given way to products from Naples, Capua and Praeneste.

Following the stern lead of the great orator and statesman Cicero, Pliny preferred unguents that smelt of the earth to ones smelling of saffron, and he scorned those who so plastered themselves with unguents that even their feet were sprinkled with perfume – a habit, he says, that the Emperor Nero learnt from one of his debauched companions. 'We have heard also of a private person giving orders for the walls of the bathroom to be sprinkled with unguents, while the Emperor Caius [Caligula] had the same thing done to his sitting-bath.'

But for all his moralizing, Pliny writes with great charm of the scent of flowers, and you can picture him sniffing at the morning air as he paced his garden, noting how some flowers smell sweet at a distance but lose their edge as you approach (the violet was one such flower, he said, by which he probably meant stocks, *Matthiola incana*). The fresh-gathered rose, he declared, 'has a more powerful smell at a distance, and dried, when brought nearer'. The smell of all plants was strongest in spring and in the morning, declining as noon approached. Young plants smelt less than old ones, and the rose and the crocus smelt best when gathered in fine weather. And while hot climates generally brought out the best scents, flowers from Egypt were weak-scented because of heavy dews from the Nile – a puzzling comment in the light of the considerable rose trade between Egypt and Rome, and the acres of roses cultivated in Roman Egypt, but one which echoes Theophrastus.[3]

Masking the odours of daily life was just one of the many practical uses of the rose to Roman householders. Roses were also soaked in wine, a recipe that required three-week-long seepings of fresh rose petals sown into linen bags and a final sweetening with honey. Only the best petals were to be used, says a recipe book credited to Apicius, who also included a recipe for making rose wine without roses, substituting a palm leaf full of fresh citrus leaves. Rose pie was another delicacy, requiring pulverized rose petals mixed with broth and strained through a colander, to which were added four cooked calf's brains (skinned and the nerves removed), eight eggs, a glass each of wine and raisin wine, a little oil and much pepper.

Considered to be 'of an astringent and refreshing nature', the rose also gave up its petals, flowers and hips to a variety of healing remedies. Roses and the contribution to medicine of antiquity's most famous pharmacologist, the Greek-born Pedanius Dioscorides, a near contemporary of Pliny, is the subject of a later chapter. But to grasp the full import of roses

to the Romans, let us linger for a moment with Pliny's thirty-two rose remedies, many specifically for female complaints and cosmetics.

In his physic as in other branches of knowledge, you sense that Pliny aimed at completeness before proven accuracy. Rose juice, he said, was injected into ears and used as a gargle for mouth ulcers, gums and tonsils. It was helpful against stomach aches, womb disorders, diseases of the rectum and headaches. Used either on its own or mixed with vinegar, it could combat sleeplessness and nausea in fever patients. Charred rose petals were used as a cosmetic for eyebrows, 'and the thighs, when chafed, are rubbed with them dried'. Ground to a powder, they soothed inflamed eyes. The flower of the rose was soporific and when mixed with vinegar and water would stop 'fluxes' in women, especially the white flux. Dried rose seed was also used against toothache, as a diuretic and in topical applications for the stomach; while inhaled through the nose, it had the effect of 'clearing the brain'. The flower heads, taken in drink, could help arrest loose bowels and bleeding, while the white parts of the petals were

Roses and other Mediterranean shrubs crowd behind the fence in frescos from the subterranean garden room of Livia, wife of Emperor Augustus, at her villa at Prima Porta near Rome. Early first century AD.

considered good for eyes. Dried rose petals could also be used as antiperspirant powders, sprinkled on the body after a bath and left to dry, then washed off with cold water. The galls of wild roses could be mixed with bears' grease and smeared on the head as a remedy for baldness, while the root of the dog rose was effective against hydrophobia from rabies.

It is an impressive list, and whatever its efficacy, the rose must have brought much comfort to Roman sickrooms.

If roses were essential to the daily lives of Roman citizens, so were they in death, when the body was adorned with flowers and a ceremonial meal was eaten at the tomb. The well-off left capital sums to pay for continued offerings of food, wine, incense, fruits and flowers of all kinds, especially violets and roses; and Roman tombs such as those at Pompeii were often planted or decorated with gardens, and situated on busy routes into the city. Roses could communicate beyond the grave, as this epitaph by the Roman poet Ausonius suggests:

> Sprinkle my ashes with pure wine and fragrant oil of spikenard:
> Bring balsam, too, stranger, with crimson roses.
> Tearless my urn enjoys unending spring.
> I have not died, but changed my state.

In an extraordinary instance of preservation, Roman burial wreaths dating back to c.170 AD survived intact in Roman tombs at Hawara in Lower Egypt, excavated in the late 1880s by University College London's first Professor of Egyptology, Sir William Matthew Flinders Petrie. Some are now held by the Royal Botanic Gardens at Kew. Tied together by unravelling strips of papyrus and date palm, the roses have darkened after nearly 2,000 years to the colour of mummy flesh.

The excavation itself was deeply unpleasant, conducted forty feet down a well in a pitch-black chamber, 'splashing about in bitter water, and toiling by candle-light'. Flinders Petrie spent a day struggling with the inner coffins, up to his nose in water as he sat in the sarcophagus, 'and then I spent another gruesome day, sitting astride of the inner coffin, unable to turn my head under the lid without tasting the bitter brine in which I sat'.

Out of this wretched toil came some of his greatest treasures: the body of the noble, Horuta, wrapped in a fretwork of beads of lapis lazuli, beryl and decomposed silver, and sixty mummies with their portraits painted on wooden panels placed over their faces. The wreaths and flowers represented another treasure, doubling the number of plants known to have grown in Egypt during Roman times. Still adorning the dead, they were found inside the coffins and graves, together with the flowers that the living had brought to the tomb scattered about the ruins of the burial chambers. 'These wreaths were often in the most perfect condition,' wrote Petrie, 'every detail of the flowers being as complete as if dried for a herbarium.' Among the many other plants found were myrtle, woody nightshade, sweet marjoram, and the juniper twigs, sedge and Egyptian sugar cane used to stuff crocodile mummies.

Helping Flinders Petrie with the dig was the Egyptologist and plant expert Percy Newberry, who described how the plant remains had survived under their skimpy covering of dust and sand. The roses had evidently been picked as buds to prevent the petals from falling. Inside the tomb the petals had shrunk into little balls, which opened when moistened with warm water to reveal their perfect state of preservation. 'Not a stamen, not an anther is wanting – one might almost say that not a pollen grain is missing.'

News of the find naturally raised a flurry of excitement across Europe, spread by eminent visitors to the dig and others to whom boxes of plants were sent. The eminent French horticulturist Charles Cochet-Cochet said that although he had received numerous rose samples from the four corners of the earth, 'I have never experienced the same emotion as I did when opening your little packet!!!' François Crépin, the director of Belgium's National Botanic Garden and a world expert on rose classification, read a paper about them to the Royal Society of Belgium. The nine blossoms sent to him evidently belonged to the same species, he judged, and resembled most closely *Rosa sancta* or the Holy Rose, now known as *Rosa × richardii*.

The species is significant. Although the Holy Rose has long since disappeared from Egypt, the eminent twentieth-century Egyptologist Ludwig Keimer found it growing in certain Coptic convents and churches in Abyssinia – now Ethiopia – at heights above 5,000 feet. It was almost

Roman burial wreaths excavated in Lower Egypt contain mummified buds of the Holy Rose, Rosa sancta, *now known as* R. x richardii, *painted here by Alfred Parsons for Ellen Willmot's* The Genus Rosa, *1914.*

certain, he said, that *Rosa* × *richardii* came to Abyssinia via Egyptian
Christians, for when Abyssinia turned Christian in the fourth century, it
took its lead from the Church in Alexandria. And so roses plot the spread
of religions as well as empires.

But the best evidence for what the garden rose meant to the Romans lay
buried for more than 1,500 years at Pompeii and Herculaneum, sealed
under a covering of lava, pumice, cinders, volcanic ash and dust when
Vesuvius erupted in AD 79, killing everyone who had remained, yet
capturing the cities' flamboyant culture of flowers in mosaics and
painted frescos, and in the pollen, seeds, carbonized woods and planting
cavities still coming to light through patient and increasingly scientific
archaeology. Today, the gardens of Pompeii and Herculaneum are
returning triumphantly to life, aided by the pioneering researches of the
American archaeologist Wilhelmina Jashemski and more recently by
the Italian botanist Annamaria Ciarallo.

Roses were everywhere in these mercantile cities of the Campanian
plain – planted promiscuously with vegetables, herbs and more flowers
in the gardens the Romans held so dear; grown for profit in commercial
flower gardens; painted on house and garden walls; hung as garlands or
worn as wreaths; revered in their hearts. 'The desire for a bit of green,
with perhaps a few flowers, seems to have been a basic part of the Roman
character,' wrote Jashemski; Italian flair had turned the Hellenistic
peristyle into a 'living, breathing garden'.

However sun-baked Pompeii and Herculaneum might appear now,
they were then set in the midst of a green Virgilian landscape, the mouth
of the River Sarno fringed with reed beds and massive pines, and
cultivated vineyards and forests reaching up the slopes of the volcano.
Pompeii's inhabitants were such garden lovers that they painted garden
scenes on their walls, indoors and out, redoubling their efforts after an
earthquake in AD 62 damaged many of the buildings.

Of all the garden paintings, three stand out as particularly exquisite.
The House of the Fruit Orchard on the Via dell'Abbondanza makes up for
its modest peristyle garden with two indoor rooms painted with spacious
gardens teeming with flowers, birds, fountains, statues and luscious
fruit trees. Here, as elsewhere, the artist framed his garden view with a

border (of hart's tongue ferns and acanthus) painted in realistic *trompe l'oeil* style. In life as in art, a lattice fence separated the viewer from the cultivated garden beyond: roses, poppies, Madonna lilies and *Viburnum tinus* grew close to the fence, while taller flowering shrubs – oleander, viburnum and myrtle – intermixed with strawberry trees and brilliant red cherries. More nature crowds into the little room off the east portico of the peristyle garden, where the roses are pink and a snake slithers up a fig tree. Half-close your eyes and you can just make out the grape arbour on the arched ceiling hung with symbols sacred to Dionysus (masks, musical instruments, drinking horns), and visited by flying cupids and birds; now only fragments remain.

The owner of the much grander House of Venus Marina loved his garden so much that after the earthquake he worked on its restoration before he finished the house, surrounding his garden with painted scenes of flowers, fruit and birds, along with a stiff-legged Mars and a crudely painted Venus drifting shorewards in a sea-shell accompanied by two *amorini*. The wall has disappeared to give a view of the sea, which will surely have given the owner much pleasure. More roses crowd the foreground of the panel to the right of Venus: one with pinkish flowers, many-petalled and slightly drooping, and another with red-and-white streaked flowers. Pompeii's chief botanist, Annamaria Ciarallo, has identified the city's candy-striped roses as *Rosa gallica* 'Versicolor' (Rosa Mundi), although others are much more cautious in trying to identify the roses of antiquity.

One of the freshest and loveliest roses in all the Pompeian garden frescos appears on the south wall of the *diaeta* or garden room of the House of the Gold Bracelet.[4] Ready to burst into song, a small brown songbird perches on a hollow reed to which is tied a prickly red rose displaying all stages of flower, from bud to full bloom. The profusion of flowers here and elsewhere in the house includes white-flowered laurels, small white chamomiles with yellow centres, lavender-coloured opium poppies, large yellow corn marigolds with notched petals, Madonna lilies, irises and hart's tongue fern, an oleander with clusters of pink blossoms, morning glories, a strawberry tree, and a young date-palm. The painted garlands are of Dionysian ivy covered with white flowers, and vine leaves heavy with grapes.

*In this fresco detail from Pompeii's House of the Gold Bracelet,
the carefully staked rose in bud and flower would have conveyed the illusion
of year-long summer to the city's inhabitants.*

Such frescos show the Pompeians to be masters of illusion, extending their gardens far into the countryside, painting garden scenes on the walls of cramped gardens and light wells, and bringing the garden indoors to private and public spaces. The frescos gave the ordinary inhabitants the chance to wander in a garden where it was always summer, the sky was always azure blue, and where native and exotic plants grew side by side. Common field daisies, periwinkles, ivy, ferns, Solomon's seal, violets and opium poppies mingle with pomegranates and plane trees from Greece, a newly introduced lemon tree from the Middle East, and the lotus, date palm, ibis and crocodile from Roman Egypt.

While some of these minglings are surely fantastic, archaeologists are now able to say what grew where by examining minute specks of pollen, seeds and carbonized woods found in the covering of *lapilli* or volcanic ash, and by the cavities left by plant root systems. In the early 1970s, archaeologists discovered a commercial flower garden in the Garden of Hercules, which grew scented lilies, violets and roses, and olives to provide the base oil in which the flowers were macerated. Archaeology tells us that Pompeian gardens really did have flimsy reed fences, and that gardeners grew decorative plants used also in medicines and wreaths. The garden of the House of the Chaste Lovers was alive with roses, juniper and artemisias, as well as mouse-ear and rose campion grown in symmetrical beds, and vines and polypodium ferns along the perimeter drains. More fragrant plants – roses, violets, irises – and olive trees were found at the House of the Perfume Maker, providing archaeological evidence to support the more fanciful frieze of winged cupids and psyches celebrating the perfumers' art in the House of the Vettii (see Chapter 16).

The catastrophic eruption of Mount Vesuvius which engulfed the remaining inhabitants (and the roses) of Pompeii and Herculaneum on the morning of 24 August AD 79 claimed another victim in Pliny the Elder, who was stationed at Misenum to the north-west of the Bay of Naples, where he held command of the imperial fleet. The scientific curiosity that compelled him to compile antiquity's greatest compendium of natural history led directly to his death, which was movingly described by his nephew Pliny the Younger in a letter to his friend, the historian Tacitus.

His attention drawn to a giant cloud shaped like an umbrella pine issuing from the volcano's summit, Pliny called for a fast sailing ship to take a closer look, inviting his nephew to accompany him if he wished – an invitation the younger man, then a youth of seventeen, sensibly declined. As he was leaving, Pliny received a letter from a panicked woman seeking rescue, thereby turning his scientific quest into a mercy dash into the area of greatest danger, dictating notes as ash and charred pumice stones rained down on the ships.

Arriving at Stabiae, south of Vesuvius, Pliny sought to calm his host's fears by taking a bath and dining cheerfully before retiring to rest and snoring loudly as the courtyard filled with volcanic debris. Waking at last, he resolved to escape the tremors that shook the buildings and sought refuge on the beach with the others, who tied pillows to their heads to pro-tect themselves from the falling stones. By now the daytime sky was blacker than night, and the sea still hostile.

'My uncle lay down there on a discard-ed sail, and repeatedly drank cold water, which he had requested. Then flames and the smell of sulphur heralding the flames impelled the rest to flight and roused him.' Leaning on two of his slaves, Pliny struggled to his feet and at once collapsed, overcome by poisonous fumes (so his nephew thought), or perhaps from a heart attack or stroke. 'When daylight was restored, two days after his eyes had closed in death, his body was found intact and unharmed. It was covered over, still in the clothes he had worn. It was more like someone sleeping than a corpse.'

So Pliny the Elder would never see his nephew's two fine villas, one near Ostia on the coast near Rome, the other in Tuscany, nor the roses his nephew planted in the translucent light of his

A nineteenth-century French portrait of Rome's great encyclopaedist Pliny the Elder, whose thirty-seven-volume Natural History *provides the best guide to roses in the Roman world.*

Tuscan riding ground, where 'the cool in the shadows is moderated by shafts of not unwelcome sunlight'.

Pliny had loved the rose as a garden flower and as a simpler, more natural ingredient in the tide of unguents and perfumes he believed was weakening the foundations of Roman society. Increasingly, however, the rose would assume its own orgiastic connotations, which would eventually bear out the truth of Horace's prophetic disquiet at 'Persian fopperies'.

Central to these concerns was the rose's close association with the goddess Venus, who, although absent from Rome's oldest pantheon, presided over all sexual dealings from the third century BC, whether between mortals and gods, or among mere mortals. Her powers grew as she became assimilated to the Greek Aphrodite and by the time the poet Ovid wrote *Fasti*, his calendar of Roman feast days setting out their mythological origins, she had taken over the second month in the calendar (April, after that of her husband, Mars). In Ovid's opening exhortation for April, addressed to Latin mothers and brides and those forbidden to wear the garb of matrons (courtesans and prostitutes), he called on them to wash Venus's statue 'from top to toe', then to dry her neck and restore her golden necklaces, 'now give her other flowers, now give her the fresh-blown rose'.

Ovid makes plain the special bond between Venus and prostitutes in his preamble to the first Vinalia (23 April), festivals dedicated to Venus and Jupiter, declaring: 'Ye common wenches, celebrate the divinity of Venus: Venus favours the earnings of ladies of a liberal profession. Offer incense and pray for beauty and popular favour; pray to be charming and witty; give to the Queen her own myrtle and the mint she loves, and bands of rushes hid in clustered roses.'

Although Ovid turned the blood of the dying Adonis into anemones, not roses as is sometimes thought, roses in the Roman world continued to exert the transformative power they had acquired in earlier pagan cultures, such as the Egyptian cult of Isis, wife of Osiris, mother of Horus and goddess of fertility. A sensational example appears in *The Transformations of Lucius* – more popularly known as *The Golden Ass* – by Lucius Apuleius, a native of the Roman colony of Madaura on the North African coast, who was himself initiated into the cult of Isis. In his satire, the hero spends much of the tale transformed into an ass – the 'most hateful beast in the universe' – and is saved only by the intervention of Isis, who tells him to wriggle through the feast-day crowds and eat the High Priest's rose garland. The ass did as he was told and 'ate those roses with loving relish'. The effect was instantaneous. 'My bestial features faded away, the rough hair fell from my body, my sagging paunch tightened, my hind hooves separated into feet and toes, my fore hooves now no longer served only for walking upon, but were restored, as hands, to my human uses . . .'

The Romans loved roses so much they duly dedicated a whole festival to them, Rosalia, which appears in calendars only from the second half of the first century AD. A movable feast held some time in May to coincide with the rose harvest, it was celebrated with much the same drunken revelry Ovid ascribed to Floralia, in which drinkers' brows were wreathed with stitched garlands and their polished tables buried under a shower of roses. 'A rakish stage fits Flora well . . . she wishes her rites to be open to the common herd and she warns us to use life's flower, while it still blooms; for the thorn, she reminds us, is flouted when the roses have fallen away.'

Long before this, however, the rose had begun to acquire a dubious reputation from its associations with drinking, debauchery and moral degeneracy. Even before Augustus transformed the Roman republic into an empire, the wearing of rose chaplets was forbidden at times of war. During the Second Punic War against Hannibal (218–201 BC), a scandalized Senate threw banker Lucius Flavius into prison for the effrontery of appearing on his balcony wearing a chaplet of roses on his head. When Cicero accused the Governor of Sicily of extortion and luxurious living in the first century BC, he criticized him especially for travelling in a litter with eight bearers, with garlands around his head and neck and sitting on a cushion stuffed with rose petals. To mask the odours of real life, he held a delicate bag of rose petals to his nose.[5] Later, Tacitus was fired by righteous anger at the debauched luxuriousness of the Emperor Vitellius as he strolled among the piles of soldiers' corpses after the Battle of Bedriacus, his way strewn with laurels and roses.

In the world-conquering Roman army, the cult of roses penetrated even into the ranks. Pliny tells us that the army's eagles and standards were anointed with unguents on feast days. By the first part of the third

Roses herald the spring in this detail from a second-century floor mosaic representing the Triumph of Neptune and the Seasons *from La Chebba in Roman Tunisia.*

century AD, the Syrian army – renowned for its degenerate tastes and love of luxury – had adopted its own rose festival, the *Rosaliae Signorum*, when the legions' standards were decorated with roses and acts of veneration were performed. Although the festival retained a vestige of religious significance, its main purpose was to give the soldiers an excuse for revelry on a grand scale; such rose carnivals were enjoying a growing favour throughout the empire, and the army was not to be outdone. The proximity of some Syrian garrisons to large towns such as Antioch had accustomed the soldiers to 'all their elaborate resources for pleasure and vice'.

But for floral excess, most shocking of all was the example set by some of the leaders of Rome. In the last years of the republic, Mark Antony famously succumbed to Egypt's Queen Cleopatra at their first meeting in Tarsus, Cilicia (modern-day Turkey), where the floors of her dining room were strewn with roses a cubit deep and spread over everything in net-like festoons. This was the glittering encounter described by Plutarch and borrowed by Shakespeare, when the Queen glided up the River Cydnus in her gilded barge, 'out of which there came a wonderful passing sweet odour of perfumes', attired as the goddess Venus surrounded by 'pretty fair boys' dressed like painted cupids and her ladies portrayed as mermaids and graces; 'and there went a rumour in the people's mouths, that the goddess Venus was come to play with the god Bacchus, for the general good of all Asia.' So said Plutarch, who heartily disliked Cleopatra, representing her love affair with Mark Antony as 'this pestilent plague and mischief'. He omitted the rose detail from his account of the meeting, however, which consequently never found its way into Shakespeare.

Antony's liking for roses paled in comparison with that of the brutal and ineffectual Emperor Nero, whose extravagances were bitterly condemned by Pliny the Elder. According to the Latin biographer Suetonius, Nero's vices simply got worse. As he sailed down the Tiber to Ostia or coasted through the Gulf of Baiae, booths furnished as brothels and eating-houses sprang up along his way. He took to inviting himself to supper with his friends, when vast sums were spent on chaplets, and on roses. At the Golden House (*Domus Aurea*) in Rome, he fitted the ceilings of his dining rooms with ingenious fretwork ivory panels, which slid back to shower his guests with flowers. An echo can be seen in the painted

Dutch-born Sir Lawrence Alma-Tadema used real blossoms as models for The Roses of Heliogabalus *(1888), which projects Roman decadence through Victorian eyes.*

ceiling of a house in Pompeii's Via dell'Abbondanza, which positively explodes with individually painted flowerheads of roses, Madonna lilies, bachelor's buttons, daisies and other flowers scattered at random against the dark background of a framed panel.

Even more notorious for smothering his guests with flowers was the Syrian boy emperor Marcus Aurelius Antoninus or Elagabalus, better known by the later Greek name of Heliogabalus, who ruled from AD 218 to 222. Castigated in some quarters for his transsexual tastes, Heliogabalus possessed a love of luxury which was punctured with a delight in practical jokes that would have turned dining with him into a

trial. 'He might serve you with wax game and sweets of crystal, the counterparts of what he was eating himself . . .; he would seat you on air cushions, and have them deflated surreptitiously . . .'

Also at his feasts, you might be served sows' breasts roasted with Libyan truffles; dormice baked in poppies and honey; peacocks' tongues flavoured with cinnamon; the brains of flamingos, thrushes, parakeets, pheasants and peacocks; a yellow pig cooked after the Trojan fashion, stuffed with hot sausages and live thrushes; sea wolves from the Baltic; sturgeons from Rhodes; fig-peckers from Samos; snails from Africa and all the rest. Guests who became befuddled through drink would wake to find themselves surrounded by lions and leopards – 'tame, of course, but some of the guests were stupid enough not to know it, and died of fright'.

To be smothered by roses seems preferable, if hardly plausible. Reputations of ancient figures depended crucially on the motives and loyalties of their early chroniclers and we know virtually nothing about Aelius Lampridius, who contributed *A Life of Elagabalus* to the notoriously inaccurate Augustan Histories, where the floral smotherings first appear (though not specifically with roses). As Lampridius tells the story, 'In a banqueting-room with a reversible ceiling he once overwhelmed his parasites with violets and other flowers, so that some of them were actually smothered to death, being unable to crawl out to the top.' Lampridius provided other explicit rose tales, however, such as Heliogabalus' taste for flavouring his swimming pools 'with essence of roses and the flowers themselves', and his habit of strewing 'roses and all manner of flowers, such as lilies, violets, hyacinths and narcissus, over his banqueting rooms, his couches and his porticoes, and then [strolling] about in them'.

The image of porticoed decadence and smothering rose petals caught the attention of one of the Victorians' favourite artists, the Dutch-born Academician Sir Lawrence Alma-Tadema, who painted his large canvas *The Roses of Heliogabalus* in the winter of 1887–8. Determined to give each petal his meticulous attention, he reputedly received weekly consignments of rose blossoms from the French Riviera at his London studio over a four-month period.[6] Enormously popular in its day, Alma-Tadema's reworking of the story links the Roman obsession with roses to a morbid Victorian sensibility that saw roses as symbolic of sensual beauty, corruption and even death. As in many of his paintings, he captures the figures with the frozen realism of a snapshot. The languid boy-emperor, his mother, a male paramour and several garlanded women watch incuriously as a sumptuous shower of rose petals engulfs the supine guests who are stretched out below them, seemingly oblivious to their impending fate.

With his taste for wide-angle perspective, epic scale and personal narratives, it is hardly surprising that Alma-Tadema should earn posthumous fame as the painter who inspired Hollywood.[7] Thus do roses link the Cleopatra of Cecil B. DeMille and the siren who ensnared the rulers of Rome, and the story of Heliogabalus indicates how a surfeit of roses carried destruction in its wake. Chapter 5 picks up this thread, investigating how the pagan rose was reborn as one of Christianity's supreme symbols. Before this, however, we must follow its journey from east to west and look at how the rose of Theophrastus and Pliny continued its steady transformation into the many-splendoured flower we know today.

Chapter Four
Of Travels and Trade

IDENTIFYING the roses of antiquity is fraught with difficulty. Even if we can begin to unravel the parentage of 'old roses'* today, we cannot be certain that these are the very same strains that bloomed at the time of Homer or Herodotus, or rained down upon Heliogabalus' luckless guests. The converging evidence of science, art and natural history nonetheless suggests that Europe's early garden roses belonged to just three groups: the Gallicas, Damasks and Albas. All belong in turn to the Gallicanae section, and all have *Rosa gallica* in their genes. Although Theophrastus and Pliny wrote of hundred-petalled roses, the group now known as Centifolia roses did not appear until very much later.

Some of the most exciting discoveries about the parentage of old roses have been made in laboratories across the globe, and especially in Japan, the United States, France, Holland and the UK. Today, genetic testing is used primarily to help rose-growers and breeders identify and protect modern cultivars, but the tests are also providing fascinating insights into how the garden rose evolved from the wild.

One of the pioneers of genetic research into roses was the UK's Major Charles Chamberlain Hurst (Dr Hurst, as he is usually known), who built on the heredity experiments of the Moravian monk Gregor Johann Mendel involving garden peas, which had resulted in his famous Laws of Inheritance. When Mendel's work was rediscovered in 1900, some

---

*The American Rose Society defines Old Garden Roses as those belonging to a class in existence before 1867, reputedly the year when the first Hybrid Tea rose was introduced.

sixteen years after his death, it explained the 'science' of genetics in a way that would revolutionize plant-breeding.

Hurst carried over this interest into roses, and from the early 1920s built up a comprehensive collection of rose species, sub-species and hybrids at the Cambridge University Botanic Garden to help in his experiments (it is still there today). He found many of the wild roses himself on collecting expeditions across England and Switzerland in the company of his wife. Enthusiastic professors and botanical colleagues contributed many more seeds and specimens (some pickled and preserved) from as far as afield as North America, Mexico, Siberia, Russian Turkestan, Lapland and Manchuria.

Hurst analysed his material in three different ways: according to taxonomy (involving a detailed examination of 100 or so characteristics), genetics (making a number of experimental crosses between different varieties) and cytology (the branch of biology concerned with individual cells). His most promising results came from counting chromosomes – the first step to identifying the genetic make-up of each individual rose.

Hurst's genetic experiments proved that real differences exist between species; and although his findings have been modified and at times overthrown, his work undoubtedly fulfilled his hope of achieving a better understanding of roses in space and time. The late Graham Stuart Thomas, Britain's great rosarian, paid tribute to Hurst by incorporating his work into his own writings on old rose varieties. The two knew each other well: as a young man, Thomas had trained alongside Hurst in Cambridge, where he reported the Major 'busy in frames and houses with his genetical experiments'.

From his experiments, Dr Hurst identified *Rosa gallica* as 'the foundation species from which most of our garden Roses have been evolved'. Found in forest fringes, fields and hedgerows, it grows wild throughout central and southern Europe, from the Loire Valley to the Ukraine and further east to Asia Minor, the Caucasus and Iraq. While it never appears in any British *Flora*, the Edwardian doyenne of English rose fanatics, Ellen Willmott, claimed that a contact of hers ('that accurate observer, the late Mr Wilson Saunders') had found it growing wild in a Surrey wood. Low-growing but erect, its thin bristly stems bear dark green leaves and medium-to-large single flowers in various shades between pink and purple. Virtually all rose authorities agree that this sweetly scented but nonetheless 'rather insignificant rose' (the verdict comes from Peter Beales) is the probable ancestor of garden roses in Europe, in recorded cultivation before 1500 at least, and probably for centuries before that.

Damascus was the supposed home of the second group of ancient roses: the Damasks, botanical varieties of *Rosa × damascena* (itself unknown in the wild), which the sixteenth-century Spanish doctor and botanist Nicolás Monardes called 'Rosae Alexandrinae', suggesting it had reached Spain from Egyptian Alexandria, or 'Rosae Persicae', indicating Iran as another possible country of origin. Although Monardes tells us that the Damasks arrived in Spain only around 1520, Damask rose water (*'aqua rosata de Damasc'*) was known very much earlier, appearing for instance in a bill of medicines supplied to the English King Edward I shortly before his death in 1307 (see Chapter 14).

Generally tall and disorderly as shrubs, Damask roses bear lax clusters of crumpled, semi-double and intensely fragrant flowers in soft shades of blush or pink. Two sorts are known: Summer Damasks, which flower only once in early summer, such as 'Kazanlik' (also known as *R. × damascena* var. *trigintipetala* and 'Professeur Emile Perrot'); and the Autumn Damask, *R. × damascena* var. *semperflorens,* known to the French as 'Quatre Saisons'. The Autumn Damask was the only western rose that regularly flowered a second time in the autumn, before the arrival of repeat-flowering (remontant) roses from China towards the end of the eighteenth century, and it has long been linked to Virgil's 'twice-blooming' rose of Paestum near Naples, although this epithet is now considered to result from a mistranslation (see Chapter 1).

Back in the laboratories and potting sheds of Cambridge, Dr Hurst attributed these different flowering patterns to genetics, concluding that the two sorts of Damask roses had different parents. While both could claim descent from *Rosa gallica,* said Dr Hurst, the Summer Damask's other parent was *Rosa phoenicia*, a white-flowered climber with a rich musk-like scent from Asiatic Turkey, Cyprus, Lebanon and into north-eastern Greece. The Autumn Damask, on the other hand (again according to Dr Hurst), sprang from a cross between *R. gallica* and the Musk rose, *R. moschata,* a vigorous late-flowering climber of mysterious origin whose native territory is variously given as western Asia, Iran and the Mediterranean lands of North Africa, Spain and southern Europe.

For sixty years, Hurst's view of the Damasks' parentage prevailed, pointing to southern Anatolia as the likely birthplace of the Summer Damask, from a cross between a wild *R. phoenicia* and a cultivated Gallica rose, such as *R. gallica* var. *officinalis.* But then a group of Japanese researchers from Hiroshima in Japan and Hope in California submitted the DNA of four of the oldest Damask roses to laboratory testing, with startling results.

The roses picked for DNA fingerprinting were two old Summer Damasks, 'Kazanlik' and the candy-striped 'York and Lancaster' (*R. × damascena* 'Versicolor'); and two Autumn Damasks, 'Quatre Saisons' and 'Quatre Saisons Blanc Mousseux'. The process involves grinding young leaves from each rose in a pestle and mortar, rejecting older foliage that might be contaminated by mould or aphids, and then mixing the ground leaves with a series of chemicals to eliminate all unwanted elements. This is achieved by spinning the extraction in a centrifuge so that solids settle at the bottom and pure liquids can be decanted. The scientists would then have looked for differences in the DNA patterns produced when the samples are loaded onto gel and submitted to an electric current; staining makes the DNA visible, so that it can be read as easily as a bar code.

What they found astonished the rose world and neatly overturned Dr Hurst's accepted theories. Instead of descending from different sets of parents, both Summer and Autumn Damask share a common ancestry involving not two but three parents: *R. gallica, R. moschata* and *R. fedtschenkoana,* a scrambling white-flowered native of central Asia from the rocky foothills of the Celestial Mountains (Tien Shan) in Kyrgyzstan and eastwards into China. A favourite with Graham Stuart Thomas (who called it 'altogether a valuable rose, interesting and charming throughout the growing season'), the rose was named after its Russian discoverers, Olga and Alexei Fedtschenko, whose son Boris would follow them into botany after his father perished in the Alps. I have it in my garden, and love it for its neat grey-green leaves and the spiced wheat-bran smell of its steady succession of creamy-white flowers.

Genetic testing has identified the true Musk rose (Rosa moschata) as one of three parents to the Damask rose. From a German medicinal herbal by Friedrich Gottlob Hayne (Berlin, 1830).

Not only did the researchers disentangle the Damasks' parentage, but they also revealed how the ancestral roses had combined to produce the common ancestor of all four varieties. The (male) pollen from *R. gallica* would first have fertilized the (female) ovule from *R. moschata*. Soon after this, pollen from *R. fedtschenkoana* would have pollinated the hybrid ovule to produce the common ancestor. After this, the roses would have been propagated vegetatively, which explains how the four roses produced exactly the same genetic fingerprint.

The Japanese breakthrough nonetheless raises new questions. First, which Gallica parent was involved: the species rose or a many-petalled garden variety? More puzzlingly, where did the cross take place, as the three parents do not apparently coexist in the wild? The species *R. gallica* is a native of southern and central Europe and eastwards into Iraq, *R. fedtschenkoana* of central Asia into north-western China, while the mysterious *R. moschata* inhabits a space somewhere in between. Did the wild rose from Kazakhstan travel westwards into the Gallica's homelands, where it happened by chance upon the *gallica-moschata* hybrid? Or did the three-way cross occur within some potentate's garden, its stock increased by early traders or travellers journeying along the northern arm of the silk roads, those ancient tracks connecting China with the West? In the taming of the wild rose, where did it all begin?

But consider for a moment the parentage of the third group of ancient roses, the Albas, which produces puzzles of its own. The classic Alba rose has single, double or semi-double flowers in shades of white or blush pink, all with a distinctive, sweetly refreshing scent and grey-green leaves. Although the great Swedish botanist Carl Linnaeus declared *Rosa alba* a species in 1793, it is in fact a garden hybrid, its parentage variously attributed to crosses between *R. gallica* and the dog rose, *R. corymbifera* (by Swiss rhodologist Hermann Christ); between the dog rose, *R. canina* and *R. × damascena* (by Dr Hurst, thrown off scent by the misleading influence of *R. phoenicia*); and a complex cross between *R. gallica, R. arvensis* and an unnamed white-flowered member of the Caninae group. Dr Hurst also tentatively added another potential parent in the white-flowered dog rose, *R. canina* var. *froebelii*, which grows in Kurdistan and possibly into the Crimea and the Caucasus.

Another Damask parent is the wild Rosa fedtschenkoana *from central Asia, seen here in* Curtis's Botanical Magazine *of 1901. The third parent –* R. gallica *– appears on page 27.*

This time it was the turn of French scientists to solve the riddle of the Alba's parentage, when they included Albas among a large-scale study of genetic variations between 100 old cultivated roses. The Albas they looked at were the three old favourites: 'Cuisse de Nymphe', 'Maiden's Blush' and 'Great Maiden's Blush', all taken from one of the great French rose gardens, the Roseraie de Val-de-Marne at l'Haÿ-les-Roses. Alba roses, it seems, are European hybrids between *R. gallica* and *R. canina* varieties; in the laboratory they clearly formed their own cluster, distinct from other groups in the study (Gallicas, Centifolias, Damasks, Portlands and Hybrid Perpetuals). Genetic analysis further proved that 'Maiden's Blush' and its French counterpart, 'Cuisse de Nymphe', are in fact identical. The French verdict on more general bloodlines was equally clear: the old Alba roses were not involved in any of the principal steps leading to the creation of modern roses. In other words, despite their assumed antiquity, the Albas represented a dead end for rose breeding.

Scientists will continue to provide answers in cases of disputed parentage. But one great mystery remains. Even if we know which species sired which progeny, where is the crucible that transmuted the wild rose into the tamed? Where, in other words, are garden roses *from*?

The most likely answer is that roses developed simultaneously in several centres – undoubtedly in China, where 'modern' rose cultivars appeared nearly 1,000 years ago in Chinese silk paintings by Cui Bai, displaying the characteristic long stem, elegant high-centred buds, double flowers, and larger leaflets[1] – but also further west. One of the most convincing works on the early history of the rose remains Charles Joret's French classic of more than a century ago, *La Rose dans l'Antiquité et au Moyen Age*. From his background as a philologist and literary historian (he was professor of foreign languages at Aix-en-Provence), Joret set about answering this question of origin by looking first at language. Joret argued that the Greek word for the rose was not indigenous; Sappho's aeolic Greek 'rhodon' was aligned rather to the Armenian '*vard*', itself suggesting links to the old Iranian (Avestan) word for a sweet-smelling flower, '*varedha*'. For Joret, this pointed to the Iranian plateau as the native home of the rose. 'Indeed,' he went on, 'it is precisely in the eastern Caucasus and Kurdistan that you will find

The roses in this c.1061 silk peacock painting by Cui Bai (also known as Ts'ui Po) already have the long shoots and high-centred buds of modern cultivars with Chinese blood.

occurring spontaneously the hundred-petalled rose, the most beautiful among the ancient cultivated varieties.'

Here in Iran, said Joret – and especially in Mazandaran Province to the north and to the south-west in Faristan (Fars) – the rose attains its greatest proportions and gives off its most exquisite scent. '*On ne peut guère douter dès lors que ce ne soit là son berceau,*' he declared (one can hardly doubt from this that here is its cradle), suggesting that from its native land, the rose travelled in one direction across Asia Minor to

Greece, and in another across ancient Mesopotamia into Syria and Palestine.[2]

Travellers to the southern shores of the Caspian Sea confirm Joret's vision of an earthly paradise where roses grow sweet and large. Here is a twentieth-century view:

The first sight of the region is almost overwhelming . . . The road [from Tehran] winds along barren slopes and up narrow valleys to cross the height of the Elburz range at about eight thousand feet. On a good day the view northward across the green-clad slopes and far over the Caspian is spectacular; patches of forest and sea may emerge from a blanket of clouds some thousands of feet below. Down the road descends, to continue through great woodlands, past the settlements of charcoal burners, and, finally, to emerge on the cleared coastal strip. Here rice is the major crop, with tea plantations scattered at intervals.

More than two centuries earlier, the merchant traveller Jonas Hanway visited the adjacent provinces of Gilan and Mazandaran on his journey from England, through Russia and into Persia. 'They enjoy here a long spring,' he wrote of Gilan (which lies immediately to the west of Mazandaran): 'their lawns and meadows are strewed with flowers, and the bushes with honey-suckles, sweet briars, and roses.' The soil, too, he judged 'exceeding fertile', producing hemp, hops and 'almost every kind of fruit without culture', from oranges and lemons to peaches, pomegranates, and grapes, 'so that a considerable part of the province is quite a paradise, notwithstanding the many great inconveniences which attend it'. By 'inconveniences' he meant the region's unhealthy climate, which spared only women, mules and poultry. Nearby Mazandaran he judged just as fruitful as Gilan, but altogether healthier.

The spread of agriculture from the Near and Middle East suggests how the rose might have travelled from its Persian homelands. Grains were the first crops, grown in the Fertile Crescent joining ancient Mesopotamia to the Levant and ancient Egypt. Olives and date palms followed; and by the middle of the third millennium BC, olives, grapes and figs had spread to the Levant and on to Greece. Fruits such as apples, pears, plums and cherries came much later – not until the first millennium BC, after the introduction of grafting. Once successfully established in its core area, horticulture then spread into new territories around the Mediterranean basin.

Like the fruit trees to which they are botanically related, the early varieties of garden rose will also have moved through Asia Minor into Greece and Macedonia, where Herodotus took dutiful note in the fifth century BC of King Midas's fragrant sixty-petalled roses.

Alexander the Great may also have contributed to the rose's gradual dispersal as he set out in his early twenties in May 334 BC, pursuing an ambition to merge Europe and Asia and taking with him the men of science whose plant observations filtered back to Theophrastus. First came his conquest of the Persians, who for two centuries had ruled an empire stretching from the eastern Aegean to the Punjab. After defeating the Persian King Darius at Issus in Asia Minor, he captured the harbour cities of Phoenicia and went on to found the first of the cities named after him, Alexandria on the Nile delta. From Egypt, his conquering journey took him to Babylon, and the great Persian city of Persepolis – which he first emptied of treasure, then set alight, possibly by accident – and on through the lush landscapes of Mazandaran Province, Charles Joret's veritable rose paradise and the cradle of Europe's garden roses.

More roses came Alexander's way as he climbed with his troops up the southern face of the Hindu Kush, on the far fringes of present-day Afghanistan. 'However hungry,' wrote historian Robin Lane Fox, 'the men must have admitted it to be spectacular. Among the wormwood and the drifts of wild roses, the late and early sunlight throws patches of blue and violet on to the last snows, lighting up the pink rock and the thick gray clumps of prickly thrift, the only local fuel.' In the Swat highlands on the borders with Pakistan, they stumbled into what they thought was Dionysus' birthplace, astonished to find myrtles, box trees, laurels and the god's own sacred plant: trailing wreaths of ivy.

The furthest east Alexander reached was the last of the Punjab rivers, the River Beas; beyond lay the Ganges, which ran down to the eastern ocean and the end of the known world. But here rain and snakes broke his soldiers' morale and they refused to go any further. Embarking some of his troops at the Indus delta for the journey home, Alexander himself marched a remnant of his army through the Makran desert in conditions

Alexander the Great of Macedon, who conquered the known world in the fourth century BC, learns that he, too, will be conquered by death. From a Persian manuscript of 1425.

of extreme hardship. Their numbers included women and children 'and a train of Levantine traders who saddled their camels with any plant that looked to be worth selling later'. There are no records to prove whether rose slips or seeds formed part of such trade, which would anyway have had to survive the rigours of the journey. But conquest inevitably eases the path of floral imperialism, even in retreat, and Alexander's journey had taken him across the habitats of many different species.

Alexander never returned to Macedonia. He died aged thirty-two in Babylon, mourning the death of his intimate friend, Hephaistion, just as Achilles had mourned his beloved Patroclus at Troy. Grief had turned Alexander to drink, and nightly debauches. The French writer André Malraux observed that he was the only man with the courage to die of his vices, but fever or poison might equally have contributed to his death.

Roses, meanwhile, continued their westward journey to Rome and the states of the Roman Empire, appearing in Egypt, North Africa, Sicily, on to southern France and as far north as climate and the spread of horticultural skills would allow. The expansion of Islam from the seventh to the twelfth centuries brought a second wave of garden roses from the Near and Middle East into western Europe, travelling the main artery of diffusion that traversed the whole of the Islamic world from east to west, beginning in north-western India and Persia, continuing south of the Mediterranean to western Africa, Morocco, and up into Moorish Spain.

Islam had arrived in the Iberian peninsula in AD 711 (92 AH according to the Islamic calendar), when a Muslim-led army of Arabs and Berbers rowed across the Straits of Gibraltar, stepping into a landscape 'shaped by Romans and then by Visigoths'. They advanced as far as Toulouse and Tours where they were checked by the Franks. The Christians did not fully recover al-Andalus (as the Muslim territory was known) until 1492, when the Moorish palace of the Alhambra in Granada fell to Ferdinand and Isabella of Aragon and Castile.

Perhaps because they came out of the desert, many of the early Arab rulers and members of the privileged castes were great collectors – of birds, beasts, plants, precious books and treasures, knowledge and ideas. They were also great gardeners, revealing their human and metaphysical aspirations in exquisite paradise gardens borrowed from the conquered Persian empire, and in a whole genre of poetry, the *rawdiya* or garden poem. And into their gardens went the rarest, most beautiful plants they could find.

As early as the eighth century, for example, the first Umayyad ruler of Spain, Abd al-Rahman, sent agents to Syria and beyond to gather rare plants and seeds, acquiring a new and superior kind of pomegranate. Some two centuries later, the rulers at Cordoba had transformed their royal plots into botanical gardens, where seeds, cuttings and roots from

New varieties of rose flourished in the gardens and botanical collections of Moorish Spain such as Granada's Alhambra Palace, drawn here in 1564 (after its return to Catholic rule) by Joris Hoefnagel for the city atlas of Braun and Hogenberg, Civitates Orbis Terrarum.

across the Islamic world were planted in experimental fields. Even after the western caliphate came to an end early in the eleventh century, the rulers of Spain's independent states would eagerly scan the great handbooks on agriculture and gardening by Ibn Bassal (c.1080), his slightly junior contemporary Abu' l-Khayr, and Ibn al-'Awwam (c.1180), looking for new plants. A practical soil scientist and agricultural scholar who farmed near Seville, Ibn al-'Awwam described roses of many types and colours in his celebrated treatise: the mountain rose, the red rose, the white rose, the yellow rose, the Chinese rose (*ward al-sini*), the wild dog rose (*nisrin*), the sky-blue rose, and another that was blue on the outside and yellow inside.[3] The list is intriguing: by 'blue' did he really mean 'red', as the late garden historian John Harvey has suggested? Or were Spain's Muslim gardeners inserting indigo and saffron into the roots of their roses to dye them blue and yellow, as Charles Joret maintained? And might this 'Chinese' rose represent the first recorded sighting of *Rosa chinensis* on European soil, 600 years before its recognized introduction, or was it a different plant altogether, such as *Hibiscus rosa-sinensis*?

As for the people who carried the new plants westwards in the wake of the Islamic conquests, they included the 'unsung heroes of this story', immigrants bringing in seeds, roots, cuttings or live plants; botanists scouting plants for the caliphs; travelling scholars; pilgrims making the *hajj* to Mecca; and merchants bringing goods to market. Although such examples of diffusion can be inferred from human behaviour, 'only the instances of caliphal plant collecting are caught in history's net', says the American landscape historian, D. Fairchild Ruggles. Yet even if much of the detail remains obscure, we are surely on the track of the rose as it moves ever westwards.

Much more suspect is the credit usually given to the crusaders for bringing roses back to Europe from the Holy Land, especially the red 'Rose of Provins', also known as the Apothecary's rose, *Rosa gallica* var. *officinalis*.[4] According to tradition, this rose was carried back from the crusades in the saddlebags of Frenchman Thibaut IV, King of Navarre and Count of Champagne, and used to found a flourishing rose industry in his native Provins producing medicines and jam. Britain's authority on hardy trees and shrubs, W. J. Bean, conceded that the story had a 'ring of truth', as Europe learned about the medical application of *Rosa gallica* from Arab works, and conserves or syrups of this rose were used to treat tuberculosis, as prescribed by the influential Arab physician, Mesuë of Damascus (see Chapter 14). Yet none of the early French writers on botany or horticulture mentions the rose's connection with the crusading knight, so where did the story originate?

While Provins's long history in making rose jam and medicines is not in doubt, the link to Thibaut arose out of civic pride, it seems, championed at the beginning of the nineteenth century by Christophe Opoix, an over-enthusiastic apothecary and proto-man of science from Provins (where else?) and repeated as gospel ever since. The puffed-up Opoix may not have originated the story, but he banged the drum the loudest for the rose's crusader origins; only at Provins, said Opoix, did the flowers conserve their beautiful purple colour, their medicinal properties and their full fragrance. Opoix's 'proof' of the illustrious history of his home-town rose included the even more startling claim that the 'belle Sulamite' in the Bible's 'Song of Songs' declared herself not simply the rose of Sharon but '*la rose qui s'apellera un jour la* Rose de Provins' (the rose that will one day be called the Rose of Provins).

A good story like this quickly takes hold, even when called into question by eminent rosarians such as Frenchman Charles Cochet-Cochet, who pointed out that as a European native, *Rosa gallica* had no need of such a long and dusty ride from the Holy Land, apparently substituting the Damask for the Gallica as the crusader's booty.[7]

But Thibaut had in any case little opportunity to botanize in the Holy Land. Described as 'an excellent poet, an ineffective warrior, and an irresolute and shifty politician', he left France in August 1239 on a crusade led jointly with the Englishman Richard Plantagenet, Earl of Cornwall, whom he never met. Most of his time in the Holy Land was spent peacefully encamped at Acre, Jaffa and Ascalon, and he fought just two battles, one a minor victory, the other a disastrous defeat, nonetheless recovering more land and castles from Muslim hands than at any time since the First Crusade.

Outside Acre, the Kingdom of Jerusalem was little more than a 'rude military settlement ... a foreign legion encamped in castles and barracks'. The crusaders had little contact with the villagers who farmed the land, brought few skilled gardeners with them, and unlike the

Christians in Muslim Spain, had no great flowering (or even mildly floral) civilization on which to draw. From the viewpoint of the Christian West, 'The Latins were scattered thinly on a narrow littoral, which they had to defend against a vast and dark background of Muhammadanism'. Crusader villages in any case grew subsistence crops to feed their hungry populations and, contrary to popular legends, there is no evidence of any speciality crops or plants of any kind being transmitted to continental Europe through the crusader kingdoms.

While Thibaut did at least make a pilgrimage to Jerusalem during his year-long stay in the Holy Land, he never travelled into Syria, where he might have experienced the Muslim reverence for flowers in general and roses in particular. Two decades or so earlier, the curious pilgrim Maître Thietmar (thought to be a Franciscan monk from Westphalia) had journeyed through the territory, noting the contrast between Frankish desolation and the fine new buildings of the Saracens. Damascus enchanted him especially; he admired its abundant fountains and artificial canals, and the fine gardens encircling the city. All kinds of fruit and other trees grew there, he said, delighting in the gardens' cool shade, the play of birds, and 'their many coloured flowers which cover them like a purple cloak'. Arriving in Damascus on St Martin's Day (11 November), he heard a nightingale sing. The roses were long since over but he found some newly opened violets 'and in my astonishment, I bought some'.

Far from relying on the crusaders to bring new varieties back from the Holy Land, the rose required Arab help to spread deep into Christian territory. But by protecting the pilgrim routes to the eastern Mediterranean, the crusaders can at least claim credit for boosting trade and opening up another route to aid the flower's cultural and geographical diffusion. Even before the crusades began, Venice had found its way into eastern markets through Byzantium, and merchants from Amalfi had established trade routes to Palestine. Now the Latin settlement of Syria gave access to the rich markets of Damascus and Baghdad, while the great trading states of Venice, Genoa and Pisa established themselves in ports along the Levant coast.

And for a century after about 1245, when the rise of the Mongols held Islam in check, the doors between East and West temporarily opened. A Genoese company sailed the waters of the Caspian Sea. A Venetian consul was settled in Tabriz, north-western Iran; and Venetian merchants such as Niccolò, Maffeo and Marco Polo penetrated deep into China. It seems that for all his bombast and shameless traveller's tales, Marco Polo really did travel the series of snaking, bifurcating routes that became known as the silk roads, which carried 'all manner of goods – gems, fabrics, spices, precious metals, weapons – as well as ideas and religions'. And tellingly for the story of the rose, the route joins all the key points in its westward passage from the Celestial Mountains of China's westernmost border with Kazakhstan, home of the wild *Rosa fedtschenkoana*, to the southern

The ancient silk roads travelled by Marco Polo – seen here in the Catalan Atlas, c.1375 – helped the rose on its westwards journey, mixing strains from central and western Asia and Europe.

shores of the Caspian sea, and onwards through Asia Minor into Europe.

Marco Polo himself is an unlikely carrier of roses. His keen mercantile eye naturally alighted on plants with a commercial value: rice for rice wine ('it makes better drink than any other kind of wine'), enormous pears, sugar cane, bamboo, timbers, mulberry trees, cinnamon, ginger and rhubarb, although not tea, strangely (perhaps he judged it too bitter for western tastes). But he had plenty of fellow travellers – Christian missionaries, Buddhist monks, Arab scouts, plant-loving merchants of all nationalities and creeds – who might have seen the value of roses that bloomed all season long.

Could this be the route travelled by *Rosa fedtschenkoana*, by chance or design to be deposited in a foreign land where it mated with a cross between *R. gallica* and the Musk rose? The story is at least more plausible than Opoix's bombastic claim, making Thibaut le Chansonnier the carrier of the Rose of Provins from the Holy Land back to his native town, where it was almost certainly growing already.

But when such a journey might have happened is not known, nor precisely where the cross took place. It must have occurred before the early sixteenth century, when we know for certain there were Damasks in Spain, but how much earlier? Might an ancestor of the *R. fedtschenkoana* that now flowers in my garden have journeyed from the Celestial Mountains more than 2,000 years ago, in time to produce Paestum's now disputed twice-blooming roses? Or was it much later, at the time of Islam's expansion westwards or the Christian West's commercially inspired inroads further east? We simply do not know. Two or three thousand years is a long time in human history, but the briefest blinking of an eye in the millions of years that mark the story of the rose.

The Symbolic Rose

Chapter Five
The Virgin's Bower

MORE than 1,200 years after Heliogabalus' murderous rose petals had rained down on his unsuspecting house guests, German artist Stefan Lochner painted his celebrated *Madonna in the Rose Bower*. All that links this painting to Alma-Tadema's orgiastic *The Roses of Heliogabalus* are the flowers: otherwise they stand at opposite poles in art.

A native of Meersburg near Lake Constance, Lochner settled in Cologne, where mystical Christianity flourished as the Middle Ages drew to a close. His painting is small, just 50 cm high, at once intimate and joyous. A blue-robed and childlike Madonna sits on a tasselled cushion within a *herber* of turf seat and flimsy pergola that supports some of the first climbing roses to appear in western art. Clearly double, their heads flat and open, the roses are of two sorts: gold-centred red roses that look remarkably like garden Gallicas, and blush-tinged white roses akin to sweet-scented Albas. On Mary's head is a jewelled chaplet or crown of single roses, ruby red and sapphire blue; she looks inwards rather than down at the Christ child on her lap, who holds an apple, the fruit of Paradise, in his left hand. About her skirts clusters a retinue of infant angels – making music, plucking a rose, praying, offering another apple from a bowl. The scene is painted as theatre: a curly-haired angel at each side draws back the red brocaded curtain, while a rosy-cheeked God the Father at the centre releases downwards the white dove of the Holy Spirit.

Lochner's painting presents an iconic image of Mary, who sits eternally in a heavenly rose arbour, the epitome of renunciation, existing in a 'timeless world peopled with gentle figures who seem to float in golden space'.[1] Mary's rose garden, too, became a commonplace of western art,

The roses in Stefan Lochner's Madonna in the Rose Bower, *c.1450, appeal to the spirit rather than the senses.*

yet in the early centuries of the Christian era, the Church fathers did all they could to outlaw this flower so tainted by pagan associations. So how did the rose transform itself from flower of Venus to the mystical rose of Christian liturgy?

Flowers – even roses – have no place in the early Christian Church. Emerging like Judaism out of the stony desert lands of Palestine and the eastern Mediterranean, Christianity valued asceticism and martyrdom, a life stripped bare; there are no flowers in the Eden of Genesis, and very few in either the Talmud or the Bible as a whole. In their rituals, the Hebrews preferred sheaves ('*gerbes*') and leaves to flowers, and as the nineteenth-century horticulturist Henry Phillips pointed out, the Israelites rejected flowers because they were associated with idolatry. 'As the gardens or sacred groves of the heathen nations were generally the scenes of their obscene revellings,' wrote Phillips in his study of floral display, *Flora Historica*, 'such public plantations, together with the erection of statues or images, were forbidden by the laws of the country.'[2]

The early Christians similarly rejected all links with the pagan practices of Rome. Roses – especially when woven into crowns and garlands – carried the taint of drunkenness, venery, idolatry and unspeakable pagan practices. 'Woe to the crown of pride,' thundered the Old Testament prophet Isaiah, 'to the drunkards of Ephraim, whose glorious beauty *is* a fading flower, which *are* on the head of the fat valleys of them that are overcome with wine!'[3] Instead of the 'fading flower', the coming of the Messiah would bring 'a crown of glory' and a 'diadem of beauty'.

Early Christian fathers such as theologian Clement of Alexandria (*c.*150–*c.*215) naturally forbade the use of crowns, especially those made of roses and lilies. Another who disapproved of crowns, although not necessarily of the flowers themselves, was the brilliant if reputedly difficult African Church father Tertullian, born a pagan at Carthage, who produced a string of ascetic and frequently controversial works after he converted to Christianity towards the end of the second century.

Tertullian wrote a diatribe against the wearing of chaplets, *De Corona,* which he sought to reserve strictly for Christian martyrs. Basing his argument on nature, Tertullian picked no quarrel with the flowers of the field that delighted the eye and the nose, organs created by God so that 'the enjoyments of the divine gifts are conveyed by the senses to the soul'.

All you had to do to enjoy them was to 'lay them in your bosom if they are so singularly pure, and strew them on your couch if they are so exquisitely soft, and consign them to your cup if they are so perfectly harmless'. But why, asked Tertullian, should heads want garlanding with flowers? 'It is as much against nature to long after a flower with the head, as it is to crave food with the ear, or sound with the nostril.' Castigating the crown-wearers as profoundly unchristian, and seductively wanton if they were women, he held out Christ's crown of thorns and thistles in direct and mocking contrast to those earthly crowns of 'laurel, and myrtle, and olive, and any famous branch . . . with hundred-leaved roses too, culled from the gardens of Midas, and with both kinds of lily, and with violets of all sorts'.

Tertullian's praise for wild roses hints at the Church's ambivalence about beauty and the sensual pleasures afforded by God's creation. For despite official disapproval, even at this early stage roses began to appear in visions of Paradise experienced by Christian martyrs. Tertullian himself edited one such account by Perpetua, a contemporary African saint, martyred in 203, and her accompanying priest, Saturus. In the priest's vision, after tremendous suffering their souls separated from their bodies and they were borne aloft by angels heading towards the east, floating upwards as if climbing a gentle slope. As God had promised, they first saw boundless light. 'And while we are borne by those same four angels, there appears to us a vast space which was like a pleasure-garden, having rose-trees and every kind of flower. And the height of the trees was after the measure of a cypress, and their leaves were falling incessantly.'

Ethereal roses feature in the legends that grew up around two other early Christian martyrs: the virginal Saints Cecilia and Dorothy. Patron of musicians since the sixteenth century, St Cecilia was a Roman martyr of the third century who refused to consummate her marriage on the grounds that she had already vowed her virginity to God. Demanding proof, as husbands will, her husband Valerian was sent to find St Urban hiding among the tombs of the martyrs on the Appian Way. On his return, he found Cecilia talking with an angel holding crowns of roses and lilies in his hand. 'Guard these crowns with spotless hearts and pure bodies,' said the angel, 'because I have brought them to you from God's paradise, and they will never fade or lose their fragrance, nor ever be seen by any except those who love chastity.'[4]

The legends surrounding St Cecilia developed only in the late fifth century, so we cannot be sure who crowned her with the roses of Paradise. But her supposed fate was gruesome enough: along with her husband and his brother, who both became Christians, she was arrested and martyred. When Cecilia refused to sacrifice to idols (the common test of a convert), she was boiled in a bath all night, and when that failed to kill her, a soldier was ordered to behead her. That, too, was botched and she lived on for another three days.

St Dorothy's martyrdom bore the same sweet smell of Paradise, and roses were once again produced as 'proof' of Christian truth. As she passed on her way to execution, probably at Caesarea in Cappadocia during the Diocletian persecutions of c.304, a jeering young lawyer named Theophilus asked her to send him the fruits of the paradise garden promised to her by her faith. Dorothy's prayers, uttered in the moments before her death, duly summoned an angel, who delivered a basket containing three apples and three roses. The legend inspired the Jacobean tragedy *The Virgin Martyr,* by Thomas Dekker and Philip Massinger, as well as Swinburne's poem 'St Dorothy', in which the basket ordered by the saintly Dorothy at her beheading contained marigolds, late peaches, red lilies and 'Great roses stained still where the first rose bled'.

Such legends suggest that in its early years, when the Church was subject to ferocious persecution and intent on defying the paganism of its persecutors, Christians welcomed the roses of Paradise but scorned the 'real' roses of the physical world. The Spanish poet Prudentius, for instance, boasted of using neither roses nor aromatic plants:

> Here no plunder of the rose
> No scent of spice smells in my nostrils.

And he praised St Eulalia for despising crowns of roses, ornaments of amber and necklaces of gold, preferring martyrdom instead and becoming, by her death, one more 'flower' in the Church's garland of martyrs.

But the rose was not to be so easily denied, and from the fourth century onwards it gradually transformed and rehabilitated itself, emerging as a Christian symbol that marked a symbolic victory of head over heart, of the soul and the intellect over the senses. That at least is the interpretation of the American academic Beverly Seaton, who argues that for pagans, flowers such as roses appealed to the heart and the biological body. In Ovid's *Metamorphoses,* for instance, flowers spring up as memorials to mortals who have died for love or been beloved by powerful gods in a kind of cosmic biology. The early Christian father Tertullian was naturally scandalized that flowers should be worn on the head, which he clearly associated with ideas and the soul, as opposed to senses and the body. But later Christian writers and artists consciously and deliberately turned flowers in general and roses in particular into just such matters of the head. Lochner's *Madonna in the Rose Bower* is simply the apotheosis of that process of transformation. Stand before it and you cannot help but respond intellectually and spiritually; these roses have nothing to do with pleasures of the senses, and Mary can quite innocently wear a jewelled chaplet of roses on her head.

And of course the situation of the Christian Church itself changed dramatically, after Emperor Constantine extended toleration and imperial favour to Christianity following his victory over rival Maxentius at Milvian Bridge in 312. The night before the battle, Constantine had dreamed that his soldiers fought under the sign of the cross. Attributing his victory to the Christian God, Constantine is revered as the first Christian emperor, although he deferred baptism until shortly before his death in 337.

Despite his hopes, Constantine's support for the Church was unable to stop the internecine squabbling among theologians and bishops, and the nature of the rose would be disputed along with every other contentious question. But it was clearly set on the path to Christian rehabilitation. Already in the fourth century, St Ambrose had Christianized the notion of Elysium as a rose garden, declaring that in Eden before the Fall, roses grew without thorns. The incarnation of Mary as the thornless rose, flourishing among the thorns of Eve, then slipped into the biblical epic *Paschale carmen* (c.430), by the Christian Latin poet, Sedulius:

Rosa alba flore pleno.   *Rosier blanc ordinair.*

White roses have traditionally symbolized the Virgin Mary. Pierre-Joseph Redouté's classic semi-double Alba rose, painted for Les Roses *of 1817, recalls the white roses in Martin Schongauer's* Madonna of the Rose Bush *of 1473.*

As blooms among the thorns the lovely rose, herself without a thorn,
The glory of the bush whose crown she is,
So, springing from the root of Eve, Mary the new Maiden
Atoned for the sin of that first Maiden long ago.

Even real roses were slowly finding their way into the house of God, after the cantankerous but immensely erudite St Jerome revoked the Church's ban on roses, encouraging the faithful to use them in church decoration. St Augustine, too, refers without censure to the use of flowers in the Church's reverence of martyrs, when a bishop bringing the relics of 'the most glorious martyr Stephen' to the waters of the Tibilis gave a blind woman the flowers he was carrying, and she instantly recovered her sight. Both incense and flowers were disassociating themselves from pagan sacrifice, and becoming acceptable accompaniments to worship. In the sixth century, the Italian bishop of Poitiers, Venantius Fortunatus (c.540–c.600), wrote a poem celebrating the glories of spring flowers, when men might decorate their doors and houses with flowers, 'and women adorn themselves with sweet roses. But you, not for yourselves, but for Christ, gather these first fruits, and you bear them to the churches, and wreathe the altars with them till they glow with colour.'[5]

The story of sixth-century St Benedict and his little rose garden, *il roseto*, illustrates how hard it is to separate fact from fantasy in the many Christian legends that grew up around the rose. Credited as the father of western monasticism, Benedict was educated at Rome, where the licentiousness of contemporary society led him to retire from the world to a cave at Subiaco. There he reputedly planted a little rose garden whose flowers delighted his senses and whose thorns he used to mortify his flesh.

A rosebud and leaves from St Benedict's garden found their way to the home of the Catholic convert and prolific American writer of the nineteenth century, Eliza Allen Starr. In *Patron Saints*, she describes the saint's garden as 'a sort of triangular plat of ground that stands out on the side of the rock a little in front of, and below, the grotto that sheltered St Benedict. The rose has been plucked many years, but still keeps its graceful stem, and mild perfume, and, almost, its beauty of color.' In Starr's retelling of Benedict's story, the saintly youth overcame temptation by throwing himself into a rose hedge, rolling on the thorns until the 'infernal temptation' left him. Seven hundred years later, St Francis of Assisi came to visit Benedict's 'wild desert', where he prostrated himself before the thorn thicket. 'After bathing with his tears the soil of this battlefield of youthful virtue, he planted there two rose-trees,' wrote Starr. 'The roses of St Francis grew, and have outlived the briars of St Benedict, and from these rose-trees I think my rose bud came.'[6]

And so from the seventh to the twelfth centuries the rose as Christian symbol proliferated, just like the roses of Sts Benedict and Francis, gathering new meanings that attached the flower sometimes to Mary, Mother of God, and at other times to Christ and Christian martyrdom. As well as the thornless rose, Mary was also the rose of modesty (*rosa pudoris*), and the mystical rose (*rosa mystica*), a title confirmed by the Marian Litany of Loreto approved in the late sixteenth century but probably much older. Latin hymns and liturgies added many more floral tributes, such as 'noble rose', 'fragrant rose', 'chaste rose', 'rose of heaven', 'rose of love' and 'never-wilting rose'. In an uncanny echo of pagan practice, roses even appeared in Mary's tomb, as described by the Italian chronicler and Archbishop of Genoa, Jacobus de Voragine, in *The Golden Legend,* one of the most popular lives of the saints in the Middle Ages. After her soul had departed from her body, Christ ordered the apostles to take Mary's body to a tomb they would find in the Vale of Jehosaphat, 'And anon she was environed with flowers of roses, that was the company of martyrs, and with lilies of the valley, that was the company of angels, of confessors and virgins.'[7]

Essential to the rose's transformation into a Marian symbol was the witty, learned and supremely eloquent St Bernard of Clairvaux, one of Mary's most ardent followers, who founded the Cistercian monastery at Clairvaux in north-eastern France in 1115. His most enduring work is an unfinished series of sermons on the biblical Song of Songs, which ranged in focus from practical issues of monasticism to a mystical confrontation between the Song's bridegroom and bride, interpreted by Bernard as Christ and his Church.

Flowers were a recurring theme. Sermon 47, on 'The Threefold Flower of Holiness', picked as its text the Song's well-loved lines spoken by

Swagged with pearls and garlanded with roses in this eighteenth-century statue painting from Peru, the Virgin of Pomata appears with St Nicholas of Tolentino and St Rose of Lima, the first Catholic saint of the Americas.

Christ in his guise as the bridegroom: *I am the Rose of Sharon, and the Lily of the valleys.* Which roses did Christ mean, asked Bernard, those of the couch, the garden, or the wild roses of the plain? He settled for wild roses, on the grounds that these were the only ones to flourish without the care or attention of man, and quickly moved on to a deeper spiritual reading of the flowers' three distinct 'blooms', which he named as virginity, martyrdom and good works, concentrating on the lily rather than the rose.

In another Lesson, he picked up Sedulius' poetic conceit about Mary and Eve, suggesting that the Virgin Mary atoned for 'the poisonous thorn' of Eve's original sin. 'Eve was a thorn,' explained the cleric, but

Mary is a rose. Eve was a thorn in her wounding; Mary a rose in the sweetening of the affections of all. Eve was a thorn fastening death upon all; Mary is a rose giving the heritage of salvation back to all. Mary was a white rose by reason of her virginity, a red rose by reason of her charity; white in her body, red in her soul; white in cultivating virtue, red in treading down vice; white in purifying affection, red in mortifying the flesh; white in loving God, red in having compassion on her neighbor.

A little confusingly, the red rose could also stand for Christ and in particular the Five Wounds of His Passion, a cult that reached its peak in the later Middle Ages. Already St Bernard was venerating the Five Wounds in his sermons on the Song of Songs, using language that would become increasingly erotic and morbid as the cult developed.

The Benedictine-educated Suffolk poet John Lydgate (c.1370–c.1450) turned the Five Wounds into a single five-petalled rose, counselling the reader in 'A Sayinge of the Nyghtyngale' to 'Make of these fyve in thyn hert a Rose / And lete it there contynuauly abyde'. His best-known poem, 'As a Midsummer Rose', contrasts the fast-fading roses of midsummer with the lasting glories of Christ, ending with a complex interweaving of different roses – the rose of the bloody field (Golgotha), the Rose of Jericho growing in Bethlehem, and the Jerusalem or Crusaders' Cross, itself made up of the Five Wounds of Christ, or of Christ and the four Gospels. All these roses merged into Christ's final Passion, when:

This fifteenth-century Flemish manuscript depicts the Sacred Heart and the Wounds of Christ cushioned on roses, from an illuminated volume of prayers relating to the lives of Christ and the Virgin.

The sunne was clips [eclipsed], and dirk in every rem [realm],
Whan Crist Jesus five welles [wells or wounds] list unclose
Towards Paradis, called the rede strem,
Of whos five woundes prent [imprint] in your hert a ros.

*

After such a surfeit of spiritual roses, it is a relief to turn to real roses growing in real gardens during the time of the Church's steady rise. Although the evidence is scanty, the idea of growing plants for food and medicine unquestionably survived the centuries of barbarian invasion and shifting migration of peoples and tribes after Rome's fall and the withdrawal of the Romans from western Europe. Botanical learning actually declined, and the medical profession virtually disappeared, but Christian monks kept alive the flames of learning, and of healing in the West. Certainly, Benedictine monks owned and tended gardens, especially for decorating their altars on feast days as the Church relaxed its prohibitions, and St Isidore, Bishop of Seville, (c.560–636) specified in his monastic rule the need for a garden within the foundation's cloister.

We can be certain that roses were planted in the gardens of central and northern Europe, following an edict issued by another great European ruler: Charles the Great, King of the Franks, better known as Charlemagne, who was crowned Emperor of what would become the Holy Roman Empire by Pope Leo III on Christmas Day, 800. Deeply Christian, despite a chaotic private life, Charlemagne extended his Franco-Germanic kingdom south into the Pyrenees and Lombardy, and east to the boundaries of Poland, and he brought uniformity and reform to government at home. He also took Europe's 'heart' northwards, away from the Mediterranean, establishing his capital at Aachen in what is now western Germany. Europe, and more particularly the Church, was slowly polarizing into East and West, as the emperors at Constantinople, true heirs to imperial Rome, grew further estranged from the western popes at Rome.

Crucial to the way Charlemagne ran his kingdom were the capitularies or government orders issued centrally to royal agents and officials, or special commissioners. One of the most important orders to survive is the *Capitulare de villis,* usually attributed to Charlemagne (although his

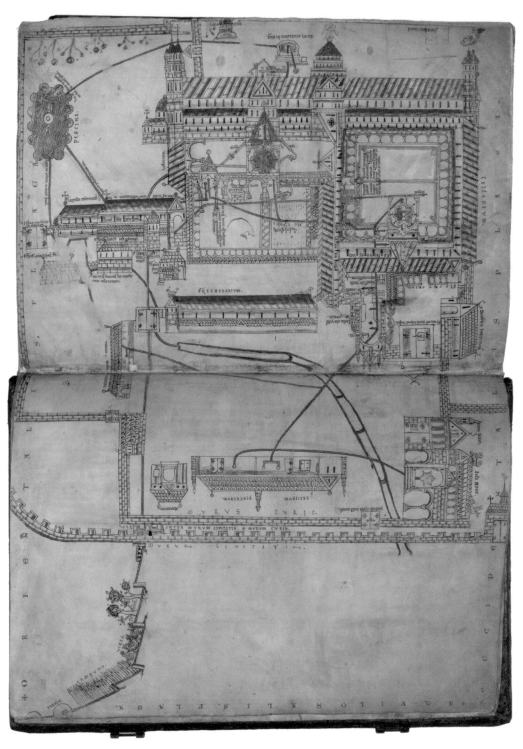

*Planted in Europe's medieval monastery gardens for their healing
and spiritual virtues, roses and lilies grow outside the precinct walls in Prior Wibert's
plan of waterworks at Christ Church Canterbury, c.1165.*

son, Louis the Pious, is another contender), intended to improve the management of royal estates. Its seventy separate provisions ranged from the principles and practice of fair treatment for all the people, to the mechanics of quality assurance and the rudiments of bookkeeping. Charlemagne (or Louis) thought of everything, even considering the plants and trees that were to be grown on the royal estates. 'It is our wish that they shall have in their gardens all kinds of plants' began the final ordonnance: 'lily, roses, fenugreek, costmary, sage, rue, southern-wood, cucumbers, pumpkins, gourds, kidney-bean, cumin, rosemary, caraway, chick-pea, squill, gladiolus . . .'

These were clearly useful gardens. All the plants listed, even the lily and the rose, could contribute to the kitchen or the infirmary, although giving these two pride of place suggests an attitude of mind that put Marian devotion before grumbling stomachs and sore heads. As revealed by John Harvey, whose patient rummaging through medieval plant lists has illuminated our knowledge of early horticulture, a good many other plants listed (such as fennel, flag iris, mallow, poppy, rosemary, rue, tansy and the sweet bay tree) were also worthy of the flower garden. Violets – a favourite flower of the age – were strangely absent, and while many of the plants would grow happily throughout western Europe, a few would survive only towards the south. Harvey also noticed that the lily was singular and the roses plural, implying more than one rose in cultivation.

Remarkably, Charlemagne's plant list is not the only horticultural survival from the time. Preserved at the great Benedictine abbey of St Gall near Lake Constance in Switzerland is the plan for an ideal monastery, drawn up some time between 819 and 826, which presents itself as a Christianized Roman villa complete with two separate gardens and a monks' cemetery planted as an ornamental orchard with fifteen sorts of trees. Roses and lilies were found next to the physician's house in the infirmary garden or *herbularius,* which had sixteen oblong beds, each dedicated to a named herb. The larger *hortus* or kitchen garden was similarly regimented, with eighteen named beds. And Charlemagne's religious and educational adviser Alcuin of York celebrated the roses and lilies of his dearly loved cell when he bid it farewell in verse: 'Thy cloisters smell of apple-trees in the gardens, and white lilies mingle with little red roses.'

But the best connection between Christian spirituality and earthy gardening practice is found in the extraordinary garden poems written by another Benedictine monk, Walahfrid Strabo (his name translates literally as Walahfrid the squint-eyed), who wrote his poetry in the calm of the abbey gardens of Reichenau where he returned as abbot in 842, a few short years before he drowned while crossing the Loire on a mission to one of Charlemagne's grandsons, Charles the Bald, whom he had tutored as a boy.

Generally known as *Hortulus* or 'The Little Garden' (Walahfrid called the collection *De cultura hortorum*), the poems are dedicated to Grimald, abbot of St Gall and one of his early teachers. In his dedication, Walahfrid pictures his mentor

> Sitting there in the green enclosure of your garden
> Under apples which hang in the shade of lofty foliage,
> Where the peach-tree turns its leaves this way and that
> In and out of the sun . . .

Inspired by Virgil, the collection is clearly written by a man who gets his hands dirty spreading 'whole baskets of dung on the sun-parched soil'. He begins by celebrating the rewards of a quiet life, not least the joy that comes to those who devote themselves to the art they knew at Paestum, acquiring the 'ancient skill of obscene Priapus' and cultivating native plants. His own little patch faced east, he tells us, a small open courtyard full of nettles which he cleared with a mattock, destroying the mole runs, breaking up the soil with a rake, then working in a leaven of manure. His garden prepared, he then describes in verse the names and virtues of thirty-five plants he grew there, from absinthe, agrimony and ambrosia to southernwood, tansy and wormwood.

He leaves the rose until last, declaring himself tired and his strength failing. It is obviously his favourite, revered for its beauty, its fragrance, and its many healing uses:

> For us the rose from year to year renews in abundance
> The yellow stamens of its crimson flower.
> Far and away the best of all in power and fragrance,

88

It well deserves its name 'the Flower of Flowers'.
It colors the oil which bears its name. No man can say,
No man remember, how many uses there are
For Oil of Roses as a cure for mankind's ailments.

Like the double red rose that Stefan Lochner would paint for his Madonna of the rose bower, this yellow-centred red rose is surely of the Gallica tribe that would produce the classic flower of healing, *R. gallica* var. *officinalis*, and the red rose of Provins. But the gardener-monk returns at the very end to the spiritual meanings of the rose and the lily, two flowers 'so loved and widely honoured' that have stood throughout the ages as symbols of the Church's greatest treasures:

> ... for it plucks the rose
> In token of blood shed by the Blessed Martyrs;
> The lily it wears as a shining sign of its faith.

And in the poem's fading moments, Strabo calls on the Holy Virgin to pick roses for war and smiling lilies for peace. Jesus, too, has come to her as a flower of the royal stem of Jesse, His fate intimately bound to the two great flowers of Christian iconography:

> By His holy word and life He sanctified
> The pleasant lily; dying,
> He gave its color to the rose.

*

The last word on Christian roses belongs, however, not to Walahfrid the squint-eyed but to Italy's supreme poet, Dante Alighieri, who ended his *Divine Comedy* with one of the most original and potent of all allegorical roses: Paradise itself as a pure white rose, vast in size and fragrant through all eternity. Situated beyond the spheres in the furthest reaches of heaven, Dante's rose of Paradise contained the two 'courts' of heaven, angels and human souls; at its heart sat Mary, Queen of Heaven, flanked by the Church's two 'roots' of St Peter and Adam. Gustave Doré illustrated Dante's rose as a vortex of winged angels swirling into a

Gustave Doré illustrated Dante's celestial rose from the Divine Comedy *as a vortex of saintly souls and angels in* The Vision of Purgatory and Paradise by Dante Alighieri *of c.1868.*

radiant sun at the eye, watched by Dante and Beatrice on a cloud. William Blake recast the rose as a sunflower – a recurring sexual symbol in his work – presided over by a scantily clad Virgin Mary as Queen of the Fallen World. But for Dante, this vision of the celestial rose would bring him to a vision of Absolute Truth.

Writing in the first decades of the fourteenth century, Dante called on three guides for his spiritual journey through Hell and Purgatory to Paradise: first Virgil, poet of enlightened reason; then his long-dead love, Beatrice Portinari, first glimpsed when Dante was a boy of nine; and finally the great devotee of Marian rose symbolism, St Bernard of Clairvaux, who conducts him through mystic contemplation on the rose to his vision of the Godhead as radiant light, which appeared as 'three circles of three colours and one magnitude; and one seemed reflected by the other, as rainbow by rainbow, and the third seemed fire breathed forth equally from the one and the other'.

The American academic Barbara Seward has called this one of the most complex symbols in literature, suggesting that Dante had attempted to concentrate in a flower no less than his answer to the riddle of the universe. Through the triumphant imagery of the rose, Dante's great epic uses earthly love as a stepping stone to spiritual love, uniting late medieval mysticism with new ideas of courtly love and looking forward to the early Renaissance that would transform Italy a century or so later. It was an astonishing performance.

Chapter Six
Sex and Sorcery

THROUGHOUT its first 1,000 years, the Christian Church had stealthily transformed the rose from an emblem of the heart to one of the head. But then a further transmutation occurred that took the rose into darker regions of the psyche. The process at work was allegory, which fused head and heart to produce a new focus on the human body and more particularly on the act of sexual union between man and woman. Long associated with Venus, now the rose became the object of desire; and even more explicitly, she came to represent a woman's sexual parts, no less in medical texts than in literary ones. The head was still involved, of course: we dream up words and symbols in our brains, turning them into stories that help explain the world to us, and ourselves. But Shakespeare's 'sweetest rose' had its origins in a very medieval conjunction between the classical and Christian worlds.

Among those responsible for this reworking of the rose were two Frenchmen, Guillaume de Lorris and Jean de Meun, who co-wrote the *Roman de la Rose,* a didactic poem of nearly 22,000 lines which became one of the most influential and controversial work of the Middle Ages. While scholars continue to dispute its meanings, its sexual imagery is obvious to even the most casual reader.

Written between 1225 and 1275 in vernacular French rather than the more learned Latin, it enjoyed singular success among medieval audiences far beyond its native France. Dante, Boccaccio and Chaucer were among its admirers. More than 100 manuscripts survive, many beautifully illuminated, and by the end of the fourteenth century it had been translated into Dutch, Italian and English.

The work was begun by Guillaume de Lorris, about whom little is known except that he came from Lorris, a village to the east of Orléans, and had completed 4,058 lines of the poem by around 1237, when his narrative breaks off; he may even have considered it finished. The poem was taken up some forty years later by Jean de Meun, poet, scholar and translator of works such as Boethius's *Consolation of Philosophy*, who was born Jean Clopinel or Chopinel at Meung-sur-Loire, a village to the south-west of Orléans. Only after Jean de Meun had added more than 17,000 lines did the poem begin to attract notoriety, lauded by some for its erudition and edifying humanism, while bitterly condemned by others as scabrous and misogynistic.

Guillaume de Lorris constructed his tale as a dream narrative, apparently written some five years after the actual dream. Wandering joyfully through a classical *locus amoenus* of river and beautiful meadow, the twenty-year-old Dream Lover comes across a large garden surrounded by high crenellated walls. Admitted through a tight wicker gate by Idleness, a lovely girl wearing chaplets of gold thread and roses, the Lover believes himself 'truly in the earthly paradise'. Here, he witnesses a carol sung by Joy and danced by figures such as Courtesy, Diversion, Sweet Looks and the God of Love, whose chaplet of roses is constantly knocked to the ground by fluttering nightingales.

Continuing further into the garden, the Dream Lover succumbs to the Fountain of Narcissus, a 'perilous mirror' out of which 'a new madness comes upon men'. Gazing into its two crystals he sees a reflection of rose bushes covered in roses and closely surrounded by a hedge. 'Mark well: when I was near, the delicious odour of the roses penetrated right into my entrails. Indeed, if I had been embalmed, the perfume would have been nothing in comparison with that of the roses.' The God of Love waits until the Lover has chosen his favourite rose, then shoots him with five arrows – an echo of the Five Wounds of Christ but in a wholly secular context. Sick with love, the Dream Lover receives instruction on how to conduct himself, but his efforts to regain the Rose meet with little success. When he snatches a kiss, Jealousy shuts away the rose bushes behind the walls of a garrisoned castle, together with the Lover's helpful companion, Fair Welcoming. Guillaume de Lorris's poem ends with the Dream Lover's lament, frustrated in his desires to capture the rose.

La conclusion du rommant

The Lover with his stiff stave walks towards the rose in this illuminated Flemish miniature from the Roman de la Rose, *produced c.1490–1500 in Bruges.*

The narrative taken up by Jean de Meun adopts a radically different tone. The sensuous garden all but disappears, its foreground turned into a literal and verbal battlefield as allegorized figures such as Reason, the Friend, the Old Woman, Nature and Genius argue their different points of view. Parading his encyclopedic learning, Jean de Meun launches into popular medieval discourses – on free will versus determinism, the influence of heavenly bodies on human behaviour, optics, the creeping power of mendicant orders, the lustfulness of the clergy and the cupidity of women. Eventually, and just before a final digression on Pygmalion's creation in ivory of the perfect woman, Venus shoots her arrow at a 'tiny narrow aperture' hidden at the front of the tower, 'where Nature, by her great cunning, had placed it between two pillars'.

Clapped on by Fair Welcoming, the Lover launches his assault on the Rose.

I set out like a good pilgrim, impatient, fervent, and wholehearted, like a pure lover, on the voyage toward the aperture, the goal of my pilgrimage. And I carried with me, by great effort, the sack and the staff so stiff and strong that it didn't need to be shod with iron for traveling and wandering. The sack was well-made, of a supple skin without seam. You should know that it was not empty: Nature, who gave it to me, had cleverly forged two hammers with great care at the same time that she first designed it.

And so he continues, commenting on the action he takes, how he knelt at the sanctuary between the two fair pillars, partly raising the curtain to know it more intimately; how he assailed it often but often failed, nevertheless discovering a narrow passageway protected by a paling, which he had to break down with his staff, certain he was 'absolutely the first' to enter by that route, until at last 'I took the bud at my pleasure . . .'

I seized the rosebud, fresher than any willow, by its branches, and when I could attach myself to it with both hands, I began very softly, without pricking myself, to shake the bud, since I had wanted it as undisturbed as possible . . . Finally, I scattered a little seed on the bud when I shook it, when I touched it within in order to pore over the petals. For the rosebud seemed so fair to me that I wanted to examine everything right down to the bottom. As a result, I so mixed the seeds that they could hardly be separated; and thus I made the whole tender rosebush widen and lengthen.

And so the story ends. After briefly thanking his friends and cursing those who held him back from committing an act that to modern eyes seems indistinguishable from rape, the Lover plucked with great delight his red rose from the rose bush. 'Straightaway it was day, and I awoke.'

Given their marked differences in tone and style, it is hardly surprising that the two parts to the *Roman de la Rose* have attracted wildly different readings. In the twentieth century, the Oxford academic and author of the *Narnia* chronicles, C. S. Lewis, saw the two works as fundamentally opposed. Guillaume de Lorris's narrative he judged an exercise in courtly love which pitted the God of Love's refined sentiments against Venus's unbridled sexual appetites, while Jean de Meun's 'huge, dishevelled, violent poem of eighteen thousand lines' plainly baffled him. Others took the opposite view, praising de Meun's outspoken realism in contrast to Lorris's 'fiddle-faddle' and linking the poem to the rediscovery of love as a disease – an idea that had returned to Europe in a cargo of Arab medical texts brought back by Constantine the African in the late eleventh century. Among his texts was a self-help manual for travellers, the *Viaticum,* which reintroduced lovesickness into European culture, along with Graeco-Arab ideas of erotic love.

Today, it is common to treat the two parts of the *Roman* as a unified whole; for all their differences in style, Guillaume's rose behaves just as sexually as Jean's. When Guillaume's Lover first sees the 'great heaps of roses' covering the rose bushes, he notices their different stages of ripening, from the 'small, tight buds' to the larger ones that were beginning to open. He likes the buds especially. 'The little ones are not to be despised; the broad, open ones are gone in a day, but the buds remain quite fresh at least two or three days.'

The bud that finally catches his eye is strangely phallic, glowing with a colour 'as red and as pure' as the best in Nature. 'The stem was straight as a sapling, and the bud sat on the top, neither bent nor inclined.' Most remarkable of all was its 'sweet perfume', which filled the entire area, and would have drawn him to it but for its barbed thorns and the nettles that blocked his path.

Later, when he snatches a kiss from the rose, he is pleased to report its gradual ripening and enlargement, although the bud was 'not so open that the seed was revealed. It was still enclosed within the rose leaves, which raised it straight up and filled the space within, so that the seed, with which the rose was full, could not appear. God bless it, it was much more beautifully open and redder than it had been before.'

With its startling imagery and topical debates, the *Roman de la Rose* reverberated down the ages, infecting the literature of succeeding generations. Its walled garden paradise appeared in Boccaccio's *Decameron,* giving refuge to the young storytellers fleeing plague-ravaged Florence, and again – explicitly – in Geoffrey Chaucer's *The Merchant's Tale* as a refuge created by the ageing Merchant for his young new wife, only to be cuckolded by his wife and her lover up a pear tree. But the garden itself was unsurpassed,

> For, out of doute, I verraily suppose
> That he that wroot the Romance of the Rose
> Ne koude of it the beautee wel devyse.

Such was its beauty, said Chaucer, that even Priapus, lecherous god of gardens, might not be able to speak of it.

While Chaucer's own moral view remains ambiguous, the *Roman de la Rose* influenced him more deeply than any other English or French work, and he liked it enough to write his own translation. A part may have survived as the first fragment of a Middle English version, *The Romaunt of the Rose*, written by several hands.

For Chaucer, as for Guillaume de Lorris, fragrance was the rose's greatest attraction:

> Toward the roser gan I go;
> And whanne I was not fer therfro,
> The savour of the roses swote
> Me smot right to the herte-rote,
> As I hadde all enbawmed be.

And Chaucer, like Guillaume, liked his roses in bud.

> I love well sich roses rede,
> For brode roses and open also
> Ben passed in a day or two,
> But knoppes wille [al] freshe be
> Two dayes, atte leest, or thre.

Yet for all his garden borrowings, Chaucer can hardly be described as a rose fanatic. His *Legend of Good Women* celebrates not the rose but the daisy; and despite the trellised alleys in the garden of *Troilus and Criseyde*, he turned to roses mainly as a simile for blushing and as a 'swoote and smothe and softe' contrast to the 'foule netle, rough and thikke'. In *The Canterbury Tales*, the Parson introduced rose bushes into his filthy tirade against the five fingers of the devil merely to have them pissed on by dogs. And while Priapus, Venus, personified Lust, Curteysie, Craft, Gentilesse, naked Beauty and others roamed the garden in the *Parliament of Fowls*, Chaucer is vague about its flowers, airily indicating a garden full of 'floures white, blewe, yelwe, and rede, / And colde welle-stremes, nothyng dede...'

But Chaucer would indirectly influence the relationship between roses and love in his 'invention' of St Valentine as the patron saint of mating birds and human lovers in the same *Parliament of Fowls,* an annual gathering of the birds for the purpose of choosing their mates:

> For this was on seynt Valentynes day,
> Whan every foul cometh there to chese his make [choose his mate].

Scholars still argue about why Chaucer chose the feast day of the martyred St Valentine (14 February) to celebrate the first matings of spring, when the weather is hardly spring-like, even under the old Julian calendar, which lagged some ten days behind today's revised Gregorian calendar. One possible explanation – that Chaucer was drawing on Christian custom that had sought to Christianize the Roman festival of Lupercalia – is now generally discounted, as Lupercalia had nothing to do with the pairing of mates. Chaucer and his friends who wrote Valentine poems about this time seem genuinely to have started a fashion that has endured to the present day.

Other late medieval writers emphatically declined to share Chaucer's admiration for the *Roman de la Rose*. One of the work's fiercest critics was the lyric poet Christine de Pizan, who turned to poetry some time after the death in 1390 of her husband, a secretary to King Charles VI of France. Writing a little over a century after Jean de Meun had completed Guillaume's poem, Christine de Pizan was scandalized by his cynical portrayal of women and by his sexual morality, not least his graphic portrayal of male and female genitalia. For this she has been called a prude, but she believed that de Meun had snared his readers with seemingly innocent imagery and then submitted them to the equivalent of literary rape. In her *Épitre au Dieu d'Amours* (Letter to the God of Loves) of 1399, she poured scorn on de Meun for employing so many murky ruses to trick a virgin,

> I can't imagine or make sense of it,
> Such force applied against so frail a place,
> Such ingenuity and subtlety.

Her mockery heralded a literary spat that ranged de Pizan and her supporter Jean Gerson, Chancellor of the University of Paris, against three royal secretaries (Jean de Montreuil, Provost of Lille, and the brothers Pierre and Gontier Col), who all championed Jean de Meun. The quarrel was conducted through increasingly heated sermons, letters and treatises. In defending de Meun's sensuality, Pierre Col went so far as to claim that the Bible sanctified the secret parts of a woman, and that de Meun was right to call a woman's 'little rosebud' a sanctuary because so too were the gates and walls of a city considered holy, and woe to anyone who used force or trespass against them. In reply, de Pizan's champion Jean Gerson wondered angrily what Bible Col had been reading to think that a woman's vulva was sanctified by custom, unless he was led astray by these words of St Luke: 'Every male that openeth the womb shall be called holy to the Lord.'[1] And when Gontier Col offered to pardon Christine de Pizan for speaking her mind like a *femme passionnée* (an impassioned woman), she retorted that she was not to be intimidated, reminding him in language reminiscent of the *Roman* itself that 'a small knife can pierce a great and swollen sack'.

Christine de Pizan's greatest weapon against her adversaries was her

Lovers converse in a garden, leaning on a rose trellis, from
Cent Ballades d'Amant et de Dame *by Christine de Pizan, illuminated c.1410–12*
by the Master of the Cité des Dames, Paris, and his workshop.

poetry, in which she called for a public repudiation of the *Roman de la Rose* and Ovid's *The Art of Love,* and recommended, like Gerson in his thunderous sermons, burning the poem she found so hateful. But far from casting roses to the flames as well, she sought to rescue the flower from its scabrous reputation by creating – in her poetry and perhaps also in real life – a chivalric 'Order of the Rose' dedicated to upholding the honour of women.

Composed in 1402, when the Quarrel of the Rose was at its height, de Pizan's poem *Dit de la Rose* positively exudes an odour of roses, brought by high-born 'Lady Loyalty' to the Parisian dinner table of Louis, Duke of Orléans, where de Pizan placed herself as an invited guest. The elegant dinner party presages a dream in which Lady Loyalty entrusts to Christine the founding of an order that would bestow its 'dear and lovely roses' only on those knights who upheld a woman's virtue and reputation, in direct opposition to Jean de Meun.

> Now he who will accept those terms
> And make that promise solemnly,
> Let him so boldly take the rose
> In which all sweetness is enclosed.

Like the authors of the *Roman de la Rose*, Christine de Pizan dealt in her poetry with abstraction and allegory. But the roses Lady Loyalty brought to the dinner party were very real and very fragrant, vases full of them, 'Vermillion, white, quite beautiful', freshly plucked that morning from her orchards. And in an irony worth savouring, the day de Pizan chose to write about the Duke's dinner party was Chaucer's invented St Valentine's day ('Escript le jour Saint Valentin'), so the arch-enemy of the allegorical *Roman de la Rose* was in turn responsible for bringing roses into the questionable celebrations of the martyred Valentine as patron saint of lovers.

The rose carried its sexual freight into later centuries. The rose in Elizabeth slang was pre-eminently sexual and came with many meanings: maidenhead, vulva, whore, courtesan, sexually used woman, syphilitic sore; to 'pluck a rose' might imply either taking a girl's virginity or pissing in the open air.[2] Did Shakespeare mean to raise a laugh among the groundlings in his audience when Juliet smiles on Romeo, declaring:

> What's in a name? That which we call a Rose
> By any other word would smell as sweet.

Or do we look for innuendo where none was meant?

Whatever Juliet intended here, for Shakespeare and his contemporaries the rose provided a convenient metaphor for a woman's ripening sexuality – a distinctly male view of sex in which the 'bud' of a girl's adolescence is soon ripe for the plucking but immediately loses its freshness as the flower opens and becomes '(over)blown'. The sentiment is charming enough when spoken breathlessly by the virgin Juliet (not yet fourteen) to her soon-to-be-lover, Romeo:

> This bud of love, by summer's ripening breath,
> May prove a beauteous flower when next we meet.

It becomes more brutal when spoken by Orsino, Duke of Illyria, to his 'boy' (in fact the lovesick Viola in disguise) in *Twelfth Night.*

> For women are as roses whose fair flower
> Being once displayed, doth fall that very hour.

In the mouth of Othello, it becomes positively murderous as he contemplates the sleeping Desdemona before smothering her in a jealous rage.

> When I have plucked the rose,
> I cannot give it vital growth again,
> It needs must wither. I'll smell thee on the tree.

And while a later poet such as Robert Herrick might exhort his (presumed male) readers to 'Gather your rose-buds while ye may',[3] Shakespeare can see the tragedy of passing time and passing beauty from a woman's point of view, as in Cleopatra's anguished cry:

See, my women,
Against the blown rose may they stop their nose
That kneeled unto the buds.

The ripening rose also provided an arresting medical image for a woman's sexual parts, thereby striking an immediate accord with Guillaume de Lorris and Jean de Meun. In his anatomical compendium of 1615, the medical practitioner and sometime steward of London's notorious Bethlem Hospital, Helkiah Crooke, described a woman's hymen as 'partly fleshy partly membranous, being compounded of Caruncles or little peeces of flesh and membranes . . . All these particles together make the forme of the cup of a little rose half blowne when the bearded leaves are taken away.' Bringing the whole of the woman's 'privity' into view,

he adjusted his metaphor to 'the Great Clove Gilly-flower when it is moderately blowne', giving it the Latin name, 'Hymen quasi Limen, as it were the entrance, the piller, or locke or flower of virginity'.[4] (Crooke raided the garden for other striking images, comparing a woman's fallopian tubes to vine tendrils and describing the ligaments of the womb as 'round like to earth wormes, reddish and hollow especially in their end'.)

The seventeenth-century herbalist Nicholas Culpeper borrowed the rose image for his directory for midwives, saying that the fleshy knobs around the hymen resemble 'the form of a Rose half blown, and therefore anciently called a Flower, and thence came the word [To deflower a Virgin]'.[5]

The image recurred in rhymes for Valentine cards of the seventeenth and eighteenth centuries, including this verse in an English Valentine primer of 1784, to

Seated Courtesan with Roses *by Nibaran Chandra Ghosh (1835–1930).*

be sent 'To a LADY, with a Rose-bud'. In the verse, the accompanying rosebud was intended to call to mind another rosebud in a different place:

> The seat where genial pleasure's found,
> With tender moss encircled round;
> Ah! would you take it in your hand,
> My throbbing soul you might command.[6]

According to the American academic Barbara Seward, Sigmund Freud also linked roses to a woman's sex. 'Blossoms and flowers in general are said to represent the female sexual organs,' she wrote, 'while the particular shape of the rose associates it most directly with the shape of the vulva. In other words, to Freud the rose of spring is first and foremost the rose of sexual love. And his theory receives ample reinforcement from primitive folk and fairy lore.'

In fact, this is not strictly true. Although Freud interpreted his patients' flower dreams in an explicitly sexual way, the flower he compared to a woman's genitalia was the camellia, not the rose, in a patient's dream that mixed together a spray of white lilies, a branch of flowering red cherry that opened into double red camellias (which Freud later misremembered as white), and a manservant combing thick tufts of hair out of a tree using a branch of wood.[7]

The rose took on a more rarefied meaning in the work of another giant of early twentieth-century psychotherapy, Carl Gustav Jung, for whom it represented psychological wholeness. Indeed, in *The Practice of Psychotherapy,* he suggested that this wholeness is part of a transcendent unity that can only be grasped symbolically, through such symbols as the rose, the wheel, or the conjunction of the sun and the moon. Jung's principal symbol of the self striving for unity and completeness was the mandala (from the Sanskrit for circle), which the Jungian analyst Philippa Campbell explains as 'a circle that contains all that is paradoxical and has at its centre the radiating rose. If we trace a mandala in our chaos we are offered a symbol that allows us to bring that which is unattended and forgotten into consciousness.'

For Jung, sexuality was just one facet of his all-embracing rose, but he

ROSARIVM

CONIVNCTIO SIVE
Coitus.

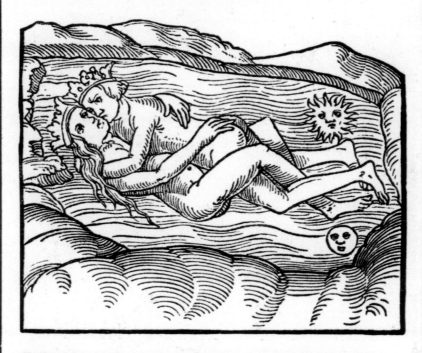

O Luna durch meyn vmbgeben/vnd suſſe mynne/
Wirſtu ſchōn/ſtarck/vnd gewaltig als ich byn·

O Sol/ du biſt vber alle liecht zu erkennen/
So bedarſſtu doch mein als der han der hennen.

ARISLEVS IN VISIONE.

Coniunge ergo filium tuum Gabricum dile=
ctiorem tibi in omnibus filijs tuis cum ſua ſorore
Beya

The union of the sun king and lunar queen from an alchemical text
of 1550, the Rosarium Philosophorum, *included by Carl Gustav Jung as an*
allegory of the psychic union of opposites in Psychology and Alchemy.

also became increasingly drawn to alchemy, the medieval forerunner of chemistry, which gave a more overtly sexual meaning to the rose. In the alchemical process, the rose stands primarily as a symbol of conjunction, the 'chymical wedding' or mystical marriage of opposites between the active masculine principle (the Red King) and the receptive female principle (the White Queen). King and Queen are often portrayed as roses, red for the male and white for the female. 'The white and red rose are synonyms for the *albedo* and the *rubedo*,' wrote Jung in his enquiry into the psychic opposites in alchemy, *Mysterium Coniuncionis,* referring to the processes of whitening and reddening after the initial blackening or degradation of matter, which the alchemists sought to turn into gold.[8] Jung was, of course, talking psychologically: for him, alchemy's chemical process came to represent the individual's progress towards psychological wholeness. But the illustrations he included in *Psychology and Alchemy* of the physical union between the Rose King and the Rose Queen deliver us straight back to the territory of the medieval *Roman de la Rose.*

Since the sixteenth century at least, the *Roman de la Rose* has attracted alchemical readings, and in his encyclopedic trawl through contemporary themes, Jean de Meun naturally threw in a reference to the principles of alchemy, without delving into the detail of its arcane practices. It would, however, be anachronistic to attempt a purely spiritual reading of the *Roman's* sexual conjunction between the Lover and the Rose. Despite resorting to the language of symbols, medieval alchemy in the West was primarily concerned with matter, not spirit, and the elusive goal of medieval alchemists was to turn base matter into gold;[9] more spiritual interpretations came later.

So the sorcery at work in the original *Roman de la Rose* was sexual rather than spiritual, and the rose at its heart remains closer in spirit to Helkiah Crooke's 'little rose half blowne' than to C. G. Jung's spiritual and psychological wholeness. Christine de Pizan thought as badly of the alchemists as she did of Jean de Meun. 'And when we have worked and worked,' she wrote in one of her many scathing attacks on the poem's defenders, 'it is all worth nothing. For the matter [*la matière*] is very dishonorable, much like certain alchemists who think they can transmute dung.'

*

While the rose in the thirteenth and fourteenth centuries had some strange bedfellows, it also added great sweetness to late medieval life. Illuminated manuscripts to the *Roman de la Rose* and de Pizan's poems project an ideal – and almost certainly idealized – world in which elegantly dressed young couples stroll gently around rose-embowered walled gardens, or sit amid the sprinkled spring flowers of a flowery mead, playing the lute, listening or quietly reading. In a British Library manuscript of de Pizan's poems, for instance, two lovers converse at the edge of a turf lawn, elbows touching as they lean on a rose trellis twined with red and white roses, their eyes not quite meeting.

No actual gardens survive from the times, so we can only speculate as to whether the illustrators painted the gardens they knew or the garden-makers came to imitate the gardens promised by romance, both the home-grown variety and the tiny walled paradise gardens of Persian miniatures, which began to appear in Europe from the last decades of the fourteenth century. Travellers would also have brought back tales of such gardens from the Arab world, including Sicily and Moorish Spain, and from the Byzantine East. Europe gained a new word, 'paradise', originally from the old Persian *pairidaeza,* an enclosure, which blended well with the enclosed garden of the Song of Songs and gave medieval minds a place in which to situate their longing for imperishable bliss.

But there were real gardens too, with practical functions (the kitchen and the medicinal garden, for instance), and the more 'aesthetic' pleasure gardens of the nobility, whose principal purpose was to delight the senses of sight and smell. We learn much about how people gardened from one of the earliest surviving garden treatises by the learned Dominican friar Albertus Magnus, son of a wealthy German lord, who wrote his treatise *De vegetabilibus et plantis* (On vegetables and plants) around 1260, adding a whole chapter on pleasure gardens (*viridariorum*) to an otherwise utilitarian work.

To produce a rich firm soil, Albertus advised first digging out the weeds, then levelling and flooding the ground with boiling water to kill any remaining fragments. Gardeners should cover the whole plot with rich turf, beaten down with mallets, and plants trodden into the grass so that 'little by little they may spring forth closely and cover the surface like a green cloth'. Sweet-smelling herbs were to surround the lawn, such as rue, sage and basil, and 'likewise all sorts of flowers, as the violet, columbine, lily, rose, iris and the like'. He also recommended the planting of sweet-scented trees, trained vines, more medicinal herbs to delight the senses of sight and smell, and the provision of turf benches and seats 'so that men may sit down there to take their repose pleasurably when their senses need refreshment'. Open to the clean and healthy winds of the north and east, the garden should also contain at its heart a clear fountain of water, 'for its purity gives much pleasure'.

In Book 7 of his treatise, Albertus Magnus included an alphabetical listing of specific plants, much like a herbal, in which he discriminated between several different kinds of roses, but identifying which ones he meant is difficult.[10] Comparing garden roses to the dog rose, he pointed out that their thorns were weaker and their leaves broader. The white rose in particular – surely a distant relative to *Rosa alba* – had a thornless main stem 'formed like the arm of a man', and many long thin branches 'just like blackberry suckers' bearing thorns that were weak and very small. The green buds with five leaves (sepals) opened into many-petalled flowers, perhaps as many as fifty or sixty in white roses. He also wrote of the five-petalled *Rosa campestris,* describing its rounded hips and saffron-coloured stamens. Some have tentatively identified this as the pure white European field rose, *Rosa arvensis,* but later in the same passage Albertus said that the flowers started green and ended up red, unlike the lily and the elder ('*sambucus*'), which might suggest Europe's native red rose, *Rosa gallica.* Even more problematic is his brief mention of a stinking rose ('*rosa foetida*'), colour unspecified, which could be the yellow *R. foetida* from the Caucasus and into the Middle East. While this rose appears in the *Book of Agriculture* of Ibn al-'Awwam, an Arab agri-culturist living in Spain at the end of the twelfth century, it is absent from all other medieval works written in Latin, but equally no other rose known in Europe has such a rank smell.

Whatever he meant by '*Rosa campestris*', Albertus must surely have known forms of *R. gallica* or its close cousin, the classic red rose of medieval gardens. The wild species is small and suckering, with few thorns and an upright habit. Its single flowers are medium to large, usually of a clear pink centre with pronounced powdery yellow stamens, and richly scented. Garden varieties include semi-double and double

Illustrated here by Sydenham Teast Edwards for Curtis's Botanical Magazine *of 1819, the field rose (*Rosa arvensis) *has been identified variously as Albertus Magnus's R. campestris, Shakespeare's Musk rose and the scrambling rose in Nicholas Hilliard's* Young Man Among Roses.

forms, all with the Gallica's characteristic flattish head and fragrance. Albertus Magnus made no mention of fragrance, although he wrote extensively of the rose's medical virtues, quoting the classical world's greatest authority on medical matters, Galen of Pergamon.

And all across Europe, roses were bringing their owners joy and sometimes profit. In the mid-twelfth century, the monks at Norwich cathedral grew roses in the main cloister garth (later returned to lawn) and transplanted a rose bush from the cloister to the tomb of William, the boy martyr, in the cemetery. Their accounts listed just four cash crops sold from the gardens: faggots, apples, nuts and roses. Among the famous gardens in Holborn, London, was the Bishop of Ely's rose garden, which he protected with high walls. Nearby, the Earl of Lincoln sold garden produce from his London garden, earning as much as £9 in 1296, which included 3s 2d from roses – either thousands of roses or a much smaller number of rose plants. To ease the ills and ailments of his patients, in 1339–40 the Infirmarer at Westminster bought the roots of roses, lilies, camomile and poppies. A century and a half later, the churchwardens at St Mary-at-Hill in London bought roses to decorate their church for Corpus Christi and garlands of roses and woodruff for St Barnabas' day, while the Grocers' Company more prudently grew their own roses to decorate their hall and garden.

Across the English Channel, Charles VI of France, brother to Christine de Pizan's Duke of Orléans, replanted his father's twenty-acre Parisian garden at the Hôtel St Pol with a hundred or so pear grafts and similar numbers of common apple trees, twelve paradise apples, 1,000 cherry trees, 150 plum trees, eight green bay trees, and 300 bundles each of red and white roses, lilies and flag iris. At his splendid new park of Hesdin, Count Robert II of Artois planted on a similarly grand scale, creating many garden areas, including a rose garden containing a little tower, just like Jealousy's castle in the *Roman de la Rose*. White and red roses crowd the frescoed gardens of the Palazzo Davanzati, celebrating a late-fourteenth-century matrimonial union.

From Paris, too, comes one of the most down-to-earth yet touching records of the late Middle Ages: a treatise on moral and domestic economy written by an ageing citizen of Paris for the instruction of his young wife. Giving the lie to Chaucer's jaundiced view of intergenerational marriages, the anonymous Goodman set down his thoughts with the 'mellow sadness of an autumn evening', amplifying his snippets of household advice with many tips for the garden (he was especially fond of violets, it seems, and knew all the different sorts of cabbages and lettuce). 'If you would keep roses in winter,' he told his wife,

take from the rose tree little buds that be not full blown and leave the stems thereof long, and set them within a little wooden cask like unto a compost cask, without water. Cause the cask to be well closed and so tightly bound that naught may come in or out thereof, and at the two ends of the aforesaid cask tie two great and heavy stones and set the aforesaid cask in a running stream.

A similar recipe for keeping roses red involved forming a dozen roses into a ball – as many as you wanted – covered with linen and tied up with thread. These should be set in a crock of Beauvais earthenware repeatedly filled with the best verjuice from the pressing of unripe grapes. When you wanted the buds to open, you should take them out of the bags and submit them to a short soaking in warm water. Other instructions taught his wife how to make rosewater without a lead alembic; how to turn rosewater red; and which were the best roses for putting in dresses – roses of Provins, he believed, 'but they must be dried and sifted through a sieve at mid-August so that the worms fall through the holes of the sieve, and after that spread it over the dresses'.

In the late Middle Ages, the rose might signify the battle between the sexes, but it could equally represent domestic harmony, uniting the concerns of good husbandry and goodwifery.

Chapter Seven
Secrets of the Rosy Cross

T HE roses of alchemy set the seeds of another subterranean movement which flourished first in Germany in the late sixteenth and early seventeenth centuries: the elusive brotherhood of the Rosicrucians, members of a society then so secret that its very existence remained in doubt.

To the uninitiated, the early history of the Rosicrucians reads like the Borgesian short story 'Tlön, Uqbar, Orbis Tertius', in which a group of intellectuals sets out to change the world not by wars or revolution but by creating an imaginary country and later a whole new planet, which they present to the world as if they really existed. 'Clues' planted in the real world – in the pages of a pirated encyclopedia, for instance, and curious artefacts that hint at other realities – exert such fascination on all who encounter them that people begin to accept this strange new mythology as fact. Borges's narrator deliberately dropped Rosicrucian names into his story, such as Johann Valentin Andreae, whom he had encountered (he said) in an essay by Thomas de Quincey, 'where I learned that it belonged to a German theologian who in the early seventeenth century described an imaginary community, the Rosy Cross – which other men later founded, in imitation of his foredescription'. Out of this swirling fog came the Rosicrucians, who owed their long-term survival to the lure of secrecy, and to their masterly adoption of the Christianized West's two most potent symbols: the cross and the rose.

The rose's long association with secrecy harks back to classical times, and the oft-repeated legend that in order to stop word of Venus's *amours* leaking into the public domain, her son Cupid bribed Harpocrates, the

God of Silence, with roses. But the story is confused. It seems that the Greeks borrowed Harpocrates from the Egyptian boy-god Horus, son of Isis and Osiris, who appears in the Pyramid texts with a finger in his mouth to signify his child status. Mistaking this gesture for an invitation to silence, the Romans turned Harpocrates into the God of Silence and Secrecy, as in the writings of Marcus Terentius Varro, who spoke of the earth and sky gods in Egypt and Rome, 'though Harpocrates with his finger makes a sign to me to be quiet'.

However tenuous the link, the rose duly became the badge of silence and discretion; and the Romans reputedly decorated the ceilings of their dining rooms with roses to remind guests that whatever was spoken under the influence of wine (*sub vino*) was also under the rose (*sub rosa*) – privileged and not to be divulged. In early modern times, the expression 'sub rosa' or 'under the rose' is thought to have originated in Germany, while in England it found its way into the state papers of Henry VIII in the penultimate year of his reign, in a letter from John Dymock, English agent in the Low Countries, to Henry's financial agent at Antwerp.[1] Invited to dine by an official of Dordrecht, then still part of the Catholic Spanish Netherlands, Dymock had been questioned on delicate matters concerning his sovereign's religious beliefs, the fate of England's monasteries, and the king's relations with his fourth wife Anne of Cleves, soon repudiated as that 'Flanders mare'. Although assured more than once that the conversation would remain under the rose, 'that is to say, to remayen under the bourde and no more to be rehershed', Dymock was arrested the next day 'lycke a trayttour or a thyffe' and thrown into jail. The correspondence rumbled on: clearly what rankled most with Dymock was that he had been questioned 'under protest that all should be under the rose' and then arrested because his Dutch accusers feared he might reveal their conversation.

By the late 1630s, the rose as an emblem of discretion had entered gentlemanly etiquette. The one-time Norfolk schoolmaster and author Henry Peacham described customs in England and the Low Countries, where 'they have over their tables a rose painted, and what is spoken under the rose must not be revealed. The reason is this: The rose being sacred to Venus, whose amorous and stolen sports, that they might never be revealed, her son Cupid would needs dedicate to Harpocrates, the god of silence.' In the secret brotherhood of the Rosicrucians, however, the rose would make the transition from silent witness to participant in the mystery itself.

Germany in the late sixteenth and early seventeenth centuries offered a fertile breeding ground for secret societies harbouring millenarian dreams of brave new worlds and spiritual regeneration. Poised between the Renaissance and the scientific revolution of the Enlightenment, Europe had been convulsed by Martin Luther's challenge to the Church of Rome, and the forces of Catholic reaction were preparing for a counter-attack that would sweep away this stubborn Protestant heresy. The tensions were especially severe in Germany's Protestant principalities, held under the repressively Catholic thumb of the ruling Habsburgs, who had arrogated to themselves the throne of Holy Roman Emperor. Those who looked for a reawakening of the spirit could also draw on Germany's strong esoteric tradition which had produced contemplative mystics such as the Dominican preacher and theologian Meister Eckhart, the magician and Neoplatonist Heinrich Cornelius Agrippa von Nettesheim, and Europe's most renowned alchemist, the physician and occult philosopher Paracelsus.

The birth of Rosicrucianism was heralded by the rise of a new star in the Protestant firmament: the handsome, gentle, intellectual but ultimately doomed Elector Palatine Frederick V, whose marriage to England's Princess Elizabeth Stuart, daughter of King James I, ushered in a brief golden dawn. Already deeply and romantically attached to each other, the couple married amid flamboyant festivities in the royal chapel at Whitehall, London, on 14 February 1613, a date that suggests St Valentine's Day had resurfaced as a celebration of love.

Wishing to prepare for his bride, Frederick hurried home to Heidelberg Castle, where the Huguenot hydraulic engineer Salomon de Caus would create fantastic gardens which heightened the strange mystical atmosphere surrounding their union.[2] The Princess Elizabeth, meanwhile, floated up the Rhine in a magnificent barge, the Earl of Arundel (and possibly the architect Inigo Jones) among her retinue. At the Palatinate town of Oppenheim she passed through triumphal arches erected in her honour, one decorated with roses to mark her association with the royal houses of York and Lancaster, while packed away in the royal baggage was the rose-decorated insignia of England's Order of the Garter, bestowed on Frederick and on his uncle Prince Maurice of Nassau a week before the wedding. Echoes of all these roses would reverberate in the rose of the Rosicrucians: here was their back story in the making.

Even before the wedding, two tracts announcing a new dawn of enlightenment had been circulating in manuscript form in the German territories. Later known as the Rosicrucian manifestos, these were eventually published in Kassel, Hesse, in 1614 and 1615. The first, *Fama Fraternitatis,* was written in vernacular German and the second in Latin, the *Confessio Fraternitatis;* both referred in their subtitles to the fraternity of the most noble or honourable order of the Rosy Cross. A third – and far stranger – Rosicrucian work appeared in 1616, published anonymously in Strasbourg: *The Chymical Wedding* (*Chymische Hochzeit*) *of Christian Rosencreutz,* an alchemical romance almost certainly written by Johann Valentin Andreae, the Lutheran pastor from the state of Württemberg in south-western Germany, later named by Borges in his story.

All three texts centred on the activities of a certain 'Father C. R.' or Christian Rosencreutz (Rose-Cross), founder of a mysterious brotherhood – apparently revived – which used a red cross and red roses as its symbols. Anti-Jesuit in focus, the brotherhood set out to found an order more truly based on Christ's teaching. Rosencreutz himself was said to be an 'illuminated man', born in Germany in 1378. During his long life he had travelled widely in search of knowledge, visiting Damascus, Arabia, Egypt and North Africa, and then crossed over to Spain to share his learning before returning to Germany, where he had studied mathematics and meditated on his philosophy. The *Fama*'s author then went on to recount the imaginary history of the imaginary order founded by Rosencreutz, and the discovery of his tomb around 1604, some 120 years after his death at the venerable age of 106.

The more erudite *Confessio* added few fresh details. Assuming knowledge of the *Fama* among its readers, it condemned East and West (meaning the Prophet Muhammad and the Pope) as blasphemers against Christ; and, scorning the books of the false alchemists, offered its followers a return to the 'truth, light, life and glory' enjoyed by Adam in

The stronghold of the Rosicrucian brotherhood sports the emblematic rose and cross to left and right of the entrance, from Daniel Mögling's Speculum Sophicum Rhodo-Stauroticum *of 1618, published under the pseudonym Theophilus Schweighardt.*

Paradise. More fevered in tone, it reflected and further stoked the excitement surrounding this mysterious brotherhood which appeared to echo Nostradamus's prophecy made half a century earlier:

> A new sect of Philosophers shall arise,
> Despising death, gold, honours and riches,
> They shall be near the mountains of Germany,
> They shall have abundance of others to support and follow them.

Actual roses appear only in the third Rosicrucian text, *The Chymical Wedding*, which could be read as a romance about a bride and bridegroom living in a 'wondrous castle' full of marvels and images of lions (clearly Frederick and Elizabeth at Heidelberg), and an allegory of alchemical processes leading to the 'mystic marriage of the soul'.

Startled to receive an invitation to a royal wedding from a trumpet-blowing winged female, Christian Rosencreutz puts on his wedding garments of white linen coat, blood-red ribbon bound crossways over his shoulder, and four red roses in his hat, a detail that recalls the rose wreath eaten by Lucius Apuleius' golden ass (see Chapter 3). On the third day of wedding festivities, the roses did indeed bring him to the attention of the Virgin, who sent over her page to request them on her behalf. After witnessing strange alchemical happenings (the beheading of corpses in their sepulchres, for instance, and their subsequent resuscitation), Christian Rosencreutz and the others prepared to leave on the seventh day, when they were declared Knights of the Golden Stone and joined a horseback procession with the King, 'each of us bearing a snow white ensign with a red cross'. Like the Rosicrucian Brothers of the two manifestos, the Knights of the Golden Stone were spiritual alchemists, and Christian Rosencreutz's journey to the chymical wedding at the magical castle offered sympathetic souls a new unfolding of the quest for the Holy Grail.

All three Rosicrucian texts created a furore, fanned by their apparent anonymity and the rumours already circulating about this very secret society. Who were the mysterious brethren of the 'Red-Rosie Cross', as Rosencreutz announced himself at the stately gates to the castle, and what was their promised illumination? How could one reach them, if their identities and addresses remained hidden? Did they really exist, or was the 'brotherhood' an elaborate hoax that was getting out of hand?

Amid all the confusion, one fact is clear: profoundly Christian in outlook – even if imbued with hermetic and esoteric ideas – the instigators of the Rosicrucian movement had struck metaphysical gold when they fused the two Christain symbols, using the rose to soften the cross of Calvary, or, in today's language of psychoanalysis, bringing Eros and relatedness into the world, which had seen too much Logos. According to this view, whenever the balance between matter and spirit becomes weighted too far towards matter and hard rationality, an 'irrational' movement such as Rosicrucianism rises up from the collective unconscious to redress the imbalance, and so the rose returns to the world.

Aside from its heraldic associations, the rose was also becoming increasingly complex and paradoxical. At once a signifier of purity and of passion, of heavenly perfection and earthly love, of Mary's virginity and charity and the excruciating Passion of her Son, it joined Dante's white rose of Paradise with the flaming red rose of the *Roman de la Rose*. In hermetic circles, too, alchemy's red and white roses came together in the mystic conjunction of the 'chymical wedding' between the Red King and the White Queen – a conjunction that appeared angelically hopeful to some, and diabolically dangerous to others.

The rose had added resonance in Protestant Germany, where Martin Luther had incorporated a white rose into his seal, claiming that it contained a compendium of his theology. At the centre of his emblem, a black cross sat within a red heart, itself placed 'in the midst of a white rose, to symbolize that faith gives joy, comfort, and peace'. In Luther's explanation to a supporter, the rose was white rather than red because 'white is the colour of the spirits and of all the angels'. The rose in turn was set within a sky-blue field, and the whole emblem encircled with a golden ring, symbolizing eternal blessedness.

Luther's rose belongs to the European tradition of emblem books such as those of Protestant theologian Daniel Cramer, which sought to guide readers through the moral maze of the world with the aid of words and engraved pictures. It may also have inspired the first pictorial

The Rosicrucian rose grows out of the cross in an engraving from the title page to English esoteric philosopher Robert Fludd's Summum Bonum *of 1629.*

conjunction of the two Rosicrucian symbols on their own – a cross encompassed by a crude whorl of five petals, set in an outer whorl of eight petals. The image appeared in an immensely long apocalyptic work of 1604, Simon Studion's *Naometria*, which used biblical measurements of the Temple of Solomon to prophesy future events.

England's Paracelsian physician and astrologer, Dr Robert Fludd, incorporated one of the most striking rose-cross images into his own writings: a double rose (composed of seven-petalled layers) growing out of a thorny cross to form the sign of Venus, in which the solar circle triumphs over the cross of matter. '*Dat rosa mel apibus*' reads the inscription (the rose gives honey to the bees), illustrated by bees swarming from nearby hives. In Fludd as in Cramer, spiritual knowledge gives succour to the soul.

But for all its symbolic potency, the rose was unable to save Frederick and Elizabeth, on whose fortunes Protestant Europe had pinned its hopes. Offered the throne of Bohemia by Protestant princes in defiance of the Catholic Habsburgs, Frederick unwisely accepted in 1619, taking Elizabeth to Prague where they reigned for just one winter, forever immortalized as the Winter King and Queen.

As Catholic forces massed at Bohemia's borders, Protestant support melted away, and Frederick's belief that his father-in-law would come to his aid proved wildly misguided: James I of England wanted peace too much to risk fighting another war, even to save his daughter's throne. Frederick's forces were crushed at the Battle of White Mountain near Prague, on 8 November 1620. The royal pair and their children fled in exile to The Hague, while Spanish forces invaded Frederick's Palatinate homeland, and the Protestant Church in Bohemia was suppressed. So began Europe's Thirty Years War, which continued the power struggle between France and the Habsburgs (much of it played out on German soil), widening into a political war that engulfed much of Europe.

After Frederick's death in 1632 at the age of just thirty-six, the widowed Elizabeth lived on in impoverished exile at The Hague. Ten years into her widowhood she had her portrait painted by Gerrit van Honthorst, her children's drawing master. Dressed in black and adorned with the pearl earrings given to her by her husband, she carries her tragedy well, her eyes unmistakably shadowed and her brow furrowed in grief. In her right hand she holds a single-stemmed rose bearing two pink roses, one healthy, the other wilted as a symbol of her widowed state. Seven years after the portrait was painted, she would lose her brother, Charles I of England, executed for high treason, but her bloodline would eventually inherit his throne through her grandson George, Elector of Hanover, at the death of the childless Queen Anne.

The Rosicrucian rose did not die, however, but rather spread its suckering roots underground, exciting controversy when it appeared in

Queen of Bohemia.

In this portrait of 1642 by Gerrit van Honthorst, the exiled 'Winter Queen' Elizabeth Stuart
holds a healthy and a withered rose to indicate her widowhood. Her marriage to Frederick the
Elector Palatine and their brief reign in Bohemia had helped to fan the Rosicrucian furore.

the Netherlands and even more so in France, imported, according to contemporary reports, by scholars and doctors returning with books from the Frankfurt Fair.

In 1623, with the King away in Fontainebleau, mysterious placards suddenly appeared across Paris, apparently written by deputies from the principal college of the Rosicrucian brothers, announcing their 'visible and invisible' presence in the city. Offering instruction 'without books or marks', in the language of their hosts, the brethren proclaimed their fervent desire to save their fellow men from the error of death – but omitted to say how they might be contacted. In an ironic twist, the young René Descartes found himself caught up in the Rosicrucian fervour. Back in Paris after disappearing from view 'somewhere in Germany' while he elaborated the first principles of his philosophic method, he had to make himself plainly visible to prove that he was not, in fact, one of the invisible brethren.[3]

The English made less of a fuss, perhaps because their character was better able to accommodate both mysticism and pragmatism. Queen Elizabeth's favourite magus, Dr John Dee, may anyway have supplied the movement's seed corn when he journeyed to Prague in the late 1580s to see the hermetically inclined Emperor Rudolph II, returning through the German lands that would witness the great Rosicrucian flowering some twenty-five years later. Among other English notables suspected of Rosicrucian leanings was the early natural scientist and statesman Sir Francis Bacon, his allegiance 'proved' somewhat ludicrously (according to one esoteric manual) by the large rosettes he wore on his shoes for the frontispiece to his history of King Henry VII – a fashion statement, surely, much like the 'provincial roses' Hamlet wears on his 'razed shoes'. Even into the Enlightenment, figures such as Sir Isaac Newton and the lawyer and antiquary Elias Ashmole could combine an interest in alchemy with membership of the Royal Society, demonstrating their ability to let the old and new sciences coexist.[4]

In Germany, the Rosicrucians kept their heads down for a century or more, but the conditions that had favoured the movement's birth also ensured its subterranean survival – an interest in alchemy and the occult, and a love of roses, both real and symbolic. They came together in Germany's greatest polymath and poet, Johann Wolfgang von Goethe, who turned to alchemy after a severe illness forced him to abandon his law studies at Leipzig University. Encouraged by the alchemical adept Susanna von Klettenberg, he read widely among occult writers and together they spent much of the winter engaged in alchemical experiments in his father's attic, when Goethe reputedly cured himself with a secret alchemical 'salt'.

Although he would later repudiate such experiments, the rose remained a constant motif in his work, from the wild rose wilfully broken on the heath by the young knave in his early poem, 'Heidenröslein', to the transformative roses celebrated by the younger angels at Faust's end, when he is reborn into wholeness and begins his journey towards heaven. He even began (but never finished) a poem featuring the Rosy Cross, and projected the magical-mystery Rosicrucian atmosphere of the *Chymical Wedding* into a fairy tale, *Das Märchen* which can be read as an allegory of the alchemical process of transformation, and especially the integration of the feminine principle. To gain inspiration from the flower itself, all Goethe needed was to look out of the window of his Garden-House at Weimar, where he had planted the sprawling climber *Rosa × francofurtana*. It grew so high that Goethe was said to have 'actually lived in the middle of a rose-bush'.

Real roses returned also to Kassel, where the two Rosicrucian manifestos had caused the original furore, in the great rose collection put together by Landgrave Friedrich II in his park at Castle Weissenstein – almost 150 different varieties by the time of his death in 1785, an enormous number for the times, including a very early *Rosa chinensis* from China (see Chapter 11). Visitors could wander into the lower rose garden, where the River Styx gushed out of the underworld into a fountain basin, their senses alive to the chirping of exotic birds, the babbling fountain and the overwhelming scent of roses. There were mutterings, too, of masonic connections, and of secret meetings among the roses, although Friedrich's conversion to Catholicism makes this unlikely.

The next Landgrave, Wilhelm IX, demolished Kassel's old castle, using its rubble to create the centrepiece of his new landscape garden refashioned in the English style: a rose island by the lake, one of the earliest plantings of shrub roses in a landscape garden. He proudly

Taf: 2.

Die Tapetenrose.

Goethe planted the Tapetenrose (Rosa × francofurtana) around his Garden-House at Weimar. Here it appears in the Allgemeines Teutsches Garten-Magazin of 1804, also produced in Weimar.

renamed his new castle and park Wilhelmshöhe, and appointed a court miniaturist, Salomon Pinhas, to paint watercolours of his magnificent roses.

Pinhas was still at work on the watercolours in 1806 when Wilhelm, by then Elector Wilhelm I of Hesse, was forced to flee his homeland, after Napoleon installed his brother Jerome as King of Westphalia and Jerome took Schloss Wilhelmshöhe for himself. The roses lived on and even found their way into Empress Josephine's collection at Malmaison (see Chapter 10). After Napoleon's fall, Wilhelm returned to Wilhelmshöhe and ordered Pinhas to finish painting his roses. In 1815 he had them bound into a quarto volume and placed in the castle library, where they lay forgotten for more than a century and a half, until plans to restore Wilhelmshöhe's park with shrub roses brought Pinhas's charming rose portraits back into the light.

The Rosicrucian rose – which blossoms to this day on both sides of the Atlantic – inspired at least one more literary prophet, the Irish poet and patriot, William Butler Yeats, who fell under its spell in the turbulent, *fin-de-siècle* atmosphere of the late nineteenth century, when Europe was awash with hermetic cults. He first joined Madame Blavatsky's Theosophists and then, shortly before the Theosophists expelled him, the Hermetic Students of the Golden Dawn, a Rosicrucian group that followed the western tradition of Kabbalistic magic rather than Mme Blavatsky's wisdom of the east. Here he progressed from the outer to the inner grade, encouraged like all initiates to meditate on the Golden Dawn's core symbol of the rose that broadly signified the flower of eternal love blossoming on the cross of sacrifice.

In line with his spiritual development, Yeats turned the rose into the central symbol of his early work, using it almost to excess – in poems, short stories, Irish folk tales, notes, dreams, verse plays, even on his book covers. By the time he brought out his first collected edition of poems (in 1895, two years after he had been initiated into the Golden Dawn's inner order), he applied the collective title of 'The Rose' to all the poems originally published in the volume of lyrics and legends, *The Countess Kathleen,* having found in them, as he himself explained, the only pathway that would allow him to see with his own eyes 'the Eternal Rose of Beauty and of Peace'.

Rosicrucian ideas permeated his next collection of stories, *The Secret Rose,* which began with a poem addressed to the 'Far off, most secret, and inviolate Rose', and which carried on the cover a gilded rose (designed by Althea Gyles) conjoining the rose and the cross, man and woman, within the folding, serpent-like branches of a stylized Tree of Life. And he set out his own interpretation of the rose in the endnotes to another volume of his poetry, *The Wind Among the Reeds,* published as the nineteenth century drew to a close. 'The Rose has been for many centuries a symbol of spiritual love and supreme beauty,' he began, suggesting that it stood also for the sun, itself a principal symbol of the divine. Just as some eastern cultures imagined the lotus growing on the Tree of Life, so for Yeats the western Flower of Life – the Rose – flourished on the same tree.

But for Yeats, the rose also stood for Ireland, and as a symbol of a woman's beauty – two personal preoccupations that became hopelessly entangled in his protracted love for the beautiful Irish radical Maud Gonne, daughter of a colonel in the British army, to whom he addressed many of his early poems. As he wrote much later in *Autobiographies*, 'I thought that for a time I could rhyme of love, calling it *The Rose*, because of the Rose's double meaning,' referring obliquely to the woman he had seen as a mortal embodiment of immortal beauty.

Yeats eventually wearied of the rose as he moved on to other symbols, and the rose came to stand for the melancholic frustrations of his early life when he seemed unable to reconcile his need for order with the messier contradictions of love and Irish politics. But 'Rosa Alchemica', the last of the *Secret Rose* stories, hints at the possibility of spiritual rebirth and of reconciling the cross with the rose, even if the story's narrator appears to have forsaken the stormy occult for the safe haven of the Catholic Church.

Written in the feverish gloom of a continent marching towards war, Yeats's 'Rosa Alchemica' is a match for Borges and the fevered dreams of the early Rosicrucians, who lived through similarly disturbed times. It draws on elements familiar to Protestant Germany of the early seventeenth century: magic and mystery, death and rebirth, spiritual and practical alchemy, the cross and the rose joined together in mystic rites that promise the dawning of a new spirit, and a new age. While

Althea Gyles's cover design for the 1897 edition of W. B. Yeats's The Secret Rose *places a four-petalled rose at the heart of the cross to signify the four elements, beneath a male and female head joined in the mystic marriage of Rosicrucianism. The three smaller roses represent the three Sephiroth or states of being at the top of the Kabbalistic tree of life.*

some may say it failed him in the end, Yeats's alchemical rose revealed the extraordinary power of the rose to reinvent itself afresh for each succeeding generation.

Europe's Old Roses

Chapter Eight

Elizabeth's Briar

THE rose in Shakespeare's day was omnipresent. Lauded throughout Europe, it had become a particularly British phenomenon after the (Welsh) Tudors had turned the roses of the English countryside into their dynastic emblem. Fêted for its beauty, its healing virtues, its political and religious symbolism, the rose had regained its own throne as the Queen of Flowers, exhaling a delicious sweetness that masked the stink of everyday life. In Shakespeare's words:

> The Rose looks fair, but fairer we it deem
> For that sweet odour which doth in it live.

Yet the Tudors should have paid more heed to the rose's darker side, which Shakespeare saw with equal clarity.

> Roses have thorns, and silver fountains mud;
> Clouds and elipses stain both moon and sun,
> And loathsome canker lives in sweetest bud.

And for the unmarried Queen Elizabeth (daughter of the executed Anne Boleyn), Shakespeare's warning was even more prescient, that the distilled rose would be 'earthlier happy' than

> . . . that which withering on the virgin thorn
> Grows, lives, and dies in single blessedness.

The political rose would prove just as fickle as the rose of love.

*

One of the most endearing guides to the rose in Shakespeare's day is the man who may have taught him much of his plant lore: herbalist and barber-surgeon John Gerard, author of one of the great herbals of Elizabethan England. For a brief few years at the beginning of the seventeenth century, Shakespeare and Gerard were near neighbours in London. Gerard had a famous garden in Holborn ('the little plot of my special care and husbandrie', he called it modestly), close to the London home of Shakespeare's patron Henry Wriothesley, the young, auburn-haired Earl of Southampton.

In 1603 or 1604, Shakespeare took lodgings a little way to the east in Cripplegate, just inside the city walls, staying with the 'mean and rather crabby' Huguenot Christopher Mountjoy, who ran a business producing highly fashionable headpieces ('tires') from his steeply gabled house on the corner of Silver Street and Monkwell or Muggle Street. The closure of London's theatres in 1603 to 1604, when plague stalked the city, gave Mountjoy's lodger plenty of time to work on his plays and coax his sonnets into shape, after he moved away from the plague-ridden stews and tenements of Southwark and came to lodge in the relatively affluent neighbourhood of Silver Street.

Already in mourning for Queen Elizabeth's death in March 1603, London had turned into a 'vast silent charnel house', hung with lamps dimly and slowly burning, where a man might be plagued by visions of corpses 'half-mouldered in rotten coffins, that should suddenly yawn wide open, filling his nostrils with noisome stench, and his eyes with the sight of nothing but crawling worms'. People died in their thousands, and those that could still walk went about most bitterly, in playwright Thomas Dekker's suitably fevered description, 'miching and muffled up and down, with rue and wormwood stuffed into their ears and nostrils, looking like so many boars' heads stuck with branches of rosemary, to be served in for brawn at Christmas'. But the herb wives and gardeners did well enough, said Dekker, who asked God to 'bless the labours of these mole-catchers, because they suck sweetness by this, for the price of flowers, herbs and garlands, rose wonderfully, in so much that rosemary which had wont to be sold for twelve pence an armful, went now for six shillings a handful'.

Had Shakespeare risked himself on London's plague-ridden streets, hc had only to step a few yards northwards up Monkwell Street to reach the hall of the Barber-Surgeons' Company to which Gerard belonged and where he was a frequent visitor, attending meetings and dinners, examining apprentices, and lobbying his fellows to develop a garden for medicinal plants on company land at East Smithfield, near the Tower of London. And had the dramatist wanted to make his way from Silver Street to Gerard's famously stocked garden on the south side of Holborn, he could drop down Cheapside, turn west along the Shambles and Newgate Market, walk up Snow Hill then across the Fleet River at Holborn Bridge, continuing past the Church of St Andrews to Gerard's house and garden on the juncture of Holborn with Fetter Lane.[1]

Herbalist John Gerard's well-stocked garden in Holborn lay outside London's city walls, south of Holborn and the knot gardens of Ely Place. Detail from the 'Agas' map, c.1561, printed in 1603.

Holborn was then little more than a village outside the city walls, in the borough of Farringdon Without. Just to the north, before the fields began, lay the gardens and great house of Ely Place, which the Queen had forced the Bishop of Ely to hand over to her 'dancing chancellor', Sir Christopher Hatton, who died in 1591. (His yearly rent for the gatehouse and garden was a red rose, plus an annual sum of ten pounds sterling and ten loads of hay for the remainder of the property.)

Although there is no evidence beyond a faint few echoes of Gerard in Shakespeare's sonnets and plays, it is tantalizing to think they might have met and talked of flowers, perhaps even of roses.

Gerard's *Herball* was published in 1597, five or six years before Shakespeare moved to Silver Street. For all its inaccuracies and unattributed borrowings, Gerard's work stands among the best-loved herbals, offering a clear sense of the man and his many botanic rambles around the capital, as well as youthful journeys further afield – to Denmark, Sweden, Poland, Livonia on the Gulf of Riga, and Russia, 'those colde countries', as he called them, where he saw wild pines growing in infinite numbers. He may also have journeyed to the eastern Mediterranean as he records conversations with the 'Merchants of the Factorie at Tripolis' about cedars growing on the slopes of Mount Lebanon.

Gerard demonstrated his love of roses by putting them first among the ornamental plants of his herbal, after he had dealt with herbs for meat, medicine and strewing. Despite its place among 'base and thornie shrubs', declared Gerard, the rose deserved 'the chiefest and most principall place' among all flowers, 'being not onely esteemed for his beautie, vertues, and his fragrant and odoriferous smell; but also bicause it is the honor and ornament of our English Scepter . . . uniting of those two most royal houses of Lancaster and Yorke.' Here Gerard is alluding to the story familiar to generations of English schoolchildren: how Lancastrian Henry Tudor gained England's crown after defeating Yorkist Richard III at the battle of Bosworth Field; and how, through marriage to Elizabeth of York, he united the warring factions of Lancaster and York. To signify this union, Henry VII took as his emblem the Tudor rose, which set the white rose of York within the red rose of Lancaster, using the potent imagery of the rose to legitimize his tenuous claim to the throne.

By Henry VIII's time, the red-and-white Tudor rose was firmly planted in the allegorical soil of England. Here, illuminated couplets by Richard Sampson, Bishop of Chester, celebrate the union of the houses of York and Lancaster and their respective roses in an English manuscript, c.1516.

But Gerard had been bamboozled by the Tudor propaganda machine, it seems, as we are today, for the 'Wars of the Roses' were no such thing – or rather, the label was applied retrospectively, condensing a complex struggle over more than thirty years into a simple conflict between two dynastic bloodlines that flowed only weakly through Henry Tudor's veins. His Lancastrian blood came through his mother, Margaret Beaufort, whose family line had sprung from an adulterous liaison between John of Gaunt, Duke of Lancaster, and his mistress Katherine Swynford, who only later became the Duke's third and final wife.

As always with the rose, the story is far from straightforward. While Henry Tudor's personal emblem was a red dragon, the red rose was, indeed, a symbol of the House of Lancaster, dating back to Edmund Crouchback, first Earl of Lancaster and a younger son of Henry III, whose wife Eleanor of Provence is said to have introduced the rose into English royal heraldry. Edmund had married Blanche of Artois, widow of Thibaut le Chansonnier's son Henri I, and in choosing his rose he may even have had in mind the famous red rose of Provins, after he was sent there to avenge the mayor's murder in a riot over taxation. But the white rose was only one of the emblems associated with the Yorkists and historians cannot even agree how they came to use it.[2] Far more potent was Richard III's white boar, under which he fought his final battle. After his death on the battlefield, when his naked and bloodied body was carried into Leicester trussed like a hog to his horse, 'ye proude braggying white bore (whiche was his badge) was violently rased and plucked doune from every signe and place where it myghte be espied'.

So runs the account given by Tudor chronicler Edward Hall, who extolled the peace descending from heaven at Henry's marriage to Elizabeth, 'consideryeing that the lynes of Lancastre & Yorke, being both noble families, equivalent in ryches, fame and honour, were now brought into one knot and connexed together, of whose two bodyes one heyre might succede'. The union sounds almost alchemical in its joining of the Red King and the White Queen.

In common with John Gerard, Shakespeare the poet accepted the roses of Tudor myth and planted them ahistorically early, inventing for *King Henry VI, Part One* an entirely fictitious scene in the Temple

Rose garden to explain how the two sides picked their roses at the very start of the conflict. The action takes place in the aftermath of the death of King Henry V, when Joan of Arc is stoking rebellion among her French compatriots against their English overlords. In London, a quarrel breaks out between Richard Plantagenet, of the House of York, and the Lancastrian Duke of Somerset, whose grandson would become Henry VII.

Shakespeare takes the quarrel out into the Temple rose garden, where the warring parties urge their followers to pick a rose to declare their support: a red rose for Somerset and the House of Lancaster, a white rose for Richard Plantagenet and the Yorkists. 'Prick not your finger as you pluck it off,' warns Somerset, echoing Ovid's metamorphoses, 'Lest, bleeding, you do paint the white rose red, / And fall on my side so, against your will'. The scene ends with a dark prophecy that the 'brawl' in the Temple garden shall 'send between the red rose and the white / A thousand souls to death and deadly night'.

As the Tudor propaganda machine geared into action, the rose underwent yet another metamorphosis: once a pagan and then a Christian emblem, now the rose in England stood firmly for dynastic succession, replacing for a time the roses of courtly or Christian love. Two of the earliest surviving songbooks for the courts of Henry VII and Henry VIII contain only such dynastic roses, celebrating the 'lyly-whighte rose' (Queen Elizabeth of York, 'a comly quene'), who sits among colourful gillyflowers and fleur-de-lis in a 'glorius garden grene', singing, 'The white rose is most trewe / This garden to rule be ryghtwis [by righteous] lawe.'

Even more lyrical is a carol by Sir Thomas Philipps, esquire to the body of Henry VII, which begins:

> 'I love, I love, and whom love ye?'
> 'I love a floure of fressh beaute.'

The flower is, of course, a rose, and the carol celebrates the birth of an heir: Henry's eldest son perhaps, the doomed Prince Arthur, or second son Henry, who would reign in his brother's place:

'I love the rose, both red and white.'
'Is that your pure perfytt appetite?'
'To here talke of them is my delite.
Joyed may we be
Oure prince to se, and rosys thre.'

Henry VIII continued the tradition at his court. The king takes credit for some twenty songs and more than a dozen instrumental pieces in another early surviving songbook, including one that begins with a lover lamenting his heavy heart. In reply, his lady talks of flowers (the 'daise delectable, / The violett wan and blo') but not of roses, as if they have been written out of love's vocabulary. Poignantly, two songs celebrate the birth in 1511 of a son to Henry VIII and his first wife, Katharine of Aragon,

A woodcut of the coronation in 1509 of Henry VIII and Katharine of Aragon
showing their emblems, the Tudor rose and the pomegranate. From Stephen Hawes's A Joyfull
Medytacyon *to all Englonde of 1509.*

widow of Henry's brother, Prince Arthur. Katharine and Henry's son lived for just six weeks, during which time madrigalist Thomas Farthing wrote this joyful round:

> Aboffe all thynge
> Now lete us synge
> Both day and nyght
> Adew mornyng,
> A bud is spryngynge
> Of the red rose and the whyght.

Written for the season of New Year festivities held to celebrate the boy's birth, another song – the lovely *Madame d'amours* – provided the exit for an elaborately staged pageant. These are its parting lines:

> Adew, adew, le company,
> I trust we shall mete oftener.
> Vive le Katerine et noble Henry!
> Vive le prince, le infant rosary.

Had the boy lived, the history of England might have been very different; and his father, the six-times-married king, would have enjoyed a gentler reputation.

By the time Henry's second daughter Elizabeth came to the throne in 1558, the rose had worked its way into every corner of Tudor life. Celebrated in poetry and plays; pummelled into salves and unguents; bunched into nosegays and stuffed into sweet bags; woven into fabrics, cushions and bags; embroidered on to wall hangings, nightcaps and gloves; stamped on to armour and coins; turned into ivory portrait boxes; painted on to ceilings; sewn on to headpieces and shoes; distilled into perfumes, oils, waters and vinegars; transmuted into mystical meanings; baked into sweetmeats, sauces and pies – the rose was inescapable.[3]

As an emblem, however, the rose remained essentially political, appearing as a stylized and crowned Tudor rose in many of the portraits through which the Queen manipulated her public image. She took

Queen Elizabeth uses a Tudor rose and a French fleur-de-lys
to project her dynastic claims in the Pelican Portrait of c.1574 by court miniaturist Nicholas Hilliard.
More Tudor roses are embroidered in black on her undershirt.

another rose as her personal emblem: the simple Eglantine or Sweet Briar (*Rosa rubiginosa*), whose shell-like blooms find echoes in the slashed sleeves to her dress in two of her most richly jewelled portraits: the Pelican and its roughly contemporary companion Phoenix portrait. Gerard described the Eglantine's flowers as 'little, five leaved [petalled], most commonly whitish, seldome tending to purple, of little or no smell at all', adding that London gardens could boast of another Eglantine with larger leaves and flowers that were 'somewhat doubled, exceeding sweete of smell'. He surely used the single variety for his own frontispiece in tribute to the Queen: his engraver, William Rogers, had decorated a portrait of the Queen as Rosa Electa with just such a border of Eglantine and double Tudor roses, an image that appeared also in the frontispiece to Henry Lyte's *Light of Britaine.*

Court artists wishing to represent the Eglantine at the time of Elizabeth used poetic licence to paint it purest white or modelled their flowers on a different rose altogether. The scrambling field rose *Rosa arvensis* is a likely candidate for the charming miniature in *Young Man Among Roses*, painted during the 1580s by the same court painter as the probable executor of the Pelican and Phoenix portraits, the Devon-born goldsmith-turned-miniaturist Nicholas Hilliard. Painted in watercolours on vellum, the small oval portrait shows a gangly lovelorn youth, hand on heart, leaning against a woodland tree encircled by a prickly white rose. Curly-haired and sporting the hint of a moustache, the young man is dressed entirely in black and white, the Queen's colours (black for constancy, white for virginity): black cloak, stiff white ruff, black-and-white doublet padded with bombast into a peascod belly, and milky-white hose that draw the eye down his impossibly long legs to his elegantly slippered feet. Even his eyes are two black dots, deep as coals.

As for the identity of the lovesick youth, he is generally thought to be Robert Devereux, second Earl of Essex, thirty-three years younger than his sovereign and eventually executed for treason after the failure of his Irish campaign. Perhaps he was already betraying Elizabeth's older-woman's heart through a marriage he kept secret from her (to Frances Walsingham, widow of his friend Sir Philip Sidney) while savouring his position as the Queen's recognized favourite.

The Eglantine slipped easily from painting into poetry, as in the

Young Man Among Roses *by Nicholas Hilliard, c.1585–95. The rose may be modelled on the scrambling field rose,* Rosa arvensis.

entertainment written by George Peele, a poet on the fringes of the court, for Queen Elizabeth's visit in 1591 to Lord Burghley at Theobalds, his grand Hertfordshire home where John Gerard oversaw the gardens. Saddened and depressed by the deaths of his mother, wife and daughter, Burghley had virtually retired from public life and the Queen's visit was intended to bring him back into the world. Burghley never appeared and the Queen was entertained instead with speeches by his younger son, Robert Cecil, as she wandered Gerard's great garden, including one from a 'gardener' who described the making of a garden in which the virtues were executed in roses:

Then was I commanded to place an arbour all of Eglantine, in which my master's conceit outstripped my cunning: 'Eglantine,' quoth he, 'I most honour, and it hath been told me that the deeper it is rooted in the ground, the sweeter it smelleth in the flower, making it ever so green that the sun of Spain at the hottest cannot parch it.'[4]

It seems that the Protestant Queen Elizabeth had replaced the Queen of Heaven in her rose arbour and taken possession of her roses, just as allegorical poet Edmund Spenser would crown his 'faire Elisa, Queene of Shepheardes all' with a crimson coronet set with 'damaske Roses and Daffadillies'(and bayleaves, primroses and violets). Shakespeare, too, would embower his fairy queen with roses, transporting her to a bank

> . . . where the wild thyme blows,
> Where oxlips and the nodding violet grows
> Quite over-canopied with luscious woodbine,
> With sweet musk-roses, and with Eglantine.
> There sleeps Titania sometime of the night
> Lull'd in these flowers with dances and delight.

The Eglantine again: Elizabeth's symbolic reach extends even to the fairy kingdom, but Shakespeare has added a Musk rose that he may have seen on his rambles through the Warwickshire countryside. He certainly did not check his botanical facts with Gerard (the play was written a year or two before Gerard's *Herball* appeared), for Gerard correctly states that the Musk rose 'flowreth in Autumne, or the fall of the leafe', unlike the other wild roses which flowered at the same time as the Damask and the red rose – in early to mid summer, when the play was first performed, almost certainly to celebrate a wedding in a noble household. Shakespeare was writing of another wild rose altogether, eventually revealed by Graham Stuart Thomas as the native *Rosa arvensis*, which 'frequents copses and bosky hedgerows, flowers with the honeysuckle, and is deliciously fragrant' the same rose as in Hilliard's *Young Man Among Roses*, perhaps.

Intriguingly, a possible link between Shakespeare and John Gerard is suggested by another rose reference, buried in one of Shakespeare's Dark Lady sonnets. The sonnet (number 54) belongs to the sequence addressed to a 'beauteous and lovely youth' and dedicated to 'Mr W. H.' (Henry Wriothesley, perhaps, the youthful third Earl of Southampton, or William Herbert, third Earl of Pembroke). Its theme is the difference between substance and show, praising garden roses (whose essence can be captured through distillation) over 'canker blooms' that

> live unwooed, and unrespected fade,
> Die to themselves. Sweet roses do not so;
> Of their sweet death are sweetest odours made.

The comparison between a cultivated rose and a 'canker bloom' has long been a puzzle. In Shakespeare's time, a canker might refer to a worm in the bud, or to one of the humble hedgerow roses such as the dog rose, *Rosa canina;* these are mostly white or pale pink in colour and very lightly perfumed. Yet Shakespeare gives to his canker blooms 'full as deep a dye' as the 'perfumed tincture' of the garden roses, suggesting a rich deep red, and he further implies that these wild roses are completely scentless. So how or why did countryman Shakespeare make such a muddle of his roses?

One possible explanation lies in Gerard, who included in the *Herball*'s long entry on the rose a strange report from a 'curious gentleman' of Leyland in Lancashire[5] about garden roses growing wild in a cornfield known as Glover's field. Whenever it was ploughed, the field yielded daily 'many bushels of Roses, equall with the best garden Rose in each respect' – which his readers would undoubtedly have read as deep red ones – but very few roses indeed whenever the field lay fallow. (He also patriotically reported the double white rose growing wild and in great abundance in many Lancashire hedges, as if York had come willingly to Lancaster.)

Gerard's later editor, apothecary Thomas Johnson, quashed this story by revealing that the rose in Glover's field was none other than the 'corne Rose' or red poppy; but it is at least possible that while writing or revising his sonnet, Shakespeare may have consulted a copy of Gerard's *Herball* and borrowed the image of scentless red roses growing wild in a Lancashire field.

Certainly the dates fit. According to current scholarship, although Shakespeare may have written the core of his sonnets in the first half of the 1590s, he continued to write and revise them into the first decade of the seventeenth century, when he was living in Silver Street. And you will find other echoes of Gerard's idiosyncratic flower descriptions in Shakespeare (the colour of ladysmock and its buds in *Love's Labour's Lost*, for instance, or Falstaff's disparaging comparison of the young Justice Shallow to a forked mandrake root) but as these contain no roses, their unravelling I leave to others.

Some nineteen years older than Shakespeare and born in Cheshire, England, John Gerard must have shown early promise with healing herbs, since he was apprenticed aged sixteen to an eminent and successful barber-surgeon in London, Alexander Mason, who became Master of the Company of Barber-Surgeons during Gerard's apprenticeship. Gerard was admitted to the freedom of the Company on 9 December 1569 on completing his training and climbed steadily through the ranks, becoming Master himself in 1607. He remained in Holborn until his death in 1612, living in a substantial house above his shop, which later passed to his wife Agnes or Anne (the names were interchangeable). In her will she refers to 'the shoppe belonginge to my said house, together with the Celler under the said shoppe, and the stall under the said shoppe'.

Gerard's marriage was solid, even good; he calls his wife a 'carefull woman' who had helped him to obtain and keep his worldly goods, which amounted at his death to the very significant sum of £551 17s 6d. She was also a 'carefull nursse', having brought him through his 'great and daungerous sycknesses', not least the long-lived ague that had struck him before the *Herball* appeared, which was cured by God rather than human intervention, 'for medicines and all other such things did me no good at all'. Together they produced a possible five children: three boys who died young – at least one of the plague – and two daughters, but only Elizabeth is known to have survived to adulthood, marrying her father's apprentice Richard Holden shortly after his admission as a freeman to the Barber-Surgeons. Father John must have been happy in his work: to one of his granddaughters he bequeathed his plaster box, with all its silver instruments, and his 'Sylver Salvatorie' (a box to hold ointments), 'to be delyvered unto her, upon her mariadge daye, so that she do marye one of my proffession'.

But it was as a gardener and herbalist that Gerard achieved lasting fame, becoming superintendent of Lord Burghley's gardens in London and Hertfordshire around 1577, and curator of the physic garden established in 1586 by the College of Physicians (his attempts to persuade the Barber-Surgeons to set up a physic garden of their own appear to have foundered). He may even have worked for the new King James I as Surgeon and Herbalist, for so he is described in a court document of 14 August 1604, recording that James's wife Queen Anne of Denmark granted him the lease of a garden plot adjoining her palace at Somerset House, on condition that he supplied her with herbs, flowers and fruit.[6]

Gerard was especially proud of his great garden which lay south of Barnard's Inn on Holborn, 'between Staple Inn and Cursitor Street, and was held of Lord Burghley by Sir Henry Willoughby, who let it to Gerrard'. (Barnard's Inn was then an Inn of Chancery attached to Gray's Inn, on the western corner of Holborn and Fetter Lane.) Here, Gerard demonstrated his horticultural talents by growing many of the new exotics then entering the country – among them a spiky cactus from the southern Mediterranean, a double white daffodil from Constantinople, the oriental plane tree, and Indian tobacco. He claimed the honour of being the first to grow the potato in an English garden, mistakenly describing the South American plants in his *Herball* as 'Potatoes of Virginia'. Splendidly ruffed and moustachioed, he even posed for the frontispiece portrait of his *Herball* holding not a rose or a lily but the flower of a highly exotic New World potato.

Gerard was so proud of this garden that he printed at least two plant catalogues – in 1596 and again in 1599 – listing over 1,000 different plants growing in his garden. A surviving copy contains delightful evidence of a botanical falling-out between Gerard and his friend, the great Flemish botanist Matthias de L'Obel. Gerard had earlier asked de L'Obel for an endorsement saying that he had seen all the plants growing in Gerard's garden. But in the second catalogue of 1599, de L'Obel had scored through his printed statement, writing '*haec esse falsissima*' (this is grossly untrue). In the intervening years, Gerard's publisher had called on de L'Obel to correct mistakes in the manuscript to

Herbalist and barber-surgeon John Gerard, from the frontispiece to the revised edition of his Herball, *which first appeared in 1597.*

Gerard's *Herball*, and after de L'Obel had made more than 1,000 corrections, Gerard hit back by accusing de L'Obel of poor English. Such prickly intemperance was typical of Gerard's character. Among several 'controversies' recorded in the Barber-Surgeons' books was a complaint made against Gerard in 1578 for claiming that a colleague's wife 'had the Frenche Pocks'. Gerard said he could prove it too, so the case was dismissed as a matter for the courts.

Roses clearly hold a special place in Gerard's heart, so let us linger with him for a moment in his Holborn garden as he savours his roses of a summer evening. His catalogue lists sixteen different varieties, from the best garden roses so beloved by his contemporaries to the humble Sweet Briar, still planted in wilder gardens. All the varieties listed in his *Herball* are here, except the dog rose of common hedgerows and the 'Rose without prickles', *Rosa sine spinis,* which he said was not then grown in England.

For his *Herball,* Gerard separated his garden roses into six basic types and we are able, at last, to identify some of their family groups with reasonable certainty, even if we cannot compare actual varieties. Until Linnaeus introduced order into the naming of plants, writers used their own names to describe their plants, which might be illustrated by woodcuts borrowed indiscriminately from other authors. Gerard's six garden roses are: white (*Rosa × alba*); red (*R. gallica*); Damask (*R. × damascena*); the lesser Province rose (Gerard described it as similar to the Damask but 'altogether lesser'); the thornless rose, mentioned by Clusius and thought by some to be a lost form of *R. × francofurtana*; and the great Province rose, also known as the great Holland rose, a sumptuously petalled *R. centifolia* of the same soft blush as the Damasks (see Chapter 9 for the genesis of this rose).

Gerard's white roses were tall, with roughly snipped leaves of 'an overworne greene colour', while his red roses grew as low bushes, their leaves 'yet of a worse dustie colour'. He singled out for special praise the 'pale red' Damask ('pink' was not yet a garden colour), which he judged 'of a more pleasant smell' than the white rose, and 'fitter for meate or medicine'. But he liked red roses best, boasting that 'We have in our London gardens one of the red Roses, whose flowers are in quantitie and beautie equall with the [great Province rose], but of greater estimation, of a perfect red colour'.

After garden roses, Gerard devoted a separate chapter to the wilder Musk roses, which had nonetheless earned a place in the garden for their colour or sweet fragrance. Among these he included two white autumn-flowering Musks (a single and a double), true varieties of *R. moschata;* and what sounds like an early variety of a mottled Damask (see later in this chapter), which Gerard described as a painter might, its large single white flowers 'dasht over with a light wash of carnation, which maketh that colour, which we call a blush colour'. An artist might equally have been tempted by the velvet rose (he called it *Rosa holosericea*), its flowers 'of a deepe and blacke red colour, resembling red crimson velvet' (with its 'yellowe thrums' (stamens), it sounds much like today's *R.* 'Tuscany', also known as 'Old Velvet'); and by the 'fair golde yellowe' of a rose he identified as *Rosa lutea,* the yellow rose. The practical gardener in him poured scorn on reports (by Matthias de L'Obel, for instance, in his herbal of 1581) that its colour was achieved by grafting a wild rose on to a yellow broom, 'for the rootes and ofsprings of this Rose have brought foorth yellow Roses', he said, which could not happen with a graft. (He was not always so sceptical.) The earliest single yellow rose to reach Europe was almost certainly *R. foetida* from Iran, probably via Muslim Spain. It smells of bed bugs, although Gerard makes no mention of this, instead describing the leaves of his yellow rose as being 'of an excellent sweet smell, and more pleasant than the leaves of the Eglantine'.

Among the Musks, he also included single and double varieties of the cinnamon rose (*R. majalis* today), which took its name from the smell of its leaves. Sometimes known as the May rose, it grows among scrub and rocks across much of northern and central Europe, and east to Siberia and Mongolia.

Gerard's third rose chapter on wild roses embraced all the varieties you might expect: Queen Elizabeth's Sweet Briar or Eglantine (*R. rubiginosa*), prized especially for its 'glittering' leaves 'of a beautifull greene colour, of smell most pleasant'; the dog rose, *R. canina,* which delighted children with its ripe fruit, as well as 'cookes and gentlewomen' for their tarts; and the Scotch or Burnet rose, which he called *Rosa pimpinella* and which we now call *R. spinosissima*. While Gerard reported wild roses growing in the borders of fields and woods in most parts of England, he

Woodcuts of the Eglantine rose, R. rubiginosa, *from John Gerard's revised Herball of 1633.*

suggested that this last kind grew very plentifully in a field 'as you go from a village in Essex, called Graies (upon the brinke of the river Thames) unto Horndon on the hill', and also in a pasture 'as you goe from a village hard by London called Knights bridge, unto Fulham, a village thereby, and in many other places'.

Altogether, Gerard described fourteen separately numbered sorts of roses in his *Herball*, eleven if doubles, singles and obviously similar types are considered together and the common dog rose ignored. Some thirty years later, the royal apothecary John Parkinson produced an equivalent list of twenty-four types of garden rose. A more orderly character than Gerard, Parkinson listed his roses according to their chronological appearance, starting with the white rose, followed by incarnate (probably blush varieties of *R. × alba*), red, Damask, and the Dutch Centifolia rose. Of the rest – and bearing in mind the caveats about comparing rose varieties named by different writers – these seem obviously new roses or new variations on the old ones: the dwarf red rose or 'Gilloflower Rose'; the Frankfurt rose, *R. × francofurtana* (a cultivar is called 'Impératrice Joséphine'); the red Hungarian rose, faintly spotted with lighter pink; the 'Chrystall Rose', 'striped and marked with a deeper blush or red, upon the pale coloured leafe [petal]'; the double yellow rose; several Musk roses, including a 'double white damaske musk rose' and the Spanish Musk rose; the great apple rose, in fact cultivated since at least the sixteenth century and so called because of 'the graceful aspect of the red apples or fruit hanging upon the bushes'; and the evergreen rose, probably *R. sempervirens* from southern Europe.

Parkinson's expanding list shows how southern roses were beginning to spread into northern Europe. While some were native to England, others came from Germany, Spain and Italy. The provenance of the double yellow (almost certainly the sulphur rose, *R. hemisphaerica*) was especially interesting. Parkinson tells us that it came from Turkey,

which first was procured to be brought into England, by Master Nicholas Lete, a worthy Merchant of London, and a great lover of flowers, from Constantinople, which (as wee heare) was first brought thither from Syria; but perished quickly both with him, and with all other to whom hee imparted it.

A second attempt at importing the rose was more successful, when it was sent to another London merchant, Master John de Franqueville, 'a great lover of all rare plants, as well as flowers, from which is sprung the greatest store, that is now flourishing in this Kingdome'. Parkinson had lost many such roses himself, but he knew of others around London who were able to grow it well, although he suspected it was too tender to survive in northern climes. Clusius recounts in 1601 how he had first encountered the double yellow rose in a pâpier maché miniature garden shown to him at the Imperial Court of Austria by a woman from Constantinople; soon afterwards he obtained the plant itself from the same city.

Wild roses were on the move, too, as we learn from Parkinson's herbal of 1640, *Theatrum Botanicum,* when Britain's native species were joined by roses from Russia, Virginia, Germany, Austria, Switzerland and France. But even if Parkinson's wild and cultivated roses are added together, their total numbers are small compared to many other plants then coming into cultivation. Later in the century, the French King's gardener at Versailles, Jean-Baptiste de la Quintinie, included in his instructions for fruit and vegetable gardens seventy-seven anemones, 225 carnations, 437 tulips and a mere fourteen roses. Only with the introduction of cultivated Chinese roses from the end of the eighteenth century would the mania for breeding new roses suddenly outstrip all the rest.

The candy-striped rose of the late sixteenth and early seventeenth centuries illustrates how hard it is to identify old roses. Frescos from Pompeii record a striped rose as early as Roman times, painted on the walls of the House of Venus Marina (see Chapter 3), but its identification remains uncertain, as does that of the striped rose Clusius described under the name *Rosa praenestina (vulgo provincalis)* in his 1583 description of plants from Austria and neighbouring regions. Both Gerard and Parkinson included one such striped rose in their works: Gerard called his 'the blush rose' and classed it with his Musk roses, pointing out that it flowered with the Damasks. Parkinson called his variety 'Rosa versicolor, the party coloured Rose, of some Yorke and Lancaster', linking it to the Damasks rather than the Gallicas. Other early sightings

Rosa gallica. β. versicolor
Rosa Mundi.

The candy-striped Rosa gallica *'Versicolor', also known as* Rosa mundi, *painted by English artist Mary Lawrance for* A Collection of Roses from Nature *of 1799.*

of these multicoloured roses are also thought to be Damasks, although not everyone agrees.

Today, these names are shared by two roses: *Rosa gallica* 'Versicolor' or Rosa mundi, a sport of the Apothecary's rose; and the Damask 'York and Lancaster' rose, *R. × damascena* 'Versicolor'. Despite the lingering tradition that Rosa mundi was named after the twelfth-century 'Fayre Rosamond', mistress of Henry II, it seems likely that *R. gallica* 'Versicolor' appeared much later, probably around 1630 and certainly before 1640 when it was painted by Nicolas Robert for Gaston d'Orléans, whose magnificent collection of watercolours developed into the *Vélins du Roi* (the King's Vellums) of Louis XIV and his successors. England's Sir Thomas Hanmer put this rose in his Garden Book of 1650, written during the Commonwealth years when he retired to his garden, as a royalist sympathizer. Calling it Rosa mundi or the 'Christmass Rose', Hanmer said this new variegated rose was 'first found in Norfolke a few years since, upon a branch of the common Red Rose, and from thence it multiplied. It is like the Red in all things, but that it is stript in great flakes with indifferent good White'. This new Gallica is clearly not the same as Gerard's painterly 'blush rose', which came in white washed with carnation.[7]

While John Gerard wrote about his roses as a gardener, his herbal was naturally intended to identify plants used in healing, and to describe their uses. How his decidedly Elizabethan views fit with medicine's gradual evolution is the subject of another chapter. But Gerard tells us nothing about how he cared for the many roses in his garden; for this we must turn to other authors such as Londoner Thomas Hill, who is credited with writing the first English gardening manual (or at least the oldest still surviving) – a tiny book, small enough to tuck into a jerkin, which he called *A most briefe and pleasaunte treatise, teachyng how to dresse, sowe, and set a garden*. Published around 1558, it appeared in a second edition of 1563 with a delightful frontispiece of a square garden within a garden surrounded by an outer paling and containing stock Elizabethan garden features such as geometric plats and flowerbeds, a simple knot, an arbour and a well.

A few years later, this treatise metamorphosed into *The proffitable arte of gardening*, clearly aimed at the growing number of middle-ranking Englishmen who could now indulge in the 'luxury' of gardening and planting the 'manie strange hearbs, plants and annuall fruits' daily coming into Britain from around the globe. Hill included his portrait in this reworking: aged about forty, he wears the unadorned flat cap fashionable among working Londoners in the mid-sixteenth century.

Hill died in the 1570s and his best-known work, *The Gardeners Labyrinth* of 1577, was finished by a friend and published posthumously under the transparent pseudonym of Didymus Mountain. Like Gerard's *Herball,* published exactly twenty years later, the book was dedicated to Lord Burghley, with an editor's apology for its 'vulgare stile'. It must nonetheless have found its market, as new editions continued to appear for at least a century. Among its charming woodcuts of gardeners at work is one showing gardeners constructing and planting a rose arbour, and another of three gentlemen sitting around a garden table laden with sweetmeats and wine, sheltered by a stout trellis thick with blooming roses.

Hill in his original writes of roses in the context of 'herbers' or arbours, which he says should be made of juniper or willow poles bound together with wires. While an arbour could support useful plants such as bryony, cucumber, gourds, melons and vines, Hill chooses to speak first of those planted 'for beauties sake', which in his view 'ought to be those of a fragrant savoure, and that growe or shoote uppe highe'. He names his three favourites: rosemary, jasmine and the 'redde Rose', which might not cover the whole arbour, yet 'the owners friendes sitting in the same, maye the freelier see and beholde the beautie of the Garden, to theyr great delyght'.

It sounds charming, exactly as one imagines a Tudor garden to be, but take a closer look at Hill's instructions on how to plant and care for those same rose trees. Gardeners should begin their work in mid-February, he recommends, in the first quarter of the moon, planting their roses in short narrow beds, 'well reared wyth a stonie and drye Earth, and not wyth Dung'. He is quite emphatic on this point, 'for neyther the slippes nor olde rootes joy in a fatte Cley, or moyst grounde, but in the drye and stonye Earthe'. You could plant bare-rooted roses, he says, or slips could be broken off from the roots, 'cutte in a slope manner at the heads, about a mans foote and a halfe long, writhed at the endes, and so sette in a slope manner, a foote deepe into beddes, well reared with a drie Earthe, and in the increase of the Moone'. As he rightly says, roses come slowly from seed, but if you wanted to grow roses from seeds, these should be planted about a foot deep in 'lyght and drie Earthe' towards the middle of March, or in February in hotter places, 'the Moone then increasing'.

Hill's advice on planting roses in a dry and stony soil runs counter to any true gardener's common knowledge, then and now. As Frenchman Charles Estienne, a near contemporary, declared in the first English translation of his celebrated *Maison Rustique,* 'It requireth a fat, sub-stantiall, and reasonable moist ground; for as for gravelly and sandie grounds, they are altogether enemies unto the Rose-tree'. And Hill says nothing of more sophisticated methods of propagation, such as grafting, layering or budding. Estienne, by contrast, gave detailed instructions for grafting and budding, suggesting that by this last method 'you may easily graft white Rose-trees in red Rose-trees, and red Rose-trees in white Rose-trees, to have Roses of divers sorts upon one and the same Rose-tree'.[8]

Hill's fumbled instructions for roses reveal him for what he is: an author of potboilers, bringing the marvels of the new sciences to an avid and credulous audience in a stream of popular works on subjects as diverse as physiognomy, astronomy, astrology, bee-keeping, palmistry and the interpretation of dreams. As he reveals himself in the frontis-piece to *The Gardeners Labyrinth,* he has plundered his material from 'the best approved writers of Gardening, Husbandrie, and Physicke', and despite his green-fingered reputation, Hill can be exposed as a horticultural mountebank, quite happy to tell you that dreaming of rose garlands out of season 'do signify good to al personnes, except those beyng sicke and to those which go aboute to hide them'. (Sick people fear such dreams, said Hill, because roses 'doe lightlye wyther and rotte', while those who seek to hide them will be found out by 'ye savoure and smell'.)

Another of his 'briefe and pleasaunt treatises', *Naturall and Artificiall Conclusions,* belonged to the tradition of 'secrets' books that mixed handy household hints with schoolboy wizardry and arcane lore. Freely admitting that the original work had been put together by 'sundry Schollers of the Universitie of Padua in Italie', Hill brought together a

The garden owner and his friends at their ease in a rose bower, from the first edition of Thomas Hill's The Gardeners Labyrinth, *published posthumously in 1577 under the pseudonym Didymus Mountain.*

ragbag of instructions: how to grow herbs with many savours and tastes, how to make beans and other seeds sprout in four hours, how to walk on water ('a proper secret'), how to kill fleas by diverse ways, how to make a hollow ring dance by itself and so on. As always in such books, roses feature in several of the recipes: how to have fresh roses at all times of the year, for instance, as well as how to turn white roses red and red roses white.

Hill surely never stopped to try the recipes himself, or he would have rejected many as unworkable. His first method for turning white roses red involved hanging the white flowers in the mouth of a pint pot filled with 'the best redde Wine', close but not touching the wine, keeping the pot tightly stoppered for a full day, 'and they will after become red of colour'. Conversely, you could turn red flowers white by holding them over the smoke of brimstone beaten into a fine powder and burnt on a new tile stone.

Another of Hill's rose recipes – 'How to have fresh Roses at all times of the yeere sundry waies taught' – was equally suspect. It involved gathering half-open fresh rosebuds at sunset ('and touch them not with the hande in gathering, but with a sharpe knife properly gather them'), laying them overnight on a board, then storing them before sunrise in a new earthenware pot, glazed inside and out, 'and stop close the mouth of that pot with clay, mired with Horse dung & flocks, all tempered well together before'. The pot should then be buried in earth, covered with dry sand, and kept free of moisture, 'and now you may have fresh roses at any time of year'.

This recipe would have appealed to all those good housewives who sought to bring the savour of fresh flowers indoors. In London especially, people lived too closely together without proper sanitation or drainage, and the stink from overflowing cesspools and polluted watercourses must have been unbearable at times. But capable housewives found ways to mask the stench. Levinus Lemnius, a Dutchman visiting England in 1560, was enchanted by the English use of herbs and flowers in the home, and wrote approvingly that 'their chambers & parlours strawed over with sweete herbes, refreshed mee, their nosegayes finelye entermingled wyth sondry sortes of fragraunte floures in their bedchambers and privie roomes, with comfortable smell cheered mee up and entierlye delighted all my sences'.

Hill was by no means the only author of the day attempting to capitalize on the market for 'secrets' books that would bring practical home-making skills and sleights-of-hand within reach of literate and relatively well-to-do housewives. A bestseller in the field was the ingenious inventor, agriculturalist and garden-lover Sir Hugh Plat or Platt, a near-contemporary of Gerard and son of a successful London brewer, who settled in Bethnal Green, London, after studying at St John's College, Cambridge, and Lincoln's Inn. Platt's *The Jewell House of Art and Nature* contains a whole book devoted to the art of distillation. It conjures up visions of the lady of the house drying her rose petals around the home, spread on clean linen on every available table and window. Better still, to dry rose leaves without a single wrinkle, Platt advised his female readers to lay out the petals of half-opcn roses (preferably red ones) in shallow boxes of washed and dried sand (specifically 'callis sand'), making sure that no petals overlapped, then to sprinkle them with another fine layer of sand and to build up four or five layers of drying roses in one box. After two hot sunny days outside, she should gently remove the dried petals by hand or with a spoon, storing them in glass jars or parchment in a warm cupboard near the stove. 'And so you may have roseleaves, and other flowers to lay about your basons, windowes, and court cupboords, all the winter long.'

More recipes for preserving and distilling roses followed in his tiny book, *Delightes for Ladies, to adorne their Persons, Tables, closets, and distillatories: with Beauties, banquets, perfumes and Waters,* considered by many to be the most charming and well-written sweets recipe book of all. Imported sugar was still an expensive luxury, so relatively few households would have been able to afford these roses preserved in syrup.

Dip a Rose that is neither in the bud nor overblowne, in a sirrup, consisting of sugar double refined, and Rosewater boiled to his true height, then open the leaves [petals] one by one, with a fine smooth bodkin either of bone or wood, and presently if it be a hot sunnie day, and whilest the sunne is in some good height, lay them on papers in the sunne, or else drie them some gentle heate in a close roome, heating ye roome before you set them in, or in an Oven upon papers, in pewter dishes, & then put them up in glasses and keepe them in drie cupbords neere the fire. You must take out the seedes if you meane to eate them. You may proouve this, preserving with sugar candie, in stead of sugar if you please.

Here are so many roses that one almost sympathizes with herbalist Nicholas Culpeper's exasperated cry: 'What a pother have authors made with Roses! What a racket have they kept.' But as a political emblem, roses had had their day. The Tudor dynasty ended with the Virgin Queen, and Stuart King James married the Scottish thistle to the red English rose, which not surprisingly lost its prominence in court circles, though without vanishing altogether.

In *The Maske of Flowers,* performed at Whitehall by the Gentlemen of Gray's Inn on Twelfth Night 1614, King and court were entertained by the spectacle of a 'Garden of a glorious and strange beauty', where Eglantine and honeysuckle twined around a 'goodly Arbour' atop a grassy mount. Involved in the masque was Sir Francis Bacon, a member of Gray's Inn, who had overseen the transformation of its gardens and walks, and who would later recommend planting thickets of Sweet Briar, honeysuckle and wild vines in the 'wild heath' of his ideal garden. But these are roses for the garden pure and simple; they carry no political freight, and neither are there political reasons to plant roses centre stage. In place of roses, the masque designers have turned to other favoured flowers to embellish the quarters of their formal garden: great pots of gillyflowers and the many-coloured foreign tulips that were beginning to cause such a stir.

Chapter Nine
Dutch Masters

THE rose that is unfolding to perfection in Daniel Seghers's (1590–1661) bouquet of flowers is unmistakably a Centifolia. Cup-shaped and darkening towards the centre, its soft pink head rests on the rim of the glass vase, anchoring the composition. Other roses droop their heads beneath a sprig of unopened orange blossom and a flamboyant flared tulip that clamours for attention, but it is the lusciously plump Centifolia rose that holds the eye: *rose des peintres,* some people call it, the painters' rose. Others liken it more prosaically to a cabbage.

John Gerard introduced this rose to British gardeners in his *Herball* of 1597, calling it *Rosa Hollandica, sive Batava* or the great Holland rose, adding its more common name for good measure: the great Province rose, 'which the Dutch men cannot endure; for say they, it came first out of Holland, and therefore to be called the Holland Rose: but by all likelyhood it came from the Damaske Rose, as a kinde thereof, made better and fairer by art, which seemeth to agree with the truth'.

Despite acknowledging the Netherlanders' hand in perfecting this magnificent rose, Gerard linked it also to Theophrastus' hundred-petalled rose, which reportedly grew on the slopes of Mount Pangaeus in eastern Macedonia, and to Pliny's Campanian roses. Such connections are now discounted, and the rose we call the Centifolia was in all probability born of Dutch horticultural wizardry in the late 1500s. It became the rose of choice for most Dutch and Flemish flower painters of the seventeenth century, resplendent enough to stand alongside the flared tulips and other exotic blooms entering Europe from Constantinople and beyond.

Daniel Seghers's Flowers in a Glass Vase, *painted in the first half of the seventeenth century, shows off the new Centifolia rose, together with a tulip, white rose and orange blossom in bud.*

Among the first to describe this new beauty was Gerard's erstwhile friend, the Flemish botanist Matthias de L'Obel, who classed it with the Damasks in his *Kruydtboeck* (*Herbal*) of 1581, calling it 'Rosa Damascena maxima' (in Dutch, the *Aldergrootste incarnaete oft Provensche Roose*). De L'Obel received his rose in Delft from Mr N. Sanders, who worked in the garden of Secretary Jan Hobote of Antwerp. When grown in good earth, it produced 'very beautiful' roses of between 200 and 300 petals, much like an average-sized double peony (*middelbaer dobbel pionie*); the whole stem resembled the 'Provence Roose' in most respects (by which he presumably meant the flesh-coloured Damask), except the wood was somewhat red. The rose was rare enough for de L'Obel to mention others who received or grew it: Secretary Willem Martiny and a woman (he describes her as '*mijn vrouwe van Aspre*') living near Gorcum in Holland.

De L'Obel may have described it first, but the Centifolia rose owed its wider fame throughout Europe to the man who also popularized the tulip: Carolus Clusius, born Charles de l'Ecluse in 1526 in Arras, southern Netherlands, and Europe's greatest botanist-scholar of the late sixteenth century. The story of how this rose found its way into art aptly illustrates the meeting of art and science through the medium of flowers, and out of this convergence came new ways of looking at the natural world. With Clusius's encouragement, the scientist's enthusiasm for careful observation inspired a whole new genre of painting: the floral still life by artists such as Jan Brueghel de Velours ('Velvet' Brueghel), Ambrosius Bosschaert the elder, Roelandt Savery and Brueghel's pupil, Daniel Seghers.

Trained first in law and then, like many early botanists, in medicine (botany did not yet exist as a science in its own right), Clusius was driven all his life by a quest for the unknown. Fascinated by plants from boyhood, he saw it as his mission to discover and observe them growing in remote regions of Europe, and to study the exotic new species coming into Europe from all corners of the world. He was also a practical plantsman, overseeing the gardens of the Habsburg Emperor Maximilian II in Vienna in the 1570s, and advising Landgrave Wilhelm IV of Hesse on his famous botanical garden in Kassel. He was, in the words of the art historian Florence Hopper, a 'proto-ecologist three hundred years in advance of his time'.

Clusius first unveiled the Centifolia rose towards the end of his long life, after he had arrived at Leiden in the United Provinces (now the Netherlands) in late 1593 to take charge of the university's Hortus Botanicus, recently established within the medical school to emulate the great botanic gardens of Pisa, Padua, Florence, Bologna and Leipzig. Although not the university's first choice as curator of the garden – that honour belonged to the Dutch botanical scholar and collector of curiosities, Bernardus Paludanus – Clusius brought with him a fearsome reputation as scholar, gardener, traveller and linguist, which placed him like a spider at the centre of a web of communications joining like-minded scholars and enthusiasts across Europe. Governing their relations was an unwritten code of reciprocity dependent on the free exchange of plants, information and pleasure in the natural world.

Influential in enticing Clusius to Leiden was the wealthy burgher Johan van Hoghelande, secretary to Leiden's board of curators and one of

Flemish scholar and botanist Charles de l'Ecluse, better known as Carolus Clusius, engraved by Jean-Jacques Boissard in 1598, after Clusius had moved to Leiden.

163

Clusius's long-standing correspondents, who lived near the university on the Kolfmakersteeg, where he cultivated a fine and extensive rose garden. For forty years or so they had exchanged plants, and it was van Hoghelande who gave Clusius his first Centifolia rose, sending him two apparently healthy plants at the beginning of 1589, although only a single root fragment survived. (Van Hoghelande was not so generous towards Clusius's other correspondents. Incensed by the rich burgher's meanness, London-based apothecary James Garet Senior complained to Clusius that he had spied in van Hoghelande's garden some beautiful flowers that were a present from Clusius himself, but 'he is so tight-fisted that I could not get any out of his hands'.)[1]

Despite their poor condition, the great botanist was clearly intrigued enough by these strange new roses to report their provenance in his collected writings on rare plants, *Rariorum Plantarum Historia,* under the name 'Rosa 60. foliorum Centifolia Batavica'. As he explained to his readers, he had seen the same roses growing that year in the Frankfurt garden of the brothers Balthazar and Charles Hoyke from the southern Netherlands. The roses puzzled him, as the Centifolias known to the ancients had tiny flowers and no scent, while these were 'bigger than [roses] from Praeneste, and almost as scented'.

To Clusius's delight, in 1591 his one surviving fragment produced a new shoot, which 'bore about forty flowers, not all of the same size, but in some I counted 120 petals, larger on the outside and tiny towards the centre, filling the place around the threads [stamens], and turned backwards into its cup; I observed the scent of the Praenestian rose, not at all like the Alba rose, and of a not dissimilar colour'. We can imagine him turning the rose in his hands, counting the petals one by one and meticulously recording what he saw. Later taxonomists such as Carl Linnaeus might prefer their plants dead and dried in a herbarium, but Clusius was inspired by a genuine love of the living organism.

Van Hoghelande also told him about two more roses of this type: a white variety, and a second, even rarer form (Clusius called it simply Centifolia Batavica II) which was 'found among those same Batavians [Dutchmen], somewhat smaller than the first, midway in size between that one and the common Praenestinian, but agreeing in respect of colour, smell and shape'. As Clusius reported, he soon received more specimens of this rarer form from two separate sources: first from van Hoghelande himself, and then 'some small shoots from that distinguished, equally learned and diligent apothecary of Delft, Theodore Clutius, a few of which have germinated healthily so that I hope they will survive: the following year one has borne a flower'.

Here we are witnessing no less than the genesis of the Centifolia rose, nurtured by the horticultural skills of men such as rose lover Johan van Hoghelande and apothecary Clutius. Better known by his Dutch name Dirk Cluyt, the latter was lured to Leiden before Clusius's arrival to begin planning and planting the university's botanic garden, so the two men would get to know each other well. Although nominally Clusius's assistant, Cluyt was the practical force behind the garden, and even gave demonstrations and lectures to the students throughout the year. Having suffered a serious fall which considerably delayed his arrival, Clusius was by now too infirm and too busy writing and cultivating his botanical network and his own plant collection to work the garden himself.

Just as Clusius was among the first to observe the Centifolia rose in a work of science, so one of his protégés was the first to record it in a work of art. That painter is Jacques de Gheyn II, whose path crossed with Clusius in Leiden in the closing years of the sixteenth century. Born in Catholic Antwerp in 1565 of a Protestant glass-painter father from Utrecht, the young Jacques de Gheyn was raised in Holland and trained as an engraver under the famous Hendrick Goltzius in Haarlem. After his father's death, dissolute company led him astray for a time, until marriage to the daughter of a wealthy Catholic family in The Hague calmed him down and gave him the financial security he craved. Now in Leiden, his engraving skills earned him the commission to produce the first printed plan of Leiden's botanic garden, which shows smartly robed and hatted gentlemen strolling in pairs among the neat arrangement of oblong order beds, and a group of students under instruction before the long enclosed gallery running along the garden's western edge. He also engraved the university's anatomy theatre, and the portrait of Carolus Clusius (then aged seventy-five) which appeared as the frontispiece to his collected works, *Rariorum Plantarium Historia*. But in the words of de Gheyn's earliest biographer, Karel van Mander, after discovering that painting is the most suitable approach to life or nature, 'the desire in him

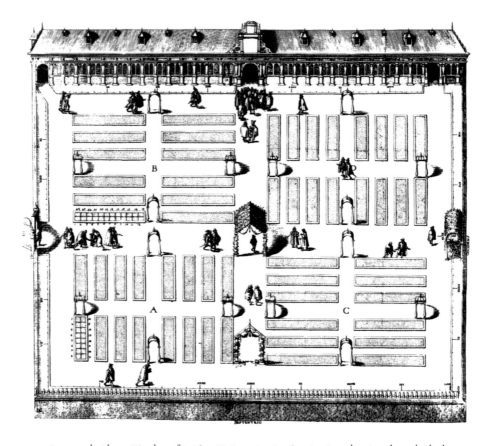

Jacques de Gheyn II's plan of Leiden University Garden *in 1601, showing the order beds where the new Centifolia roses were grown.*

to paint became more and more powerful so that he abandoned engraving and printing and lamented the time he had wasted'.

It must have been Clusius who introduced Jacques de Gheyn to the rewards – aesthetic, scientific and material – of painting flowers from life. The earliest surviving portrait of a Centifolia rose appears in an album of twenty-two watercolours of flowers and animals, which de Gheyn drew and painted with infinite care between 1600 and 1604, when he sold it to Emperor Rudolf II, Maximilian's successor and a renowned Renaissance collector of natural and artificial wonders, who had moved the Habsburg court from Vienna to Prague. As well as flowers and art, emperor and artist shared a fascination with sorcery and witchcraft.

Today, the album survives as one of the great treasures of the Frits Lugt Collection at the Institut Néerlandais in Paris. Measuring just 234 × 182 mm (a little over 9×7 inches), it is preserved in a nineteenth-century binding of black leather richly embossed with gold. Art historian Claudia Swan judged the luminosity of its painted forms 'still extraordinary, set off against the milky white of the prepared vellum on which they are painted'. Roses appear in six of the twenty-two folios, and Centifolia roses in two of these: a study of the rose viewed from the side and the front, its cut stem and a leaflet slipping over the composition's frame, which has been carefully drawn in gold ink; and a composition shared with an Austrian briar rose (*Rosa foetida*) and a lily. Again, the Centifolia's stem and leaf extend beyond the frame, as if the painted roses are stepping off the page. The album's other roses include a Damask (*R. × damascena* var. *semperflorens*), a semi-double Eglantine (*R. rubiginosa*), a simple dog rose, several Albas (*R. × alba* 'Alba Maxima' and 'Great Maiden's Blush'), a Frankfurt rose (*R. × francofurtana*), and an Apothecary's rose, (*R. gallica* var. *officinalis*).

For his album, de Gheyn also carefully painted many of Clusius's favourite rare bulbs and flowers: tulips, iris, anemones, more lilies, nigella, double columbines, narcissi, alpine flowers such as trollius and the dainty star-shaped alpine squill (*Scilla bifolia*), ranunculus, crocus, pinks and hepatica. His attention to detail owes much to the miniaturist's techniques he had learned from his father, informed by Clusius's scientific eye. De Gheyn's Centifolia rose, for instance, is said to be remarkably similar to a dried herbarium specimen of 1620 preserved in the Bodleian Library, Oxford; both display the Centifolia's unmistakable cup shape, reflexed outer petals and long projecting sepals. The artist's obvious delight in his subjects translates into living portraits which far outshine the crude illustrations in Clusius's own published writings.

To find his flowers, de Gheyn had only to visit van Hoghelande's rose garden, or stroll with the other smart gentlemen among the neat order beds of Leiden's botanic garden, where Cluyt had planted the roses in a bed of their own in the second quadrant, on the eastern side of the garden. Most of the roses he chose to paint were already growing here by 1594. The great Centifolia and a white variety also appeared among

The first botanical painting of a Centifolia rose, by Jacques de Gheyn II, contained in an album of flowers, insects and animals sold in 1604 to Habsburg Emperor Rudolf II.

mixed plantings in other areas of the garden; these were clearly no ordinary shrubs.

Rudolf's purchase of de Gheyn's flower album reflects its value as a work of art and as a collection of rarities. Rudolf could enjoy its portraits in Prague's frozen winters, when the flowers it celebrated were long dead. As such, it made a fitting addition to his collection of natural and artificial marvels, which demonstrated his mastery over nature. Well known for his interest in rare plants, trees and flowers, Rudolf would later commission the Dutch merchant and collector Emanuel Sweert to prepare one of the earliest florilegia or flower books illustrating the many new plants arriving from Turkey and the New World. In its opening pages, Sweert confided to the reader his own love of plants, which he brought to the Emperor 'because his Majesty was the world's greatest admirer and amateur of all rarities and worldly artifices'. The Centifolia rose naturally took pride of place in the page devoted to Dutch roses, which included Albas, a Damask and a double yellow rose now identified as *Rosa hemisphaerica*; Clusius identified Vienna as the source of the double yellow's introduction to the West.

While de Gheyn was painting his watercolours on vellum, he began to experiment with oils, developing a technique that allowed him to distinguish colours in all their variety. He then applied the knowledge gained about pigments to his first botanical portraits, incorporating many of the flowers he had modelled for his little vellum album, which functioned as an artist's sketchbook. Perhaps he made a copy for himself as he continued to reproduce the same flowers long after he had left Leiden for The Hague, including the Centifolia rose viewed from the side.

In his day, Jacques de Gheyn was championed by the influential Dutch statesman and poet Constantijn Huygens (his neighbour in The Hague), whose father had unsuccessfully sought de Gheyn's services as an art teacher to the Huygens boys. The artist's high contemporary reputation was reflected in his earnings: 600 guilders to paint a special flower piece for the French Queen, Marie de' Medici, on her visit to the United Provinces in 1606 – more than the cost of some houses and as much as a master carpenter might earn in a year.[2] But not everyone valued his talents so highly; English diplomat George Gage considered they remained essentially those of an engraver rather than a painter, as he remarked to

Sir Dudley Carleton, English ambassador at The Hague, suggesting that 'howsoever you esteeme there your Jaques de Ghein, yet wee preferre by much Brugel, because his thinges have neatnesse and force, and a morbidezza, which the other hath not, but is cutting and sharpe (to use painters phrases) and his thinges are to[o] much ordered'.[3]

The story is often told that the Dutch invented flower painting in Antwerp because paintings came cheaper than flowers. Unable to afford the high prices commanded by the strange new tulips arriving from Constantinople, a lady is said to have approached the artist Jan Brueghel to paint the precious blooms instead. As an explanation of the origins of the art form, the story is almost certainly untrue. Brueghel's earliest known flower paintings are contemporary with Jacques de Gheyn's magical flower album, yet German painters were painting flowers at least fifty years before this, and even earlier works may not have survived.

But despite de Gheyn's lucrative commission for Marie de' Medici – and the even more astronomical prices achieved by a handful of later artists such as Jan van Huysum – most flower paintings sold for meagre fees, far below the wildly speculative prices paid for feathered tulips and other rarities. Paintings of all kinds were plentiful enough to decorate the homes and shops of even modest burghers, as noted by the keen-eyed Peter Mundy, an employee of the East India Company who travelled tirelessly through Europe and the East in a state of mild astonishment. Even butchers and bakers hung paintings in their shops, he said, 'yea many tymes blacksmithes, Coblers, etts., will have some picture or other by their Forge and in their stalle. Such is the generall Notion, enclination and delight that these Countrie Native[s] have to Paintings.'[4]

The growing popularity of flower painting in the Netherlands marked the emergence of the *stilleven* or still life (its literal meaning is 'things lying still'), a term that first appeared in the Northern Netherlands around 1650, although compositions of flowers, fruit and other lifeless objects had been painted for many years before this. The influence of science on art was part of the story. Important, too, was a very Dutch appreciation of the pleasures of the physical world. The Dutch even had a word for showing off such beauties, *pronken,* and for the sumptuous still lifes that fed this sensibility, *pronkstilleven.*

For centuries, flowers had appeared in western art primarily for the messages they conveyed; in the case of roses, these usually revolved around ideas of heavenly or earthly love. Now, in a century characterized as the Dutch Golden Age, Dutch and Flemish artists were painting portraits of flowers, pure and simple, letting the beauty of the flowers speak for itself. Of course, some of the old associations remained: ideas of '*vanitas*', of the fleeting pleasures of life compared with the eternal joys of heaven, of the hand of God in creating all these lilies of the field. Individual artists might still communicate their religious beliefs through their works. Jan Davidsz. de Heem added Eucharist chalices, crucifixes, watches and skulls to his opulent fruit and flower pieces, for instance, and the Dutch remained wedded to the emblem books of writers such as Jacob Cats, who frequently used roses to illustrate commonplace moral precepts. But in the new genre of still-life painting, artists for the most part could concentrate on looking and seeing and painting what they saw.

Most famous of all the early flower painters was the kindly Jan Brueghel the Elder, youngest son of Pieter Brueghel the Elder, painter of peasant scenes. Born in 1568, the year before his father died, Jan was taught to draw by his grandmother and later worked in Italy, establishing his studio in his native Antwerp. His nickname of 'Velvet' could refer to his love of rich materials, velvet coats especially, or the velvety sheen of his paintings. Of all the fashionable flowers he painted, roses were his favourites. Like his pupil Daniel Seghers, he used them to anchor his paintings, while also favouring lilies, stocks, viburnum, iris, orange blossom, fritillaries, newly arrived tulips and crown imperials.

Brueghel was unusual in painting his flower compositions from life. Later artists cheated the seasons by making studies of individual flowers and then arranging these into compositions that could not possibly occur in nature. Look carefully at *Flowers in a Glass Vase*, painted by another pupil of Brueghel's, Ambrosius Bosschaert the Elder. Surely the prominent Damask rose, blush-pink and softly opened, would flower later than his flowers of spring – the yellow and white narcissi especially, but also hyacinth, snakeshead fritillary, columbine and his exquisitely feathered tulips? Brueghel was both more honest and more patient. In August 1606 he wrote to the secretary of his patron, Cardinal Federico Borromeo of Milan, complaining of problems with a garland he was painting entirely from nature, without help from his pupils. Already the blooms were fading, so he would have to wait until the next growing season to complete the picture.

He was also prepared to travel for his art. 'I have begun on a bouquet of flowers for Your Eminence,' he wrote to the Cardinal in April of that same year. 'The result will be a success and very lovely because of both the naturalness and the exceptional beauty of the various flowers, many of which are here unknown or extremely rare; for this reason I went to Brussels to draw from life some of the flowers not to be found in Antwerp.'

The gardens Brueghel visited in Brussels would have included the Archdukes' garden mentioned by English gardener John Tradescant in a letter of 1610 to English agent William Trumbull, requesting a number of rare plants for his new employer, Robert Cecil. Tradescant's wish-list included three roses: 'Rosa icanadine', which he had received the year before, 'but it is dead' (did he mean 'incarnadine', crimson or flesh-coloured, such as the lovely blush-pink Alba rose 'Great Maiden's Blush'?); the evergreen rose, *R. sempervirens;* and the thornless rose, which he called 'Rosa Sina Spina'. Brueghel may also have visited the Brussels nurseryman Mr John Joket, from whom Tradescant requested several pretty white flowers that would have graced any flower painting, including a dainty paradise lily, a spring-flowering pulsatilla, and a silvery-white star-of-Bethlehem.[5]

Daniel Seghers shared his master's love of roses, especially those in bud or just opening into flower. Born in Antwerp but raised in Holland in the reformed faith, Seghers returned in 1610 to Antwerp where he joined Brueghel as an apprentice. It is said that Brueghel brought him back to the Catholic faith, and in January 1615 Seghers was received into the Society of Jesus at Malines (Mechelen in Belgium), finally taking his vows some ten years later. For the rest of his life he rose at 4 a.m. (an hour earlier in summer), repeated his office and then devoted his day to painting, stopping only when princes called to view his work. Visiting in 1635, Archduke Ferdinand of Austria, Governor of the Spanish Netherlands, described how he was taken to the room 'where a lay brother painted flowers from nature, so live that the hand was tempted to gather

Jan Brueghel the Elder painted the flower garden and landscape and Pieter van Avont the figures in this Holy Family of c.1620.

them'. Another of his callers was the future Charles II of England, then in exile after the execution of his father; and in a well-deserved judgement, Constantijn Huygens called Seghers '*le peintre des fleurs et la fleur des peintres*' (the painter of flowers and the flower of painters).

But however 'real' the flowers might appear, Seghers and his fellows were engaged in a careful manipulation of reality through art. Far from contenting themselves with accurate botanical description, they under-stood that creating the illusion of reality demanded the application of artificial rules that would translate three dimensions into two. The art of Dutch and Flemish flower painting can be seen as the gradual refinement of rules to represent a rounded bouquet of flowers, so real that you might ache to gather the flowers in your arms, like Archduke Ferdinand, and breathe in the heady scents.

Throughout the seventeenth century and well into the next, the illusion became ever stronger – in paintings by Jan Davidsz. de Heem, for instance, or the early works of Rachel Ruysch, another great rose-lover, who produced ten children and was still painting in her eightieth year. But after the rules had pushed art to the furthest boundaries of 'reality', the artists simply got bored and threw them away, concentrating instead on purely decorative effects. Jan van Huysum's *Flowers in a Terracotta Vase* in London's National Gallery sets his exuberant bouquet within a light-filled niche, making a deliberate nonsense of the rules of perspective. A nest of birds' eggs apparently hovers on a perpendicular plane. Two double yellow roses hang their heads over the vase, as if gloating at the displaced Centifolias lying on the base beside a glistening bunch of grapes that holds the eye with its sparkle. Flowers and petals explode in a riot of pinks, poppies, peonies, narcissi, hyacinth, marigolds, con-volvulus, auriculas, tulip, iris, peaches, more grapes, more roses and a double yellow hollyhock in the honoured top-right position. It was painted over two years, in 1736 and 1737. The artist had at least followed Brueghel's lead in waiting for the flowers to come into season, so that he could transpose them directly from nature on to his canvas.

All these artists painted their favourite flowers, but their choices also reflected changing tastes as the popularity of individual flowers waxed and waned. Tulips were naturally prominent in the mid-1630s as tulip fever raged, slipping back towards the shadows when the fever suddenly

Jan van Huysum combined flowers that bloom in different seasons for Flowers
in a Terracotta Vase, *on which he worked from 1736 to 1737.*

died. A second wave of speculation over hyacinths produced similar effects towards the end of the century. Speckled fritillaries were common until about 1650; thereafter came other favourites such as double hollyhocks. But roses were a constant throughout: Centifolias, Albas, Damasks, yellow roses (singles and doubles), which clearly represented the best that gardens could offer, and the simple dog rose from the wild. Gallicas were largely absent, as if they lacked the voluptuous roundness that so appealed to Dutch tastes.

However often the Centifolia rose appeared in the canvases of the Dutch masters, its parentage remains something of a mystery. Throughout much of the twentieth century, the notion persisted that it was directly related to the hundred-petalled roses of Theophrastus and Pliny. The old-rose expert Edward Bunyard believed that the rose known to the Ancient Greeks and Romans became very rare, possibly even extinct, until it reappeared in Holland some time in the 1580s, perhaps reintroduced through Asia Minor by the Turks.[6] Another respected authority was less certain, suggesting that it 'is not known, and perhaps never will be, whether the Holland rose was raised in the Low Countries or imported from somewhere in the southern Europe or the eastern Mediterranean'.

The Centifolia's alternative name of 'Province Rose' (present even in Gerard) only added to the confusion. Some called it the 'Provins Rose' (in fact the Gallica), and others the 'Rose de Provence', implying an origin in southern France. The English rose expert John Lindley attempted to set the matter straight by equating Linnaeus's *Rosa centifolia* with Philip Miller's *R. provincalis*, but his prose became so convoluted he tied his meaning in knots.

Without finally resolving their parentage, genetic testing has at least demonstrated that Centifolia roses belong with other European roses, such as the Damasks and the Gallicas, as distinct from the Chinese roses that came to Europe from the end of the eighteenth century. In his pioneering Cambridge studies, Dr C. C. Hurst had declared the Centifolia a complex hybrid between the Damask parents and *R. canina*, either as a cross between the Autumn Damask and an Alba, or by some more complicated process. But he was wrong about the Damask parents (see

Chapter 4), and the best evidence to date suggests that *R. × centifolia* is a garden hybrid, closely related to *R. × damascena,* and that it was raised in the Low Countries in the late sixteenth century and improved by fixed mutation up to the eighteenth century. Some scientists further suggest that the presence of *R. fedtschenkoana* in its genes might explain the spontaneous mutation that produced the Moss roses so popular with the Victorians, many of which belong to the Centifolia group, among them the bright crimson 'Henri Martin', bred by Laffay in France.

And although Dutch flower painting had to some extent exhausted itself with the unfettered displays of Jan van Huysum, the line of artistic succession continued, chiefly through the Dutch painter Gerard van Spaendonck, who moved to Paris and painted flowers for the French King, and through van Spaendonck's most famous pupil, the clumsy Belgian with the large hands, Pierre-Joseph Redouté, who carried on painting through the Revolution and the Reign of Terror, eventually putting his skills to the service of his greatest patron, the Empress Josephine, at her beloved Malmaison on the outskirts of Paris. And Redouté would become one of the most celebrated rose painters of all.

Chapter Ten
Memories of Malmaison

WHEN Englishman Seth William Stevenson visited the Château de Malmaison in the summer of 1816, the year after Waterloo, Empress Josephine's beloved home on the outskirts of Paris was already suffused with the 'chilling breath of neglect'. Napoleon had begun his final exile on St Helena, and his repudiated Empress was two years in her grave. On the winning side in the perennial skirmishing between the English and the French, Stevenson wished not to gloat but rather to compare the *quantum* of English blessings with those of a 'great and rival state'. And despite Malmaison's evident neglect under the absentee ownership of Josephine's son by her first marriage, the young visitor from Norwich pronounced himself delighted with the house and estate, 'so congenial to the dictates of nature, and to the spirit of true taste'. As he was fortuitously visiting at rose time, Stevenson has also bequeathed to us one of the very few first-hand accounts of Malmaison's roses, whose potent memory was soon to whip the French into a frenzy of '*rosomanie*'.

After admiring the château's restrained elegance, Stevenson set out on a tour of its grounds, laid out 'completely *à l'Anglaise*' and displaying everywhere the 'desired *capabilities*'. Here was everything you might desire: novelty, perfectly judged views, little '*cassinos*' peeping through the trees, conservatories and forcing houses for fruit, and productive gardens 'which equally abound with supplies for the *bouquet* and the *kitchen*'. The roses formed part of this artfully natural landscape, for, as Stevenson discovered, 'along a valley between the gardens and the house, a canal is made to wander with the easy windings of a natural stream; its banks were covered with rose trees in bloom, and other flowers; and here

Empress Josephine grew roses along the winding stream of Malmaison's park, seen here in a watercolour of the Temple of Love by Auguste Garneray, painted before 1824.

and there shaded with cypresses, willows, and lilacs'. Close by, a cascade issued from a rockwork grotto, and after a patch of gloomy shade the delighted visitor reached a 'choice *morceau*' of Greek architecture – a Temple of Love containing a pretty figure of Cupid inscribed with this dedicatory couplet:

> Qui que tu soit, voici ton maître:
> Il l'est, le fut, ou le doit être.
> [Whoe'er thou art, thy master see; He is, or was, or ought to be.]

Stevenson's impressions of Malmaison were coloured by what he had discovered about the moral character of its previous owner. Shown around the house by a middle-aged man in a dark green livery who introduced himself as the Empress's old *maître d'hôtel,* the visitor from Norfolk courteously remarked that he had always understood the Empress to be very kind and good to her family and to her servants. '"Sir, (replied the man with quickness), she was good to *every body* (*elle etait bonne à tout le monde),* and every body loved and respected her."' The man's tone was zealous and affectionate, 'and the gardens which we were then entering had not the fewer charms in my eyes, for having been arranged in their present enchanting stile by a person whose taste was equalled by her benevolence'.

'*Adieu, Mal Maison,*' murmured the young Englishman on quitting the estate, reminded by distant glimpses of the Aqueduct de Marly and the Château de St Germain of the links between Napoleon's short-lived sovereignty and the former seats of dynastic kings. Had Josephine remained his wife, he reflected, she might have 'softened the stern and stubborn stuff of his vaulting ambition' with some of her own regard for suffering humanity. Then 'the reign of Buonaparte, instead of impoverishment and humiliation, might have heaped blessings upon France'. So even to her country's former enemies, Josephine was viewed as a benign influence on her erstwhile husband, praised for her goodness and taste and for the exemplary meekness with which she endured her fate: to be discarded for a younger wife who might bear a son to ensure Napoleon's dynastic succession.

Already the Josephine myth was at work, and the dead Empress found her star hitched to a variety of causes that gained added lustre from her name. So it was with Josephine and roses. She liked them, of course, and grew them at her beloved Malmaison – along the winding stream, in her cutting garden, in planting boxes brought out at rose time or, if they were rare enough and especially tender, in her several glasshouses for exotics requisitioned from as far afield as Australia and the Cape of Good Hope. She even fretted over their care when she was away from the house, writing to her *dame de palais,* the Countess d'Arberg, to make sure her roses were being properly watered.

But there was no rose garden at Malmaison, and had you visited out of rose season, you could be forgiven for ignoring roses altogether. Those who visited Malmaison before and after Stevenson make no mention of roses in their eulogies of Malmaison's many botanical splendours. In his

1808 guide to the new gardens of France and her ancient châteaux, for instance, French author Alexandre de Laborde described the château's situation across the bridge of Neuilly and through a countryside planted with roses and fruit trees, but he gave no hint of roses growing within the palace grounds.

Nor do roses appear in the breathless description by Polish traveller Baron U. T. von Uklanski, shown around Malmaison by Josephine's resident botanist and garden superintendent, Aimé Bonpland, who had previously travelled around Latin America with the German naturalist and explorer Alexander von Humboldt. Like his imperial employer, Bonpland was in love with exotics and took much delight in showing off Josephine's splendid temperate glasshouse, the *Grande Serre Chaude*. The Baron was instantly seduced. 'From all sides the most beautiful flowers smile on the visitor,' he recorded. 'Seville orange-scented *Clerodendron fragrans* with its large umbels, the splendid *Calla aethiopica*, the palm-like *Jucca gloriosa*, the attractive fan palms, the large-leaved banana, the wonderful Indian bean tree from America, with a trunk resembling that of the Yucca-palm and banana-like leaves.'

Bonpland also showed him Malmaison's exotic menagerie tucked away in a shrubbery, and talked of plans to introduce many rare breeds. During his visit, the Baron was surprised by Malmaison's solitary kangaroo, which jumped the ditch in a desperate bid for freedom but succeeded only in breaking both its forelegs. It must have survived or been replaced, as the inventory at Josephine's death listed a kangaroo, a llama and seven black swans among the exotic fauna at Malmaison.

The year after Stevenson's visit, a deputation of Scottish gardeners visited Malmaison in the autumn, long after most European roses had stopped flowering. Although they noticed extensive rose plantations on their drive from Paris, they make not a single reference to any roses at Malmaison itself. In all other respects, their impressions mirrored those of Seth Stevenson: of a fine estate slipping into neglect, hastened by the damage wreaked by Prussian cavalry who entered the house a few hours after Napoleon had passed through as he fled, defeated, from the Battle of Waterloo. Was it the same *maître d'hôtel* who pointed out the smashed mirrors, slashed paintings and Napoleon's shattered writing desk, broken open in the soldiers' frantic search for gold?

Like Stevenson before them, the Scottish gardeners walked around the English-style grounds, admiring the scattering of exotic trees near the house (including a fine *Magnolia grandiflora*; a longleaf pine from the southern states of North America; Chinese privet; Persian lilac, *Melia azedarach*; and a sweet orange). 'In the time of Josephine,' they noted, 'the flower-garden was among the richest in Europe; for that Empress was an unwearied patroness of botanical collectors, who in their turn enriched the garden at La Malmaison with their vegetable treasures.'

The Scottish contingent included obvious rose-lovers, as they went on to describe the collection of roses in the Luxembourg gardens in Paris, arranged in formal squares 'quite in the manner of a London sale-nursery' and interplanted with chrysanthemums to prolong the flowering season. And they dutifully visited the nursery of M. Noisette, where 'The *roses* are disposed in groups or families, according to the general characters of their foliage and flowers, and the original species from which they are supposed to have been derived.' Noisette's collection had swollen to some 600 varieties placed into twenty-six groups – an enormous list for that early date. 'Many of these, of course, have but slender claims to distinction,' they added with mild disapproval. 'But he is constantly making experiments and raising new varieties from seed, and he collects from every quarter. A new rose of considerable beauty, allied to Rosa Indica, but with pale and sweet-scented flowers, has lately had the name of the Rose de Noisette bestowed upon it.' They even added a note about the new Bonne Nouvelle nursery near Rouen, established in 1817 by the English firm of Calvert and Co., which boasted a catalogue containing nearly 900 varieties of rose – a number which could easily be inflated with 300 or so Scots roses from Messrs Austins of Glasgow, they suggested patriotically.

But of Josephine's roses, the Scottish gardeners remained resolutely silent. Nor do they refer to the notion that she set out to collect every rose then known – a claim that has since slipped into accepted truth without any supporting evidence.

Until she took possession of her new Malmaison estate in 1799, Josephine displayed no special passion for plants or animals, beyond the usual floral affinities of her class and sex. Born Marie-Joseph-Rose de

Tascher de la Pagerie in 1763 to a family of white Creole plantation owners on the French Caribbean island of Martinique, she travelled to Europe aged eighteen to marry the aristocratic Alexandre de Beauharnais (her paternal aunt had been his father's mistress). The marriage produced two children: a son, Eugène, who would eventually inherit Malmaison, and a daughter, Hortense. Both parents were imprisoned during the terrors of the French Revolution, and Alexandre was guillotined in July 1794. Josephine survived, and on her release reputedly became the mistress of several prominent politicians.

When she first captivated Napoleon, he was a little-known general in a worn, ill-fitting uniform. They married in 1796, and, ironically for her later reputation, her new husband changed her name from Rose (as she was generally known) to Josephine. His passion was at first greater than hers. Often apart, they each took lovers and Josephine's love for her husband was apparently without depth until the darkening days leading up to the couple's divorce in 1810. He had nonetheless crowned her as his Empress in March 1804, when his ardour had cooled and her failure to produce an heir was already threatening their union.

Malmaison at the time of Josephine's purchase was a typical country house of the *ancien régime*. Its previous owner had already begun to lay out the park in the English style, to which Josephine added the crowning touches of her exquisite taste. Well known for her extravagances, Josephine poured money – first the state's and later her husband's – into her new home, spending as much as thirteen times the original purchase price on improvements to the house and grounds. Josephine herself was often away, but when in residence Napoleon

Empress Josephine in a charcoal sketch by Pierre-Paul Prud'hon, undertaken perhaps as a study for his subtly melancholic portrait of the Empress at Malmaison begun in 1805.

visited regularly during the first three years and together they planted the magnificent cedar of Lebanon that still stands to one side of the château's garden façade, celebrating Napoleon's victory at Marengo.

Exotic trees and plants were Josephine's special passion; and as Alexandre de Laborde approvingly commented in his contemporary guide, 'The continual care that has been taken to augment this fine collection, has rendered Malmaison the true botanic garden of France.' Her special collections included heathers from the Cape, housed in their own small greenhouse,[1] and she did much to popularize camellias, dahlias and pelargoniums.

The great hothouse that so enthused the Polish Baron von Uklanski was situated at some distance from the house rather than the more usual winter garden attached to the main apartments. Josephine overcame

Interior view by Auguste Garneray of Josephine's great hothouse at Malmaison, which combined a section for plants and a tasteful salon for guests.

this deficiency by constructing her glasshouse in two halves: a part for plants, and a 'tastefully furnished salon', decorated with costly vases and pictures, where guests could enjoy the sights and scents of her magnificent plant collection, as well as fine views out to the park and her Seville orange trees reflected in the waters of a bright pool. If you were lucky enough to be shown around by Josephine herself, she would dazzle you with her botanical knowledge, rattling off the names of rare plants which her skilled gardeners had persuaded to grow in France's northern climate. And as she confided to the French count who accompanied the British politician Charles James Fox to Malmaison in 1802:

'It is here I would like to be enthroned, among these vegetal peoples . . . here is the hortensia [hydrangea] that recently took its name from my daughter, the soldanella of the Alps, the Parma violet, the Nile lily, the rose from Damietta. These conquests over Italy and Egypt will never be the enemies of Napoleon, but here are my own conquests,' she added, pointing to a beautiful jasmine from her native Martinique. 'The seed planted by me reminds me of my home-land, my childhood and my adornments as a young girl.' And indeed, as she said this, her Creole voice struck one visitor like music full of expression and tenderness.[2]

Josephine's courtiers were less impressed by the Empress's botanical performances. One of her ladies-in-waiting – clearly bored to tears by a lifestyle she castigated as 'amphibian' – describes how every day, weather permitting, they would visit the glasshouses, taking always the same route and talking always of the same things. 'The conversation revolved around botany,' recalled Mlle Georgette Ducrest, 'a science *so interesting* to Her Majesty, whose prodigious memory prompted her to name all the plants: almost always the same phrases repeated at the same hour, which rendered our promenades tiring and tiresome.' As soon as she set foot in Malmaison's pretty walks, which had seemed so charming on her first day, the pleasure-loving Mlle Ducrest admitted to being overcome with violent and uncontrollable yawns. Then, after examining the rarest of flowers right down to their stamens, the party was expected to admire the Empress's famous black swans, which Mlle Ducrest judged infinitely less beautiful than the common white variety. 'At this point we listened again to the chamberlain's speech on the difficulties of naturalizing them, and his solemn assurance that they could acclimatize only at Malmaison.'

Yet however much Josephine's botanical passions bored her ladies-in-waiting, it would be wrong to dismiss them as mere whim. Her hothouses welcomed many rare plants from territories conquered by her husband. Josephine herself arranged for her superintendent Bonpland to make a clandestine visit to Vienna's Schönbrunn Palace to see what plants might usefully find a home at Malmaison. Many more plants and animals – including the famous black swans – came back with Captain Nicolas Baudin from his expedition to Australia and the South Seas, sanctioned by Napoleon just four months after he came to power as First Consul. This was botanic imperialism on a grand scale. And as Josephine showed through her many letters, she was not simply an avid collector of exotica for herself, but wanted to distribute her introductions more widely – an impulse she shared with Thomas Jefferson, then President of the United States of America, who ranked his introduction of the olive tree and dry rice to South Carolina on a par with writing America's Declaration of Independence. 'The greatest service which can be rendered in any country,' he believed, 'is to add an useful plant to its culture.'[3]

The Empress wrote to anyone she thought might help in her quest for new plants: local dignitaries, colonial governors, French diplomats abroad, and individuals to whom she proposed exchanges, such as hardy magnolias for seeds from the Dutch East Indies. A frequent mediator was the diplomat Louis-Guillaume Otto, created Comte de Mosloy by Napoleon, whom she thanked in June 1801 for doing all in his power to advance her design of naturalizing useful plants in France. She reminded him of her hope that the British King's gardener at Kew might supply some 'curious seeds', despite mounting hostilities between Britain and France. Josephine was clearly not one to let international politics stand in her way, and a few months later she wrote again to Otto, saying that she would call on him as soon as harmony was restored between the two nations. 'Do you not think that the King of England might consent to give me a few plants from his fine garden at Kew?' she asked, hoping that Otto might present the idea with his accustomed *délicatesse*.

At least two roses were proposed as part of Josephine's efforts to naturalize exotic plants on French soil: an unnamed variety intended for a Préfet in the Alpes-Maritimes, which flowered constantly and which she thought might be grown outdoors in Nice. The second rose – sent to Toulon in the Midi by Bonpland – was the white 'Lady Banks' rose, *Rosa banksiae* var. *banksiae*, brought to England from China in 1807 by William Kerr and named in honour of Lady Banks, wife of the eminent naturalist Sir Joseph Banks (see Chapter 11). Thornless, evergreen and flowering profusely in early spring, it is not fully hardy and needs warm sun to flower.

But no roses – not even the new exotics from China – appeared in the two books Josephine commissioned to immortalize her botanic rarities at Malmaison and her estate at Navarre. As the first of these works, *Jardin de la Malmaison*, was published in 1803, she must have ordered its compilation soon after she took possession of her Malmaison estate, fired by similarly sumptuous works celebrating the botanical treasures of another Parisian garden belonging to the amateur plantsman and rose enthusiast, J. M. Cels. In any case, she approached the same team: the former priest and distinguished botanist Étienne Pierre Ventenat to provide the words, and the 'Raphael of flowers', the Belgian illustrator Pierre-Joseph Redouté, to execute the illustrations. They had included three roses for Cels, no doubt at Cels's own request (he was known to have introduced several exotic roses into France): two Chinese roses (one they called *Rosa diversifolia;* and the white Macartney rose, *Rosa bracteata,* a native of south-east China and Taiwan, introduced into Britain in 1793 after Lord Macartney's mission to China); and a rose called '*Rosa kamtchatica*' from the Kamchatka peninsula of north-eastern Russia (today often listed as *R. rugosa* var. *kamtchatica*).

But Josephine can have issued no such instruction for her garden book, which suggests that her rose collection did not yet contain rarities to match her novelties from Australia and the Cape. Certainly, the majority of Chinese roses were slow to reach France. France's own East India Company had shut down some twenty years before the French Revolution, and apart from Cels's introductions, most Chinese and Asian roses came to France either through British hands or via France's outposts overseas.

Ventenat died in 1808 and Josephine then turned to the experienced

The Empress is about to step into her carriage in a view of Malmaison's garden façade by Auguste Garneray.

gardener and plant-hunting botanist Aimé Bonpland, appointing him superintendent of her estates at Malmaison and later at Navarre. Bonpland continued the tradition of immortalizing in print the Empress's stupendous collection of exotics from all five continents: Moutan peonies from the mountains of imperial China; a purple foxglove from the Palatinate; giant heathers from the Cape; a yellow-flowered banksia from Australia; mimulus from Peru; and a hothouse acacia from an unknown land ['Patria ignota'], which he thought might have been one of the plants he brought back himself after his expedition with Humboldt. These are the plants for which Malmaison was justly famed during the Empress's lifetime and which featured in the inventory of plants growing at Malmaison at the time of her death; but of roses, scarcely a mention. Like Ventenat, Bonpland ignored Malmaison's roses;

and the work that most obviously celebrates Josephine's love of roses – Pierre-Joseph Redouté's *Les Roses*, published some years after her death – owes little to her direct influence, as we shall see.

So where and how did Empress Josephine acquire her reputation as a rose-lover, and which roses did she grow? Flattery undoubtedly played some part in bolstering her reputation as a serious rose-grower. In his flowery dedication to the *Jardin de la Malmaison*, Ventcnat had hailed her taste for flowers and her success in reuniting at Malmaison the rarest plants on French soil, naturalizing plants 'which had not yet left the deserts of Arabia and the burning sands of Egypt'. These, he said, provided 'the gentlest memory of the conquests of your illustrious husband, and the most amiable proof of your studious leisure hours'.

Later writers specifically linked her to roses, both in her lifetime and in the decades after her death in 1814. Since the rose was the 'Queen of Flowers', it was natural for the French to see in the rose the 'emblem of the Sovereign they cherish'; so wrote M. Lelieur, administrator of the imperial parks, nurseries and gardens in a little book devoted to the culture of rose trees and other shrubs, which he published the year after Josephine's divorce, when her standing with the French people appeared in no way diminished.

The botanist Auguste de Pronville went further, placing Malmaison among the select few gardens around Paris with a significant rose collection. The others he mentioned, in a work aimed at bringing order into the messy business of classifying the new rose hybrids, were the royal gardens of the Luxembourg and the Trianon (but emphatically not the École du Jardin Royal), and the private nurseries of Cels, Noisette and Godefroy at Ville d'Avray. Pronville published his work the year after the Scottish gentlemen visited Malmaison without recording a single rose, so he either looked harder than they did or deliberately amplified his memories.

By 1824 – some ten years after her death – Josephine was credited with igniting in the French a passion for growing roses, and for wresting the commercial advantage away from the English and the Dutch. Such was the verdict of the French rose-grower J. P. Vibert, who declared himself no particular admirer of the English but wanted to be fair, 'even at some cost to our amour-propre'. The English were born with commercial instincts and could sell just about anything, he suggested. 'By birth they are no more intellectually favoured than we are, and their climate is considerably worse. But with them, the taste for ornamental plants is shared by a large part of the leisured and even wealthy classes.'

Vibert was basing his arguments on custom, class and social snobberies. In his view, one shining example stood out in France: Josephine Beauharnais (he was using her name under the *ancien régime* in subtle deference to France's temporarily restored monarchy), this 'virtuous woman' who had rendered such service to the culture of ornamental plants in France, and who had gathered about her at Malmaison one of the richest collections of plants and shrubs. 'Roses were a special favourite of hers,' he wrote, adding that she did not consider it beneath herself to show particular consideration to a humble rose-grower such as André Du Pont, a postal worker and France's foremost amateur rose grower. Soon her influence spread beyond her immediate locality, he claimed, and it was really from this time that one can date all the important discoveries in the genus, improvements in their culture, and an increase in the number of rose-lovers. Here is myth-making at work: Josephine's moral character gaining credit for and further disseminating a love of Josephine's 'favourite flower'.

In another two decades, her reputation as France's premier rose enthusiast was secure. Not only was she credited – along with postman Du Pont – of igniting in Paris a 'great impulsion' towards rose-growing, but her garden at Malmaison was praised for reuniting 'all that Holland, Belgium and Germany possessed that was most beautiful of this kind'. (Britain's absence from this list can no doubt be explained by another crisis in Anglo-French relations.) By now, the notion that Josephine grew all known roses at Malmaison had firmly taken root.

Art played its part, too, in cementing Josephine's reputation as a rose-lover, and in particular one of the most celebrated works of botanical illustration: Pierre-Joseph Redouté's *Les Roses,* released in instalments and published in three volumes between 1817 and 1824. It is hard to reconcile the work's exquisite delicacy with the caricature sketched for us by his contemporary, François Joseph Grille, who talked of the artist's 'thickset body, elephant members, a head heavy and flat like a Dutch cheese, thick lips, muffled voice, hooked fingers' and altogether repulsive appearance.[4] What he lacked in good looks he more than compensated for by his talent and evident charm, however.

Born into a family of painters from Saint-Hubert in the Belgian Ardennes – his great-grandfather, grandfather, father and two brothers were all painters – Redouté had gravitated before the Revolution to Paris, where he practised drawing in the Jardin du Roi, received elementary instruction in botany from amateur botanist Charles-Louis L'Héritier de Brutelle, and worked his way into court circles. Gerard van Spaendonck asked him to take over some flower paintings for the Vélins du Roi, then incorporated into the King's Library, while Queen Marie-Antoinette gave him free access to paint the flowers in the Petit Trianon. He survived the Terror by keeping his head down (as did his two brothers) and devoting himself to his art. In the year the French king was guillotined, he quietly exhibited his first flower paintings in watercolour, and went on to win the competition to continue the botanical vellums that had now transferred to the Jardin des Plantes. Painting flowers while Paris burned was an excellent way of staying out of trouble and he remained on good terms with all sides, as illustrated by the strange – and probably apocryphal – story that the doomed King Louis XVI and Marie-Antoinette summoned him one night to their prison at the Temple to paint a rare cactus in bloom.

All three Redouté brothers soon found employment with the Bonapartes: brother Henri-Joseph followed Napoleon to Egypt, Antoine-Ferdinand decorated Josephine's reception rooms at Malmaison, while Pierre-Joseph became her special protégé, producing plates for Ventenat's *Jardin de la Malmaison* and his own resplendent work on the lily family (published in instalments between 1802 and 1816), and watercolours on vellum for Josephine's bedchamber. The year after the Empire was declared, Redouté was appointed 'Flower-Painter to the Empress' at an annual salary of 18,000 francs; yet despite this princely sum, he always needed more.

While Josephine was undoubtedly the inspiration and driving force behind *Les Liliacées*, it seems that painting roses was the artist's own ambition. The work began to appear only in 1817, three years after her death. The author of the accompanying text was the cultured and genial

Claude Antoine Thory, once a parliamentary lawyer who had signed the decree to arrest the revolutionary Jean-Paul Marat, and now a gifted amateur botanist with a fine rose garden at Belleville on the outskirts of Paris. The two friends would often meet in a café to discuss progress on the work and to check each other's contributions.

Redouté already had a number of roses in his portfolio, among them the Chinese and Russian roses he had painted in the Montrouge garden of M. Cels. He had also bought a country house in Fleury, a hamlet near Meudon, and planted a rose garden of his own. He was proud of his roses, but there is no record of him following the example of the English botanical artist Mary Lawrance, who actually sold some of her roses.[5] Several of his prize creations found their way into *Les Roses*, including a supposed cross between *Rosa spinosissima* and *R. glauca*, which Thory named *Rosa redutea* in his honour; *R. gallica caerulea*, a Provins rose with bluish petals, obtained from the painter's sowing at Fleury; and *R. rubiginosa Flore semi-pleno*, raised during the family's earliest days at Fleury and widely distributed around France and abroad through the nursery trade (the names are those given in *Les Roses*).

The whole family became avid rose-spotters on their rambles around Meudon and the environs of Paris, and *Les Roses* is full of charming references to their discoveries. They found *Rosa villosa* in the woods near Meudon; *R. leucantha* among bushes at the foot of the slope bordering the road from Meudon to Bellevue; and *R. andegavensis* in the boundary hedges to General de Montcera's estate. In 1817, close to the pheasantry, Redouté's daugher Josephine found *R. tomentosa*, which until then had escaped the researches of M. Tuillier, 'or perhaps that clever taxonomist had seen in the rose only a variety of *R. villosa*'. Even brother Henry became involved, bringing back from the Ardennes *R. pimpinellifolia Mariaeburgensis*, which he had found growing wild near their grand-father's native haunts.

For several years, Redouté and Thory tramped round all France's famous rose collections in and around Paris, inspecting, drawing, describing, comparing as many roses as they could find. In total, they prepared plates for a relatively modest number of roses: just 169, less than one third of Noisette's tally although considerably more than the 100 or so they had originally intended to include. They duly recorded their sources in the introduction to the first volume: these included government collections in Paris, Sèvres and Versailles; the gardens of the most skilful nurserymen and enlightened amateurs, among them Messieurs Thouin, Le Lieur, Du Pont, Cels, Vilmorin, Noisette, Descemet and Biquelin; and rare varieties from the magnificent glasshouses of M. Boursault. French and foreign botanists supplied them with other roses that were too tender to flower under Parisian skies; among them was M. De Candolle who had written the text for the first four volumes of *Les Liliacées*. Even Bonpland and his exploring companion Alexander von Humboldt had told them about a new rose they had found in Mexico. (Disappointingly, it was almost certainly a dog rose introduced to Mexico by the Spanish in the sixteenth century, and known as the *Rosier de Montezuma*.)

One name is missing from the list: Josephine's Malmaison, supposedly the garden that brought together all the roses known in France, and intimately familiar to the artist. In the whole of *Les Roses*, Redouté draws our attention to just two roses he painted there. The first (in Volume I) is the little bicoloured *Rosa berberifolia* (now *R. persica*), a native of Iran, Afghanistan and the steppes of central Asia, brought back from Iran by André Michaux and first coaxed into flower in France by the green-fingered Cels. 'The engraving shows the flower as we painted it several years ago, growing on vigorous stock in the gardens of Malmaison,' wrote Thory about Redouté's distinctive watercolour, which shows the bright yellow flower in various stages of opening and a single petal marked by its characteristic purple eye.

Redouté's second Malmaison rose is a superb Gallica, dark and velvety like the petals of *R. 'Tuscany Superb'*. Thory called it *Rosa gallica Purpurea velutina* and in French *le Rosier de Van Eeden*, describing it as a 'magnificent variety of Provins rose, obtained from seedlings by Van Eeden, clever nurseryman in Harlem [Holland], with which he decorated, in 1810, the beautiful gardens of Malmaison'. Redouté's watercolour is one of the finest plates in the book. He must have taken his easel to Malmaison and painted it before 1814, as Thory explains that after Josephine's death this beautiful rose disappeared from Malmaison, and they had no idea where it might be multiplying on ungrafted stock. 'It is in abandoning the rose to its own devices that such magnificent

Rosa Berberifolia   *Rosier à feuilles d'Épine-vinette.*

P. J. Redouté pinx.   Imprimerie de Rémond   Chapuy sculp.

The little bicoloured Rosa berberifolia, *now known as* R. persica,
*one of only two roses definitely painted at Malmaison by the great Belgian botanical
artist Pierre-Joseph Redouté for Les Roses (1817–24).*

Rosa Gallica Purpurea Velutina, Parva.   *Rosier de Van-Eeden.*

P.J. Redouté pinx.   *Imprimerie de Remond*   *Langlois sculp.*

Redouté's other rose painted at Malmaison for Les Roses: a velvety Gallica rose similar to
'Tuscany Superb', which he called 'le rosier de Van Eeden' after its Dutch suppliers.

flowers were obtained at Malmaison,' explained Thory, 'which is still Van Eeden's practice today at his fine nurseries of Harlem.' Yet for all the beauty of Redouté's image, it could never match the original, because 'Painting lacks the colours faithfully to reproduce the nuances that one perceives in the flowers of this shrub, which illustration and text together can only feebly portray, even though the painter has employed all the resources of his art.'

Thory was not exaggerating his artist's skill. Redouté's *Les Roses* represents the pinnacle of botanical illustration, combining a high degree of botanical accuracy with artistic flair and magnificent technical artistry. Countless ordinary reproductions leave you ill-prepared for the brilliance of the original, and Josephine would surely have marvelled over its exquisite workmanship had she lived long enough to applaud its publication. Redouté used an intaglio process known as stipple engraving, by which thousands of minute dots are pressed into a soft copper plate. His innovation was to use a technique that allowed him to apply all his colours on a single plate, instead of four successive plates. By this means, his flowers literally sparkle on the page with 'all the softness and brilliance of *watercolour*'.

But to add more names to the list of roses definitely grown at Malmaison beyond Redouté's paltry pair, we must rummage through surviving garden accounts and notes made by careful visitors. In Malmaison's flower garden, for instance, the French rose expert M. Auguste de Pronville saw a Damask rose he identified as '*Rosa damascena carnea*' – quite possibly (he thought) the same rose painted by Mary Lawrance under the name 'damascena Imperial Blush Rose'. Notebook in hand, he also diligently spotted a variety of Scotch rose (*Rosa spinosissima*) he judged of botanic rather than garden value; another rose he called *Rosa mollisima* (*R. mollis* or *R. villosa*); and a botanical curiosity that left him cold: a rose without any petals at all. In one of Josephine's glasshouses he spied Redouté's little yellow-flowered *Rosa berberifolia* with its bright purple spot.[6]

The French rose expert François Joyaux has scoured the National Archives in Paris for other roses definitely grown at Malmaison, identifying wherever possible their modern names. Those from unnamed suppliers include the alpine *Rosa pendulina,* the Four Seasons rose,

R. virginiana, three Moss roses, and a Centifolia rose known as 'Unique'. A certain M. Catoire supplied a dwarf rose apparently from the tropical island of Java, which almost certainly originated elsewhere.

More roses came from one of Malmaison's chief supplier of exotics: the London firm of Lee & Kennedy, which operated from the Vineyard at Hammersmith and which Redouté knew well from his stay in London through the winter of 1786 to 1787. Hailed by the famous British gardening writer J. C. Loudon as 'unquestionably the first nursery in Britain, or rather the world', the firm developed a close, if deferential, relationship with Josephine through the good offices of partner John Kennedy, son of the original Lewis Kennedy – so close, in fact, that he named one of his twenty-one children Josephine in her honour. Their professional relationship apparently ignored the fluctuating hostilities between the two nations, giving rise to the strange rumour (current in the 1840s) that 'the late Mr. Kennedy was provided with a passport to go and come as he pleased during the war, in order that he might superintend the formation of [Malmaison's] garden'. He certainly visited in 1802, before Britain imposed the blockade on French ports, supplying plants and giving advice; and the firm was still supplying Josephine with plants in November 1811, when the British press reported that 'Curious plants, to the amount of 700*l.* value, have been lately shipped at Portsmouth for the *ci-devant* Empress Josephine. They are the produce of a nursery garden at Hammersmith; from which she also got a supply in 1803, to the amount of 2600*l.*'[7]

Given relations between Britain and France, the plants faced a difficult journey. Like any prudent housewife, Josephine kept a close eye on her precious consignments. In February 1802 she sent Citizen Otto a list of plants that had perished on the journey, asking him to arrange with Lee & Kennedy for their replacement. More than two years later, she told her banker to inform the nursery that their charges were too high, as they had agreed not to bill her for useless plants, and part of their recent consignment had suffered so much in transit it was beyond use. 'I have proposed to reduce their bill to twelve thousand francs,' she told him, 'and with that sum they should consider themselves very well paid. If they refuse, I shall settle their bill in full, but they shall cease to supply me.'

One can only suppose that John Kennedy meekly agreed to reduce his charges, as Hammersmith plants continued to cross the Channel, including four Chinese roses which arrived in 1813. These were an unidentifiable *Rosa chinensis* (a name given to several varieties); the vigorous, lilac-pink *R. multiflora* 'Carnea'; *R. semperflorens* (introduced into Britain in 1792 as 'Slater's Crimson China'); and the white Moss rose, *R. × centifolia* 'Muscosa Alba', a sport of the common Moss rose known in England as 'Shailer's White Moss'.

Writing in 1817, Thory tells us that the white Moss rose was introduced into cultivation 'about four or five years ago' by the English nurseryman Shailer, and came to France via the actor and rose enthusiast Jean-François Boursault; although not widely grown, it was also found in the nurseries of Vilmorin, Cels and Noisette. (Other sources give the rose a much earlier introduction into England.) If Thory's dates are right, Josephine would have planted her white Moss rose long before Boursault, so that by buying directly from Lee & Kennedy, she was able to obtain unusual roses before they became generally available in France. But by 1813, Chinese and other exotic roses were on sale in France, so why Josephine risked ordering them from England is a puzzle. Perhaps she simply wanted the best, and French rose growers had not yet overtaken their English or Dutch counterparts. She was also collaborating with the English nursery on a plant-collecting expedition to the Cape, collecting heathers, bulbs and other plants, so adding roses to her plant consignments was simply convenient.

As well as being London's premier supplier of exotics (together with the upcoming Loddiges nursery of Hackney), Lee & Kennedy prided themselves on their roses. Responding to a request from Kew to supply a list of plants introduced by the nursery, particularly heathers and proteas, the nursery offered to supply a recently compiled list of their roses as well, with the proviso that 'the names we give them are so unbotanical that it can be but of little use'. The letter was written on 24 October 1808, almost certainly to King George III's gardener, William Townsend Aiton, who was then revising his father's list of plants growing in the royal gardens, *Hortus Kewensis*. The nursery duly supplied their handwritten list of some 220 roses and the names had indeed changed from the plainer labels of the previous century, when they were indicative of geography, colour, botanical characteristic, smell, type or situation. Many of the old favourites remained, of course, but here were names like 'Triumphant', 'Celestial', 'Burning Coal', 'Sanspareille', 'Supreme Beauty', 'Grand Triumphant', 'Illustrious', 'Admirable', 'Refulgent', 'Paradise', 'Elysian', 'Bijou', 'Delicious', 'Dauphine', 'Imperial Blush' and 'Rose Peruque'.

Nurserymen everywhere were clearly adopting the Dutch habit (begun with their tulips) of baptizing their new cultivars with fanciful names to catch public attention, even when the plants themselves were little different from the old. Serious horticulturists such as correspondents to France's *Le Bon Jardinier* might grumble about the trivializing habit of calling flesh-coloured roses 'Cuisse de Nymphe' (nymph's thigh) or 'Cuisse de Nymphe Ému' (thigh of an aroused nymph) for the slightly pinker version, but they could not stem the tide of ever more florid varieties appearing in nursery catalogues. All they could do was to insist on some link between the plant and its name, reserving names like 'Jeanne d'Arc' and 'La Duchesse d'Angoulême' for white or very pale roses, for instance, and 'La Comtesse de Genlis' or 'Ninon de l'Enclos' (a famous salon wit and courtesan) for roses with superb flowers in more flamboyant colours.

To augment her supplies from England, Josephine would undoubtedly have turned to Parisian rose growers such as Cels, Boursault and Vilmorin (described in 1813 as 'the first to have procured the complete collection of roses'). One of her largest suppliers was indeed the postal worker André Du Pont, who had a 'rich garden' at 8 rue Fontaine-au-Roi in the Faubourg du Temple. Du Pont grew the rose with no petals that had so disconcerted Pronville at Malmaison, and bills show that he supplied Malmaison with large numbers of roses (but sadly not their names) in 1808 and 1809 – perhaps as many as 2,500 rose trees in the two seasons. About this time Josephine was also exchanging roses with her sister-in-law at Kassel. In November 1809, Queen Catharina wrote to inform her 'dear sister' Josephine that the King – Napoleon's brother Jérome Bonaparte, created King of Westphalia – 'could not take the roses with him, because the hasty departure, according to the gardener, would have harmed the plants. Today I am having them sent to Monsieur de la Valette's address, and he will deliver them to you.'[8]

By 1813 Du Pont's catalogue contained 218 different roses – almost exactly the same number as Lee & Kennedy, although Du Pont's total stock was said to number more than two and a half times that.[9] In that same year, however, retirement from the postal service forced him to give up his house and garden in the Temple and seek cheaper premises – a great loss to the capital's amateur rose growers, as they could no longer buy their favourite roses from him. Du Pont's stock went to the Luxembourg gardens, which developed a fine reputation for roses under its director, M. Alexandre Hardy, who bred the pure white, green-eyed Damask he named 'Madame Hardy' after his wife. English rose-grower William Paul described the Luxembourg under Hardy as having 'the most splendid collection in France' and its director as being 'very courteous to foreigners'.

Another Parisian rose-grower forced to give up his collection in infinitely more tragic circumstances was Jacques-Louis Descemet, who came from a family of horticulturists that had cared for the garden of the Apothecaries of Paris since the seventeenth century. The rose-grower Vibert credited him with creating more than 200 interesting varieties (his father's catalogue of 1782, by contrast, had offered just twenty roses for sale).[10] But the Descemet nurseries at Saint-Denis succumbed to the changing tides of war, first in 1814 when Russian troops occupied Saint-Denis, causing much damage to the nurseries, then again in July 1815, when the invading troops menacing the nursery came from the old enemy, England. This time Vibert rescued some 300 varieties and perhaps as many as 10,000 young seedlings among Descemet's 'precious collection', transporting them to his own nursery garden at Chennevières-sur-Marne, where most happily survived. Distressed by the lack of support from the French state, Descemet exiled himself to Odessa in the Crimea, where he became director of the city's botanical garden and built up a fine new collection of roses on Russian soil.

Josephine did not survive the end of Empire. After Napoleon's crushing defeat by the Russians and his first abdication, she received her country's enemies as visitors at Malmaison, including Alexander I of Russia, his brothers Nicholas and Michael, and Frederick William, King of Prussia. It is said she caught a cold showing Alexander around her gardens, and soon succumbed to a high fever. She died at Malmaison on 29 May 1814, just before her fifty-second birthday.

Napoleon came briefly to Malmaison after the slaughter of Waterloo, three days after his second abdication and before his final exile to St Helena. Standing before a thicket of roses, he is reported to have said to Josephine's daughter, Hortense, 'Poor Josephine! I cannot get used to living in this place without her! I always seem to see her emerging from an avenue of trees to gather these plants which she loved so much.' His words fit the myth well: of the charming, silvery-voiced Creole whose memory will be forever linked to the Queen of Flowers.

Josephine left no will. Malmaison's inventory of contents took forty days to prepare, producing an estimated value of 3 million francs. The last day was devoted to rare plants around the house, in the park, and in the glasshouses. Only one possible rose is mentioned by name: 'Rosa Metalcupa', included with 220 hothouse plants such as eucalyptus and the evergreen *Magnolia grandiflora*. It may not even have been a botanical rose. Her rose collection as a whole was clearly not considered special enough to be given a commercial value.

The Empress also left many debts. Her son Eugène de Beauharnais inherited Malmaison but lived in Munich, and he began selling off precious objects from the estate to settle the family's debts, much to Napoleon's long-distance fury. By the time Eugène died in 1824, the inventory's value had reduced to some 97,000 francs. The estate was sold within a few years, most of the glasshouses were pulled down, and botany came to an end at Malmaison.

But all the time Josephine's reputation was spreading as a champion of roses. *La Rose de Malmaison*, painted c.1866 by French artist Hector Viger and now hanging at Malmaison, offers a rosy-tinted memory of happier times. Against a backdrop of the Temple of Love, a uniformed Napoleon hands a rose to his seated wife, who sparkles in white satin, surrounded by a languid group of female family and friends, including her daughter Hortense, Napoleon's scandalous sister Pauline Borghese, and the Countess d'Arberg, who had taken charge of rose-watering in Josephine's absence. Several hold cut roses in their hands; more roses can be seen growing in the garden beyond.

Painted half a century after her death, La Rose de Malmaison
*by Jean-Louis Victor (Hector) Viger sets the seal on Empress Josephine's reputation
as France's most iconic rose lover.*

After passing through several hands, Malmaison reached its nadir
during the Franco-Prussian war of 1870, when enemy troops pillaged the
house and the inhabitants of Rueil-Malmaison stole from the now empty
palace. 'Only two obelisks remain standing,' wrote a visitor in 1895, 'the
waterfall is no more than a puddle beneath a thicket of old horse
chestnuts and conifers, below which are the rocks illustrated by Prudhon
in his portrait of Joséphine ... As for the palace itself, it remains
abandoned.'

Malmaison was saved for the nation by the enormously wealthy financier Daniel Iffla, known as Osiris, who bought and restored the house and the remaining sliver of park, donating it to the state in 1904 on condition that Malmaison opened to the public as a museum dedicated to memories of the Napoleonic era. Josephine's rose collection was imaginatively recreated by French rosarian Jules Gravereaux – at his fine garden in L'Haÿ-les-Roses (now the Roseraie du Val-de-Marne); at Malmaison itself; and in print in a work illustrated by entirely fictitious plans and engraved views of Empress Josephine's rose garden, looking for all the world like a garden of the *belle époque*.

As no catalogue existed for Josephine's roses, Gravereaux turned to contemporary lists of rose growers such as Du Pont and Descemet, claiming (without evidence) that 'she possessed all the roses known during the First Empire'. His list of 197 roses, further refined by François Joyaux, nonetheless provides a fascinating glimpse of First Empire roses. Gallicas predominate, with names redolent of Josephine's court: 'Belle Sultane', 'Beauté Insurmontable', 'La Tendresse', 'Grand Napoléon', 'Agathe de la Malmaison', 'Joséphine', and the velvety 'Van Eeden' rose so memorably painted by Redouté. There are also many Centifolias, Albas, Damasks, Musk roses and a smattering of the new 'Bengal' roses originating in China that would so transform roses in the West. Among the ornamental rather than historic roses planted at Malmaison was, of course, the blush-pink Bourbon 'Souvenir de la Malmaison', its petals shading into the palest of pink face powders – a rose the Empress can never have known, as it was created some thirty years after her death.

Josephine would be distressed by the state of her garden today. While the house has been lovingly restored and breathes the air of restrained elegance that so enchanted Seth William Stevenson nearly 200 years ago, when I visited in June 2008 the rose gardens to either side of the château were a melancholy sight, although I am assured its maintenance is being steadily improved. Thistles and weeds grew among the roses, which no one had attempted to deadhead for days. The lawns, too, were matted with dandelion and clover, and when I asked a young gardener for help in identifying the rose varieties used, he was sadly unable to oblige.

But wander into what little remains of the park and something of Josephine's magic returns. On a sunlit summer afternoon it is possible to imagine her appearing between the trees, talking of botany to her entourage and of the roses that have become her emblem, even if she herself would perhaps have preferred to be remembered for her startling Antipodean exotics and her giant heathers from the Cape.

Roses of East and West

Chapter Eleven
Chinese Whispers

THE first Chinese rose to make its recorded appearance in Britain belonged not to a gardener but to the apothecary James Petiver of Aldersgate Street, London, a collector of natural and artificial curiosities and a friend of Sir Hans Sloane, whose own vast store of treasures would become the founding collection of the British Museum. The year was 1702. 'Rosa CHUSAN. glabra, Juniperi fructu,' wrote Petiver in the descriptive catalogue to his collection. '*This* Rose *I have received from* Chusan *and* China, *but not with Fruit, till* Dr Sloan[e] *was pleas'd to give it to me.*'

The dried rose specimen took its place among Petiver's treasure trove of insects, shells and plant material gathered together from home and abroad, including a flowering variety of the Chusan tree, also donated by that '*worthy Communicative Gentleman* Dr Sloane'; an enormous subtropical insect brought back from the Bay of Bengal by Mr John Fox, a surgeon with the East India Company; and a bituminous fossil discovered in a Yorkshire coal pit by another '*Curious*' medical gentleman. For the first unequivocal record of a Chinese rose in Britain, it is easy to miss.

Petiver's Chusan rose came from Dr James Cunningham or Cuninghame, a physician with the British East India Company and one of the first Europeans to go botanizing in China. Before sending back his rose, he had already made one journey there, sailing in 1697 and sending back specimens to Petiver and other learned friends of his circle, such as Sloane and the royal botanist Leonard Plukenet. After this first journey, Petiver praised Cunningham as a '*Learned* and most *industrious Promoter* of *Natural Philosophy,* and extremely well qualified for such a Design; as I am very sensible, by the curious *Remarks* he hath made on most of the

Plants, &c he hath observed'. Cunningham had also procured for him Chinese paintings of nearly 800 plants 'in their *Natural Colours,* with their *Names* to all, and *Vertues* to many of them'. This work and others like it served to whet European appetites for the glories of Chinese flora, especially when the trickle of living plants brought proof that these were real flowers and not mere flights of fancy.

Cunningham found his rose on his second trip east, when the East India Company was setting up a trading base or factory at Chusan (Zhoushan), an island off the coast of north-eastern Zhejiang a little south of Shanghai. From here, Cunningham also sent back the first detailed description of the tea plant that was to assume such social and economic importance to Britain. But Cunningham's fate was to foreshadow that of many other collectors and explorers who put their passion for natural history before their personal safety. After surviving two uprisings against the unwelcome British presence – on the island of Pulo Condore, off Cochin-China (South Vietnam), and later on Borneo – Cunningham got as far as Bengal and then vanished along with his ship on the long voyage home.

Thirty years later, a crimson China rose of unknown origin appeared in the herbarium of the Leiden naturalist, Jan Frederik Gronovius, a friend and mentor to the Swedish botanist Carl Linnaeus. He called it 'Chineesche Eglantier Roosen' and it was later used as the type specimen for the red China rose, *R. chinensis.* More news of Chinese roses reached Europe some twenty years later via a pupil of Linnaeus, the Swedish pastor and naturalist Pehr (Peter) Osbeck, for whom Linnaeus had secured a passage to China as chaplain to the Swedish East Indiaman, the *Prins Carl.* Setting off from Göteborg in Sweden in November 1750, Osbeck travelled via Cadiz and the Cape of Good Hope to Canton (Guangzhou) where he stayed for four months and more.

Osbeck is one of the first Europeans to give a sense of what sailing into a Chinese landscape was like, past the green rice fields on both sides of the river, as far as the eye could reach, the fine woods of many different trees, the beautiful hills and valleys, towards the customs houses built partly on 'hard stony ground' and partly on stilts jutting into the river. Near the entrance to the first customs house, Osbeck found roses growing among hibiscus and a pomegranate tree – all 'tokens of the taste

An eighteenth-century colour lithograph of rice cultivation in China, showing the landscapes described by early western visitors such as the Swedish pastor, Pehr Osbeck.

this nation has for all sorts of plants to adorn their habitations. You will scarce meet with a family either in town or in the boats without some herbs or trees in flower-pots, if not for use, yet for the sake of pleasure.' Adorning their windows were January-flowering narcissi, Chinese lilies, and little potted trees – sweet oranges, especially.

But despite the haunting beauty of its landscape, China was a frustrating place for Europeans, who were kept outside the city of Canton and allowed through the city gates only with express permission, in covered chairs. Osbeck nonetheless managed to spy through the curtains as he was carried through the long, crooked streets, paved like courtyards without any gutters. Dogs, hogs and chickens impeded their path but the streets were surprisingly clean, he noted, 'because poor people continually go about with baskets and gather up all the filth'. Walking anywhere was difficult, for although the 'persons of rank' taught their children virtue and honesty, 'the common sort of people train their children up with their dogs; for which reason neither of them can bear strangers'. Strolling with friends on the edge of the suburbs, Osbeck and his companions attracted a crowd of clamouring boys who made them feel uncomfortably like 'ambassadors from the moon' and when they reached the Street of the Millers, pelted them with stones, sand and grit.

While Osbeck proved himself an acute observer of Chinese flora, he had little success in bringing live plants back to Europe. A precious tea-shrub, carefully potted for the voyage, fell victim to the firing of cannons and general jubilation as the ship weighed anchor for home, 'and was thrown over-board without my knowledge'. Those plants that survived the tumult of leaving generally perished around the Cape of Good Hope. But his dried herbarium specimens fared better, among them his rose; and he gave all his rich haul to his mentor Linnaeus, who was then putting the plant world in order with his new system of binomial plant names that gave all plants a family name and an identifying species name. Linnaeus used some fifty of Osbeck's specimens when compiling the first edition of his revolutionary *Species Plantarum*, which appeared in 1753, the year after Osbeck's return from China, but not apparently this rose. Instead, Linnaeus gave Petiver as a reference, which may mean he glimpsed Cunningham's Chusan rose among the herbarium of Sir Hans Sloane, to whom Petiver had bequeathed his natural history treasures.

Far from bringing order to the rose family, however, Linnaeus muddled his geography so hopelessly that he called the Chinese rose *Rosa indica,* apparently assuming that India and China were synonymous. The confusion provoked the British rosarian John Lindley into wondering precisely which rose Linnaeus intended by the '*indica*' label, 'since his specific character and description will agree with no species from China at present known; and the figure of Petiver which he quotes to this . . . belongs to a widely different plant, very nearly allied to *R. Banksiae*'.

*

Unless you are a botanist, it is hard to get excited about dried specimens of any flower, and Chinese roses were slow to infiltrate the West. They may even have made a fleeting appearance in sixteenth-century Italy, as the Florentine artist Agnolo Bronzino gave his Cupid a fistful of very Chinese-looking roses in his *Allegory with Venus and Cupid,* painted between 1540 and 1550. And when the French essayist Michel de Montaigne visited the gardens of the Jesuits at Ferrara in November 1580, he was given a rose from a remarkable rose tree that produced flowers all year round – a distinctly Chinese virtue.[1] But these are isolated sightings, and the provenance of the roses is unconfirmed.

The traffic in roses had many hurdles to surmount, not least the Chinese suspicion of foreigners. A few years after Osbeck's visit, the Chinese Emperor effectively restricted all foreign trade to Canton, further confining western traders to the narrow strip of land by the river where they built their factories. Even if you managed to secure living plants from Chinese nursery gardens or merchants, the rigours of sea travel were more than likely to kill them. For plants that survived the journey, Europe's little ice age of the sixteenth to mid-nineteenth centuries dealt a further blow to tender species, and even in hothouses many failed to flower properly, so most Europeans had little idea of the marvels that awaited them.

But slowly, in their various guises, Chinese roses began to appear among the plant lists of curious gardeners and dedicated nurserymen throughout Europe.[2] Philip Miller, gardener to the Society of Apothecaries at Chelsea, is supposed to have included a *'Rosa sinica'* in the seventh edition of his *Gardeners Dictionary* of 1759, but this was in fact a hibiscus, then known as 'Rosa sinensis'. Princess Augusta, Dowager Princess of Wales, was actually growing a *'Rosa indica'* by 1768, when it appeared in the first list of exotics and rare native plants growing in her garden at Kew. In the same year, a 'Rosa chinensis' was drawn and described by botanist Nicolaus Jacquin in Vienna: this is clearly a herbarium specimen, with leaves, seed head and no flowers. Empress Josephine's favourite London suppliers, the Hammersmith nursery of Lee & Kennedy, was selling the 'China Rose' (*Rosa indica*) by 1774, three years before the Hackney firm of Loddiges compiled a catalogue for their German customers containing forty-one roses, including *'Rosa indica,*

Chinesische Rose, the Chiney Rose'. By the end of the 1770s, Lancashire gentleman John Blackburne had planted two Chinese roses in his garden near Warrington (his gardener called them *Rosa chinensis* and *R. indica*) – one more than the celebrated plantsman Dr Fothergill, who grew only Linnaeus's *R. indica* in his garden at Upton in Essex. The French nursery of Descemet had a *'Rose de Chine'* by the early 1780s at least, and by 1781 the pink form of *Rosa chinensis* had travelled back to the Netherlands with the Dutch East India Company, and was planted in the botanic gardens of Leiden and Haarlem. At the end of the decade, the royal gardener William Aiton also included just one Chinese rose (this time named *Rosa sinica,* and mistakenly linked to Philip Miller's hibiscus) in his catalogue of plants growing in the King's garden at Kew.

Occasional sightings of such rarities hint at the wondrous novelty of these strange new roses from the East. In 1782 Baroness d'Oberkirch, a childhood friend of Goethe and of the future Russian Empress Maria Feodorovna, visited Dutch Haarlem, where a famous gardener introduced her to her first Chinese rose, a shrub that 'produces magnificent flowers, of which the petals are soft as velvet, but odourless. He told us that it was called the Chinese Rose, and had been imported within the last year with great care.' The occasion was memorable enough to record in her memoirs, published two generations later.

The reason for all the excitement is clear. Chinese roses really did bring qualities that were startlingly new to Europe and the West: these were the lightest of silks compared with the crumpled Damasks of old Europe, in radiant new colours that included bright reds, scarlets and yellows, as well as the purples, pinks and whites common to the West. Their leaves, too, were a lustrous green and their elegant buds more pointed. While many lacked fragrance, a select few carried a fresh and delicate scent – of tea, according to the French (and to Mrs Gore, author of *The Rose Fancier's Manual* of 1838, who described a pale pink Tea rose as 'very agreeably scented with the odour of Pekoe tea'), or the 'faint sweet smell, at least in a warm room, resembling that of the Harebell'. And in contrast to most European roses, which bloomed only once in early summer, Chinese roses brought the precious gene of remontancy that kept them flowering month after month in an apparently everlasting display.

Unlike the wild strains of central Asian roses such as *R. fedtschenkoana* that had already found their way into Europe's gene pool, these new varieties were almost all the product of China's advanced horticulture, which was then the best in the world in terms of knowledge, techniques and the numbers of cultivars raised. For 1,000 years or more, the Chinese had been cultivating many large-petalled roses of the kind Cui Bai painted on silk in the Song dynasty c.1061 for 'Loquat and Peacock', in which a double pink high-centred rose flowers on an upright bushy plant between two peacocks (illustrated in Chapter 4). In his *Plants and Flowers in Luoyang,* written in AD 1082, Shihou Zhou documented thirty-seven varieties of rose – not as many as the tree peony's impressive 109, but many more than the scant handful recorded more than a century and a half later by Europe's sage, Albertus Magnus. And before Albertus was even born, the poet Yang Wanli celebrated the Chinese rose's perpetual flowering in verse:

> No flower can bloom for ten days, people say,
> While the Chinese rose blooms day by day.

Of course not all the new arrivals could endure northern Europe's cold wet climate, and many succumbed to disease. But their arrival coincided with Europe's increased knowledge of plant-breeding, and they would create a veritable explosion of new 'types' as rose-breeders across Europe and America vied with each other to create the next new sensation. Towards the end of the 1820s, the British rosarian Henry Andrews predicted that the genes of Asia and Europe would soon become so blended it would be impossible to tell which had played the greater part in any individual parentage – 'but *n'importe lesquelles;* for whilst the one is most esteemed for its smooth shining foliage, the other will always be considered as more unequivocally fragrant'.

Britain was to play a major role in bringing Chinese roses to Europe, through the medium in which she felt most comfortable, foreign trade, spurred on by the scientific and practical curiosity of men such as Sir Joseph Banks, botanist, explorer, patron of the natural sciences, President of the Royal Society, friend and adviser to King George III and virtual director of the King's garden at Kew, facilitator par excellence.

A key figure in Britain's botanical imperialism, Sir Joseph Banks chose William Kerr as Kew's first plant collector in China. Wood engraving of Banks from the Picturesque Atlas of Australasia, *1886.*

Although slow to enter the China trade, by the mid-eighteenth century Britain had inched her way to a predominant position. The Portuguese had been the first to penetrate Chinese defences at the beginning of the sixteenth century, establishing their trading factories at Ningbo, then Amoy (Xiamen), then Canton, and finally at Macao (Macau), which remained in their administrative control until its handover to the People's Republic of China in 1999. They were swiftly pursued by Jesuit missionaries who successfully insinuated themselves into the imperial court at Peking (Beijing), helped by their skills in astronomy, physics and chemistry. The Russians, too, gained a foothold in Peking. Then came the Dutch and the Dutch East India Company (Vereenigde Oost-Indische Compagnie or VOC), the earliest and initially the most successful of Europe's colonial trading corporations.

Despite their growing strength in the China trade, the British still smarted like everyone else under the restrictions on their movements and, consequently, on their freedom to do business. Western traders were penned for the short winter trading season into their Canton factories, where tea had replaced silk as the major cargo. Once the fleet set sail for Europe, they retired to the limited freedoms of Macao, where they could at least roam the neighbouring islands. Yet according to a former superintendent, their situation was at best 'so uninviting, or rather so miserable, in that country, that it requires some resolution, and no small zeal in the cause of science, to encounter the obstacles and annoyances that meet one at every step'.

Determined to win concessions from the Chinese, the British sent two diplomatic missions to the Chinese Emperor; the first set off in 1793, led by colonial administrator Lord Macartney and armed with much helpful advice from Sir Joseph Banks, who wanted to find out as much as he could about Chinese know-how in all spheres of science, manufacturing and the arts. Bank's attitudes towards the Celestial Empire displayed Europe's customary cultural arrogance tinged with a modicum of respect for practical achievements, as he confessed in a letter to Lord Macartney: 'The Chinese appear to me to possess the Ruin of a state of Civilization in which, when in Perfection, the human mind had carried all kinds of knowledge to a much higher Pitch than the Europeans have hitherto done.'

Banks was particularly concerned to find out all he could about plants, and how the Chinese gardened. To his friend Sir George Leonard Staunton, secretary to Macartney's embassy, he sent detailed notes on gardening, both to help prepare the embassy members for what they might find, and to focus their attention on plants and practices in which he took a particular interest. Intent on discovering how the Chinese managed to accelerate flowering times and to stunt the growth of trees, he also asked them to look out especially for the sacred lotus, the Yulan magnolia, tree peonies and garden flowers that are 'equal in splendor & attraction to our Roses Lilies & Jasmines'.[3] He even sent in advance a small quarto volume of Chinese plant illustrations, addressed to Dr Alexander Duncan, then his chief contact at the Canton Factory, and marked with crosses to signify his interest. Four crosses indicated 'an ardent wish' to acquire the plant for British gardens, while a single cross meant that he simply wished it to be examined in its living state.

The embassy failed to live up to expectations, however, either politically or botanically. As Lord Macartney's party travelled northwards largely by water, the opportunities for botanizing were rare. They did at least gain an audience with the Emperor, overcoming the hurdle of protocol by agreeing to kneel before him as they would to their own sovereign, instead of kowtowing in the Chinese fashion. But the Chinese refused to relax trading conditions for foreigners and the embassy returned home empty-handed. The dried plant specimens collected for Banks came without notes and often without flowers or fruit, which rendered them botanically useless. Staunton's four geographical plant lists were similarly ill-defined. They found no roses in the provinces around Peking or Tartary; an unspecified 'Rosa' in the provinces of Shantung and Kiangnan (Jiangnan); and both 'Rosa indica' (whatever they meant by it) and 'Rosa – another species' around Canton.

But rose lovers can be grateful for the splendid new rose they brought back: the wild Climber *Rosa bracteata*, which bears very large single white flowers with a mass of golden yellow stamens, vicious thorns and glossy evergreen leaves. 'This plant, although a native of China and the northern provinces of India, is nevertheless tolerably hardy in our gardens,' was the rosarian John Lindley's verdict, 'producing its fine milk-white flowers in profusion during the greater part of the summer.' Commonly known as the Macartney rose, it is usually credited to Sir George Staunton, although John Haxton, one of the embassy's two gardeners, is the more likely discoverer.

The second embassy to China under Lord Amherst set off in 1816 and was even less successful. As no compromise was reached over the kowtowing ceremony, Amherst failed to achieve an audience with the Emperor. The mission's official naturalist and chief medical officer, Dr Clarke Abel, suffered a brain fever early in the journey, which considerably hampered his efforts to botanize, and he then lost virtually all his specimens when his frigate was shipwrecked on the voyage home. His one recorded sighting of a rose climbing the walls of Nanking was small compensation.

Banks's disappointment at the earlier botanic failings of diplomacy

The garden of a wealthy Chinese merchant, c.1800–1805. William Kerr found many of his plants in Chinese nursery gardens and gardens such as these.

no doubt strengthened his resolve to send his own man to China as Britain's first resident plant collector. 'Botany advances rapidly,' he wrote to a fellow naturalist in April 1803. 'I am in hopes just at this time of sending a Gardiner to China to reside there some years, & send over to Kew annual supplies of the beautifull & valuable produce of that Country.'

Banks's plan was in fact already well advanced. The man chosen was William Kerr, the son of a nurseryman from Hawick in the Scottish borders, already working at Kew and previously selected for an abortive plant-collecting mission to South America. Having known Kerr for some years, Banks judged him 'a considerate & a well behaved man'; others were even more glowing in their praise. The old China hand Dr John Livingstone would later extol Kerr's 'most perfect acquaintance with the habits of plants', judging that he possessed 'a competent share of Botanical knowledge, much natural shrewdness, and bodily strength'.

The plan hatched by Banks, William Aiton at Kew (the son of the garden's original superintendent) and the directors of the East India Company was to ship Kerr out to China under the wing of David Lance, the Canton factory's former supercargo (superintendent) who was then returning to the East as emissary to Cochin-China. Lance would school Kerr in the precautions he should take when dealing with the Chinese, 'to prevent them from taking umbrage'. Even the King was involved. As Banks wrote to Kerr:

As his Majesty has been graciously pleased to select you from among your Fellow Gardiners & appoint you to the very desirable office of collecting the Plants of Foreign Countries for the use of the Royal Gardens ... your inducements to diligence & good conduct are as great as can possibly be held out to any young man whatever.

The East India Company was to pay all Kerr's expenses incurred in travel, living and transporting the plants back home. The royal purse paid Kerr's salary (£100 a year), while Kerr himself would need to find money only for his clothes. As these were far cheaper in China than in England, said Banks, 'you can then have little reason for money on your own account, & you must always remember, that the less you indulge yourself in the supply of unnecessary wants during the time of your pilgrimage in foreign parts, the more reserve you will make for future Indulgence.' It was to prove a prophetic warning.

Kerr immediately got busy, his head full of the instructions showered on him by the indefatigable Banks, who had – as always – thought of everything, from the way he should pot up his plants ready for shipment home (either in boxes that would fit into his newfangled plant cabins, or in large Chinese pots), to the tin tickets he should use to identify his plants, and the wild plants he should seek at Macao and Danes Island, where he was to be as industrious as possible, 'because you have little chance of being allowed to Botanize in any other part of the Chinese Empire'. As good information held the key to success in any plant-collecting venture, Banks gave Lance the same book of Chinese plant drawings that had accompanied Macartney's embassy (at least it used the same system of crosses), while Kerr took with him lists of desired plants and trees drawn from missionary sources; one of Kew's great desiderata was a carnivorous pitcher plant known locally as the 'pig basket plant'. Banks even supplied a list of plants in Chinese characters prepared by Staunton's son, another Sir George and one of Britain's first sinologists. For his part, Kerr was to provide a full account of the plants he was sending home, writing short letters to Banks and much longer ones to Aiton, carefully setting out the plants' cultivation requirements concerning climate, soil, even 'the kind of manure generally used to promote their fertility, and the manner in which it is applied'. After the Staunton fiasco, Banks was leaving nothing to chance.

Intriguingly, the plant trade with China went both ways. Loaded on to the ship with Kerr went an assortment of European plants (including roses) intended to test the efficacy of Banks's specially designed plant cabins for housing plants on deck, and to encourage plant exchanges with Chinese gardeners and merchants. A plant-lover himself, Banks realized that the best way to prise a desired specimen out of any collector's hand was to offer something in return.

Kerr left England on 29 April 1803, the latest possible date to catch the winds that would take them eastwards to China around the Cape of Good Hope. The journey took five months and doubtless prepared Kerr for the hardships and disappointments to come. In late September they hit a typhoon in the China Seas, which wreaked havoc on the plants they were carrying, and many were washed overboard. When the winds abated, Kerr made frantic efforts to save them, planting up the survivors in fresh compost; although a few showed signs of life when they finally reached Canton, they were much too exhausted to revive. 'All that now remains is an Apple Tree a Pear Tree and a Rose,' wrote Kerr to Aiton, 'the Rose is now in good health & I hope soon to be able to propagate it. The Apple and Pear Trees are both in a very sickly state, & I fear will not recover.' The eventual fate of China's first imported European rose is not known.

Kerr himself had little time to recover from the journey, as the ships were leaving soon for Europe and he needed to collect as many new plants as he could to please his royal masters. Lance had immediately obtained for him a small piece of garden ground from one of the Canton merchants, but it was far from ideal. Situated about a mile from the English factory, it could be reached either through 'long intricate narrow & crowded streets', or by boat through the equally crowded waterways. It was very small, bounded on one side by the river and on the other three by houses, so that it 'has servd little other purpose yet than a convenient place for Potting and keeping the Plants sent home'.

Despite his grumbling, Kerr was quietly pleased with himself, boasting to Aiton that more plants had left Canton in his first season than at any one time before, carried by virtually every ship's captain in the fleet: 'no doubt my Mission has excited their attention to this as well as a kind of emulation'. As he was not allowed to roam freely, he bought most of his plants from the Fa-Tee nursery gardens about three miles higher up on the other side of the Pearl River from the foreign factories. It was where Europeans habitually went for their plants, supplemented by those they acquired from merchants' gardens. The nurseries delivered cut flowers, rented out potted flowers, and sold seeds and plants to suit the tastes of their Chinese and, increasingly, European customers. While Europeans generally heaped scorn on the 'insignificant intricacy' of Chinese gardens, they had nothing but praise for the 'arrangement and neatness of their nurseries, the unceasing care bestowed on their potted collections of plants, and the great value set upon some of them, even among themselves'.[4]

Lord Macartney's party had passed a pleasurable afternoon at one of these nursery gardens at the end of their mission, admiring 'the rare, the beautiful, the curious, or the useful plants of the country; which are sent to Canton for sale'. Although their western eye picked out the 'much esteemed *Rosa Sinica*' among many choice plants, Chinese 'florimania' worshipped other stars, particularly the sacred lotus (*Nelumbo nucifera*), moutan tree peonies, chrysanthemums, camellias, sweet-scented olive (*Olea fragrans*), jasmine (*Jasminum grandiflorum*), and myrtle-like plants such as the downy myrtle (*Rhodomyrtus tomentosa*). They also had a taste for dwarf trees, known as '*Koo-Shoo*'. Kerr's friend Dr Livingstone reported to London's Horticultural Society a gruesome parallel among young children, who were sometimes kidnapped, he said, to turn them into human *Koo-Shoos* for the profit of exhibiting them. 'Their limbs, trunk, and head are moulded into an infinite variety of strange unnatural forms, and their eyes are not unfrequently [*sic*] put out.' He does not appear to have witnessed such 'horrible practices' himself, but he claimed good authority for his report.

Buying plants for shipment home was not as easy as it sounds. The soil of the nurseries was alluvial clay, broken into small half-inch cubes – a bad medium for nurturing the plants through the traumas of their long journey home, so purchases needed to be repotted well in advance of departure. Kerr could at least do this in his small garden, but he found dealing with the Chinese nurserymen altogether more difficult. Reluctant at first to commit himself to learning the Chinese names of the plants he wanted, he quickly discovered it was the only way to avoid being cheated over prices or the plants themselves. As he complained to Aiton, 'If a Chinese List is presented, if the Plants are either scarce or not in the possession of the owner, others are without hesitation substituted in their place.'

Kerr sent his main consignment back to Kew in the Honourable East India Company's ship the *Henry Addington,* under Captain John Kirkpatrick. As required by Banks, he wrote descriptive notes to help identify his new plants, referring when necessary to the book of Chinese drawings Banks had given to Lance. This first haul included seven sorts of cultivated roses and two wild varieties. Six of the former were grouped together under the Chinese name *Yeut-quai-faa*; in Banks's book, it merited just a single cross. 'This is a delicate little flower of a light red or blush colour,' explained Kerr, '& is certainly different from the one resembling it in England. In the same Box are the following different sorts, Viz No 5/2 *Pac-yeut-quai faa*, a variety of the preceding with white flowers. No 5/3 *Muck hung* a large running sort not shiny.' For the remaining three, he simply wrote their Chinese names as best he could: *Tsut-See-mui, Mui quai* and *Soi-yang-fei*. His other cultivated rose had pale yellow flowers and was 'highly valued': he called it *Wong-li-tsun*.

The two wild roses came with plants he had collected on Danes Island soon after their arrival, mostly from rocky or gravelly places. One he described simply as a rose with white flowers, and the other as a red-flowered variety of *Wong-li-tsun*. All were despatched in a growing state, planted in small purpose-built boxes to fill up the plant cabin.

Banks must have been delighted when he went with the King to Kew to inspect Kerr's first consignment from Canton, much of which had survived, including the Chinese juniper (*Juniperus chinensis*), the tiger lily (*Lilium lancifolium*), and the heavenly bamboo (*Nandina domestica*). Tending the plants throughout their voyage home was the Derbyshire miner John Allen, returning from Australia; his expert care reinforced the advantage of sending plants home with a skilled gardener, as other shipments had succumbed to the rigours of the journeys and the added hazards posed by French men-of-war in Britain's continuing war with France. Storms and changing temperatures tended to kill off many plants even before the ships broke their voyage at St Helena. Others fell victim to rats, lack of sunlight, and dousing with salt spray; or they struggled bravely to Europe, then quietly expired at the watermen's rough handling.

Kerr's roses were a disappointment, however. Only two survived from that first journey: the cultivated *Mui quai* and the white-flowered wild rose, but in the roll-call of attributions Kerr takes credit for neither. Perhaps they expired in the English climate, or perhaps one star was indeed all they merited, and they were allowed to fade away. Undeterred, Kerr sent more roses the following season aboard the *Winchelsea* under Captain Campbell, 'who is himself fond of Plants', which gave Kerr hope that they might survive, especially as he had had plenty of time to establish his plants in their planting boxes. Among the roses, he packed another specimen of *Wong li-tsun,* with its clusters of delicate pale yellow flowers, which was considered 'most scarce and valuable'. Another he described as a very distinct sort, 'a running or straggling growing plant, without Thorns, when not cultivated in Pots in a dwarf State, is generally trained upon Walls, or trailing where it has a good appearance when in flower'. The flowers had a little smell, he added, and appeared in February and March.

Two more were quite distinct despite their similar Chinese names, which distinguished them only by flower colour: *Pai-moui-quai*, a rose that produced small, 'inodorus' double white flowers in February and March; and *Hang-moui quai*, whose fragrant purple flowers appeared in May and June. 'This is one of the most esteemed Sorts,' declared Kerr, 'it seldom produces any Suckers from the root, and is generally propagated by grafting upon some of the more common sorts.'

Despite his hopes, these roses are unlikely to have survived their passage to Europe. Banks broke the news personally to Kerr, saying he was sorry to inform him 'that the Plants dispatched by you on board the *Winchelsea* have been as unfortunate as the former ones were fortunate, scarce one of the whole collection having reached Europe alive'. The circumstances were judged 'unavoidable' – it had been a particularly tempestuous voyage as far as St Helena, where the *Winchelsea* had had to await the rest of the China fleet and a naval escort to conduct them safely back to England – and no blame was attached either to Kerr or the ship's captain. The disaster nonetheless convinced Banks that 'unless a Person in some degree conversant in Gardening has the charge of the Plants, they will not be likely to succeed'. Indeed, Kerr was sending so many plants home, they would need constant supervision, and he asked Kerr to find a Chinese gardener – possibly in the employment of Canton's leading merchant, Puan Ke Qua – to travel to London with the plants, staying at Kew, where he could work if he chose, and returning with a freight of European garden plants for China.

The new arrangements may explain the survival of the one Chinese rose for which William Kerr takes credit: the white Banksian rose brought to England in 1807 and fittingly named after his patron's wife, Lady Banks. Its flowers are like those of a double cherry blossom, their scent 'most agreeable, being exactly like that of the sweetest violet'. The name naturally made it a favourite at Spring Grove, the Bankses' home at Isleworth to the west of London, where it reputedly flowered for the first time, transformed by Banks's gardener Isaac Oldaker from an 'insignificant green-house plant' into a 'hardy and splendid creeping shrub'. Experiment played a hand in its transformation, demonstrating that it flowered best when planted in open ground against a southerly or westerly wall and trained like a fruit tree. The French rose-grower, Boursault, obtained a plant from England in 1818 and turned it out of its pot into a border of heath mould in his Paris conservatory, where it flowered the following year and grew to a length of forty feet or more, producing a great mass of tightly packed fragrant flowers.

Back in China, things were not going well for William Kerr, however.

The white Banksian rose, Rosa banksiae *var.* banksiae, *is William Kerr's one recognized rose introduction, of 1807. From an anonymous watercolour in the Reeves collection of Chinese paintings held by the RHS Lindley Library.*

He kept himself busy enough, sending plants and seeds not just to Kew but also to Dr William Roxburgh at Calcutta's Botanic Garden,[5] and to the island of St Helena, which it was hoped would develop into a staging post for eastern plants destined for the west; Banks had a vision of botanical imperialism that cast William Kerr as one its footsoldiers. But the latter had always hated the constrictions of Canton, declaring that there could be 'no place more unfavourable to Botanical researches than the European Factories at Canton situated almost in the middle of a great and populous Town'. Only the kindnesses he received from Company officers and the 'indefatigable industry of the Chinese' made life bearable.

For a time, Macao held out the prospect of 'more pleasure', and on David Lance's suggestion he travelled in search of plants to Manila and the Philippines, but the expedition was not a resounding success. On returning to Macao, he lost many plants to a storm, and for all his pains he received a carefully worded rebuke from Sir Joseph Banks, who did not 'entirely approve' of Kerr leaving 'the Post where you were placed' and going off to Manila. The problem was climate. Banks wanted plants that would survive at Kew, such as 'those of the Northern Provinces of China which were the particular objects of your Mission'. The moutan peony was now flowering well outdoors, he said pointedly, proving that one northern plant was worth a hundred others that required a hothouse to keep them alive in England.

Kerr continued to put together his plant consignments, sending much the same roses as before: two yellows, one purple and one white in February 1806 by the *Hope* under Captain Pendergrass (the *Hope*'s owner was then Sir Abraham Hume, who would later take credit for introducing 'Hume's Blush Tea-scented rose'); and in January the following year, by the *David Scott* under Captain Zooke, his fragrant white Banksian rose, which he called *Pac-mue-huung*, which he said was similar to an earlier rose he had sent, except for its colour, and 'this is much more fragrant'. But he seems to have lost heart. The careful plant descriptions disappear. His grasp of time falters: in his plant lists for Aiton, first he muddles the months, then the years, then the years disappear altogether. Many of his seeds received at Kew are identified only by their Chinese names, no further clues given as to their identity or germination requirements.

Rumours of his condition reached Sir Joseph Banks from Thomas

Manning, a Chinese scholar and the first European to enter the Tibetan city of Lhasa, who arrived in Canton in spring 1807, shortly before Kerr decamped to Macao. 'He and I are upon a very good footing together', wrote Manning to Banks.

I don't think he is happy here but I may be deceived by his natural manner & disposition. He has, I perceive, no one for him to associate with here. (I don't mean to say anything against the Steward, who has a very pretty little shop at the top of the Hong.) I shall try & throw a little sunshine now & then upon his dull hours.

Kerr's friend Dr John Livingstone was convinced that money lay at the root of Kerr's problems. He remembered Kerr's vigour when they had travelled out to China together in 1803, having watched his friend scale mountains under a burning sun, leaving Livingstone to seek 'a friendly shade', where Kerr would join him with the fruits of his labour. But three or four years later, after Livingstone's appointment as assistant surgeon to the factory at Canton, the change in his friend was dramatic. Kerr's salary was too small to cover his needs, Livingstone reported to London's Horticultural Society, which lost him respect in Chinese eyes and forced him to consort with 'inferior persons'.

According to Livingstone, Kerr's £100 a year was barely sufficient to cover his washing and left no money to buy any new clothes to wash. Travelling from his garden to the factory for meals occupied much of his time, especially in hot weather. By degrees he became indolent, so that instead of collecting plants, planting them in a proper soil, and taking care of them afterwards, he began to put off every labour, 'and not infrequently habits of intemperance, and the natural consequence falls, bruises, and sprains rendered him unable to do anything for days and weeks'.

So Kerr was drinking and perhaps worse, ground down by poverty and loneliness. Money was certainly a constant anxiety in his letters to Aiton and Banks, and despite assurances that the King was taking a patriotic interest in his efforts, Kerr must have felt abandoned on foreign soil. Yet he did not crack completely, nor did he lose all credibility with his masters. Instead of recalling him, as Kerr must surely have hoped, Banks resolved to send him to Ceylon (Sri Lanka) as superintendent of a new botanic garden the King had graciously decided to establish there, 'for the benefit of the commercial interests of the Island, and for the advancement of the Science of Botany'. On the face of it, the new posting was a reward for Kerr's 'good conduct' and the success with which he had conducted his business at Canton, but expediency offers another possible explanation. Banks needed someone to put together a collection of Chinese plants and transport them to the new garden: who better than his resident plant collector at Canton? Banks's letter to Kerr anticipates his retirement, suggesting that he would continue to serve his country with honour as long as his health permitted, and when age or infirmity rendered him unfit for public duty he would be able 'to retire with a sufficient independance [*sic*] & end your days in ease & comfort'.

Kerr never saw his homeland again. To his credit, although he had to drag his heels in Canton for another two years, he regained much of his old vigour. Once en route for Ceylon, some eight and a half years after he had first set foot on Chinese soil, he wrote encouraging letters to Livingstone from Malacca and Calcutta, full of plans for the new garden. And to the King's garden at Kew he sent boxes of plants from Colombo, their contents labelled in Latin and properly described, apart from those that were simply '*Incognita*'. His industry was impressive, and Banks received encouraging reports about his progress. But then came the 'melancholy news' of his death in November 1814, following a tour of the northern part of the island with the President of its Council and former Chief Justice, Sir Alexander Johnston. Johnston himself broke the news to Banks, explaining that for ten days Kerr had suffered a severe fever, which terminated in an inflammation of the brain. 'It may afford his family some consolation for his loss to know that every care was taken of him during his illness & that his remains as a mark of respect were attended to the grave by most of the civil & military servants at the place.' He died without leaving a will, and Johnston arranged to send his papers and botanical works home to Banks, 'in order that you may do with them whatever you think proper'. His other property amounted to some £700 to £800, although 'we do not know if he has any debts'.

Whether or not he felt any responsibility for Kerr's death, Banks chose not to replace his resident collector at Canton. Kerr had all but exhausted the stock of new varieties available through the Fa-Tee nurseries, and

Banks anyway had an avid – if amateur – correspondent and collector in John Reeves, who came to Canton as Assistant Inspector of Tea for the Honourable East India Company just as Kerr was leaving. For thirty years – long after Banks's death and his own retirement from the East – Reeves was the driving force behind the introduction of Chinese plants to the West, and scarcely a ship left Canton without a portable greenhouse bristling with new treasures collected directly or indirectly by the zealous Reeves.

With Reeves's help, the baton was passed from Kew to London's Horticultural Society, where the rosarian and botanist John Lindley was fast moving up the administrative ladder, first as Assistant Secretary of the Society's garden at Chiswick, then as Assistant Secretary to the Society as a whole. Particularly concerned to introduce and disseminate ornamental exotics, Lindley recognized the importance of making drawings of plants growing in their native countries. The Society chose China for its first such collection, and John Reeves, 'a corresponding and very active member of the Society', as its overseer.

Although the Reeves collection was sold off (apart from volumes on chrysanthemums and peonies) when the Horticultural Society faced financial difficulties in the late 1850s, it is now back in the Society's care. Thirteen exquisite watercolours of roses survive in one of the smaller volumes: an extraordinary record of the China roses then most coveted in the West. In style, the watercolours blend East with West: these are Chinese roses refracted through a European lens intent on botanical accuracy, but executed with Chinese fluency and flair. Here is Kerr's double white Banksian rose, painted on light Chinese paper. Other varieties still sought in the West were executed on heavier papers from Europe, which Reeves must have brought with him from England. Seven of the thirteen roses are now identified as various forms of *R. chinensis;* the others are the white and yellow Banksian roses, *R. laevigata* (the 'Cherokee' rose), *R. multiflora, R. × odorata,* and *R. roxburghii* f. *normalis* (*R. microphylla*).

As well as aiding identification by collectors or purchasers, the painted flowers made communication between Banks and Reeves much easier. 'I mentioned in my former letter that we have no red Rose like the one you mention,' wrote Reeves from Canton in November 1820, 'but in my enquiries I have fallen upon two others new to me, one a dark red as Drawing sent to the Horticultural Society and another a small dwarf rose of a pink colour: both of them I shall endeavour to forward to England in the present season.'

Kerr's friend Dr Livingstone continued to chivvy the Horticultural Society into sending their own man to China, with the blessing of the East India Company. He should be resident at Macao, in Livingstone's view, and paid a commission for every new plant successfully introduced into Britain. Such a plan would overcome the torpor induced by life out East, and concentrate minds on the problems of transportation. By Livingstone's calculation, 1,000 plants were lost for every one that survived the journey to London; at an average cost of 6s 8d per plant (including chests and sundries), this meant that each new introduction was costing in the region of £300 – three times poor Kerr's annual salary.

The Society responded by sending out to China first John Potts (in 1821) and then (in 1823) one of its most successful botanical collectors, John Damper Parks, who was asked to bring back as many varieties of chrysanthemums as he could find, and also to lose no opportunity of securing the yellow Banksian rose (*R. banksiae* 'Lutea') which had become well established in Calcutta's Botanic Garden and which the English wanted for themselves. Parks duly complied, and soon the members of London's Horticultural Society heard news of a 'very handsome [yellow] variety of Rosa Banksiae, brought from China for the Society in 1824 in the Lowther Castle East Indiaman'. Flower colour was not the only difference. This new variety had shinier leaves and although not fragrant, its flowers were smaller and its petals 'arranged with greater regularity one above the other'. Relatively hardy, it flowered in open ground at the beginning of May, a fortnight before the common sort. It also propagated easily from cuttings; indeed, as Livingstone assured the Horticultural Society, 'it is common practice with the Chinese gardeners, to engraft a cutting of R. Banksiae with any other kind that they wish to encrease [*sic*], and then to plant the cutting so grafted'.

From this same journey, Parks brought back a second yellow rose that was to prove revolutionary in western rose breeding. Commonly known as 'Parks' Yellow Tea-scented China', this was one of four Chinese cultivars (known as the 'stud Chinas') which reputedly gave their genes to virtually all modern roses. Already known to collectors through the Chinese drawings of roses, its first flowering in Britain was eagerly awaited, and when its pale sulphur-coloured flowers finally appeared at Chiswick, they were greeted with rapture. Lindley judged it 'one of the finest varieties of China Roses known in the gardens, and so entirely different from any other, that it may be considered an important addition to our collections. It appears to be hardy, but thrives in a conservatory, where it expands [and] flowers better than in the open air.'

Parks' Yellow China was chronologically the last of the stud Chinas to reach Europe. The name was coined by Britain's Dr C. C. Hurst, whose researches at Cambridge would start to unravel the parentage of European roses. Turning his attention to modern garden roses, Hurst concluded that the Chinese part of their ancestry came not from China's wild roses (generally once-flowering climbers) but from their cultivated offspring that had evolved through mutation, cross-breeding and selection over a thousand years of Chinese floriculture, developing a gene for continuous flowering which they then transmitted to the West through hybridization with our western roses, and thereby 'changed them as by a magic wand'.

It was Hurst's contention that just four China roses were responsible for this transformation. The first two to arrive are thought to be cultivated varieties of *Rosa chinensis* var. *spontanea*: the blush pink 'Parsons' Pink China' and the darker 'Slater's Crimson China', while the later two are thought to result from crosses between *R. chinensis* and *R. gigantea*. All three wild parents belong to the Chinenses (Indicae) section of the subgenus Eurosa (Rosa).

Hurst's view has not been comprehensively challenged, although more recent chromosome counts of the early imports and crosses have achieved different results, and his theory offers a reductionist view of what was undoubtedly a more muddled process. Not only did early breeders achieve their crosses by open pollination and without documentation, but many early China imports died out in Europe, including at least two of the four stud Chinas. While these were later 'rediscovered' in the warmth and relative isolation of Bermuda, their exact relationship to their lost ancestors must remain open to question. Botanically, too, the theory may not tell the full story. In his study of climbing roses, the rose expert Charles Quest-Ritson suggests that the gene for repeat-flowering may have come from

One of four roses known as the 'stud Chinas', Parks' Yellow Tea-scented China came to Britain in 1824 with John Damper Parks, sent out by the Horticultural Society of London. From the Reeves collection of Chinese paintings.

醉嬌妃 Tsuy yong Fee.

Rosa semperflorens : Var. Bash red.

Another of the four stud Chinas from the collection of plants painted by Chinese
artists for the East India Company employee, John Reeves: Slater's Crimson China, introduced
c.1792 into the exotic garden of Mr Gilbert Slater in Leytonstone, London.

a mutation of one of the Synstylae group of roses such as *R. multiflora* and *R. moschata*.

But Hurst's theory of the four stud Chinas neatly encapsulates the revolution in European rose-breeding provoked by these exotic blooms and it is worth examining the roses he named. First to arrive by some accounts was the silvery pink 'Parsons' Pink China', also known as the Pale Pink China or the Blush Chinese Rose, and described by Henry Andrews as 'one of the greatest ornaments ever introduced to this country'. Various dates are given for its introduction, some as early as the 1760s. Aiton tells us that Sir Joseph Banks introduced it to Kew in 1789 (in which case this may be the rose he is said to have brought back from the Netherlands), although Andrews suggests that it was first seen in 1793 in the Hertfordshire garden of John Parsons, the son of a wealthy City brewer. Soon after, it was acquired by the London nursery firm of James Colvill on the King's Road, then the fashionable hub of nursery gardening in west London, and 'it has been ever since increasing in estimation'.

It soon found its way to Paris, and from there is believed to have travelled westwards to Charleston in South Carolina and eastwards to the French island of Bourbon (La Réunion), becoming respectively a grandparent to the French Noisettes (through a cross with *R. moschata*) and to the Bourbon roses (through a cross with an Autumn Damask). In England, meanwhile, it spawned the Dwarf Pink Chinas known there as Fairy Roses, which crossed to the Continent as the Bengal Pompons and begat the first of the Poly-Poms. If indeed the same Pink China was involved in all this activity, it clearly lived up to its name and a form is still grown today as the much-loved 'Old Blush'.

More usually credited as the first of the stud Chinas was 'Slater's Crimson China', which arrived in Britain some time between 1789 and 1792, bound for the famous garden of exotics cultivated at Knot's Green, Leytonstone, by Mr Gilbert Slater, managing owner of two Indiamen ships and a passionate collector of exotic plants. When the buds burst into flower, they caused a sensation: large, semi-double and a vivid crimson, they continued blooming all year, earning this rose the name of '*Rosa Semperflorens,* Ever-blowing rose'. Curtis's *Botanical Magazine* judged it 'one of the most desirable plants in point of ornament ever introduced to this country'. As Slater was generous with his cuttings, the rose soon spread among the principal nurserymen around London and was expected, within a few years, to 'decorate the window of every amateur'.[6] At one time credited as a parent of the original Portland rose, R. 'Portlandica' (impossible, as this rose predates the China's introduction) it almost certainly passed on its bloodlines to the old Hybrid China and Portland groups, and through them to the modern Hybrid Teas. Considered lost in Europe, it was rediscovered in the 1950s growing in Bermuda as the 'Belfield' rose, and reintroduced elsewhere. (Roses were not Slater's only passion, it should be said. He grew enormously fat through over-eating and died of an obstruction in his kidneys just a year or two after welcoming his rose.)

Third – and most distinctly fragrant – of the four studs was 'Hume's Blush Tea-scented China', which was closest to R. gigantea in its genetic make-up. 'This elegant plant was imported from the East Indies in 1809 by Sir A[braham] Hume, Bart.,' enthused Henry Andrews, 'and is a great acquisition to the British gardens.'[7] He classed it as one of the ever-blooming varieties, with the unusual addition of an agreeable scent 'which very few China roses possess'. Its unfurling flowers offered another surprise, when the elegantly pointed and apparently purply red buds opened into rounded flowers of a soft blush-pink, sometimes nearly white. The rose made an elegant addition to Hume's growing collection of Chinese plants in his garden at Wormley Bury near Broxbourne in Hertfordshire. Although his famous rose disappeared from cultivation (possibly re-emerging as the Bermudan rose known as 'Spice'), its fragrance lingers on through the bloodlines passed through the old pink Tea roses and the Hybrid Chinas to the modern Hybrid Teas.

'Parks' Yellow China' completed the foursome. Crossed with an original blush Noisette, it sired the old yellow Tea roses and yellow Noisettes, passing on the yellow colouring found in the Yunnan form of R. gigantea.

Pink, crimson, blush and yellow: here is the fresh new palette that the Chinas offered to the West, together with their smaller habits, shiny dark green leaves, papery petals, smooth stems, occasional reddish prickles and that elusive whiff of tea. Three of the studs definitely feature in Reeves's painted collection of roses: 'Slater's Crimson', 'Hume's Old

Blush', and 'Parks' Yellow', while Reeves's 'Yuet Qui' (identified as 'Rosa indica Monthly Blush') is surely the fourth, 'Parsons' Pink'.[8] Reeves's Chinese names also suggest that William Kerr might have attempted to import all except 'Parks' Yellow' in his first consignment of plants for Kew.

But the four studs were by no means the only Chinese imports coming to Europe. William Townsend Aiton was growing a good half dozen Chinese roses at Kew by 1810 compared to his father's one. As well as Macartney's *R. bracteata,* Kerr's white Banksian rose, and the first three stud Chinas, these included the bramble-flowered Chinese rose, *R. multiflora,* introduced by Thomas Evans of Stepney in 1804, which became a parent of the Floribunda roses. The literature on Chinese roses was also expanding. Lindley in 1820 described a dozen identifiably Chinese species in his monograph of roses, plus two more of uncertain origin. Eight years later, Henry Andrews included around twenty Chinese beauties in the second volume of his work on roses, some reared in British nurseries (chiefly the King's Road nursery of James Colvill, but also his Chelsea neighbour J. Knight, Lee's Hammersmith Nursery, and Messrs Whitely of Fulham and Kensington). More Chinese or Bengal roses were coming to Britain from France. Andrews included a hardy purply-pink variety with incurved petals he called 'Rosa Indica incurva', imported originally from France under the name Bischon or Bichon's rose, as well as a single Indian rose sent as seed from France to Knight's nursery in 1816. Presumed to be a species rather than a cultivated variety, this last was probably a seedling selected in Europe from an imported cultivated variety. Selective breeding was beginning to produce other new varieties, including a white China rose raised at Mr Knight's nursery from the seed of the Macartney rose, 'but nothing like its parent'.

More China hybrids can be found in Redouté's great work *Les Roses,* which appeared in three volumes between 1817 and 1824. In all, he painted some two dozen China roses and hybrids, giving us an early glimpse of 'Rosa Noisettiana', the first of the Noisette roses bred in America by Philippe Noisette (from a Musk rose and a Pink China) and sold in France through the Paris nursery of his brother, Louis Noisette. Redouté also proudly painted a rose he bred himself from the seed of an ordinary Bengal rose: 'Rosa Indica caryophillea', he called it, or 'Le

Bengale-oeillet' (the Bengal Pink) on account of its carnation-like flowers, coloured a fine bright crimson.

Not all the Chinese roses lived up to their initial promise, however. Imagine the surprise of rose-lovers who had paid a guinea, sight unseen, for the 'Blue Rose' imported from China around 1810 to the gardens of Lord Milford. When the flowers finally opened, they were not blue but a 'red purple' that became distinctly less brilliant as it faded, turning to a cold purple. Although it lacked that touch of celestial blue, Andrews nonetheless judged it a 'graceful and very abundant flowering Rose'. Evans's 'multiflora' rose, originally thought to be yellow, exceeded expectations in its abundant flowering, even if it proved to be flesh-coloured.

Among other early introductions are two roses painted by Reeves's Chinese artists: *R. roxburghii,* the Chestnut rose; and the evergreen, single-flowered *R. laevigata,* native to central China westwards into Sichuan, which cropped up mysteriously in North America as a supposed native, known as the Cherokee rose, and was later adopted as the floral emblem of the state of Georgia (See Chapter 13).

From the mid-1820s onwards, excitement shifted from finding new roses overseas to breeding them at home, inflaming the rose mania throughout Europe and America which is the subject of a later chapter. Plant-collecting in China stopped altogether in 1839 when Britain launched the first of the infamous Opium Wars to force the Chinese to accept imports of opium from British India and thereby balance the books of Britain's trade with China. After the humiliating treaty of Nanking (Nanjing) had prised open the China trade, Britain and the West engaged in a more brutal form of botanic imperialism which saw the theft of tea plants from China to boost Britain's interests in India.

The old plant-hunting passions resurfaced at the same time, and the long-retired John Reeves galvanized the Horticultural Society into sending a new man into China: another Scot, Robert Fortune, who arrived in China in 1843 on the first of four visits, less than eleven months after the Treaty was signed. He received the same annual salary as Kerr – just £100 – and when he asked for more, received the sharp rebuke that 'the mere pecuniary returns of your mission ought to be but a secondary consideration to you'. Fortune nonetheless managed to persuade the Society to let him take firearms, and he was also able to take advantage of the new glazed 'Wardian cases' for transplanting his precious plants and seedlings.

Fortune experienced an eventful trip, during which he survived gales and attacks by thieves, pirates and more pirates. Like Kerr before him, he visited Canton's Fa-Tee gardens, which he judged especially bright in springtime when they are 'gay with the tree paeony, azaleas, camellias, roses, and various other plants'. He also called in at the East India Company's small riverside garden, 'not more than sixty paces each way', surrounded by walks and a clump of trees in the middle. 'Since Mr Reeves's time no one seems to have paid any attention to the plants here,' he reported sadly, 'and if there ever were any rare species, they are now all lost.'

Among the many plants Fortune sent back to the Horticultural Society were two roses he found around Shanghai: *Rosa anemoniflora* (now *R. × beanii*), probably a hybrid between *R. banksiae* and a form of *R. multiflora*; and a *R. rugosa* (native to northern China and elsewhere) with sweetly scented semi-double flowers of a rich purple. He also sent them two more roses he found on his second visit to a mandarin's garden at Ningbo: the five-coloured rose (almost certainly *R. multiflora* 'Grevillei', which bears large trusses of flowers in a bewildering range of colours from deep lilac to soft pinks and even white, all at the same time), and the yellow beauty that became known as 'Fortune's Double Yellow'. This last rose was a particularly fine sight. On entering the mandarin's garden one fine morning in May, he was struck by a mass of yellow flowers completely covering a distant part of the wall.

The colour was not a common yellow, but had something of buff in it, which gave the flowers a striking and uncommon appearance. I immediately ran up to the place, and, to my surprise and delight, found that it was a most beautiful *new double yellow climbing rose*. I have no doubt, from what I afterwards learned, that this rose is from the more northern districts of the empire, and will prove perfectly hardy in Europe.

Increasingly, however, collectors in China were interested not in garden roses but in their wild ancestors. The first European to find *Rosa chinensis* growing wild, in the valleys above Ychang in western Hubei, was

Fortune's Double Yellow rose, sent home by plant hunter Robert Fortune,
who saw it blooming in a mandarin's garden in Ningbo, Zhejiang Province. Painted by Alfred
Parsons for Ellen Willmott's The Genus Rosa *(1910–14).*

the 'insignificant-looking little Irishman' Dr Augustine Henry, who came to China in 1881 in the service of the Chinese Maritime Customs at Shanghai, then moved to Hubei as medical officer. Lucky enough to collect in an entirely new field, he employed first one then two local collectors and went out into the field himself, sending back his first collection to Kew in 1886.

Henry was proud of his find, which he described for the *Gardeners' Chronicle* of 28 June 1902 under its old Linnaean name of 'Rosa indica'. 'The only wild specimens known are those collected by me in the glens near Ichang in Central China; and I have no reason to doubt that they are truly wild.' The rose then disappeared from view until Graham Stuart Thomas encouraged his friend Mikinori Ogisu, a Japanese botanist working in China, to search for it again. Ogisu rediscovered the rose growing wild in secondary forests on dry, west-facing slopes in southern Sichuan.

Wild roses continue to gladden the heart of visiting botanists and collectors. Early in the twentieth century, the naturalist 'Chinese' Wilson found roses growing wild wherever he went in western China, at their best in April: *Rosa laevigata* and *R. microcarpa* in fully exposed places; *R. multiflora*, *R. moschata* and *R. banksiae* on the cliffs and crags of glens and gorges, the last two scrambling high into the trees and trailing a festoon of flowers. As he wrote of his travels, 'To walk through a glen in the early morning or after a slight shower, when the air is laden with the soft delicious perfume from myriads of Rose flowers, is truly a walk through an earthly paradise.'

More recently, botanist Martyn Rix and writer-photographer Roger Phillips travelled to Yunnan Province and Sichuan in their quest to unravel some of the mysteries of the China bloodlines. They found roses very similar to all the four stud Chinas growing in China's hinterland and concluded tentatively that the cultivated roses brought back by William Kerr and others from Canton had in all likelihood been bred elsewhere. But the absence of records among the early Chinese hybridizers and the fact that so many of the early Chinese imports were allowed to die out in Europe supports the view expressed by Mikinori Ogisu 'that the origin of the China roses is still shrouded in mystery'.

Chapter Twelve
The Prophet's Rose

You could easily miss the signpost to Boulge church, which directs you down a pitted concrete road between Suffolk wheatfields bordered with old-fashioned hedgerows. Take the first turning right and there at the end of the track, beneath impressive chestnut trees and churchyard yews, is the flint-and-brick church of St Michael & All Angels. The church itself is not the attraction, despite its quaintly Victorianized interior, but rather a pink granite grave in the overgrown graveyard. The grave belongs to Edward FitzGerald, whose rendering into English of the medieval Persian *Rubáiyát of Omar Khayyám* earned poet and translator lasting fame in the West by welding the epigrammatic quatrains of a Farsi scholar, mathematician, astronomer and free-thinker into a unified 'poem' whose languid orientalism and wistful hedonism perfectly suited Victorian tastes.

Ever the self-willed outcast, FitzGerald chose as his final resting place not the family's mildly Gothic mausoleum but the plainer grave to one side that lists his dates of birth (31 March 1809) and death (14 June 1883), but gives no hint of his brief marriage to a poet's daughter or his lasting relationship with a Lowestoft fisherman. He had spent his formative years on the estate living in a two-roomed cottage just inside the gates to his parents' home at Boulge Hall. Here he would sit all day long in his dressing-gown, smoking a pipe in his book-filled study as he worked on his Persian translations, the door open 'to let in the odour of the cowslips or the garden flowers'. A friend of Alfred Lord Tennyson and other members of the Cambridge Apostles, he published translations of Farrid ud-Din Attar's *Bird Parliament* and Jami's *Salaman and*

Absal and also made a selection of works by fellow Suffolk poet and radical George Crabbe, but it is for Omar Khayyám's *Rubáiyát* that he is remembered.

FitzGerald's slim volume is a masterly example of the transformative power of translation, which planted real roses in place of the more meta-phorical ones of Khayyám's original, making their inevitable withering doubly poignant.

> Iram[1] indeed is gone with all his Rose,
> And Jamshyd's Sev'n-ring'd Cup where no one knows;
> But still a Ruby kindles in the Vine,
> And many a Garden by the Water blows . . .

In FitzGerald's verse, roses appear and disappear with the spring, and flourish best at scenes of conquest and slaughter:

> I sometimes think that never blows so red
> The Rose as where some buried Caesar bled;
> That every Hyacinth the Garden wears
> Dropt in her Lap from some once lovely Head.

The tone is melancholy yet not mournful, regretful but not especially morbid. The nightingale can still make the rose blush, and the rose's vanishing beauty recurs like a refrain:

> Each Morn a thousand Roses brings, you say;
> Yes, but where leaves the Rose of Yesterday . . .

Separated in time by some seven and a half centuries, these two men are united in death by the same little shrubby Damask rose which the artist-traveller William Simpson had found in 1884 growing on Omar Khayyám's tomb in Nishapur, north-eastern Iran, and whose seeds he brought back to London's Kew Gardens for propagation. Employed as a special artist by the *Illustrated London News,* Simpson had stumbled across the poet's tomb while on a mission to Persia with the Afghan Boundary Commission. In October 1893, a few admirers planted the rose

'Dust into Dust, and under Dust, to lie, Sans Wine, sans Song, sans Singer, and – sans End'.
Illustrator Gilbert James chose butterflies and scattered rose petals to illustrate death in this 1909
edition of the Rubáiyát of Omar Khayyám translated by Edward FitzGerald.

on FitzGerald's grave in Boulge churchyard in the name of the Omar Khayyám Club.

More than thirty years later, the rose was clearly flourishing and already the quiet Suffolk churchyard had become a place of pilgrimage for a small band of FitzGerald devotees. In the late 1920s, the minor poet and author Godfrey Mathews recounted his own visit to FitzGerald's grave one lovely September evening, when he was fortunate to meet the church sexton and guardian of the rose tree, the aptly named Mr Bloom, who not only knew FitzGerald but had helped to bury him. 'He seemed rather puzzled to know why so many people came to see the grave,' wrote Mathews, 'and did not seem very enthusiastic about the Rubáiyát,' claiming that '"The Fitz-Geralds were a queer lot." *Sic transit gloria mundi.* Queer the Fitz-Geralds all were, if by queer is meant eccentric.'

In the churchyard's deepening shadows, Mathews stood beside the grave of one of 'the master craftsmen of our language', imagining that Omar felt the same tinge of sadness when he wrote these lines about the rose and the nightingale:

> Yet Ah, that Spring should vanish with the rose!
> That Youth's sweet-scented manuscript should close!
> The Nightingale that in the branches sang,
> Ah whence, and whither flown again, who knows!

A similar sadness pervades the churchyard today, which evokes in the visitor a sense of timelessness (of manorial Suffolk and lofty chestnut trees) and of time passing. Mown paths lead through the long grass and thistles of the churchyard to FitzGerald's grave, its rose reduced to a weakling sucker through a combination of neglect, poor growing conditions and the attentions, perhaps, of too many curious pilgrims. But you can read the story of Omar's rose on a tin plate attached to its protective wire cage and contemplate the scene from the shade of a spreading cherry tree. A tangle of pink roses blooms freely in another corner of the churchyard.

'The poet of Khorassin [Khorasan, Khayyám's home province] simply accepted the Universe as he found it,' wrote Mathews, 'and said why bother when we do not and cannot know anything about ultimate things.'

Roses permeate Muslim culture, just as they permeate FitzGerald's verse and Omar Khayyám's original quatrains. So it comes as a surprise to discover that the flower itself makes no appearance in the Qur'an, Islam's holy book containing the divine revelations received by the Prophet Muhammad in the last twenty years of his life.

The plants that do appear are all typical of Arabian oases and the eastern Mediterranean – plants such as the date palm, olive, grape, pomegranate, fig, Christ's thorn (*Ziziphus spina-christi*), tamarisk, the toothbrush tree (*Salvadora persica*), henna, ginger, lentil, onion, garlic, Sahelian acacia *(Acacia seyal)*, sweet basil, euphorbia, and the spreading cedar of Lebanon (*Cedrus libani*)). The rose is mentioned only metaphorically in Surat 55, which says that on the Last Day the sky is rent asunder and turns rose-red like ointment.[2]

Roses are absent, too, from the paradise gardens promised by the Qur'an as a reward to believers and martyrs. Instead of a flower garden, the Qur'an dangles before the eyes of believers a place of green shade and gurgling fountains, plenteous fruits and cool pavilions, where the pious recline upon brocaded couches. Adorned with bracelets of gold and dressed in green garments of silk and brocade (green is the traditional colour of Islam), they find themselves among 'maidens restraining their glances [the virginal *houris* of Paradise, formed according to a seventh-century source from the four substances of musk, camphor, ambergris and saffron], untouched before them by any man or jinn ... lovely as rubies, beautiful as coral'.[3] As a vision of paradise on earth, it is both aristocratic and acutely attuned to the longings of a desert people.

But while the Qur'an plants no actual roses in Paradise, Muslim tradition in the *Hadiths* or collected sayings of the Prophet has given the rose a spiritual origin. According to these sources, as the Prophet made his heavenly journey into the divine presence to receive revelation, some drops of his sweat fell to the ground, from which sprang the first fragrant rose.

The idea gave the great thirteenth-century Persian mystic poet and

A Persian miniature of the Prophet Muhammad in the gardens of
Paradise with roses and songbirds.

theologian, Jalal al-Din Muhammad Rumi (better known to the West as
Rumi), this vision of the mystical rose:

> Root and branch of the roses is
>   the lovely sweat of Mustafa,
> And by his power the rose's crescent
>   grows now into a full moon.[4]

Later *Hadiths* added further elaborations, suggesting that droplets of
sweat falling from different parts of the Prophet's body created the
different varieties of rose. When the Prophet saw a rose, they say he
kissed it and placed it on his eyes. He also regarded the rose as a
manifestation of God's glory; and mystics such as Ruzbihan Baqli from

245

Shiraz experienced the divine glory in clouds of roses. 'The red rose is part of the splendour of God; everyone who wants to look into God's splendour should look at the red rose,' wrote Baqli, placing the rose at the heart of the mystic experience.

Muslims and Christians were not the first peoples to dream of Paradise as a garden, or to live their lives anticipating a return to the promised abode. Established in the southern part of Mesopotamia (present-day Iraq) from the fourth millennium BC, the Sumerians located their creation myth in a paradise-land known as Dilmun, described as 'the place where the sun rises' and 'the Land of the Living'.

And the garden we think of as essentially Islamic in character, with its cooling water and shade and quadripartite division or *chahar bagh,* is in fact pre-Islamic and essentially Persian in origin. You can still trace its outline in the runnels and watercourses of Cyrus the Great's garden at Pasargadae, built in the sixth century BC on the Iranian plain of Morghab, where the encircling hills hold you as if in the palm of a giant hand. During the Prophet's lifetime, by contrast, the gardens of Arabia were little more than date palms and water. But after the Prophet's death the Arab armies of Islam began rapidly to expand their territories, defeating the Persians in AD 642. From their desert origins, they overran centres of high civilization and immediately began to assimilate the best the conquered lands could offer in material and intellectual gains. And so the new religion grafted itself on to an older, stable civilization with a culture of gardens at its heart.

More conquests followed and the 'Islamic' garden travelled up from North Africa into Spain, al-Andalus, and eastwards into central and southern Asia, overlaying and adapting local traditions with Persian forms and a Persian love of flowers. Wherever they went, the early Muslim rulers created fabulous earthly gardens that gave a glimpse of the heavenly gardens to come: at Basra, Damascus and Nisibin in Mesopotamia; at Tunis, Algiers, Tlemcen, Fez and Marrakesh in North Africa; at Seville, Cordoba, Toledo, Valencia ('the scent-bottle of al-Andalus') and Granada in Moorish Spain; at Khumarawaih in Egypt; at Kabul, Srinagar and Lahore in Mughal Afghanistan, India and Pakistan; at Alanya and Istanbul in Turkey.

Ottoman Sultan Mehmet II, Conqueror of Constantinople, savours a rose in this portrait executed c.1480. The artist is reputedly Shiblizade Ahmed, a pupil of Sinan Bey.

As Chapter 4 described, many of those early Muslim rulers stand out for their love of plants and roses were undoubtedly among their treasures. Ibn al-'Awwam's immense *Book of Agriculture*, compiled in the late twelfth century, so astonished the prolific Scottish garden writer and designer J. C. Loudon that he concluded that the plants grown in Moorish Spain were 'more numerous than those which were cultivated by the Greeks and the Romans'.[5]

Also noted for their garden culture were the Mughals, starting with Zahir ud-Din Muhammad – known to the world as Babur – who claimed descent from Tamerlane (Timur the Lame), the creator of a garland of gardens around his capital at Samarkand. Heading eastwards from his homeland in Uzbekistan, Babur conquered Samarkand for a time, moved on to Herat in western Afghanistan, then advanced into northern India, defeating the Muslim rulers of Delhi in 1526 and founding the Mughal dynasty. Wherever he went, Babur created gardens that marked his claims to the territory, even 'in unpleasant and inharmonious India . . . In every corner were beautiful plots, and in every plot were regularly laid out arrangements of roses and narcissus.'

Roses were Babur's special passion. He gave his three daughters by Dildar Begum names connected to the rose – Gulrang (Rose Coloured), Gulchihra (Rose Face) and Gulbadan (Rose Body). Yet roses were also linked to his ox-like warrior nature. 'My heart is steeped in blood like a rosebud,' he wrote on a springtime excursion to the tulip-filled plains and mountains around Kabul. 'Even if there were a hundred thousand springs, what possibility would there be of its opening?'

Throughout the Muslim world, a love of roses burned most strongly in the Persia of old. 'We in England tend to regard the rose as our national flower,' wrote Vita Sackville-West, Bloomsbury luminary and chatelaine of Sissinghurst, 'so it is salutary to be reminded that the Persian poets adopted her quite as early as we did.' She also pointed out that *gul*, the word for 'rose' in Persian, is also the general word for a flower, 'thereby implying that the rose is pre-eminent among all flowers'.

Early travellers recorded their impressions with wide-eyed astonishment, among them the author, traveller and parliamentarian-turned-royalist Sir Thomas Herbert, who dutifully paced the Persian gardens;

*Mughal Emperor Babur (1483–1530) supervises the laying out of
one of his favourite quadripartite gardens, the Bagh-i-Vafa in Kabul, from a
Mughal miniature in the Baburnama, c.1590.*

recorded their many fine trees; admired the 'Flowers rare to the eye, sweet to the smell, and usefull in physick'; criticized the women (some of whom he called 'the most nasty, pocky Whoers you shall find in any place'); blushed scarlet at the pederast portraits of Faraharbad; and all but swooned at the magnificence of the King's antechamber at Ashraf, being especially impressed by its cooling water tanks surrounded with 'Goblets, Flagons, Cesternes [cisterns], and other Standards of pure massie gold, some of which were fill'd with Perfumes, other some with Rosewater, with Wine some, and others with choisest flowers'.

A more painstaking recorder of Persian society and its flowers was Jean Chardin, a French Protestant jewel merchant and traveller who spent much of the 1660s and 1670s in Persia, including ten years in Shah 'Abbas's glittering new capital of Esfahan, before eventually settling in London. His French sophistication nonetheless clouded his opinion of Persian gardens, for he saw little art in their straight alleyways, water tanks and random planting of fruit trees and roses. 'They know nothing about flower beds, green arbours, mazes, terraces and the other adornments of our gardens,' said Chardin scornfully. 'This is mainly due to the fact that Persians do not walk in their gardens as we do, but are content to have the view and breathe in the air. For that they seat themselves in a part of the garden when they enter and stay put until they leave.'

But for Persian flowers Chardin had nothing but praise, judging their vivacious colours 'generally handsomer' than those of Europe and India, especially those witnessed on his travels to the less drought-ridden eastern province of Mazandaran, which 'is nothing but one continu'd Parterre, from September, to the End of April'. His journals paint a dazzling canvas of spring and summer flowers: tulips, anemones, ranunculi, single and double jessamines, crown imperials, hyacinth, lily-of-the-valley, violets, pinks, mallows, jonquils, daffodils, the great clove gillyflower – and Persian roses, of course. 'The Rose, which is so common among them, is of five sorts of Colours, besides its natural one [and what might that be?, mused Vita Sackville-West], *White*, *Yellow*, *Red*, which we call the *Spanish Rose*, and others of two Colours, viz. *Red* on one Side, and *White* or *Yellow* on the other. The *Persians* call these *Roses Dou Rouye*, or Two Places. I have seen a *Rose-Tree*, which bore upon one and

Watercolour of people in a garden with roses in the Persian Qajar style by Mirza Hadi Ibn Mirza Habib Ramzi, 1835, illustrating a masnavi poem about the royal gardens of Sa'adatabad, Esfahan.

the same Branch, *Roses* of three Colours, some *Yellow*, others *Yellow* and *White*, and others *Yellow* and *Red*.'

More than a century after Chardin, Persian roses were still dazzling western visitors such as the artist and traveller Sir Robert Ker Porter, whose painterly eye recorded the voluptuous scenes in the (vacant) lodgings of the women and female slaves, all '*couleur de rose*', and especially the immense marbled hall of the great bath, where the 'fair bathers' could recline on the finest carpets and where 'gathered roses strew the floor in every direction, contrasting their natural beauties with their gilded imitations on the walls. Such profusions of this lovely flower, within and without the dwellings of Persia, cannot but remind the foreign visitor at every step, that he is in the land of Hafiz, – of the nightingale and the rose.'

In Tabriz in north-western Iran, Ker Porter marvelled at the beauty and fragrance of rose trees shut away within walled gardens, which spread their perfume for such a distance that 'the traveller, riding alone through the dark-hued streets, is often lost in wonder, of whence such sweet breath can proceed'. Indeed, he declared after visiting the Negarestan garden in Teheran where he saw two fourteen-foot rose trees 'laden with thousands of flowers', exquisitely perfumed: 'I believe that in no country of the world does the rose grow in such perfection as in Persia; in no country is it so cultivated, and prized by the natives.' Gardens and courts were crowded with roses, he reported, rooms ornamented with great bunches of them, and every bath strewn with flowers in full bloom. 'Even the humblest individual, who pays a piece of copper money for a few whifs of a kalioun, feels a double enjoyment when he finds it stuck with a bud from his dear native tree!'

Twentieth-century visitors were similarly impressed. Vita Sackville-West well understood the place of the rose in Persian life after she travelled to Persia in 1926 to visit her husband Harold Nicolson, on his posting to the Teheran Legation. As she wrote in her short memoir, *Passenger to Teheran*:

Imagine that you have ridden in summer for four days across a plain; that you have then come to a barrier of snow-mountains and ridden up the pass; that from the top of the pass you have seen a second plain, with a second barrier of mountains in the distance, a hundred miles away; that you know that beyond these mountains lies yet another plain, and another, and another; and that for days, even weeks, you must ride, with no shade, and the sun overhead, and nothing but the bleached bones of dead animals strewing the track. Then when you come to trees and running water, you will call it a garden. It will not be flowers and their garishness that your eyes crave for, but a green cavern full of shadow, and pools where goldfish dart, and the sound of little streams. That is the meaning of a garden in Persia, a country where the long slow caravan is an everyday fact, and not a romantic name.

Although she claimed to have hunted unsuccessfully for a proper garden in her early days in the country, the imperious Vita soon began to appreciate the joys of even the most dilapidated Persian garden when set against 'the enormous geographical simplicity that lies beyond'. And once she had experienced the exuberance of the native wildlings, she came to understand the reputation of Persian roses.

Huge bushes, compact, not straggling like the English dog-rose, spattered with flame-coloured blossom; the ground carpeted with fallen petals – this is the first impression, then a closer scrutiny reveals the lovely shape of the separate flower, the pure, early shape of the briar-rose, of a pristine simplicity which our whorled hybrids, superlative though they be, can never excel; and, allied to that early, naked design, a colour such as all our cross-fertilisation fails to produce: the interior of the petal red, but lined with gold, the two together giving a glow of orange, a burning bush.

The rose she describes with such simple brushstrokes is *Rosa foetida* 'Bicolor', commonly named 'Austrian Copper' in deference to the intro-duction from Vienna of its parent species attributed to the great sixteenth-century Flemish botanist Carolus Clusius. Vita liked it so much she took a root home with her from Teheran to grow in her own garden. A close cousin is the double form, *R. foetida* 'Persiana', which has globe-like flowers of a rich golden yellow, much like the sulphur rose, *R. hemisphaerica* which Vita said was 'much esteemed for its musky scent and its value in the making of rose-water'.

Among her many Persian stories, Vita relates her visit to Kum [Qom]

Rosa sulfurea

Rosier jaune de soufre

P.J. Redouté pinx.

Imprimerie de Rémond

Langlois sculp

The sulphur rose, Rosa hemisphaerica, *painted by Pierre-Joseph Redouté*
for the first volume of Les Roses *(Paris, 1817).*

on the road from Esfahan to Teheran where she and her companions stayed with 'a tall, black-bearded man of incomparable dignity'. They found their breakfast laid out on a small ledge outside their sleeping room, with cushions of emerald-green velvet and a bunch of brilliant, single yellow roses, and were afterwards led by their host through a labyrinth of streets to a closed door. Inside the courtyard stood the tree from which the roses had been picked, taller than a man, and smothered in wide, single yellow roses, more like a butterfly than a flower. 'It was the magic bush of the Arabian Nights; I looked about for the Singing Fountain and the Talking Bird; a goldfish darted in the tank.'

Their host stood there smiling, lit by some extraordinary pride 'that he was showing us something that held a romantic, secret place in his life, something apart from the homeliness of his dwelling-house, a separate thing'. A young woman appeared briefly with a child in her arms, cried out and vanished, 'and the court returned to its warm empty silence and the sole sentinel of the yellow rose'. Still smiling, 'as a showman who for a second time has drawn aside a curtain and let it fall again', their guide ushered them back into the street. No one remarked on what they had seen, and 'we strolled towards the bazaars, talking of Russian traders on the Caspian'.

Vita Sackville-West may have understood the rose's secret power over Persian hearts, but she had much less sympathy with the rose in Persian poetry, complaining that the great poets Hafez and Sa'di sang frequently, 'even wearisomely', of roses. 'Everywhere you look is a flower bed and a rose garden, and wherever you turn in a palace and a pavilion,' wrote one poet of the great Persian ruler of the early nineteenth century, Fath 'Ali Shah, but he could equally have been writing of Persian poetry.

As the flower of springtime, the rose is naturally the flower of lovers, evoked to celebrate the beloved's physical attributes, especially the cheeks but also the face and breast, while the rose bush (*gulbun*) signifies the nose, and the rose garden (*gulistan*) the face. Other flowers are praised too, of course. In his eleventh-century poem *Vis*, Fakhr al-Din Gurgani likened the features of the baby girl to fresh lilies growing in the gardens of Paradise, her hair to violets, her eyes to narcissi, her cheeks to jonquils, her face to the tulip, her black locks to ripe grapes, her chin to apples, her breasts to pomegranates – and not a rose in sight.

Profane poets might see flightiness in the rose's short life and wayward behaviour but to the devout the rose represents the divine Beloved, celebrated for almost a millennium as the perfect manifestation of God's glory. The rose's pre-eminence is particularly marked in Persian mystical literature; to the great Sufi mystic Rumi, it appears as the likeness of the 'soul at peace':

Like a rose I smile with my whole body, not only by the way of the mouth, for I am, without myself, alone with the king of the world.

'This idea leads Rumi to advise the lover that he should learn to die with a smile like the rose,' wrote Professor Annemarie Schimmel, a renowned German scholar who saw it as her life's work to awaken an understanding for Islam. 'Slowly dropping its petals and leaving behind its fragrance, the flower fades away in perfect serenity.' The thought connects with Hermann Hesse's poem 'Sterbende Rosen' ('Dying Roses'), which talks of 'drinking death in a kiss', and with Shakespeare's distilled roses. Although the rose garden dies in the autumn, its scent lingers on in rosewater and essence of rose.

Rumi also introduced a mystical interpretation to the classic association of lovers, nightingale and rose – the lovelorn bird who sings its sweet song in honour of the eternal rose, eternally separated but in Rumi the duality is finally resolved:

The nightingale of those whom He grants a mystical rapture
has its own rose garden in itself.

For Rumi and for so many poets of the Muslim world, the constant admiration for the rose 'forms the warp of images'. It lies behind the titles given to poetic and mystical works, among them Sa'di's *Gulistan* or *Rose Garden* (written c.1258) and the *Gulshan-i raz* or *Secret Rose Garden* (also known as the *The Rose Garden of Mystery*) by the fourteenth-century Sufi mystic, Mahmud ibn 'Ad al-Karim Shabistari. For Annemarie Schimmel, one of the loveliest accounts of spiritual roses was written by a little-known

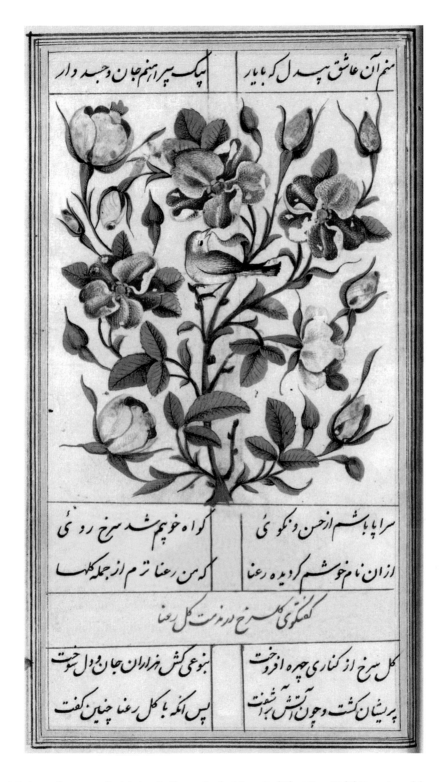

سخن آن عاشق بیدل که بیار | اینک سپهر بهتم جان و جسد وار

سراپا باشم از حسن و نکو ئی | گواه خویم شد سرخ رو ئی
ازان نام خوشم کردیده رعنا | که من رعنا ترم از جمله گلها

گفتگوی گل سرخ در مذمت گل رعنا

گل سرخ از کناری چهره افروخت | نموعی کش هزاران جان و دل سوخت
پریشان کشت و چون آتش برافروخت | پس آنکه با گل رعنا چنین کفت

A Qajar-style rose-and-nightingale illustration by Mirza Hadi Ibn Mirza Habib Ramzi to celebrate the royal gardens of Sa'adatabad, Esfahan.

Turkish folk poet of the seventeenth century, Ümmi Sinan, who described the 'city of roses' which he visited in his vision. 'Here, everything is roses, the mills and the waterwheels, the water and the dam, the fountains and the grain, the walls and the marketplace, and eventually he sees Khidr, the mysterious prophet, sitting in a tent of roses and understands that even weeping is "the rose of those whose hearts are nightingales".'

As Vita Sackville-West implied, roses run through the veins of two of Iran's most revered poets, Sa'di (Musharrif al-Din Muslih), writing in the thirteenth century, and Hafez (Shams al-Din Muhammad), writing a little over a century later. Both were born and died in the southern city of Shiraz, and today their mausoleums attract admirers of all ages. Evening is the best time to visit, when daylight fades and whole families, groups of friends and discreet young couples flock to pay their respects. Hafez's tomb is especially popular, its approach lined with floodlit roses, the bright red-and-orange kind you see everywhere in Iran, and the atmosphere is close to electric.

Among Hafez's many western translators was the British traveller and archaeologist Gertrude Bell, who first visited Teheran in 1892. There are roses in nearly half the Hafez poems she chose: sad roses, joyful roses, wind-blown roses, roses-and-nightingales (several), fleeting roses, lovers' roses, hopeful roses, purple roses, spring roses and dawn roses, as here:

> In the clear dawn, before the east was red,
> Before the rose had torn her veil in two,
> A nightingale through Hafiz' garden flew,
> Stayed by to fill its song with tears, and fled.

More modern poets continue this love affair with the rose.

> . . . If you allow me flight
> I will become a flower
> in the rose garden of poetry . . .

So wrote the fiercely independent Forugh Farrokhzad, whose manners and developing modernism shocked the male-centred Iranian society of the 1950s and 1960s (she died in a car crash in Teheran aged just thirty-two, when she apparently failed to yield at an intersection). 'Red Rose' is one of her earlier poems:

> He took me to the rose garden,
> And in darkness, he threaded
> a red rose in my ruffled hair
> And made love with me
> On a red rose petal.

From this union grew another red rose, her unborn child, 'Below my heart and deep inside my loins', a rose that was 'Red as the flags of revolution'.

Amid so much praise for the rose, it is oddly refreshing to detect the occasional voice of dissent. Compared with myrtle, for instance, the rose can appear disloyal, her life as fleeting as a smile. 'How long is the life of a rose?' asked the leading Urdu poet Mir Taqi Mir. 'The bud heard my question and smiled.' And in the well-developed Arabic literary debate between the narcissus and the rose – a contest usually decided in favour of the rose – one notorious ninth-century poet voiced a contrary opinion, comparing the rose to a mule's anus with remnants of faeces at its heart.[6]

Today, Iran continues to take more pleasure in its roses than any country I know. The roses themselves are often fairly ordinary; what strikes you most is their abundance, especially in and around Shiraz in the southern province of Fars, which declares itself the 'city of roses and of poets'. But throughout Iran, roses are grown haphazardly wherever there is space – in hotel gardens and municipal plantings, in cemeteries and cramped urban courtyards, in palace gardens and cheap cafés, on roundabouts and roadsides; there are even roses growing along the central reservation of the highway leading up to Qamsar near Kashan. In the early morning during the rose season you will encounter men at work between the traffic harvesting the Damask roses for Qamsar's distilleries, as we discovered in late April 2009 when we were privileged to witness a primitive distillation, guided by a coachload of Iranian tourists from Teheran and a chance encounter in our hotel lobby with a high government official.

You will find the same surfeit of roses in Iranian art, and the familiar pairing of nightingale and rose, lover and beloved. Known as *gul o-bulbul* (rose and nightingale), the motif was especially popular in the richly decorative art of the nineteenth-century Qajar dynasty, when it proliferated on every available surface from ceilings to book covers, from mirror casings to cash boxes. Particularly exquisite are the richly glowing pen-boxes made of papier mâché then painted and lacquered, a technique borrowed from the Chinese and later developed into an art form.[7]

If you crave still more roses, look closely at Iran's public buildings, secular and religious. Nowhere does the Qur'an expressly forbid the representation of living things, and while such a prohibition soon arose in much of the Muslim world, on the grounds that creating life through art is an act of competition with God, Iran follows the minority branch of Shi'a Islam where no such reticence applies. Mosques, museums, cafés, palaces, bath-houses and shrines all have roses to delight the eye, whether huge bouquets in silk or plastic honouring the mausoleum of many a remembered imam, or rose patterns traced in tiles both indoors and out. Stand under the great central dome to Esfahan's magnificent royal mosque (now the Imam Mosque), constructed on the orders of Shah Abbas, and you cannot fail to be awed by the magnificent gold-on-blue floral tracery that turns the space into a great golden rose basket (the actual flower is abstracted, more like a lotus).

And when you have had your fill, step outside and look across to the dome of its sister mosque, the Sheikh Lotfollah Mosque, which is smaller, more understated and – to my mind – even more exquisite. Around the biscuit-coloured wash of the dome's outer brickwork runs a bold branching rose-tree inlaid in black and white. In the 1930s, the British traveller Robert Byron saw in it a hint of William Morris, especially its thorns. He was even more entranced by the foliage pattern inlaid on the dome's interior network of compartments, and the twirling arabesques on the deep ochre stucco of the walls. 'Each part of the design, each plane, each repetition, each separate branch or blossom has its own sombre beauty,' declared Byron. 'But the beauty of the whole comes as you move.' Byron the gentleman aesthete and begrudging traveller admitted that he had never before witnessed such splendour. The richness of other great interiors was three-dimensional (Versailles, the porcelain rooms at Vienna's Schönbrunn, St Peter's in Rome, and the Doge's Palace in Venice), but in Esfahan's Mosque of Sheikh Lotfollah, 'it is a richness of light and surface, of pattern and colour only. The architectural form is unimportant. It is not smothered, as in rococo; it is simply the instrument of a spectacle, as earth is the instrument of a garden.'

So the story of the rose in Islamic cultures is one of profusion and diffusion. The rose's presence is at once physical, metaphorical and metaphysical, whether planted in gardens or commemorative tombs; celebrated by poets, artists and mystics; transformed into rosewater and attar of roses; painted on to pen boxes or embedded in religious architecture. Its virtues bring benefit to mind, body and soul.

Looking upwards into the interior dome of the Sheikh Lotfollah Mosque in Esfahan, begun in 1615 for Shah 'Abbas I. The light at certain times casts a peacock's tail from the centre.

Is it possible to weary of the rose's infinite possibilities? That old Arabia hand T. E. Lawrence expressed a desire to turn his back on roses for the purity of the desert. In his classic of the Arab campaign, *Seven Pillars of Wisdom,* he describes how his Arab guides took him to see a Roman ruin in the plains of northern Syria, reputedly built by a prince as a desert palace for his queen.

The clay of its building was said to have been kneaded for greater richness, not with water, but with the precious essential oils of flowers. My guides, sniffing the air like dogs, led me from crumbling room to room, saying, 'This is jessamine, this violet, this rose.'

But at last Dahoum drew me: 'Come and smell the very sweetest scent of all,' and we went into the main lodging, to the gaping window sockets of its eastern face, and there drank with open mouths of the effortless, empty, eddyless wind of the desert, throbbing past. That slow breath had been born somewhere beyond the distant Euphrates and had dragged its way across many days and nights of dead grass, to its first obstacle, the man-made walls of our broken palace. About them it seemed to fret and linger, murmuring in baby-speech. 'This,' they told me, 'is the best: it has no taste.'

Chapter Thirteen
American Beauties

Early in October 1986, the most powerful man in the western world stood on the lawn of the White House Rose Garden and solemnly declared the rose the National Floral Emblem of the United States of America. No one pointed out that the English had beaten him to it by some 500 years. The applause was suitably enthusiastic, even if the garden's few remaining roses had wilted after a long hot Washington summer. It was the year of Chernobyl and the unravelling of the Iran–Contra affair.

'Americans have always loved the flowers with which God decorates our land,' declared President Reagan in a short, emotional address that linked the rose to America's prehistoric and revolutionary past, and to its most cherished values. 'More often than any other flower,' he added (you can imagine the slight quiver in his voice), 'we hold the rose dear as the symbol of life and love and devotion, of beauty and eternity. For the love of man and woman, for the love of mankind and God, for the love of country. Americans who would speak the language of the heart do so with the rose.'

Reagan's performance was as polished as ever, betraying his skills of old-fashioned oratory and the actor's knack of leavening with emotion the words penned by his reliably capable speechwriters. As the President went on to explain:

The study of fossils reveals that the rose has existed in America for age upon age. We have always cultivated roses in our gardens. Our first President, George Washington, bred roses, and a variety he named after his mother is still grown today. The White House itself boasts a beautiful Rose Garden. We grow roses in all our fifty States. We find roses through our art, music, and literature. We decorate our celebrations and parades with roses. Most of all, we present roses to those we love, and we lavish them on our altars, our civil shrines, and the final resting places of our honored dead.

In America, roses clearly merit presidential attention, but like much else in the story of the rose, the reincarnation of George Washington as a rose-breeder exaggerates the case a little. The 'Mary Washington' rose belongs to the Noisettes, a class not created until after Washington's death; and while the first President was an avid experimental gardener, his copious diaries tell us little about roses, except that he used the wild sorts for hedges.

A passion for roses was more obvious with America's other great gardening President of the revolutionary era, Thomas Jefferson, but Reagan may have judged him too liberal a model for his roses speech. The principal author of the Declaration of Independence, Jefferson had also served as Governor of Virginia and (in the 1780s) as Minister to France, dying patriotically on 4 July 1826, exactly fifty years after the adoption of his historic Declaration.

Gardening was one of Jefferson's most absorbing interests, and he kept a special memorandum book intended as a diary of his garden at Monticello, his great estate near Charlottesville, Virginia, recording all the changes he observed in nature. Roses appear in the first of Jefferson's 'gardener's diary' entries for 1767, a little before his twenty-fourth birthday, when he records planting 'suckers of Roses, seeds of Althaea [the Rose of Sharon, *Hibiscus syriacus*] & Prince's feather [*Amaranthus hypochondriacus*]'. Roses and Sweet Briar next appear in 1771 among a tangle of shrubs and fruits planted on open ground to the west of his estate, where the wild shrubberies also contained alder, barberry, cassioberry (a native viburnum), hawthorn, wild honeysuckle, hazel and ivy. Later, he would plant seeds of the naturalized Cherokee rose (*Rosa laevigata*) received as a gift from the revolutionary patriot John Milledge, Governor of Georgia. 'Goliah stuck sticks to mark the place,' he noted in his Garden Book, referring to one of his slaves, for despite his declared anti-slavery views, Jefferson was perennially short of money and relied on slave labour to run his extensive estates.

Jefferson was also very fond of fine garden roses, and during the many years in which he was absent from home on government business, he ordered more roses for his Monticello plantings. In 1791, much taken with the maples he had seen in Vermont while touring the north as George Washington's Secretary of State, he requested the pioneer nurseryman William Prince of Flushing, Long Island, to send him all the sugar maples he had. After receiving Prince's nursery catalogue, he placed a second order which included classic ornamental roses from Europe, requesting three each of 'Roses Moss Provence. yellow. rosa mundi: large Provence. the monthly. the white Damask. the primrose.

Thomas Jefferson's estate of Monticello near Charlottesville, Virginia, where he planted European roses, Sweet Briar and seeds of the Cherokee rose. A nineteenth-century copy of a painting by George Cooke.

musk rose. cinnamon rose. thornless rose. 3 of each making in all 30'. He asked for the plants to be shipped from New York to Richmond Virginia, addressed to the Richmond merchant Mr James Brown, who would pay the freight charges. The shipment was on its way by early November, although Prince sent only two plants of each requested variety, reducing the total number of roses to twenty. When Jefferson returned to Monticello in 1794, after an effective absence of ten years, garden roses featured among the few ornamental shrubs he included in his master plan to restore the estate, which he had found in a deplorable state.

In the White House, too, he liked to surround himself with birds and roses. We catch a charming vignette by the now-forgotten novelist Mrs Samuel Harrison Smith, wife to the proprietor of the *National Intelligencer* and a prolific chronicler of the early years of Washington society. In the window recesses to his private apartment, Jefferson had an indoor garden where he kept 'the flowers and plants which it was his delight to attend and among his roses and geraniums was suspended the cage of his favourite mocking-bird, which he cherished with peculiar fondness, not only for its melodious powers, but for its uncommon intelligence and affectionate disposition'.

And crucially for botanic relations between the Old and New Worlds, Jefferson took part in the plant exchanges which began in the earliest days of settlement and continue to this day. While stationed in Paris in the mid-1780s, 'roses of various kinds' featured among the vegetables and ornamental plants he sent back to his close friend Francis Eppes in America, along with gillyflowers, pinks, double tulips, crown imperials, ranunculus and martagon lilies. Once back in Washington – and now president – he wrote to one of his frequent suppliers, the Washington nurseryman Robert Bailey, saying that a friend in France had asked him to procure a long list of seeds and native plants, including 'Wild roses of every kind, $\frac{1}{2}$ bushel of each'. His French friend was the Comtesse Noailles de Tessé, aunt to the Marquis de Lafayette, who had to wait a year for her precious shipment because of the difficulty of arranging transport to Europe through Washington's only local port at Alexandria. The box measured about 13 cubic feet and was naturally very heavy.

*

Right from the earliest days of settlement, roses feature in the accounts of European adventuring to the fledgling colony. Life was then a grim matter of survival: food and the pursuit of profit took precedence over mere gardening (and the Virginian settlers would have saved themselves much grief if they had planted more food and less tobacco, the wonder crop that promised to make them rich). But the allure of roses played a part too. If at first the discovery of wild roses in the Edenic landscape revived reassuring memories of home, the introduction of European roses to the gardens of the New World would just as plainly bear witness to its increasing civility.

The flamboyant settler Captain John Smith omits roses from his earliest impressions of Virginia, despite his lyrical descriptions of its lush forests and the Indian encampments planted 'in the midst of their fields or gardens, which are small plots of ground'. But the colony's official secretary, William Strachey, included roses among the spring herbs found in Virginian woods, 'good for broathes and salletts'. He also put 'a rose' and 'a rose tree' in his Algonquin dictionary of more than 800 words intended for those wishing to 'truck and Trade with the People', translating the flower as 'Pussaqwembun' or 'Pussagweinbun' and the tree as 'Pussaqwembunameindg'.

The *Mayflower* pilgrims similarly found roses growing wild after their first terrible winter in New England. 'Here are grapes, white and red,' reported William Bradford and Edward Winslow, 'and very sweet and strong also; strawberries, gooseberries, raspas [raspberries], &c.; plums of three sorts, white, black, and red, being almost as good as a damson; abundance of roses, white, red and Damask; single but very sweet indeed.' Some fifty years later, visiting Englishman John Josselyn included these wild roses among native remedies for burns and scalds, noting the presence of 'Wild Damask roses, single but very large and sweet, but stiptick [astringent]'.[1]

The most lyrical description of wild roses comes from the early colonist Daniel Denton, a Yorkshireman by birth, who wrote one of the first English-language descriptions of Long Island. After listing an abundance of native fruits and herbs, he moved on to the flowers, declaring that 'Yea, in *May* you shall see the Woods and Fields so curiously bedecke with Roses, and an innumerable multitude of delightful Flowers, not only pleasing the eye, but smell, that you may behold Nature contending with Art, and striving to equal, if not excel, many gardens in *England.*' All common diseases of the country might be cured by one or other of its native plants, he declared, remarking without apparent irony on the surprising decline in the numbers of the native population 'by the Hand of God, since the *English* first setling of those parts'.

By the time Denton wrote his tract to encourage new colonizers, North American roses were long familiar to the elite of England's gardeners. 'Rosa Virginiana' was one of twenty-seven rose varieties recorded in the Lambeth garden of the celebrated plantsman John Tradescant the elder in 1634. A contact must have procured the specimen for him, as he never made the Atlantic crossing himself. His apothecary friend John Parkinson also included a Virginian rose in his great herbal of 1640 ('Virginia' was not then geographically precise.) He called it *Rosa sylvestris Virginensis,* the 'Virginia Bryer Rose', and described it as having:

divers as great stemmes and branches as any other Rose, whose young are greene and the elder grayish, set with many small prickles and a few great thornes among them, the leaves are very greene and shining small and almost round, many set on a middle ribbe one against another somewhat like unto the single yellow Rose: the flowers stand at the toppes of the branches consisting of five small leaves [petals], of a pale purple or deepe incarnate colour like unto those of the sweet brier, which fall away quickly as they and others doe.[2]

European roses were also making the reverse crossing westwards across the Atlantic as a mark of North America's increasing sophistication. In 1633, a London contact of John Winthrop, the plant-loving first governor of Massachusetts, offered to send him English roses and even at this early stage cultivated roses were blooming in the more important gardens further south in Virginia. Calling at the riverside home of George Menefie, Jamestown's official merchant to the colony, a Dutch visitor admired his two-acre garden 'full of Provence roses, apple, pear, and cherry trees, the various fruits of Holland, with different kinds of sweet-smelling herbs, such as rosemary, sage, marjoram, and thyme'.

The same steady civilizing influx of European roses was evident all along the eastern seaboard, from New England in the north down to Carolina in the south. John Josselyn in New England (1672) noted the herbs, vegetables and flowers imported from Europe and how they adapted to the region's climatic extremes. Parsnips grew to a 'prodigious size', while bloodwort fared 'but sorrily'. Sweet Briar or Eglantine he classed among the plants that thrived exceptionally well, 'and *English Roses,* very pleasantly'. The Musk rose, too, grew 'as well as in *England*'.

Dutch and French Huguenots brought their floral expertise to New Netherlands and the lands about the Hudson and Mohawk Rivers, introducing 'the white and red roses of different kinds, the cornelian roses, and stock roses; and those of which there were none before in the country, such as eglantine'. The process of beautification continued after the English had taken over New York. Here is a description by Gabriel Thomas, a pioneer in William Penn's colony, of John Tateham Esquire's 'Great and Stately Palace' at Burlington, west New Jersey, 'which is pleasantly Situated on the North side of the Town, having a very fine and delightful Garden and Orchard adjoying to it, wherein is variety of Fruits, Herbs, and Flowers; as Roses, Tulips, July-Flowers, Sun-Flowers (that open and shut as the Sun Rises and Sets, thence taking their Name), Carnations, and many more; besides abundance of Medicinal Roots, Herbs, Plants, and Flowers, found wild in the Fields'. Tateham's house was just one of the 'Fair and Great Brick Houses' on the outskirts of Burlington, 'which the Gentry have built there for their Countrey Houses'.

The same story was repeated further south in Carolina, where settlers were gradually turning their attention from agriculture to horticulture. Sent out to Carolina in 1680 by royal command to enquire into the state of that country, the gentleman clerk Thomas Ashe reported that while the colonists' early efforts had been devoted to cultivating their plantations and raising cattle, 'now their *Gardens* begin to be supplied with such *European Plants* and *Herbs* as are necessary for the Kitchen, *viz. Pottatoes, Lettice, Coleworts, Parsnip, Turnip, Carrot* and *Reddish:* Their Gardens also begin to be beautified and adorned with such *Herbs* and *flowers* which to the Smell or Eye are pleasing and agreable, *Viz.* The *Rose, Tulip, Carnation* and *Lilly, &c.*'

Some fifty years later, roses played a part in one of the most significant

*The wreath of cultivated roses signifies both wealth and virtue in this portrait of Deborah Glen,
daughter of a wealthy American army colonel, shortly before her marriage to John Sanders in 1739.*

and best documented Atlantic plant exchanges: between the London cloth merchant Peter Collinson and his fellow Quaker John Bartram, a Pennsylvanian farmer with a house and land by the Schuylkill River, on the outskirts of Philadelphia. Both men were passionate about botany, and largely through Collinson's efforts Bartram was eventually rewarded with the appointment of botanist to the English King George III.

Their correspondence reveals both the joys and disappointments of transatlantic plant exchange. In 1739, Bartram wrote to Collinson with a mild complaint that 'the rose seed thee sent mee proves to be ye common single red rose & that thee sent for ye double blossomes was our common single sort we have plenty of ye Damask provence white cinamon & double & single red rose but I never saw ye yelow rose yet'. For his part, Bartram supplied seeds and specimens to Collinson, who was in touch with all the 'curious' plant collectors in Britain. As well as sending Bartram wish-lists of American plants and finding clients for his precious seeds, Collinson also advised him on practical matters such as dress, urging him to go 'very Clean, neat & handsomely Dressed to Virginia' because its people looked perhaps 'More at a Man's Outside than his Inside'.

Collinson introduced Bartram to Philip Miller, the curator of the Society of Apothecaries' physic garden at Chelsea and author of the hugely successful *Gardeners Dictionary* (1731 and many subsequent editions). Miller and Bartram did not correspond directly until the 1750s, when Miller sent Bartram some seeds with a basket of roses and cedar cones, explaining that he was enclosing 'a few plants of some of our best sorts of Roses, which I wish may prove such as you have not already; for, as I am unacquainted with what has been sent you from England, so I am at a loss to guess what I should send'.

The following summer Bartram wrote back to say that the roses sent in a basket with Norway maples had all died, but most of the other roses were growing prodigiously and full of flowers, although he was still pining for a yellow rose. 'I think there is one sort Something differing from ours,' he confided to Miller, 'but I cant see ye austrian nor ye single nor double yellow rose which would be a rarity as I think we have them not.'

*

George Washington, later first President of the United States, at the rose-bedecked home of Quaker farmer and botanist John Bartram in 1774, painted by American artist Jean Leon Gerome Ferris (1863–1930).

The roses John Bartram sent to Philip Miller included wild varieties such as the swamp rose, *Rosa palustris,* a moisture-loving counterpart of *R. carolina* found in boggy sites from Nova Scotia southwards to Florida. Not all natives were quite what they seemed, however. Even experienced botanists could be confused by a plant's apparently native origins – witness the strange story of the Cherokee rose. This rose was 'discovered' by the great French botanist and plant explorer André Michaux, who came to America in 1785 armed with a commission from the French King, Louis XVI, in the same year that the French explorer and naval officer Jean-François de Galaup de La Pérouse set out around the world. Both men would perish in their explorations. La Pérouse and his entire

272

expedition vanished somewhere in the Pacific in 1788. Still botanizing, Michaux died of fever in Madagascar, just as his American *Flora* was going to press in Paris.

As the first trained botanist to explore extensively in North America, Michaux arrived with a mission to collect seeds and plants to enrich the gardens and forests of France, which had been seriously depleted by naval wars with the English. His American *Flora* lists four native roses, which he called *Rosa caroliniana*, from Georgia and Carolina; *R. setigera* (the prairie rose) from southern Carolina; *R. pensylvanica* (*R. palustris*) from the swamps of Pennsylvania and New England; and *R. laevigata* (the Cherokee rose) from Georgia, a vigorous climbing or trailing evergreen that produces pure white single flowers in spring, large and fragrant with fluffy golden yellow stamens.

But the Cherokee rose is not native to America at all. It comes from China, where it was illustrated by Chiu-Huang Pen Ts'ao in his *Famine Herbal* in the early fifteenth century. Leonard Plukenet, Royal Professor of Botany and gardener to Queen Mary, first introduced it into European literature under the name *Rosa alba Cheusanensis* in a work of 1705. How it

Cherokee Roses, *1889, by Martin Johnson Heade. Long considered an American native, this rose is actually* Rosa laevigata *from southern China.*

273

had spread across the southern American states by the time of Michaux's journey is a mystery. Did it come in the early waves of settlement? Were its seeds among the transcontinental exchanges of plant enthusiasts such as Collinson and Bartram? Did it reach Spanish America via the Arabs and Moorish Granada in mainland Spain? Or does the Cherokee rose endorse the controversial claim that Buddhist monks from China first set foot in America (probably Mexico) in the fifth century, according to the account of returning monk Hoei-shin in AD 499?[3]

This Chinese native was still masquerading as an all-American champion in 1916, when the Georgia Federation of Women's Clubs persuaded the state legislature to adopt the Cherokee rose as the floral emblem for Georgia. In a foretaste of President Reagan's floral patriotism, the Georgia state legislature located the original Cherokee rose firmly 'among the aborigines of the northern portion of the State of Georgia', claiming that it was 'indigenous to its soil, and grows with equal luxuriance in every county of the State'.

Mythic histories continue to stick to this very tenacious rose, linking it to the 'Trail of Tears' that marked the US government's forcible removal of more than 16,000 Cherokee Indian people from their homelands in Tennessee, Alabama, North Carolina and Georgia, sending them to Indian Territory in what is now Oklahoma. Hundreds of Cherokee died during their trip west, and thousands more perished from the consequences of relocation. According to the legend of the Cherokee rose, when the Trail of Tears began in 1838, the Cherokee mothers were grieving and crying so much they were unable to help their children survive the journey. The elders prayed for a sign that would lift the mothers' spirits to give them strength. The next day a beautiful rose began to grow where each of the mothers' tears fell – white for their tears, and gold-centred in recognition of the gold taken from Cherokee lands. (A state history guide also claims for this rose seven leaves on each stem for the seven Cherokee clans, when in fact it has just three leaflets on each stalk.)

Dubious botany and myth-making tendencies have followed the rose into California, this time confusing genuine natives with European imports and introducing a note of nostalgia for the state's Spanish past.

California joined the Union only in 1850. Until then, it was part of the Spanish Americas, ever since the 1500s when Spanish sailors and explorers claimed for Spain first lower California (Baja California, now part of Mexico) and then the rest of what would become known as Alta California. It became a colonial province of New Spain in 1769, and so it remained until Mexico gained independence from Spain in 1821, and for twenty-five years California functioned as a remote northern province of the new Mexican state.

Until the arrival of the Spanish missionary fathers in 1769, the Spanish came to Alta California mostly as visitors. Roses featured in many of their letters, providing a convenient shorthand for a hospitable and pleasant land ripe for colonial exploitation. When the Spanish soldier, explorer and diplomat Sebastián Vizcaíno sailed into San Diego's natural harbour in 1602 on his way up to Monterey, he made no mention of the roses growing in the San Diego valley. But his accounts written a few months later from Mexico pointedly added *Rosas de Alejandria* (roses of Alexandria) to the trees and shrubs found at the port, which others on the same voyage called *Rosales de Castilla* (rose bushes of Castile).

Then, in 1769, the first of the mission fathers arrived, among them the small and dynamic Franciscan priest from Majorca, Father Junipero Serra, who had taken charge of the missions in Baja California the previous year, after King Carlos III of Spain had forcibly expelled the Jesuits from New Spain. Serra then travelled northwards, establishing the first mission in Alta California at San Diego with the dual aim of advancing the interests of Spain and converting the native population to Roman Catholicism. In just over fifty years, the Spanish fathers advanced up the coast as far as Sonoma, building a string of twenty-one missions in strategic sites such as San Juan Capistrano, San Gabriel, San Luis Obispo, Carmel, Santa Cruz and San José.

Father Junipero Serra had been in San Diego less than forty-eight hours when he mentioned roses in letters to two fellow priests, re-marking on the wild grapevines and *Rosas de Castilla* which filled the nearby river valley. His letters echo the descriptions of another Franciscan, Father Crespi, who wrote of the plain dotted with wild grapevines in bloom, and of the 'many Castilian rose bushes with very fragrant roses' which he found growing on the willow-covered banks of the San Diego River, and 'which I have held in my hand and smelled'. The same descriptions occur again and again: of wild grapes, and abundant Castilian roses growing in thickets by streams and other wet places, sweet-smelling and flowering in panicles, with hips that could be eaten after roasting briefly in a slow fire.

The name '*Rosa de Castilla*' belongs to no officially recognized tribe, so it is not at all clear which rose was meant. Some say it was either a Summer or an Autumn Damask, others a Gallica rose, while a Cuban provincial dictionary of the 1860s suggested that a rose known as the *Rosa de Castilla* at the west end of Cuba was called the *R. Alejandria* in the east – an intriguing echo of the early Spanish reports. From their descriptions it is probable that the Spaniards were describing not a true-blooded Spanish rose from Castile but an American native such as *Rosa californica*, which grows in just such thickets by canyons and streams, although it is not especially sweet-smelling. The priests and explorers brought the name from Spain, not the rose.

Spanish missionaries nonetheless introduced seeds of vegetables, flowers and flax, and the following decade saw 'shrubs for pleasure'

Today, California's Spanish mission houses are bathed in rose-tinted light. This photograph of the San Diego mission c.1915 suggests a harsher reality.

brought to California from France, including 'Roses-hundred leaves' (probably the Centifolia rose) by La Pérouse when he visited California in 1786. And the 1824 annual report for Sonoma – the last of the missions to be founded – specifically mentions *Rosales de Castilla* among the trees, vegetables, grapes and shrubs planted in the new mission orchard that year. These roses almost certainly came from Spain and once introduced, Spanish roses found their way to most if not all of California's missions, invariably called *Rosas de Castilla*.

Today, roses play their part in reinventing for the Spanish missions a benign history of 'benevolent priests baptizing indigenous peoples, establishing agriculturally successful communes, and maintaining an ideal of integrated living'. The reality was somewhat darker, especially for the Native Americans working for the Spanish fathers who some see as having been virtually enslaved; and although roses of every type now fill the colourful gardens of restored missions such as San Juan Capistrano, these functioned in their heyday as frontier outposts where basic subsistence came before beauty. Recording their long years of decline, early photographs show the missions as bare, dusty places with little more than the odd bush or tree to indicate a garden.[4]

The same rose-tinted light bathes the Californian cattle ranches or *ranchos* of the Mexican era, before California joined the Union as its thirty-first state. 'I have often been asked about the Mission and ranch gardens,' wrote Guadalupe Vallejo in 1890, suggesting they were more extensive and of greater variety than most people imagined. A niece of General Vallejo, Alta California's highest-ranking officer, Guadalupe was a famous beauty, born in the Mission San José in the last years of Mexican rule. Believing that 'there never was a more peaceful or happy people on the face of the earth than the Spanish, Mexican, and Indian population of Alta California before the American conquest', she describes in fine detail the mission orchards of her childhood, with their olive trees and gracious avenues, and the gardens of Alta California. These she remembers as 'gay with roses, chiefly a pink and very fragrant sort from Mexico, called by us the Castilian rose, and still seen in a few old gardens. Besides roses, we had pinks, sweet-peas, hollyhocks, nasturtiums which had been brought from Mexico, and white lilies.'

Aiding the romanticization of the rose-embowered *ranchos* and southern California's Mexican-Spanish past was the phenomenally successful novel *Ramona,* by Helen Hunt Jackson, first published in Boston in 1884. Part love story, part social tract, *Ramona* tells the story of an orphan, the child of a white father and an Indian mother, who is raised by a foster mother, Señora Gonzaga Moreno, in ignorance of her true parentage. Falling in love with an Indian herder called Alessandro, the heroine is forced to exchange the picturesque life of the Mexican upper classes for the privations and cruelty experienced by Alessandro's people.

Although Jackson wrote *Ramona* to draw attention to the plight of mission Indians at the hands of the US government, readers fell in love instead with the novel's idealized vision of the recent past and went looking for the settings it described, including Señora Moreno's *rancho* with its low adobe house and wide verandas massed with yellow-flowered musk roses. 'The Señora's passion for musk she had inherited from her mother,' wrote Helen Hunt Jackson. 'It was so strong that she sometimes wondered at it; and one day, as she sat with Father Salvierderra in the veranda, she picked a handful of the blossoms, and giving them to him, said, "I do not know why it is, but it seems to me if I were dead I could be brought to life by the smell of musk."'

One of the old Spanish-Mexican estates to claim itself as the home of Mrs Hunt Jackson's *Ramona* ('the *Uncle Tom's Cabin* of the Indian') was Camulos, 1,400 acres of valley forty-five miles north-west of Los Angeles, on the lower edge of Ventura County. The owners rushed out a booklet for would-be tourists that included a poem to Camulos, which painted it in suitably romantic terms:

> Across the dim placita,
> Where passionate roses blow
> And sober cypress stand their guard,
> The fountain plashes low . . .

Not everyone was convinced, however. The British Library's copy of the promotional booklet contains an undated newspaper cutting from the *Daily Globe* which cast the story in a rather different light. 'RAMONA IN REAL LIFE,' begins its series of headlines. 'Helen Hunt's Heroine

Sells Baskets to Tourists. Allesandro Stole a Horse. She is a Squaw with a Taste for Drink. Beautiful Romance Was Written About Very Ordinary Characters.' According to this more jaundiced view, the woman on whom Hunt Jackson based her novel would show herself only if you bought her photograph or some Indian trinkets. 'She is not pretty at all, as the story reads, but is rather homely, even for a squaw, is lazy, dowdyish in dress, and too much addicted to the drinking of firewater.'

Back east, meanwhile, the rose was also gaining ground in a way that owed much to hard-nosed commercialism and only a little to myth-making. In a charming compendium written in the 1930s, the pioneer old-rose collector Mrs Frederick Love Keays linked the story of America's old roses to the country's wider history: its colonial origins up to 1789; the federal period from 1789 to 1840; and then the 'Great Forty Years' (1840 to 1880), when the United States pushed outwards over the continent and 'masterly rose culture startled an unsuspecting world'.

The federal period was indeed revolutionary, politically and horticulturally. The beginnings of the Union (Delaware was the first state to ratify the Constitution, in 1787) coincided with the explosive introduction of China roses into Europe, which soon found their way across the Atlantic. Chapter 17 tells the story of the French Noisette roses, which originated from a new rose bred in America by Charleston rice farmer John Champneys and which went on to sire a new class of rose named after its subsequent nurserymen-breeders rather than the rice farmer.

It was nonetheless a cause for patriotic celebrations, as the Noisette class would spawn much-vaunted favourites such as the lemon-white 'Lamarque' and the brilliant yellow 'Maréchal Niel', roses that festooned the walls and verandas of southern and Pacific coast homes, 'and along the Riviera millions of their flowers breathe incense, telling to the American traveler, in their mute way, that his country has done something for rose culture of which he may be proud'.

Another early American rose was named 'Harison's Yellow' (*R.* × *harisonii* 'Harison's Yellow') after the man who discovered its vigorous suckers on his land, the wealthy New York lawyer and amateur horticulturist George F. Harison. Marketed by a New York nurseryman, the rose (a hybrid *R. spinosissima*) appeared in nursery catalogues from about

1830 and, according to folklore, moved westwards with the pioneers of the 1840s and 1850s who took the rose with them as a memory of home. 'There was hardly a pioneer mother who didn't include a rooted piccc of "Harison's Yellow" with the treasures she brought for her family's new home out West,' wrote Clair G. Martin, curator of roses at California's Huntington Botanical Gardens. 'Even today, one can almost follow the immigrant trails across the country to Texas, California, and Oregon by simply mapping plantings of "Harison's Yellow".'[5]

Other rose historians agree. Roy E. Shepherd claims that today 'these plants and their progeny are to be found, still thriving, amidst the ruins of many an abandoned homestead, mining camp, and cemetery'. Whether the roses accompanied the pioneers on their trek west or whether enterprising nurserymen sprang up wherever they saw a demand is open to question, however. Pioneer literature invariably stresses the hardships of the trek west, and roses were part of the mythology of arrival rather than the journey itself. 'The journey became more and more rugged; women took to wearing bloomers instead of long dresses and even went barefoot much of the way.' So wrote Jen Carlson in her pioneer history of Drain, Oregon, *Wagon Trains Lead to Roses in December*. Roses in fact appear only in the title, the dedication and the endnote, which talks of Mrs Carlson's success in capturing 'the spirit of this small town nestled in the most beautiful valley between Pass and Elk Creek where the roses still bloom to warm our hearts as they did our early settlers of Oregon when thcir wagon trains stopped to rest'.

But from the early years of the nineteenth century, the thriving centres of the east coast were clamouring for new flowers and plants to adorn houses and gardens, and business was ever ready to meet demand. The dozen or so known wild and imported roses stocked by Thomas Jefferson's supplier, Prince's nursery at Flushing, Long Island, had multiplied to an incredible 1,630 varieties by the time the founder's great grandson William Robert Prince published his *Manual of Roses* in 1846. In a rival catalogue of the same date, Boston seed merchants and nurserymen Hovey & Co. could claim only 773 varieties, still an 'immense collection' which they split into two divisions and many classes. As well as the old-fashioned Gallicas, Damasks, Albas, Centifolias, Sweet

Briars and Moss roses, here were the new Chinese progeny: Hybrid Chinas, Hybrid Bourbons and a whole division of the latest 'perpetual or autumnal roses, blooming June till November', including Hybrid Perpetuals and the tender Chinese or Bengal roses.

Hovey's Boston catalogue rightly boasted of the 'great expense and labor' involved in assembling the collection. 'A visit to Europe, and a personal inspection of the collections of the principal cultivators of Roses in France, has enabled us to procure all the finest new varieties as soon as they are offered for sale,' proclaimed the firm's proprietor. Some were being offered to the American market even before they went on sale in England.

North America's mania for roses produced three books in the mid-1840s devoted solely to their culture. The first to appear was *The Rose Manual* by the Philadelphia nurseryman Robert Buist, beating Prince's manual by some two years. Originally from Scotland, Buist had trained in Edinburgh at the Royal Botanic Garden and, like many other leading figures in American horticulture, had travelled to America to achieve fame and fortune in the first half of the nineteenth century. As a nurseryman he was best known for camellias and roses, two wildly popular classes of plants that featured in his earlier venture into print, *The American Flower Garden Directory,* first published in 1832 and substantially revised a few years later. The number of varieties he quotes is astonishing: nearly 1,000 varieties of *Camellia japonica* alone, and as many as 2,000 cultivated varieties of garden rose.

Buist was especially entranced by the tender hybrid Chinese roses, produced at first by chance crosses 'but latterly, from the regular impregnating process. The superb varieties of this fine division, give a combination of all that is grand and beautiful in roses. Their flowers are of the most elegant forms and richest colours; their foliage of great luxuriance, and their branches flexile and vigorous. They are of first rate importance for covering pillars and trellises: their shoots frequently growing from six to ten feet in one season: these shoots may be thinned out year after year, *but never shortened.*'

Out in the garden, Buist discouraged his readers from planting roses indiscriminately among other shrubs, preferring to place them in small groups of similar colours or arranged according to leaf size and manner

Spring 1896

THE STORRS & HARRISON CO.

Painesville, OHIO

The nursery trade across America capitalized on rose mania. A catalogue cover for 1896 from Ohio nurserymen Storrs & Harrison, which claimed to be the largest combined nursery, florist and seed business in the world.

of growth. Another 'desirable and fanciful method' he proposed was to plant them within mounded 'baskets of roses' edged with 'wire, willow, or any other substitute, in imitation of basket work' – an idea he may have borrowed from English landscapers such as Humphry Repton. The more vigorous Moss or Provins roses could be trained to cover an area of several square yards, he suggested. And for southern gardens, he proposed fences of Noisette and China roses and a profusion of Sweet Briar, noting that a fence 300 feet long 'would cost only about one hundred and twenty dollars'.

Throughout the nineteenth century, America nursery catalogues continued to chart the rose's unstoppable rise as American and European breeders added ever more new and splendid varieties. American names creep into the lists; among the earliest (1843) were two roses bred by Samuel and John Feast in Baltimore using the native Prairie rose, *Rosa setigera,* as a parent: the clustering pale-pink 'Baltimore Belle', and the brighter pink 'Queen of the Prairies'.

As the century progressed, the taste grew for darker, richer colours such as 'Général Jacqueminot' (also known as 'General Jack'), a Hybrid Perpetual with Chinese genes bred by Roussel in France in 1853. A Boston catalogue of 1875 described this rose as 'Brilliant velvety scarlet-crimson; superb, glowing, and effective color, with a rich fragrance, which commands immediate notice'. Then largely grown by the florists of Boston and New York and used for the choicest bouquets and flower baskets, it was fetching as much as $1.00 a stem.

American nurserymen made much of price and profit as an indication of beauty and 'worth'. In another trick adapted from Humphry Repton, the nurseryman D. M. Dewey from Rochester, New York, opened his leather-bound catalogue for 1872 with two contrasting postcard views of the same property. The first showed an 'Unpleasant Home' before its owners began to patronize the nurserymen, while the second showed the same house adorned with ornamental conifers, weeping tree, bordered paths, veranda, Chinese gothic tower, roof finials, creeper, carriages, outbuildings and a distant plantation – 'As it will be A Pleasant Home, after patronizing the tree dealers'. The benefits were commercial and aesthetic, as the catalogue's opening parable made clear. The owner of the splendid new house had (we are told) paid for his improvements out of profits from his orchard, which compensated for occasional lean years in his field crops.

Even if nurseryman Dewey omitted roses from his vision of arboreal bliss, he inserted fine plates of the best roses into his catalogue, including American and French favourites such as 'Baltimore Belle', 'Queen of the Prairies', 'Coquette des Blanches', 'Général Jacqueminot', 'Maréchal Niel' and three old moss roses: 'Glory of Mosses', 'Perpetual Red Moss' and 'Perpetual White Moss'. Only the last is still generally available, usually known as 'Quatre Saisons Blanche Mousseuse'.

In nineteenth-century America, flowers – and especially roses – were seen to have moral worth as well. The very first American book devoted wholly to growing flowers – Roland Green's *A Treatise on the Cultivation of Ornamental Flowers* of 1828 – started from the premise that ornamental gardening is one of the most innocent, healthy and, to some, 'the most pleasing employment in life', its rural scenes 'teaching us to "look through nature up to nature's God"'. Flower gardening was, moreover, particularly appropriate for young ladies ('the fair daughters of America'). 'It teaches neatness, cultivates a correct taste, and furnishes the mind with many pleasing ideas.' As to the rose, 'This favorite flower is worthy of all the care and attention that can be paid to it', said Green, recommending the outstanding collection of Messrs G. Thorburn & Son of Liberty Street, New York, while omitting to point out that Messrs Thorburn were in fact co-publishers of his little tract.

But moralizing with roses could all too easily turn mawkish. A book of 'Christmas roses' intended as a New Year's gift to young people contains an overly sentimental tale of two young children who live with their widowed mother. When the boy falls sick at Christmas time – and no doctor is prepared to attend the dying boy – the girl's tears conjure up a figure in shining robes and a gift of pure-white Christmas roses from the Christ-child. The boy is miraculously cured, and the Christmas flowers planted in the garden attract buyers offering a high price, thereby restoring the family to health, happiness and a measure of prosperity. Whether the buyers would enjoy such good fortune is debatable, however, for as the fable notes at the end, 'the healing virtues and restoring power were imparted to the Christmas

GENERAL JACQUIMINOT.

D. M. DEWEY'S SERIES
COLORED FROM NATURE

AMERICAN
FRUITS AND FLOWERS

The much admired Hybrid Perpetual 'Général Jacqueminot' from The Specimen Book of
Fruits, Flowers, and Ornamental Trees Carefully Drawn and Colored from Nature for the Use
of Nurserymen, *published in 1872 by D. M. Dewey, nurseryman from Rochester, New York.*

roses only when conveyed by a heavenly visitant to the homes of peace and good will'.

Roses also played a part in philanthropic moves to brighten the lives of the urban poor. *Bootblack with Rose* of 1878, by the British-born American realist painter John George Brown, is almost unique among nineteenth-century American paintings in putting a rose in a male hand, that of a poor working lad on the streets of New York who looks fondly at his rose while waiting for custom. He may have got his rose from the Ladies Flower and Fruit Mission, founded in the early 1870s to distribute donated flowers to the poor and sick in the city's tenements and hospitals. The great Danish-born photographer and social crusader Jacob Riis would also later form an organization to distribute flowers to the poor. Writing to the editor of the *New York Times* in 1888, he suggested that well-to-do commuters should gather flowers from their gardens and take them into the city, where the 'pleasure of giving the flowers to the urchins who will dog their steps in the street crying with hungry voices and hungrier hearts for a "posy" will more than pay for the trouble'.[6] The rose gardens at New York's two botanic gardens resulted from the same philanthropic impulse: Brooklyn Botanic's Cranford Rose Garden courtesy of Mr and Mrs Walter V. Cranford (Cranford's engineering firm built much of Brooklyn's subway system), and the Peggy Rockefeller Rose Garden at the New York Botanical Garden.

By 1900 the rose reigned supreme among flowers and among all classes of American society. Its secret lay in its variability. Exquisite cut blooms were bought only by the wealthy, of course, but the rose in its many guises was also the flower of choice for the humblest homesteader. Its easy rooting and promiscuous habits made it the most democratic of flowers (overgrown cemeteries are now a favourite source for old rose collectors). Even the urban poor were not excluded. And if patriotic gardeners spurned too much European refinement, American hybridizers were using native stock to breed roses suited to the American climate (see Chapter 17).

Sometimes a simple name change was all it took to turn an immigrant rose into an all-American native, as happened in the case of the plainly French rose 'Madame Ferdinand Jamin', a Hybrid Perpetual rose of startling carmine colour but finicky tastes bred in the 1870s by Lédéchaux.

After it had crossed the Atlantic and changed its name to 'American Beauty' in a masterly marketing ploy by the Washington nursery Field Brothers, it became synonymous with the youthful beauty of American womanhood. Wholesale prices rocketed to $3.75 for a single cut stem (a price that reflected its contrariness); it soon became the official flower of the District of Columbia, and 'Americans forgave it all its faults'. Now rarely seen in retail catalogues, it gave its name to Sam Mendes's film *American Beauty* (1999), although the British director actually used a different rose in the film, preferring the richly saturated red of classic valentine roses whose careful illumination underscores the film's mythic qualities. When the middle-aged hero in the throes of a mid-life crisis fantasizes about his school-age daughter's friend, she is naked, surrounded by deep red rose petals, while the roses that surround his suburban home mask the hollow reality at its core.

A cigarette card c.1895–1900, linking the 'American Beauty' rose to timidity in a series on floral beauties and the language of flowers.

In his manipulation of reality, Mendes was simply drawing on America's long tradition of using roses to create a myth and a mood that could be projected into the future as well as the past. California, for instance, had used roses to great effect in its efforts to lure new settlers across the deserts and the Rockies to America's paradisiacal West Coast, where skies are forever blue and roses always in bloom.

On New Year's Day, 1890, Pasadena's Valley Hunt Club organized its first winter procession of flower-laden horses and carriages that would become the Tournament of Roses Parade. Its message to the frozen Midwest was plain: why endure the discomforts of winter when here in California roses bloom even in January? Called the 'Dead of Winter' festival the following year, it had to be hurriedly renamed the 'Orange' Tournament in 1892 after a severe frost damaged the roses, but the very next year the parade was back to roses and so the tradition has remained, expanded over the years into a full-scale downtown parade celebrating civic pride.

The young literary radical Hamlin Garland, originally from West Salem Wisconsin, describes the euphoria of his first visit to the Pacific Coast, where he had been invited to lecture for an anti-poverty society, taking his elderly parents to visit their Californian relatives. After travelling through barren desert and mountains, his brain 'drunken full of desolation', they had suddenly burst out 'among green orange and lemon trees and little cottages in mute little green gardens. The air was very warm . . . We moved out upon the walk like people in a dream.'

Present at the fourth Tournament of Roses parade of 1893, Garland perfectly captures its flamboyant pageantry of prancing horses, Mexican horsemen in broad hats and Spanish señoritas in swirling dresses, accompanied by a constant medley of martial music. 'The sun shone but the shadows were cold,' he wrote in his dog-eared notebook. 'The field swarmed with carriages decked with winter roses and evergreens – Great Lilies, burning Carnations, and nasturtiums.' Though Garland could admire Pasadena's wealth and luxury only grudgingly, you sense his seduction by this modern Promised Land of perpetual roses.

Before he was elected President, Ronald Reagan was Governor of California, which perhaps explains his attachment to the rose and the mythologizing that surrounds it. He would also have appreciated the presidential associations of the White House Rose Garden, where he fittingly stood to declare the rose his country's National Floral Emblem.

The White House has had a rose garden on its current site since 1913, when Edith Roosevelt's colonial garden of boxwood parterres filled with roses and old-fashioned flowers gave way to the more architectural style preferred by Woodrow Wilson's first wife Ellen, who called on designers Beatrix Farrand and George Burnap to help with the redesign. Farrand was largely responsible for the East Garden, and Burnap for the Rose Garden to the west, which borders the Oval Office and the West Wing and was known at first as 'The President's Rose Walk'.[7] A painter in her own right, Ellen Axson Wilson used the treillage behind a statue of Pan to hang her canvases during White House garden parties, and she was particularly fond of the Rose Garden, which had for her a 'suggestion of Italy', with its 'roses in profusion, and masses of small multicolored flowers bordering the paths'.

With their customary flair, the Kennedys had the garden redesigned in 1961, bringing in their old friend Rachel Lambert Mellon, the horticulturist, art collector and wealthy second wife of the equally wealthy philanthropist Paul Mellon, to create a more open space for outdoor ceremonies, and an oblong lawn bordered by flowerbeds that were intended to contain a concentration of American plants. Edged with low hedges of boxwood and divided into diamond-shaped compartments with thyme, the long beds feature a series of 'Katherine' crab apples and small-leafed limes, and a saucer magnolia (*Magnolia* × *soulangeana*) placed at the garden's four corners. Spring bulbs give way to roses and other flowers, which provide an ever-changing backdrop to the garden's ceremonial occasions. Directly adjoining the Oval Office, the garden also has more informal uses. When I visited in late June 2008 in the last months of President George W. Bush's administration, a couple of footballs on the lawn awaited the presidential couple's Scottish terriers, Barney and Miss Beazley.

As I had been warned, there are not many roses in the White House Rose Garden and in Washington's humid heat, the ones in flower (including the low-growing cluster-flowered R. 'Laura Bush' in various shades of orange) were struggling a little. While some roses remain in the garden for several years, the First Lady makes her selection each year from seasonal planting plans submitted to her, and makes suggestions of her own. Nancy Reagan loved red. Laura Bush favoured Floribundas and Hybrid Teas in big splashes of colour. Michelle Obama put vegetables before flowers, creating a new kitchen garden on the White House's south lawn and planting no new roses in the first year of her husband's administration.

Although I was assured that planting is in no way partisan, the roses tell a different story. Of the garden's ten rose varieties evident at the time of my visit, five celebrated Republican presidents or their wives: 'Pat

Nixon', 'Barbara Bush', 'Ronald Reagan', 'Nancy Reagan' and 'Laura Bush', mostly Hybrid Teas in colours ranging from burgundy red through red, orange and apricot, to pale pink. Of the remaining five roses, the oldest (but still classed as a new rose) was the apricot-yellow Hybrid Musk 'Francesca', bred in the UK by the Rev. Joseph Pemberton. Two were white roses: the hugely successful 'Iceberg', a Floribunda rose bred by Kordes of Germany; and a lemon-scented Hybrid Tea, 'Pope John Paul II'. The final two added more splashes of colour: another red Hybrid Tea, 'Opening Night', bred by Jackson & Perkins's Canadian-born Keith Zary; and Kordes's 'Crimson Bouquet'.

The Kennedys had favoured old varieties such as Moss roses, Bourbons and Hybrid Perpetuals, as well as later Rugosas, Shrub roses and Hybrid Musks. Among the many roses planted at one time or another since the (Democratic) Johnson administration and no longer found in Laura Bush's planting scheme were the ever-popular 'Mister Lincoln', 'American Beauty', 'First Lady Nancy', and the blowsy 'Dolly Parton, which blooms in flushes through the season. But gone, too, were any roses named after Democrats, including 'Lady Bird Johnson', 'John F. Kennedy', and 'Rosalyn Carter'. What presidents or their spouses choose to plant is clearly a matter of personal taste, but with roses it seems the personal shades into the political.

And the story of America's roses mirrors that of its immigrant peoples flocking over from Europe and all points further east, attracted by this brave new land where even the flowers promise to be bigger, brighter and more commercially successful. North America's roses show us, too, how truly cosmopolitan this flower can be; whether its bloodlines originate in China, Asia, the desert oases of the Middle East, Europe or America, we claim it as our own.

The Useful Rose

Chapter Fourteen
A Cure for Divers Ills

In September 2008, a world congress on osteoarthritis heard enthusiastic reports of a breakthrough in medical research that would bring relief to sufferers of this painful condition, which is caused by abnormal wearing of the cartilage that cushions the joints and a decrease in lubrication. According to researchers from the Frederiksberg Hospital at the University of Copenhagen in Denmark, relief would come in the form of a patented rose-hip powder containing the active ingredient GOPO(R) (glycoside of mono and diglycerol). In clinical studies, patients taking the powder were able to reduce their reliance on potentially dangerous painkillers, and they reported better moods, energy levels and sleep. The powder was not simply effective in reducing inflammation, said the researchers, but also appeared able to protect cartilage cells from inflammatory assault and self-destruction.[1]

In the West, the notion that roses might soothe or cure human ills dates back to the ancient Greeks at least and the pharmacology of Pedanius Dioscorides, who is honoured as the father of medical botany, just as his earlier compatriot Theophrastus is revered as the father of botany. Written in the first century AD – and probably shortly before Pliny's death in AD 79 – Dioscorides' five-part treatise *De Materia Medica* is celebrated as the most influential treatise on herbs ever written.

Born in Anazarbus (Anavarza) in what is now Turkey, close to the centre for pharmacological study at Tarsus, Dioscorides acquired his knowledge of medicines while travelling around the Roman Empire, leading, in his own words, 'a soldier's life'. This implies that he was a soldier's physician, but he writes as much about women's ailments as manly wounds and may simply have toured the Eastern Empire as an itinerant physician. Dioscorides was interested first and foremost in the raw stuff of medicine, plants especially (he also wrote about minerals and animals), their range of uses, and how to use them to best effect. Know your plants was Dioscorides' message to his fellow healers, because 'the man who will observe his herbs oftentimes and in divers places, will acquire the greatest knowledge of them'.

With its varied uses, the rose was for Dioscorides an essential ingredient in the physician's store of remedies, as it would remain for many centuries. He writes in *De Materia Medica* of two sorts of rose: the cultivated rose, which he named in Greek *rhodon,* and the common dog rose (*cynobastus* or *oxyacantha*), which he described as 'a shrub much bigger than a common bush – almost the size of a tree. It bears leaves a great deal broader than myrtle, and has strong hairs around the sprigs, white flowers, and somewhat long fruit like the kernel of the olive. When this is ripe it grows red and the stuff within is downy.' This common rose had relatively few uses in Greek medicine, although the dried fruit (minus its 'downy stuff') could be taken as a drink in hot wine to stop discharges from the intestines.

The cultivated rose by contrast was good for sore eyes, ears and gums, aches and pains of various descriptions, sundry inflammations, wounds, diarrhoea, spitting blood – and cosmetics. Each remedy required a different preparation, as his text below shows, and he provided equally precise instructions on how roses should be gathered and stored.

Rhodon [roses] cool and are astringent, and dried roses are more astringent. The juice must be pressed out of them whilst they are still young, first cutting off that which is called the nail (which is the white that is in the petal), and the rest must be pounded and pounded in the shade in a mortar until it becomes thick, and then put in jars for eye salves or suppositories. The leaves are also dried in the shade. They must be turned over now and then least otherwise they putrefy or grow mouldy. Dried roses (boiled in wine and strained) are good for headaches, as well as the eyes, ears and gums, and pain of the perineum, intestine, rectum and vulva, applied with a feather or washed with the liquid. The same (without straining) bruised, boiled and applied, are good for inflammation of the area below the ribs, moistness of the stomach and *erysipela* [streptococcal skin infection]. Roses (dried and pounded into small pieces) are sprinkled on the thighs. Thcy arc put in compositions called *antheræ* [medicines extracted from flowers] and in wound antidotes. They are burnt for medicines to make the eyelids look pleasing. The part of the flower that is found in the middle of the roses (dried and sprinkled on) is good for gum discharges. The heads [hips] (taken in a drink) stop loose intestines and blood-spitting.

In his *De Materia Medica,* Dioscorides explains how to make rose oil, rose pomanders, and rose wine. Making rose oil was both messy and time-consuming. First you must take 5lb 8oz of bruised, boiled and strained *Juncus odoratus* (a kind of rush), adding it to 20lb 5oz of oil. Then you must add to the oil 'a thousand counted dry rose petals', rubbing your hands with honey and stirring the mixture up and down while gently squeezing the petals. After leaving the mixture overnight, you should make the first pressing. The strained roses were then to be thrown into a small washing jar, mixed with thickened oil, and strained again as the second pressing, and so on for a third and fourth time, on each occasion rubbing the inside of the jars with honey. You could also add the same number of new dried rose petals to the oil. 'The oil can take this addition of roses seven times, but by no means any further.'

Once made, rose oil was able to cool a heated stomach, loosen the bowels (when taken as a drink) and much else besides. 'It fills up hollow boils, and makes soothing medications for malignancies. It is a rub for penetrative ulcers, catarrh in the head, and heated eruptions; and a lotion for headache as well as a mouth rinse for the start of toothache. It is good rubbed on for eyelids that have grown hard, and it is good given as a suppository for *rosiones* [gnawing corrosion] or irritations of the intestines and the vulva.'

Dioscorides's charming recipe for deodorant rose pomanders required exotic ingredients such as myrrh and nard (*Nardostachys jatamansi* from the foothills of the Himalayas, often known as Indian spikenard) and could, he said, be worn around women's necks in place of necklaces. Rose wine required a pound of dried, pounded roses to be bound in a linen cloth and seeped for three months in eight pints of grape pulp. After that it should be strained and stored in clean jars. Taken as a drink after meat, it could aid digestion and stomach disorders as well as

*A healing red rose from the Byzantine Juliana Codex, also known as the
Vienna Dioscorides, an exquisitely illuminated early sixth-century copy of* De Materia
Medica *by Greek pharmacologist Pedanius Dioscorides (c.40–90* AD*).*

diarrhoea and dysentery, and mixed with honey it was good for sore throats.

For all his careful instructions on how roses should be prepared and used, Dioscorides has little to say on how they achieved their effects, beyond his simple statement that roses are cooling and astringent, and that dried roses are more astringent than fresh ones. Although he did not entirely agree with all its details, he is here reflecting the ancient theory of humours set out by Aristotle and Hippocrates, and further elaborated (after his time) by another Greek physician, Galen, whose medical theories held western medicine in a virtual stranglehold for a millennium and half.[2]

In the ancients' view of man and matter, the body was tied in to the workings of the universe through a quadrilateral scheme in which everything is ultimately linked: the four elements (air, fire, earth, water); the four elementary qualities (hot, dry, cold, wet); the four humours of the body (blood, yellow bile, black bile, phlegm); the four seasons (spring, summer, autumn, winter); and the four ages of man (childhood, youth, adulthood, old age). Each element, they believed, resulted from the action of elementary qualities, one active and one passive. Representing these elements in the body were the four humours, which also dictated an individual's temperament (sanguine, choleric, melancholic and phlegmatic): blood was hot and wet like air; yellow bile hot and dry like fire; black bile cold and dry like earth; and phlegm cold and wet like water.

Illness arose from an imbalance of humours; and since all foods were also composed of the four elements, diet played an important role in maintaining health, as did medicinal herbs or 'simples', on the allopathic principle of curing by opposites. Patients suffering from melancholia, for instance (which indicated a temperament that was cold and dry), were advised to eat foods that were hot and wet; while a hot dry cough could be cured by a cold, moist remedy. Galen took this further by specifying different degrees of intensity from one to four, with one being the most gentle.

For Galen, the rose was 'of a waterish hot substance, joined with two other qualities: that is to wit, binding and bitter. The flower is more binding than the roses' selves be, and therefore it drieth more.' Galen's judgement is here transmitted through the mid-sixteenth century herbal of William Turner, the Northumbrian divine and Dean of Wells in Somerset; it should be remembered that as roses are hot and wet, their effect is cooling and astringent.

Much medical knowledge was lost when the Roman Empire collapsed and Alexandria's great library – the ancient world's greatest storehouse of knowledge – subsequently foundered. No trace remains of Aristotle's writings on botany, for instance; other ancient texts were saved in the Eastern Roman Empire, copied by Byzantine scholars, and later in the Arab world, where they were translated into Arabic and profoundly influenced developing Arab medicine before returning to Europe through the translations of men such as Constantine the African.

The route taken by Dioscorides' *De Materia Medica* perfectly illustrates the interrelatedness of the great empires of the West and the Middle East, and reinforces the pre-eminence of the rose in matters of healing. The oldest (but incomplete) copy known to have survived is the exquisitely illustrated Juliana Codex, made in the early sixth century for a Byzantine princess, Juliana Anicia, daughter of Emperor Olybrius and a great patron of the arts. Its illustrated red rose looks much like a cultivated Gallica, perhaps even a forerunner of the Apothecary's rose (*Rosa gallica* var. *officinalis*): semi-double, it has prickly stems and the characteristic centre of pronounced golden stamens.

After passing through many hands, the Juliana Codex was revealed to the West in 1562 by Ogier Ghiselin de Busbecq, the Holy Roman Emperor's ambassador to the Sublime Porte, who wanted to buy it for the Emperor despite its worm-eaten state, but was frightened by its price of 100 ducats. 'It belongs to a Jew,' he wrote in his *Turkish Letters,* 'the son of Hamon, who, while he was still alive, was physician to Soleiman [Suleiman the Magnificent] . . . I shall not cease to urge the Emperor to ransom so noble an author from such slavery.' The Emperor gratifyingly took heed and the work (known as the Vienna Dioscorides) is now one of the treasures of the Austrian National Library in Vienna.

Other copies survived through translations into Latin, and later (from the Greek original) into Arabic. As early as the eighth century, the Ummayad Caliphs at Damascus had commissioned translations of Greek medical works from Nestorian Christian physicians, and they took this

Gathering red and white roses in Tacuinum Sanitatis, *a medieval handbook of wellness written in Latin and based on an eleventh-century Arab treatise by the Christian physician Ibn Butlan of Baghdad.*

interest to Muslim Spain when they were ousted from Damascus in 750 AD. But the 'translation movement' really gathered pace under their successors, the Abbasid caliphs at Baghdad who oversaw a tremendous expansion in the scientific knowledge of the Arab world.

The first Arabic translation of Dioscorides was undertaken during the reign of the tenth Abbasid caliph, al-Mutawakkil (847–61), the inadequacies in its plant names revised first by an Arab Christian and son of a pharmacist (Hunayn), and later in 1083 by another scholar (al-Husayn b. Ibrahim al-Natili). Al-Natili not only reworked the text but claimed authorship of all the illustrations, including the fine healing rose, *al-ward*. While similar in some respects to Juliana's, the Arab rose is more stylized, bearing single oval leaves rather than leaflets, and its many-petalled flowers are both red and white.

Two of the main figures of Islamic medicine introduced the rose into their works: the Assyrian Yuhanna Ibn Masawayh (known to the West as Mesuë), and the Persian philosopher-physician Ibn Sînâ (Avicenna), who sought to improve on Greek theories by studying the concrete, and who produced both a *Book of Healing* and his encyclopedic *Canon of Medicine*. Both authors agreed with the Greek view of the rose's healing virtues, here put forward by Mesuë as 'translated' by England's William Turner:

The rose is cold in the first degree and dry in the second, and is compounded and made of two divers and separable substances: of a watery, which is measurable; and of an earthly binding, giving unto it much matter; but of an airish sweet and spicy; and fiery and fine, of which cometh the bitterness, the redness, the perfection, and the form or beauty.

The rose in Islamic medicine performed many functions, as it had done for the Greeks. Considered to quieten the yellow bile, it was used internally for stomach disorders and tuberculosis, and externally in soothing ointments. The Arabs' early mastery of distillation (see Chapter 16) made rosewater a vital ingredient in their pharmacology, usually blended with other medicinal herbs and spices such as aloes, saffron, musk, camphor and clovers. Distilled rosewater was used to treat migraine, nausea and anxiety, and especially in eyewashes.

The rose also played a more general role in the 'Prophetic medicine', based largely on the recommendations of the Prophet Muhammad, which sought to preserve and restore the health of body and soul. Patients were to be given foods they liked and never forced to eat; drinks should be simple and of a moderate temperature, 'such as drinks made of waterlily and apple and moist rose'. An equally important principle of treatment was that patients should receive medicines and foods to which they were accustomed, so that the people of desert lands and the tillers of soil 'would gain no benefit from draughts of water-lily (*nilufar*) or dried rose, nor smilax (*mughla*), and it would have no effect whatever on their constitutions'.

While medicine flourished in the Islamic cultures of the Middle East and Spain, rudimentary medical knowledge in Europe's dark ages was kept alive largely through the monasteries, which developed infirmary gardens of healing plants – among them roses, as we know from the plans for the idealized monastery of St Gall in Switzerland, and the little garden planted lovingly tended by Walahfrid the squint-eyed, who planted roses for their symbolic value and for their precious oil, a 'cure for mankind's ailments' (see Chapter 5).

The rose that became known as the Apothecary's rose – and was probably even then the rose most used for healing in much of Europe – is a cultivated form of the red Gallica, *Rosa gallica* var. *officinalis* (the '*officinalis*' tag denotes a plant considered to have medicinal properties), also known as the 'Rose de Provins' (see Chapter 4). No one can say when it first found its way into the sickroom. Low-growing yet bushy, it bears large, semi-double flowers and is highly scented.

Just such a medicinal rose survives in another early manuscript herbal: the magnificent *Tractatus de herbis*, probably produced in Naples or Salerno towards the end of the thirteenth century, and certainly before 1317. The vibrant scarlet of its petals leaps off the page, even if the plant itself stays a little flat, as if drawn from a pressed specimen laid out on the artist's table. This rose, too, is semi-double, having more than the five petals of the single wild variety. Its leaves are composed of five rounded leaflets, and the stems bristle with slender prickles. At the heart of the flower are the Gallica's characteristic golden

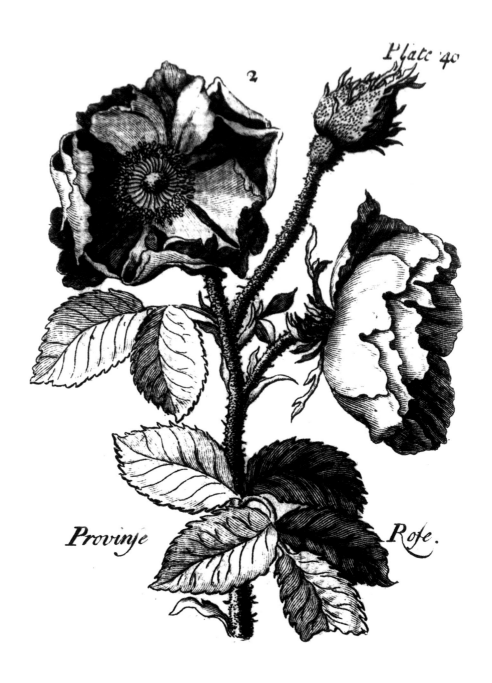

Plate 40

2

Provinſe

Roſe.

The Apothecary's rose Rosa gallica *var.* officinalis, *also called the Provins rose after the French town where it reputedly grew best, from an English translation of Pierre Pomet's* A Compleat History of Druggs, *1712.*

stamens, separately illustrated to show how conspicuous they are.

Damask roses were also used in European medicine but almost certainly from a later date than the native Gallica, as the Damask rose came from further east and travelled westwards only slowly. The earliest record of the Damask rose in Britain dates back to 1306, when it appears in an urgent wish-list of remedies dispatched to London with the King's apothecary to treat Edward I, then travelling northwards through his kingdom. The King was suffering from a disorder of the legs and had reached some four miles north-west of Hexham, where he halted before proceeding to Lancercost. Although his condition stabilized for a time, he would die the following year at Burgh-by-Sands near Carlisle, after suffering an attack of dysentery.

'Aqua rosata de Damasc' (Damask rosewater) was among the costly items requested from London, along with medicaments made from pearls, jacinth and coral; the oils of wheat, ash and bay; and pomegranate wine. Pomegranate rind boiled in wine was used in cases of dysentery, but the fruits were very expensive, at 60 shillings for six pomegranates, besides the cost of bringing them from London. The physician required 40 lb of rosewater at a cost of £4. Such a high price suggests that it was imported, probably from Arab lands, as rosewater was one of the 'minute spices' of oriental or African origin traded in small quantities at high prices in medieval Mediterranean markets. As rosewater had so many uses, it is impossible to say whether the royal physician used it to make up compound medicines, or to bathe his sovereign's legs.[3]

Unspecified sorts of roses feature, too, in the first printed medical book by an Englishman (although not the first written): the *Rosa Medicinae* or *Rosa Anglica* by John of Gaddesden, court physician to Edward II and one of the physicians mentioned by Chaucer's Doctor of Physick in *The Canterbury Tales.* Explaining why he named his book after the rose, he said that just as the rose had five petals, so his book had five parts, covering fevers, injuries, hygiene, diet and drugs – much of it, naturally, borrowed from Dioscorides and other ancients. 'And as the rose overtops all flowers, so this book overtops all treatises on the practice of medicine.'

John of Gaddesden's best-known cure (used – apparently successfully – on Edward II's son) was the red-light treatment for smallpox, which involved wrapping the patient in a red cloth and allowing only red objects around the bed. Roses played a less spectacular but nonetheless welcome role in curing medieval ills. He judged them to be particularly useful for travellers, urging them in warm weather to take frequent nibbles of 'sugar of roses, or violets, or waterlilies', or a number of other conserves and candies. Or they could make a drink from 'sugar and vinegar or from pomegranate wine, or syrup of roses or violets or water-lily'. Wayfarers should take with them camphor, roses or violets, to smell when the air was hot or foul-smelling; and if they had an aversion to hot baths, they could gently bathe their extremities in a decoction of roses, violets and camomile.

Rosewater also appeared in a remedy for weak sight, as it would for the next four centuries and more, although the mixture John of Gaddesden proposed called for a fairly strong stomach. In addition to rosewater, it contained tutty (a crude oxide of zinc) quenched fifteen times in the urine of a virgin youth, balsam, white wine, marjoram, fennel, spikenard, pepper, aloe-wood, all mixed in with the gall of a crow, a swallow or a hen, and then rubbed with honey. Taken partly as food and partly as an eyewash, it would allow the patient 'to see small letters to the end of his life'.

John of Gaddesden wrote *Rosa Anglica* for surgeons and physicians, rich and poor alike, 'so that there shall be no need for them to be always running to consult other books, for here they will find plenty about all curable disease both from the special and the general point of view'. The trend in medicine was towards greater specialization, however, and as medicine became more organized throughout Europe, its pecking order became more pronounced, with physicians at the top, followed by the barber-surgeons, then the apothecaries, and right at the bottom the 'silly Hearb-women' who collected herbs from the fields and hedgerows. As most people could not afford the services of a physician, they turned instead for help to a virtual army of empirics, mountebanks, herbalists, astrologers and uroscopists, and to the healing remedies passed down from generation to generation. Roses were the stock-in-trade of virtually everybody, from the loftiest physician to the most blatant quack.

Aiding the spread of plant knowledge at a professional level were the great herbals which appeared across Europe throughout the sixteenth and seventeenth centuries, conceived as handmaidens to healing and inspired by a new curiosity about plants. Still in thrall to the theories of Dioscorides and his Muslim 'improvers', the herbalists and protobotanists brought the benefits of close observation to their plant descriptions. In Germany, their number included Otto Brunfels, recognized by Linnaeus as one of the 'Fathers of Botany'; Jerome Bock, who described his plants in the plain, racy German of the people; and the Bavarian Leonhart Fuchs, whose *De Historia Stirpium* of 1542 was written in a 'singularly pure and fine Latin'. In the Low Countries, Rembert Dodoens published his *Cruijde boeck* in 1554, which was swiftly followed by Clusius's translation into French, and later by Henry Lyte's translation from French into English. Other notable botanists across the continent included Matthias de L'Obel (the Low Countries); Pietro Andrea Mattioli (Italy); Nicolás Monardes (Spain); and in Switzerland, Konrad Gesner and the brothers Jean and Gaspard Bauhin. As well as relying on ancient authorities, each botanist exchanged ideas and information with the others, so that it is sometimes hard to disentangle their separate contributions, and their works were often illustrated with the same printers' blocks.

The rose appeared in all these early herbals and there is little to distinguish their descriptions, apart from the growing number of varieties covered. An early botanist such as Fuchs restricted himself to just two sorts of roses – the wild and the cultivated. 'The rose is known to everyone,' he began. 'It sends out shoots marked with dusky spots, and full of thorns; the leaves are divided, dark and rough.' Clusius's French translation of Dodoens, which appeared fifteen years later, borrowed Fuchs's woodcut (but reversed) and described five different cultivated sorts (white, red, Province, dark red Provins, and a single pink rose smelling of cinnamon); the Musk rose; and the wild rose. All the authors then commonly borrowed from Dioscorides and other Greek, Roman or Arab authorities in describing the rose's healing properties.

London printer Richard Banckes was the first to bring out a herbal in Britain written in English. Probably derived from an untraced medieval manuscript, it contained no illustrations and needed to explain to readers on the title page that the alphabetical listing of plants was a 'newe mater / the whiche sheweth and treateth of ye vertues & proprytes of

Many early herbals 'borrowed' woodcuts from Leonhart Fuchs's De Historia
Stirpium *of 1542. Its back page shows artist Albert Meyer drawing a plant held by
Heinrich Fullmaurer, who transferred the drawings to woodblocks.*

herbes / the whiche is called an herball'. His little book gave roses a
substantial entry of three pages: 'This is the reed Rose,' it began. 'It is
colde in the fyrst degre & dry in the seconde degre. Dry roses & grene
[fresh] roses be used in medycynes / and of grene roses be made many
confecyons', which he then proceeded to describe.

Banckes clearly found a market, because just the following year, in
1526, a rival brought out *The Grete Herball*, translated from the French
and charmingly illustrated on the title page with a man tending his vines

and his good wife gathering roses in her apron. Much like Banckes's herbal, this one offered perfect knowledge and understanding of herbs and their gracious virtues, 'which god hath ordeyned for our prosperous welfare and helth'. A work of healing rather than botany, it gave general directions on collecting roses for medicine ('They that have a pale / wane / whytysshe or blacke colour ought not to be put in medycyne, whan they be so gathred thei ought to be somwhat dryed in the sonne / and may be kept thre yeres'), and then described separate rose cures for different ailments: to cleanse the stomach, for the bloody flux, several remedies for flux of the womb, and for overheated livers, head pains, sore gums, faint hearts, vomiting, swooning, and for the eyes. *The Grete Herball* also gave garbled instructions on making rosewater, admitting that the process could be described only if you had witnessed it (which the author presumably had not).

The English had to wait for William Turner to read an original herbal written in English that combined a genuine understanding of plants with scientific knowledge. Born in Morpeth, Northumberland, and educated at Cambridge, Turner vigorously pursued his interests in medicine, plants, natural history and divinity, demonstrating how a love of plants and pugnacious nonconformity in religion often went hand in hand. Imprisoned for preaching without a licence and twice forced to seek exile in continental Europe for his religious views (under Henry VIII and again under Catholic Queen Mary), he travelled through Holland, Germany, Italy and Switzerland studying botany and medicine, collecting plants, making friends with other plant-lovers, writing religious books later banned for heresy in England, and embarking on the herbal that would eventually earn him the title of 'Father of English Botany'. Returning to England on the accession of Elizabeth I, he was restored to his post as Dean of Wells but remained defiant to the end, condemning the bishops as 'white coats' and 'tippet gentlemen'.

Turner's greatness as a botanist lay in his powers of observation and his delight in identification. Writing in English was just as important to him, as he wanted passionately to share his knowledge of plants, making it available to all. He also had little faith in the so-called learning of his fellow professionals. How many English surgeons and apothecaries could read Pliny in Latin or Dioscorides and Galen in either Greek or

Latin, he asked? And how many lives were put at risk because they could not tell the herb-gatherers precisely which herbs they wanted? 'Were it better, that many men shuld be killed, or the herball shuld be set out in Englysh?'

Unlike many of his contemporaries, Turner was not a natural rose fanatic. He omitted the flower altogether from his very first listing of herbs, written in Latin; added it to his slightly extended version giving the names of herbs in Greek, Latin, English, Dutch and French; and included only the Eglantine rose or Sweet Briar in the first volume of his herbal, published in 1551. Here, he passed on Pliny the Elder's comment that the Eglantine's root was good against the biting of a mad dog, and that powdered rose gall was a remedy for hair loss caused by red scall. 'Eglentine seemeth to have been first called in Greke Kynorhodos because: the roote heled them that were bytten of a mad dog,' he explained.

The medicinal rose made a much fuller entry in Turner's second volume to his *Herball*, published a decade or so later. Much is already familiar, as Turner repeated the properties of the rose as seen by Dioscorides, Galen and Mesuë; he even used the same reversed woodcut from Leonhart Fuchs showing a five-petalled rose. But look closely and you will see how complicated curing with simples could be. First and most obviously, the number of available roses had grown, from Dioscorides' one (cultivated) variety to Mesuë's two (the red and the white), and now 'there are found divers other kindes as Damaske roses / incarnation roses / muske roses / with certayn other kindes / whereof is no mention in any olde writer'. Different roses displayed different virtues, as did different parts of the plant, and all the various concoctions.

As Turner carefully explained, rose juice was hot because it had separated from the cold, earthy body, and could therefore purge and scour. Best taken from fully open flowers, the juice of roses cleared 'yellow choler of gall' from veins and arteries; scoured the heart and the liver; strengthened the heart and stomach; healed the trembling heart; and was good in cases of jaundice and choleric agues. But roses were a 'gentle medicine', needing 'helpers' such as whey, honey and spikenard to purge effectively.

Dried roses, on the other hand, were colder and more binding,

The husbandman tends his vines while his wife gathers roses in her apron.
Woodcut from the title page of The Grete Herball *of 1526, which was largely based on*
Le Grand Herbier, *a French translation of an original Latin work.*

especially flowers only just opening, and white rather than red roses.
(White roses could not purge, according to Turner, and some herbalists
avoided them altogether.) The yellow anthers at the heart of a rose were
considered especially binding, while the best roses for medicine were
those with fewer petals and plainer flowers.

Rose oil and distilled rosewater cured much the same ills: binding
loose substances, reducing hot aches and burning, strengthening the
throat and the uvula, reducing drunkenness, and making men sleep.
Vinegar of roses likewise reduced all kinds of inflammations and
burnings, bringing comfort and strength to the sick.

Syrups made from rose juice or whole roses were gentle purgatives, while rose sugars scoured less and strengthened more. Distilled rosewater strengthened but did not purge, because 'roses, specially being fresh, can abide no seething, for their purging and scouring virtue is driven away by the fire; the juice of roses, by measurable seething, is made more finer and scoureth more mightily'.

Given the state of Tudor stomachs, Turner's patients would often have received rose remedies from his hand, including the Duke of Somerset, who hired him as his chaplain and physician during the reign of Edward VI. But Turner's faith in the rose's healing qualities positively pales beside that of his near contemporary William Langham, who described himself as a 'Practicioner in Phisicke' in his alphabetically arranged and helpfully indexed directory to Elizabethan herbal remedies, *The Garden of Health.* To Langham's eyes, the rose was an extraordinary cure-all, good for general aches, backache, belly griefs, bladder griefs, cleansing the blood, bloody flux, weak brains, sore breasts, bruises, chaps, colic, digestion, ear griefs, eye griefs, facial deformities, fainting, hot fevers, fluxes, frenzy, fundament griefs, gum griefs, gout, heart disease, headache, falling hair, holy fire, hot griefs, jaundice inflammation, the King's evil, liver griefs, womb trouble, melancholy, mouth cankers, nose bleeds, piles, private parts, kidneys, St Anthony's fire, general sickness, shingles, skin deformities, sleeplessness, spitting blood, stomach griefs, kidney stones, strangury, swellings, swoonings, toothache, thirst, vomiting, tongue ulcers, stopped urine, white discharges, windiness, worms and wounds.

Each ailment has its own rose remedy; most give a sense of soothing gentleness. 'Roses doe comfort the heart, & rejoyce the blood,' he tells us. 'The Rosed Hony doth both comfort & expell melancholy & flegmatike matter, and taken with water wherein Fennell seedes have bene sodden, and a little salt put thereto, doth purge the better . . . For madnesse and heate of the head, stampe Housleeke and Roses with womans milke, and apply it to the forehead & temples.' These remedies may not have cured mankind's manifold ills, but they surely cannot have done much harm.

By the time of John Gerard, author of a much loved if occasionally slapdash Elizabethan herbal, roses were firmly established as one of the most versatile ingredients in the Tudor medicine chest. Like Turner, Gerard took pains to explain that different roses, and different parts of the plant, had different qualities. The dried and powered flower stamens he recommended especially to ships' doctors – perhaps from his own experience – to cure the dysenteries and diarrhoeas that ravaged crews at sea. Powdered stamens dissolved in red wine with a little ginger could stop white or red fluxes in women, he said; but for an outbreak of bloody flux on board, ships' doctors could dissolve the powder in any liquor that came to hand.

Apprenticed to a barber-surgeon, a Freeman and later Master of the Company of Barber-Surgeons, Gerard had busied his hands with healing, herbs and horticulture; for all his failings as a man and an author (attributable perhaps to an impatient, choleric temperament), he is an excellent guide to how the Elizabethans viewed their health and how they practised their medicine. Expanding on advice in earlier authors, he recommended roses as a gentle remedy, good for purging the stomach (Musk and Damask roses especially), removing 'those excrements which stick to the bowels, or that in the first and neerest vaines remaine raw, flegmaticke, and now and then cholerick' (even excrement had its humours, it seems). Distilled rosewater was taken to strengthen the heart, refresh the spirits, and for any ailment that required gentle cooling (a virtue, too, of rose syrup).

Eyes in particular could benefit, as rosewater 'mitigateth the paine of the eies proceeding of a hot cause, bringeth sleepe, which also the fresh Roses themselves provoke through their sweete and pleasant smell'. The effects seem psychological as much as physical; and patients would surely have appreciated Gerard's suggestion of adding rosewater to 'junketting dishes, cakes, sawces, and many other pleasant things, [which] giveth a fine and delectable taste'.

Gerard instructed readers in the art of making different sorts of rose syrups, and a conserve of roses that had the opposite effect of binding stomachs that were moist and raw. He also proposed a morning feast of musk petals eaten 'in maner of a sallade, with oile, vineger & pepper, or any other way according to the appetite & pleasure of them that shall eat it'. The aim was to purge the belly of 'waterish and cholericke humours' in a way that was both gentle and surprisingly precise: the petals of twelve to fourteen Musk flowers would produce six to eight stools, he tells us, and so pro rata. Painters and cooks could try his method of making a yellowy liquid from white Musk flowers, used as a colour wash for miniatures, or to colour meats and sauces. But he drew the line at passing on recipes for 'Sugar roset, and divers other pretie things made of Roses and Sugar, which are impertinent unto our historie, bicause I intend neither to make thereof an Apothecaries shop, nor a Sugar bakers storehouse, leaving the rest for our cunning confectioners'.

Gerard left the humble dog rose until last. Although similar in their virtues, wild roses were little used in physick if garden roses were to be found, despite Pliny's recommendations. At least the hips of dog roses gave much delight to children, cooks and gentlewomen with a taste for tarts, he said slyly, 'the making whereof I commit to the cunning Cooke, and the teeth to eate them in the rich mans mouth'. But on the link between rose hips and osteoarthritis he remained resolutely silent.

Chapter Fifteen
The Housewife's Friend

G ERARD's great *Herball* of 1597 ran to 1,392 pages in the original and
1,630 pages in apothecary Thomas Johnson's revised version of
1633, each entry bursting with information about finding, identifying
and growing plants, and their many uses in medicine, cooking, gardening and running a household. Its sheer size put it beyond the pockets of
ordinary folk, even if they valued its contents. Books could scarcely get
much fatter than this, and after Gerard came a parting of ways. As more
plants came in to Europe from east and west, and as knowledge became
more specialized, the herbal developed into different forms, depending
on whether the interests of authors and their readers lay in plants, medicine or family matters. Roses, for a time, featured in all of them.

The serious (and wealthy) herbalist or curious plantsman might have
turned to apothecary John Parkinson's 'masculine' herbal *Theatrum
Botanicum,* which he dedicated to King Charles I, in contrast to his more
'feminine' book of garden flowers, *Paradisi in Sole Paradisus Terrestris*
(Park-in-sun's terrestrial paradise, a terrible pun), dedicated to Queen
Henrietta Maria. The herbal appeared in 1640, just two years before the
outbreak of civil war – not a time to think of planting garden roses. But
he included a growing number of wild roses and delved deeply if
conventionally into the healing properties of wild and garden roses.

Parkinson put all his writings – whether about herbs or flowers – into
a godly context, declaring that God had inspired in Adam 'the knowledge
of all naturall things', later passed on to Noah and posterity, which Adam
had used to give names to all living creatures, according to their natures,
and to determine 'both what Herbes and Fruits were fit, eyther for Meate

*Placing horticulture within a godly context, the frontispiece to
Stuart apothecary John Parkinson's* Paradisi in Sole Paradisus Terrestris
of 1629 shows roses and vines clambering up the trees.

or Medicine, for Use or for Delight'. After Parkinson came the proto-scientists such as Robert Morison and John Ray, who produced works of botany rather than herbals, and science detached itself gradually from the divine.

Sophisticated herbals and learned plant treatises were not the only sources of information on healing with plants, however. Adam's knowledge of all natural things – and especially of herbs fit for meat or medicine – inspired a whole parallel tradition of do-it-yourself books for the housewife, who was responsible for looking after her family's health just as she looked after their stomachs and made the house smell sweet. If she could read, she could turn to one of the many books of 'secrets' – usually small enough to slip into a purse or pocket – offering snatches of household lore, some plain and simple, others more arcane or downright fantastical.

We have already encountered such books written by contemporaries of John Gerard and William Shakespeare. One that inclined more towards health was John Partridge's *The Treasurie of commodious Conceites, and hidden Secrets, commonly called, The good Hus-wives Closet of provision, for the health of her household*. By 1584, it was already on to its fourth edition, and dedicated to an assistant in Gerard's Company of Barber-Surgeons. Fifty years later, a new edition identified its readers as 'Courteous Gentlewomen, honest Matrons, and vertuous Virgins', claiming to have been printed originally at the request of a 'Lady of great calling, and now augmented with some rare conceits not before published'.

In its tightly packed pages, the good housewife could look up the healing virtues of the rose, and follow the many rose recipes for the kitchen and the constitution. The rose appears variously as rose vinegar, conserve of roses ('good against blacke Choller and Melancholie. Conserve of white Roses doth loose the bellie more then the red'), and Damask water (excellent for lifting tarts, apple mousses, or almond butter, and for perfuming gloves).

From Partridge, she could also learn how to add roses to a number of other flowers, spices, herbs and good Gascon wine in a 'soveraigne water' named after Master Doctor Stevens, 'a man of great knowledge and cunning' who effected many cures with it over a long period and 'kept it always secret, till of late, a little before his death, a speciall friend of his, did get it in writing of him'. The recommended dose was a spoonful taken on an empty stomach once every four days, 'for it is very hote in operation'. It sounds as good a quack medicine as any, apparently able to comfort the spirits; soothe internal disorders; cure contracting of the sinews; aid conception in barren women; kill worms in the belly; guard against gout, toothache, all kinds of stomach problems, cold dropsy, stones in the bladder, canker and stinking breath; and help preserve at least the illusion of eternal youth. (An Archbishop of Canterbury apparently drew such goodness from it that he lived until he could no longer drink from a cup, but sucked his nourishment through a silver straw.) Not surprisingly, Dr Stevens Sovereign Water remained a classic in various guises for at least a century. It even travelled to the American colonies (minus its roses) where it surfaced in *The Compleat Housewife* written by Eliza Smith, who had worked as a cook for more than thirty years in 'fashionable and noble Families', dying around 1732.

Being a good housewife involved not only learning the right recipes; she must also develop the right frame of mind. For help, she could turn to Gervase Markham, an English soldier, poet and author who hit on a rich vein of 'how-to' books, aimed initially at the 'perfect Husbandman' and later at the perfect housewife.

In Markham's eyes, a knowledge of physic came immediately after moral virtues in a housewife's armoury of skills, since 'the preservation and care of the family touching their health and soundnesse of body consisteth most in her diligence'. Such knowledge was to be soundly practical: how to make and administer medicines, how to prevent an outbreak of sickness, and how to take away 'the effects and evill of the same, when it hath made seasure on the body'. Careful to placate the jealousy of physicians, Markham suggested that of course the art of physic was far beyond the capacity of most skilful women, 'lodging onely in the brest of learned Professours', but our simple housewife could nonetheless learn from them ordinary rules and medicines, which she could put to the service of her family.

Roses naturally featured in many of Markham's remedies for all the usual ailments, principally as rosewater, oil of roses, powdered rose

Roses were a staple of the kitchen and of the distillery. Frontispiece to the tenth edition of The Compleat Housewife: or, Accomplish'd Gentlewoman's Companion *(London, 1741).*

hips, and conserve of roses – good against fevers but not strong enough for the plague – or in this novel cure for a stitch in the side: 'take Doves dung, red Rose leaves, and put them into a bag, & quilt it: then thorowly heat it upon a chaffingdish of coales with Vinegar in a platter, then lay it unto the pained place as hot as may be suffered, and when it cooleth heat it againe'. Another recipe for headache involved heating together two spoonfuls each of rosewater, camomile juice, woman's milk and strong wine vinegar, steeping a dry rose cake in the resulting liquid, adding grated nutmeg 'then breaking it into two parts, bind it upon the temples of the head, so let the partie lie downe to rest, and the paine will in a short space be taken from him'. Two handfuls of red roses and of camomile could also be added to twenty live swallows and a handful of twenty other plants and herbs – including Roman wormwood, French mallows and cotton lavender – to make oil of swallows. And in the kitchen, the housewife cook would always have rosewater to hand for adding to spice cakes and sugar plate, marchpane and Genoa paste, or for candied fruits.

When she gave birth, the woman of the house will have welcomed roses at her confinement, taken with the water of fenugreek seed, chickpeas and maidenhair, all beaten together and dampened with the oil of blue fleur-de-lis to provoke labour. If she bled excessively – and if her purse were large enough – the midwife may have anointed her womb and her 'secrets' with an ointment made from oil of roses, the scrapings of ivory and of goat's horn, red coral, white frankincense and white wax. Or she might have had her arms bound straight and strong, a hot cupping glass placed under her breasts, linen cloths soaked in vinegar laid on her belly between the navel and her private parts, and a little round bag filled with red roses and other blood-staunching ingredients, 'the quantity of a mans thumb, the which shee shall put into the privie parts'. (As well as roses, the bag might contain pomegranate flowers and rind, amber, Armenian bole, white frankincense, galls, and other more exotic *materia medica*, beaten to a powder and tempered with red wine.) For four or five days after the birth, she may have fortified herself with a comfortable potion of dried red rose petals and other ingredients in wine, sack or muscatel, four spoonfuls to be taken daily. And if she failed to produce enough milk, she could wash her breasts with wine in which mint, roses and violets had been seeping (oil of white lilies or violets would do equally well, mixed with musk, incense and laudanum).

Roses were also gentle enough to administer to her newborn child for flux and diarrhoea, in a plaster of rose seeds, cumin and anis, laid on the child's belly. If the infant's stools turned red or yellow, 'then give it to drinke of the Syrope of Roses, or of Crabbes, or else of Pomegranats, tempered with a little Mynt-water'.

From the mid-seventeenth century, however, flowers and medicine were beginning to part company, in books at least, as the more 'botanic' herbals developed into flora, while the more medical texts turned into fully fledged pharmacopoeia. At the crossroads stood two splenetic individuals – supporters of different medical theories – who snarled at each other from across the divide: William Coles and Nicholas Culpeper.

Born in 1626, some ten years after his rival, William Coles was more obviously a plantsman than a medical man, devoting many years to his favourite pastime: 'simpling', the growing or gathering of plants for herbal remedies. Once a member of New College Oxford, although not obviously learned, he subscribed to sympathetic medicine and the doctrine of signatures, believing that God had not only given plants a distinct form, but 'hath also given them particular Signatures, whereby a Man may read, even in legible Characters, the use of them'.

Coles dedicated his first tiny pocketbook, *The Art of Simpling,* to a fellow herbal enthusiast whom he had not yet met: Elias Ashmole, who would later bully Oxford University into building the Ashmolean Museum to accept his outstanding collection of curiosities, much of it amassed by the gardeners and collectors, the John Tradescants. Coles also used his book to hit out at Culpeper, promising not to deceive his readers with a few empty notions, as Mr Culpeper had recently done, relating nonsensical stories when it was obvious to all and sundry 'that he understood not those Plants he trod upon'.

As a flower of the garden more than the field, the rose plays only a modest role in Coles's book on simpling, but achieves far greater prominence in the expanded treatise he brought out the following year – *Adam in Eden: or, Natures Paradise* – which he divided anatomically into four parts, treating of plants appropriate to the upper, middle and lower body parts, and then to the limbs. In Coles's pharmacology, roses belonged to the eye section of the first group of upper-body plants, after plants used to treat the head in general, the brain and falling hair. (His first plant is the walnut, 'the perfect Signature of the Head' in all its particulars, from the outer husk to the inner kernel, which 'hath the very figure of the Brain'.)

Coles's other 'eye' plants included fennel, vervain, celandine, rue, eyebright, clary and hawkweed; but his logic soon breaks down. As well as eyes, roses could also work on ears, throats, gums, bottoms, lower bowels, wombs and contemporary illnesses such as St Anthony's fire, a dreaded madness caused by eating rye bread contaminated with ergot fungus which produced headache, vomiting, diarrhoea, gangrene of the fingers and toes, and the sensation of being burnt at the stake. And despite criticizing Culpeper for plagiarism, Coles borrowed many remedies from other authors, including the red rose cake strapped to the temples overnight to ease headaches, and a gentle reminder of rose-water's general benefits for the sickroom, which he may have lifted from Culpeper himself.[1]

Another shining example of a radicalized plantsman, Nicholas Culpeper was the son of an educated clergyman who had died just before his son was born in 1616. In his short life, Culpeper studied at Cambridge; eloped and lost his bride-to-be to a lightning strike; went to London, where he became apprenticed to an apothecary; and as a natural rebel, he took the side of the Parliamentarians against the King (London was then rabidly anti-royalist). His longest-running battle, though, was with the College of Physicians, which held the medical profession – and the spread of medical knowledge – in an iron grip.

Apothecaries were allowed to prepare only those medicines prescribed by the College in its 'bible' of medical remedies, the *Pharmacopoeia Londinensis*. As this was written in Latin, it effectively kept knowledge out of the hands of the unlearned. Taking the contrary view that medicine should work for the public good rather than private gain, Culpeper used his education to translate the *Pharmacopoeia* into English, and to add information about how the medicines were to be used, thereby revealing the 'secrets' of the medical fraternity and rubbishing any views and remedies with which he disagreed. It was clearly a political act and brought Culpeper lasting fame, if not exactly fortune.

To his grounding in Galenic theory, Culpeper added a dubious brand of astrological medicine that aligned ailments and their cures to different planets; plants, too, were linked to their planetary counterparts – and different roses came under different planets, according to Culpeper's precise directions: 'Red Roses are under *Jupiter,* Damask under *Venus,* and White under the *Moon,* and Province under the King of *France.*'[2]

Perhaps their several planetary influences explain why roses feature so prominently in Culpeper's medicine. To William Langham's long list of ailments soothed by roses he even added a few more, including the French pox and leprosy itch. As for the Damask water acquired at such expense for the medieval King Edward I, by Culpeper's time it 'is chiefly used for Fumes to sweeten things, as the dried Leavs thereof to make sweet Pouders, and fil sweet Bags, and little use they are put to in Physick, although they have some purging quality'.

Seventeenth-century engraving of radical herbalist Nicholas Culpeper, who included a 'pother' of roses in his work.

Culpeper's translation of the physicians' bible gives us a privileged glimpse into the more bizarre remedies of 'orthodox' medicine, such as sparrows' brains to provoke lust; ash from the head of a coal-black cat burnt in a new pot and blown daily into the eyes of a patient suffering from cataracts; and the skull of an unburied man, beaten to a powder and taken in betony water, to relieve palsies and epilepsy. Culpeper included some outlandish remedies of his own, recommending 'The Heart of a Lark being bound to the Thigh of those that have the collick helps them; it doth the like also, being beaten'.

But Culpeper's *Pharmacopoeia* also introduces us to the standard medical practice of his time. Employing in their medicines three kinds of roses (red, white and Damask), London doctors placed the rose among their five cordial flowers, along with violets, borage, rosemary and balm. They laid down strict rules for how roses and other plants should be prepared, whether in vinegars, decoctions, juleps, syrups, electuaries (a medicinal paste, of the consistency of honey), lohochs (a type of linctus, thicker than a syrup but not as thick as an electuary), powders, pills, sugars, troches (a pastille made into any shape, usually little flat cakes), oils and ointments.

Culpeper judged many of the doctors' recipes unnecessarily complicated. Their ointment of roses, for example, required much mixing of well-washed hogs' grease with fresh red roses, letting the mixture stand for seven days, boiling, straining, adding more fresh roses and repeating the operation, then adding red rose juice followed by more boiling and straining. 'You need do no more than let it stand till it is cold,' said Culpeper sharply. And he took particular exception to a rose syrup made with black hellebore roots, warning that hellebore should never be boiled, or very little. 'The Syrup rightly used purgeth melancholly, resisteth madnesse, I wish the ignorant to let it alone,' he said. He found the physicians' recipe for an electuary of rose juice, a violent purgative, to be equally dubious. 'I would not willingly have my Country men do themselves a mischief; let the Gentry study Physick: then shall they know what belongs to it. A lazy Gentry makes block headed Physitians.' But most rose recipes passed without comment, including a delightful concoction for consumptive patients, which mixed the fruits of figs, prunes, jujubes and sebesten (an East Indian fruit) with the flowers of roses, violets, borage and half a handful each of maidenhair, hops and endives, plus two drachms of liquorice, all cut and bruised and boiled in spring water until reduced by one third.

For all their lauded virtues, roses could not halt the consumption that forced Culpeper to his sickbed, his condition exacerbated by his furious smoking and the bullet wound to his chest he had received fighting for the Parliamentarians at the Battle of Newbury, from which he had never fully recovered. Writing feverishly to the last, he died in 1654, aged just thirty-seven, a few weeks after Oliver Cromwell had accepted the title of

Lord Protector for life, and the egalitarian ideals for which Culpeper had battled all his life were beginning to lose their lustre.

London cannot have had much use for roses during the stern years of Cromwell's rule, when merrymaking and all things pagan were rigorously proscribed. They make a triumphant comeback in the years immediately after the restoration of King Charles II, when royalist sympathizer John Evelyn proposed a radical plan to banish from the city all noxious industries such as the brewers, dyers, soap and salt boilers, and the lime burners, ringing the city with sweet-smelling plantations of 'fragrant and odiferous *Flowers* . . .', among them Sweet Briar and honeysuckle, 'the Common *white* and *yellow Jessamine,* both the *Syringa's* or *Pipe-trees;* the *Guelder-Rose,* the *Musk,* and all other *Roses, Genista Hispanica'.* The areas between the palisaded fields were to be planted with borders of herbaceous flowers such as lilies, pinks, carnations and violets; and the interlying fields with green vegetables but not cabbages, 'whose rotten and perishing stalks have a very noisom and unhealthy smell'.

It was a wonderful plan – part environmental tract, part royalist allegory – prompted by a walk Evelyn had made in the King's palace at Whitehall, where he stepped into a 'presumptuous Smoake' that choked the area around Scotland Yard, and Evelyn's royalist sympathies prompted concern for the health of his King, who had long been accustomed to the excellent air of France, where he would have enjoyed the 'odiferous wafts which flow from *Fontenay* and *Vaugirard,* even to *Paris* in the season of *Roses'.*

Evelyn's was not the only voice crying out against filthy air: another contemporary who took a scientific interest in the subject was Robert Boyle, the Irish natural philosopher, physicist, inventor, gentleman scientist and one of the first modern chemists. Boyle's sickly childhood also gave him a very personal interest in what he called 'medicinal experiments', which he collected together for the use of families living in the country. Boyle may have been a Fellow of the Royal Society, but the dawning of the Enlightenment did not immediately banish from medicine the weird and the wonderful. One of his remedies for dysentery required the thighbone of a hanged man ('perhaps another may serve, but this was still made use of'). Fond of using dung in his medicines – including human excrement, at times – he recommended as a tested remedy for sore throats stuffing good sea salt down the leg of a well-worn and unwashed worsted stocking, tied about the patient's neck all night.

Roses and rosewater appear in many of Boyle's remedies: as a conserve or gargle for sore throats; as a nightly hair powder (Damask roses powdered with the flowers of betony, marjoram, sage and roses, together with nigella seeds and lignum aloe powder); as a remedy for toothache and loose teeth; and as a linctus of honey of roses mixed with *album graecum* or 'white Dogs-turd, burnt to a perfect whiteness', to be let slowly down sore throats.

Boyle's eyes were particularly troublesome. Coming to London to recover from fever and dropsy provoked by bad weather and even unhealthier Irish inns, he had caught another fever raging in the capital, which left him with a 'Sense of Decay in my Eyes, which during my long Sickness I had exercis'd too much upon critical Books stuff'd with Hebrew, and other Eastern Characters'.[3] Not surprisingly, he sets down more than a dozen rose remedies for eyes that are sore, bloodshot, inflamed or weeping, among them Lady Fitz-Harding's eyewater, which mixed white rosewater with eyebright water, sifted white sugar candy and aloes, and 'which lately cur'd an almost blind Person, whose Eyes look'd like Glass'. Other ingredients Boyle the chemist added to his rose remedies for eyes included rotten apples and wormwood tops, tutty, frogspawn, coral, pearl, white breadcrumbs, and the flowers and seeds of a veritable physic garden.

While Boyle experienced some conflict between science and his deeply held religious principles, for others such as the reforming Christian cleric John Wesley (1703–1791) faith could also bind together moral and medical precepts. Following Boyle's example, Wesley published a small book of primitive physic, written in plain words and designed to give medicine back to the people – a gesture that was every bit as radical as Culpeper's translation of the physicians' bible. And like the early herbalists, he wrapped his medicine in a Christian coat. According to Wesley, Adam and Eve's fall from grace in the Garden of Eden may have introduced the seeds of wickedness and pain, of sickness and of death to human experience, but God (the 'Great Author of Nature') had

A Damask rose from Elizabeth Blackwell's A Curious Herbal *of 1737, undertaken to help release her husband from a debtors' prison. Its 500 specimen plants (drawn, engraved and coloured by the author) came mostly from the Apothecaries' garden at Chelsea.*

nonetheless found ways of lessening man's pain, through exercise, diet, plain living, plenty of cold baths and that old unfashionable medicine, prayer.

For each ailment, Wesley proposed a sequence of possible cures, starting with the simplest (often a cold bath, even for blindness), and moving on to the more complicated. A last-ditch cure to prevent a relapse of the falling sickness, for instance, was to administer a pill or two of '*powder'd Toad*' before and after every new moon, while anyone apparently struck dead by lightning was to be plunged immediately into cold water, and if that failed, '*Blew* strongly with Bellows down his Throat'.

Wesley proposed roses in just fourteen of his 725 remedies, mostly in the form of rosewater for eyes, throats and mouth cankers, but also as a conserve for violent coughing and bruised eyes; as rose petals boiled or mixed with egg whites for displaced wombs, and headaches; as an oil for itch; as dried Damask petals for a gentle purging; as an ointment of white roses to dissolve hard swellings; and as dried and powdered haws to be taken in white wine every morning to cure the stone.

Out of so many remedies, it was a meagre haul. The rose and its many preparations were beginning to lose favour in the sickroom, it seems, as they continued to do throughout the eighteenth and nineteenth centuries. Even householders were omitting the rose from their medicine chests, finding space for medicinal stalwarts such as rhubarb, senna, prepared crabs' claws, peppermint and cinnamon water, syrup of poppies (and of oranges and lemons), laudanum, almond oil and wax plasters, but not for roses in any form. Roses were losing favour, too, in the kitchen; and their continued inclusion in works of pharmacology was aesthetic rather than medicinal, as trust in their healing properties was fast waning. Arab physicians might have prescribed conserve or honey of roses for consumptive patients, said a later 'improver' of *Culpeper's Herbal*, but always in combination with other ingredients and a regime of fresh air, so who could impute recovery wholly to the rose? The 'pother' of roses was fast dying down.

By the 1870s, some eighty years after Wesley's death, cultivation of red roses (*Rosa gallica*) for the drugs trade in England had shrunk to a mere ten acres around Mitcham in Surrey, and further crops in Oxfordshire and Derbyshire. Mitcham could also boast eight acres of Centifolia roses to supply London druggists, supplemented by supplies from the market gardens of Putney, Hammersmith and Fulham; and more roses were grown commercially in continental Europe, especially at Wassenaar and Noordwijk in the Netherlands, around Hamburg and Nuremberg in Germany, and in the villages around Paris and Lyons in France. But the overall picture is one of decline, and even Provins roses (still grown for medicinal use) were no longer held in quite the same esteem.

Hips from the dog rose underwent a similar demotion. Country people might gather them still, as they had since the days of Galen and Dioscorides, and their popularity might be holding steadfast among Native Americans such as the Blackfoot people, and even growing in countries such as Turkey, but western pharmacists valued rose hips chiefly as a means of adding bulk to pill masses, electuaries and pharmaceutical confections. As for all the claims made for roses down the ages, surprisingly few records survive of their use in English folk medicine: just one remedy for treating colds and sore throats with rose hip syrup, and another from Essex, where cuts were treated with crushed rose leaves, although more recipes may result from Kew's interest in ethnomedicine and its current study of medicinal plant use in England in the first part of the twentieth century.[4]

By the 1930s, the process was virtually complete. When Maud Grieve published *A Modern Herbal* in 1931 – based on pamphlets she had written during the First World War, checked and augmented by her editor's scouring of American herbal literature – the rose was still fêted for its marvellous history, but medically emasculated and valued officially for its aesthetic properties alone. 'Red Rose petals are official in nearly all Pharmacopoeias,' wrote Mrs Grieve. 'Though formerly employed for their mild astringency and tonic value, they are today used almost solely to impart their pleasant odour to pharmaceutical preparations.' The British Pharmacopoeia allowed just three rose preparations: a confection, an acid infusion and a fluid extract, while the United States also endorsed a syrup of red rose, used to add flavour and smell to other syrups and mixes, and honey of roses, prepared from clarified honey and fluid extract of roses. Rose hips, too, were stripped of their cooling and astringent properties, and employed medicinally only to prepare the confection of rose hips used in conjunction with other drugs, 'the pulp being separated from the skin and hairy seeds and beaten up with sugar'. Thus was ancient medicine laid low.

Yet Mrs Grieve clearly loved her roses and helpfully suggested suitable red roses to replace the officially prescribed *Rosa gallica*, which had virtually died out as a pure strain in the frenzy of rose breeding that followed the introduction of China roses to the West. (Today, *Rosa gallica* var. *officinalis* is once again available from specialist rose-growers.) She looked for roses that would yield a fragrant rose-coloured infusion, somewhat astringent, when seeped in boiling water. Her choice fell on six Hybrid Perpetuals: 'Eugène Fürst' (ragged-edged, crimson-purple and highly scented); the acclaimed 'Général Jacqueminot' (a fine clear red, and scented); 'Hugh Dickson' (deep red and sweetly scented); 'Richmond' (light carmine to scarlet, and scented); 'Ulrich Brunner' (rosy carmine, fading to pink with age, sweetly scented); and 'Liberty' (scarlet-red). Only the last is no longer generally available in Britain.

Maud Grieve's herbal harks back to the old strain of household compendia, updated with the latest herbal science. As well as explaining how medicines were made, she devoted much attention to the rose in perfume (see Chapter 16), and passed on recipes for pot-pourri and sweet jar (a moist form of pot-pourri), crystallized roses, and rose-petal sandwiches, a delightful treat that recalls John Gerard's salad of musk petals.

Put a layer of Red Rose-petals in the bottom of a jar or covered dish, put in 4 oz. of fresh butter wrapped in waxed paper. Cover with a thick layer of rose-petals. Cover closely and leave in a cool place overnight. The more fragrant the roses, the finer the flavour imparted. Cut bread in thin strips or circles, spread each with the perfumed butter and place several petals from fresh Red Roses between the slices, allowing edges to show. Violets or Clover blossoms may be used in place of Roses.

Despite the intervention of science, the old belief in the efficacy of roses refused to die down completely. After nutritional scientists declared that wild rose hips contained higher concentrations of vitamin C than any other fruit or vegetable (according to *Flora Britannica*, a cup of rose-hip pulp provides more vitamin C than forty fresh oranges), wartime children in the 1940s were fed spoonfuls of rose hip syrup to replace citrus fruits and other sources of vitamin C. Britain's Ministry of Health initiated a voluntary collection scheme that marshalled schools, scouts, girl guides, and children's gangs to scour the hedgerows for the ripened hips, especially in the north of England where the vitamin content was reputedly highest. By the end of the Second World War, more than 450 tons of rose hips were harvested annually and used to fortify Britain's children.

Even this claim was disputed, however. In 1990, a German regulatory commission poured cold water on the use of rose hips to prevent and treat colds, flu and flu-like infections. Declaring the use of rose hips in treating or preventing vitamin C deficiency as 'questionable', in view of what it called the drug's low and rapidly decreasing vitamin C content, the commission could also find no clinical evidence to substantiate claims that rose hips helped in a string of complaints familiar from the old herbals, such as those affecting the bowel, stomach, digestion, kidneys, lower urinary tract and eyes. Having drawn a blank, it could conclude only that the therapeutic use of rose hips 'cannot be recommended'; and it handed responsibility to the food and vitamin industry for deciding on the suitability of rose hips as a dietary supplement. At least the commisson raised no objections to the use of rose hips as a taste enhancer in herbal teas.

In line with these views, most modern handbooks of clinically tested herbal remedies omit roses altogether, leaving them to the wilder fringes of New Age healing, such as the French '*terrain*' concept which turns its back on the 'doctrine of specificity', looking instead at the condition and nature of fluids in the whole body in a way that draws together the ancient Greek system of humours with elements of traditional Chinese medicine[5] and the Ayurveda healing system of India. According to practitioners, the leaves and flowers of the dog rose are sweet and warm, while their fruits are sour and warm, and when administered in sufficient doses, the leaves and flowers 'have a therapeutic effect on anguish with sensations of emptiness in the chest, corresponding to a vacuity of Heart yang'. (The British physician Dr Edward Bach similarly recommended wild roses as a flower remedy for those who drift resignedly through life.) Under the same system, Damask and Centifolia roses are considered to have antidepressant and aphrodisiac properties, able to stimulate vaginal secretions and sperm production and to

103.

ROSA CANINA, *Linn.*

D.Blair F.L.S. ad nat. del. et lith.

M & N. Hanhart imp.

Rose hips included for their use as a medical confection
in Robert Bentley's Medicinal Plants *of 1880.*

alleviate a number of conditions including constipation, anxiety and uterine bleeding.

The rose is indeed still valued in Ayurvedic Indian healing, which seeks to restore imbalances in an individual's physical and mental states. Ayurvedic healing works through all the senses and the rose is used in a number of treatments: combined with herbs in proper diet (taste); aromatherapy (smell); colour therapy (vision); and in herbal oil massages (touch). Only sound is absent, although according to one of the many transformational movements to originate in India, 'the falling of each rose petal, one by one, is compared to the human surrender to God in all aspects of life'. And many of Ayurveda's specific rose remedies recall the cooling, soothing, cleansing treatments of early western and Islamic medicine, used especially for eyes, digestion and female reproductive systems.

The recent Danish research into the efficacy of rose hips in treating osteoarthritis (see Chapter 14) suggests that it is time to re-evaluate the healing power of roses. Interest in rose hips and the seeds they contain is clearly growing, and more trials are producing the kind of randomized, double-blind, placebo-controlled evidence required by science.[6] It seems strange, nonetheless, that none of the old herbalists and ancient pharmacologists picked up the connection between wild rose hips and the searing pain of osteoarthritis – not even William Langham, whose Elizabethan healing garden gave the 'fruit' of the rose as a remedy for various forms of bleeding, and for kidneys, but whose remedies for dealing with various aches and pains were largely topical, such as rose cakes stepped in warm wine, or sour breadcrumbs mixed with vinegar and rose petals and applied to aches and swellings. We can only hope that anyone enduring painful joints would have been cheered by one of John Gerard's rose-hip tarts or Maud Grieve's rose-petal sandwiches.

Chapter Sixteen
Heaven's Scent

O F all the senses, the late Enlightenment philosopher Immanuel Kant judged smell the most dispensable. Equating it to taste at a distance, he maintained that it 'does not pay us to cultivate it or to refine it in order to gain enjoyment; this sense can pick up more objects of aversion than of pleasure (especially in crowded places) and, besides, the pleasure coming from the sense of smell cannot be other than fleeting and transitory'.

Perfumers and rose-lovers would surely prefer the verdict of a philosopher such as Jean-Jacques Rousseau, who named smell as the sense of the imagination. The problem for florists and philosophers alike remains one of definition, as smell is the most elusive of all five senses. Western languages have no words that uniquely label different smells (as they do for colours and textures), so these can be described only by association and comparison. Furthermore, smells connect directly to the primitive part of the brain and are linked to emotion rather than cognition. In trying to smell the memory of a rose, we can recall our associated emotions, but few if any of us can recreate it with the 'inner nose' as the inner ear or eye can for other sensations.

Gertrude Jekyll, England's most revered gardener of the early twentieth century, had a fine nose for bad smells, catching a whiff of dirty hen-house in the butterfly flower, *Schizanthus,* and mangy dog in the Pyrenean lily. But on the spiced-pinks smell of the old Cabbage rose, *Rosa × centifolia,* she lost her sharp tongue, declaring simply that 'it stands alone as the sweetest of all its kind, as the type of the true Rose smell'. And while she tells us that the calyx of the Moss rose (a Centifolia sport)

332

has its own delicious scent, of a more 'aromatic' or 'cordial' character, she saves herself further trouble by declaring that these roses are 'so well known that one need say no more than that they should never be neglected or forgotten'.[1]

As with all the senses, the psychology and chemistry of smell go hand in hand. Although perceptions and preferences naturally change with the times, certain fragrances stand as reference points across the ages; one such is the scent of rose, celebrated from the Greeks on-wards as the lightest and sweetest of perfumes, able to give actual relief from 'heaviness and discomfort, even from that caused by other perfumes'. To better understand the rose's enduring fascination, it is instructive first to unravel changing ideas about what smells are, and what effect they exert.

Plato maintained that smells cannot be classified, and that there are only two sorts of smell: good smells and bad smells. In order to align the body's five senses to the four elements of water, air, fire and earth, he linked smells to vapour, an intermediate state between water and air. The Greek-born physician Galen followed suit (see Chapter 14), further implying that some smells carry earthy or fiery qualities.

For nearly two millennia, philosophers and natural scientists have wrestled with the nature of these 'vapours', and how to categorize their different types. In his encyclopedic *Margarita philosophica* of 1503, German humanist Gregor Reisch counted eleven different smells which he ranked in this order: aromatic, salty, bitter, sharp, vinegary, astrin-gent, briny, oily, sweet, insipid and stinking. By 1865, the English perfume expert Eugene Rimmel – a reporter of the perfumery jury at the Great Exhibition, and Britain's first historian of perfume – had counted as many as eighteen different 'types' for pleasant smells alone, starting with rose (where else?).

Others were concerned less with counting smells than with under-standing their effects. A decade before Rimmel's *Book of Perfumes*, the London perfumer Septimus Piesse provoked the mirth of chemists by transcribing smells in the chromatic scales of music. After lengthy experiments, Dr Piesse drew up a list of the volatility and strength of different odours, and produced a gamut of odours most used in perfum-ery. As his descendant Charles H. Piesse, explained:

French postcard of a perfume bottle, c.1905.

Scents, like sounds, appear to influence the olfactory nerve in certain definite degrees. There is, as it were, an octave of odours like an octave in music; certain odours coincide, like the keys of an instrument. Such as almond, heliotrope, vanilla, and clematis blend together, each producing different degrees of a nearly similar impression. Again, we have citron, lemon, orange peel, and verbena, forming a higher octave of smells, which blend in a similar manner. The analogy is completed by what we are pleased to call semi-odours, such as rose and rose-geranium for the half note; petit-grain, neroli, a black key, followed by fleur d'oranger. Then we have patchouly, santalwood and vitivert, and many others running into each other.

According to Piesse, rose appears at the top of the bass or F-key, making a harmonious bouquet when mixed with musk, tuberose, tonquin bean, camphor and jonquil.

However dubious his chemistry may have been, Piesse's musical smells linked Shakespeare's idea of music as the food of love, creeping over the lovesick Duke Orsino 'like the sweet sound / That breathes upon a bank of violets', to the correspondences between the senses extolled by symbolist writers such as Baudelaire and J.-K. Huysmans. In his morbidly *fin-de-siècle* novel, *À rebours* (*Against Nature*), Huysmans gives us the anti-hero Des Esseintes, skilled in the arts of perfumery, who mixed a chaotic blend of feuding ingredients to create a 'collective perfume, unexpected, and strange, in which there reappeared, like a persistent refrain, the ornamental opening phrase, the scent of a great meadow fanned by the lilacs and the lime trees'.

The twentieth century saw order return to the chemistry of smell, notably in the experiments of German psychologist Hans Henning, whose exhaustive researches into the perceived smells of more than 400 separate substances produced a prism that could capture all smells on its surface (or so he claimed): spicy, resinous and burned at one end; fragrant, ethereal and putrid at the other. Two US chemists – Ernest Charlton Crocker and Lloyd F. Henderson – condensed the prism still further to a square comprised of just four primary smells: fragrant, acid, burnt and caprylic or goaty.

Shifting the focus of enquiry from chemistry to psychology, in the early 1950s the German chemist Paul Jellinek mapped an odour-effects diagram with four cardinal points indicating the four basic odour types (which he defined as sweet, acid, bitter, and alkaline) and their corresponding effects (narcotic, anti-erogenous, stimulating and erogenous). Other odours and their effects were accommodated between the cardinal points. 'Floral', for instance, appeared close to 'sweet', before passing through 'fruity', 'watery' and 'green' to 'acid'; travelling from 'sweet' to 'alkaline', by contrast, the odours passed through 'balsamic' and 'honey-like' to 'fecal' and 'urinous'.

Very much a man of his time, Jellinek proposed his perfumed landscape to support his theory that all perfumery is rooted in the sexual drive, and that perfume is worn primarily to enhance sexual attraction, either by masking unpleasant odours or using erotic ones. According to Jellinek, not only do perfumery's main ingredients (flowers, civet and musk) have a sexual function, but perfumery itself has developed under the dominance of this drive, so that 'it unequivocally remains sexuality's servant'.

The rose played a crucial role in his argument. Having noted that poets of all civilizations and at all times have celebrated the erotic effect of 'sultry' floral odours such as rose, orange blossom, orchid, tuberose, jasmine, lilac and lime blossom, he turned his attention to the erotic effect of various smells, concluding that the most erotic are those reminiscent of human body odour. In flowers, this calls for a relatively high proportion of the chemical indol, a component of animal faeces whose purpose in flowers is to attract insects. Indol is present in the flower oil obtained from jasmine blossoms, it seems, but absent from the rose, which in Jellinek's view 'exhibits an almost purely narcotic effect, barely modified by erogenous and stimulating nuances'. So how did the rose – and especially the red rose – earn its title as the 'flower of love'?

Jellinek found the answer to his own rhetorical question not in the rose's smell but in its colour and shape, which link directly to (predominantly male) sexual experience. In his seriously argued view, the rose ranks among the most aphrodisiac of smells because its narcotic effects make men more receptive to the erotic images it evokes, which are reminiscent of women, and of love.

The opulently rounded shapes of the petals of a rose in full bloom are suggestive of the mature female body and their rich red color evokes thoughts of lips and kisses. The austere form of the bud before blooming, which only subtly hints at the rounded abundance and fragrance of full maturity, and its opening to amorous life, exhuming a ravishing scent are external manifestations of the flower's life processes which man sees and senses and which stimulate his erotic fantasy.

As Jellinek's son conceded in a revised edition of his father's work, such bold statements about why certain smells excite us are no longer made today. The more we know, the less certain we feel; and we remain a long way from producing a general theory about the effect of smell on human behaviour and experience. Jellinek *père* may have been forty years ahead of the field in exploring the effects of erogenous odour complexes and materials, but when it comes to finding common triggers to olfactory experience, we are still sniffing in the dark.

Yet in these and many other experiments, the rose stands as a reference point for the floral fragrance *par excellence*. American researchers naturally included the rose among six wildly different scents they wanted to test in a 1980s global survey of smell recognition, conducted through the worldwide readership of *National Geographic* magazine (the other scents were sweat, banana, musk, cloves and gas). Some 1.5 million members responded: the rose proved its pedigree by achieving near-unanimous detection among women (99.5 per cent, equal with cloves) and scoring almost as well among men (99.0 per cent, 0.1 per cent more than cloves). In terms of recognition, cloves beat the rose into second place, correctly identified by 84.5 per cent of women and

81.6 per cent of men (the scores for cloves were 89.6 per cent and 83.2 per cent respectively). As the researchers explained, they had chosen cloves precisely because they are easy to detect and familiar to cultures around the world, and the smell of roses is complex, composed of many individual ingredients: if you miss one, your nose detects another.

In selecting their rose fragrance, the researchers opted for a 'typical' scent specific to no single strain. But as any true rose-lover will tell you, each rose has its own very particular scent that varies according to the vagaries of weather, soil, climate, time of day and age; even on the same bush, finicky growers maintain that different blooms have subtly different scents. And with some roses, the leaves smell too. The Sweet Briar, *Rosa rubiginosa,* spontaneously releases a fruity smell on a warm day, and by a gentle wind after light rain. Crush the innumerable oil glands in the lower parts of the leaves and it smells of English pippins.

As the English statesman, philosopher and garden-lover Sir Francis Bacon knew only too well, many roses release their fragrance best when smelt close at hand, yet 'the *Breath* of Flowers, is farre Sweeter in the Aire, (where it comes and Goes, like the Warbling of Musick) then in the Hand'. Determined to track down the sweetest-smelling flowers and shrubs to plant in the sweet walks so beloved by the courts of Queen Elizabeth and the early Stuarts, he must have tramped the length of his garden at Gorhambury in Hertfordshire, or perhaps nearby at his cousin Robert Cecil's Hatfield House, marshalling his favourites into a top ten for his celebrated essay *Of Gardens,* with further suggestions for plants to crush underfoot.

For Bacon, double white violets came top of the flowers that spontaneously perfume the air, followed by the July-flowering Musk rose. By this, he presumably meant the native *Rosa arvensis,* the same rose that graced Titania's bower, rather than the true Musk, *Rosa moschata,* which flowers in late summer and autumn.[2] Sweet Briars came fifth, after dying strawberry leaves and vine flowers, and garden roses nowhere at all, for 'Roses Damask and Red, are fast Flowers of their Smelles; So that; you may walke by a whole Row of them, and finde Nothing of their Sweetnesse; Yea though it be, in a Mornings Dew.'

Most rose growers are happy to savour their roses in the hand, although few take the business quite as seriously as the French rosarian

Dr Raoul Blondel, who submitted a thesis on the 'odiferous products of roses' to Paris's faculty of medicine in the late 1880s. His instructions on how to smell a rose cover a full page. First, he said, you should take a Cabbage rose and smell it slowly and circumspectly, taking care not to crush any of the scent glands in its stalk (pedicel). Draw the rose's fragrance into your nostrils in little bursts, alternating with pure air so as not to fatigue the membranes ('*papilles spéciales*') in the nose that receive and interpret the particles emitted by the flower. This gives you an odour of exquisite *finesse* for which the term 'suave' ought to be invented, said Blondel – the absolute and irreducible odour of rose. Continue smelling the rose and you receive a second odour, much less easy to define, comparable to the smell of pinks in Rimmel's eighteen-part classification. Persist in smelling and your nostrils will detect only a vague sensation of freshness; from this point on, your exhausted membranes will no longer transmit any real sensations at all.

For all his laborious smelling, when he tried to express in words the scent of the Cabbage rose, Blondel was forced like writers before him to resort to equivalences: the leaves release no special smell of their own, he said, until rubbed between the fingers, when they emit a distinct smell of cloves ('*une odeur carophyllée*' – carophyllene is the main component of clove oil). The glandulous calyx secretes a resinous liquid that smells at once of turpentine and pepper. The flower's many petals exhale a smell that is 'gentle, exquisite, a little fleeting, almost imperceptibly mingled over time with a clove-like scent, corresponding well with what we have called the "odour of Rose"'. He earned his doctorate with precision but hardly with poetry.

Aside from the Cabbage rose, a few rose varieties have no smell while others have been compared to a veritable store-cupboard of fruits, spices, flowers and sundry substances: violets, raspberries, banana, melon, peach, lily of the valley, lilac, hyacinth, cucumber, apricots, mignonette, cloves, nutmegs, aniseed, moss, damp earth, musk, face powder, sun-ripened fruits, Russian leather – even bed bugs, coriander and rancid butter.

The herbalist Maud Grieve had a good nose, although she borrowed freely from other writers without attribution. In a pamphlet on roses and pot-pourri published in the 1920s, she recognized three types of rose

Original watercolour drawing of the Moss rose, Rosa x centifolia
'Muscosa' for Curtis's Botanical Magazine *of 1788. Very popular in Victorian times, Moss roses secrete additional scent from their mossy glands.*

smells: the Cabbage rose, the Damask and the Tea rose, judging many roses – especially among the Hybrid Perpetuals and Hybrid Teas – to fall somewhere between the three. You cannot smell tea in the so-called Tea Roses, she decreed, judging that many lack fragrance altogether while others emit delicately fruity odours. The China rose she found astringent, refreshing and somewhat 'citrine' (did she mean citrous?); while 'Gloire de Dijon' (a cross between an unknown Tea rose and 'Souvenir de la Malmaison') 'has such an undefinable odour that any comparison is impossible'. And although the yellow Banksian rose has no smell, the clustered white varieties reminded her of the quite different Noisettes. Matching the scent to the name clearly exasperated her at times. The rose she knew as *Rosa muscosa* or the Musk rose (now *R.* × *centifolia* 'Muscosa') has 'a fine odour of pinks and none whatsoever of musk, in spite of its name, but the Hybrid Musk "Pax" with semi-single pure white blossoms tinged with lemon in bud, has a strong real musk perfume'.

Mrs Grieve's recommended roses yielding the purest and finest scents are well worth considering today; varieties still widely available include: the Rugosa Hybrids 'Blanc Double de Coubert' and 'Conrad Ferdinand Meyer'; the Hybrid Perpetuals 'Fisher Holmes', 'Général Jacqueminot', 'Hugh Dickson' and 'Ulrich Brunner'; the Noisette 'Maréchal Niel'; and the Hybrid Teas 'Gloire de Dijon' and 'La France'.

Currently, the best noses straddle the worlds of perfumery and rose-growing. One of the most perceptive is Robert Calkin, a retired perfumer who advises the English rose grower David Austin; among his favourite roses is the centuries-old Autumn Damask known as 'Quatre Saisons' (*R.* × *damascena* var. *semperflorens*): 'If sunshine had a smell this would be it,' he says. His other favourites include the Portland rose, 'Comte de Chambord'; the Hybrid Musk 'Buff Beauty' for its ability to fill a garden with its fragrance; and the Tea rose, 'Lady Hillingdon', whose scent he compares to a freshly opened packet of slightly tarry China tea.

As Calkin has demonstrated, the chemical composition of the rose fragrance is immensely complicated. More than 400 separate constituents make up the essential oil extracted from the flowers of the rose variety used in the Bulgarian rose industry, the Damask rose 'Kazanlik' (also known as *R.* × *damascena* var. *trigintipetala* and *R.* 'Professeur Emile Perrot'), and the total number of ingredients found across all rose varieties is likely to be higher. Smelt on their own, most of the components would not be associated with the rose, and many would be regarded as unpleasant, but together they constitute what we perceive as the 'unity' of the rose – a perfect blend, not just a mixture.

Staying with 'Kazanlik', we find that some 85 per cent by volume of its essential oil is made up of just four materials: the so-called rose alcohols, phenylethyl alcohol, citronellol, geraniol and nerol.[3] The main ingredient of commercial rosewater, phenylethyl alcohol, has a soft character typical of the paler Gallicas. Citronellol is wonderfully warm and vibrant, best smelt in Rugosa Hybrids such as R. 'Blanc Double de Coubert'. Geraniol is a little sharper, carrying a hint of geranium leaves as the name suggests, while nerol is harsher and fresh. Another ten or so ingredients make up a further 10 per cent of the oil, while hundreds more are present in tiny proportions in the remaining 5 per cent. Minor constituents can nonetheless influence the fragrance. Bulgarian rose oil, for instance, owes much of its 'true rose-like odour' to the presence of beta-damascenone, detectable in very low concentrations.

Other rose fragrances come from different mixes or different constituents altogether. For instance, the hint of damp, tarry greenhouse in R. gigantea, the Chinese ancestral species that sired many of our Tea roses, comes from dimethoxy toluene, which accounts for a full 50 per cent of its fragrance. A further 10 per cent comes from its other main ingredient, dihydro-beta-ionol, which smells of violets and earth. The same material is also found in R. chinensis, another presumed parent of the Tea roses and grandparent to the Noisettes. Robert Calkin says it can be best detected, together with the related ionones, in his favourite Hybrid Musk, 'Buff Beauty', and in the scented Banksian roses, further suggesting that 'the Banksians, with their intense violet character, may also have been involved somewhere along the line in the Tea rose ancestry'.

Blending two species or near species can produce some remarkable scents, says Calkin, such as the 'exquisitely simple fragrance' of 'Stanwell Perpetual', a cross between the Autumn Damask and the Scotch briar, R. spinosissima, which has fully double quartered blooms in the softest of blush pinks; and the amber-yellow verbena-scented R. 'Agnes', bred in Canada from a cross between R. rugosa and the yellow Persian rose, R. foetida 'Persiana'. Occasionally the parents' chemistry throws up something completely new, such as the anis character in R. 'Splendens' (also known as the 'myrrh-scented rose') arising from 4-vinyl anisole in crosses between the field rose, R. *arvensis* and a variety of R. *chinensis*. The Bourbon roses sired originally on the island of La Réunion (then known as the Île Bourbon – see Chapter 17) are mostly fruity in character; the silvery-pink 'Madame Pierre Oger' has one of the sweetest scents.

A French grower who has also joined forces with a professional perfumer to map the 'olfactory landscape' of the rose is Henri Delbard. Together they have devised a pyramidal map which puts the most volatile 'head notes' of the fragrance at the apex (the citrus scents of lemon, mandarin and bergamot; and the aromatics of aniseed, lavender and citronella). These express the perfume's spirit, according to Delbard. Next comes the scent's heart or personality, in descending notes classified as floral (rose, jasmine, lilac and so on), green (grass, ivy, leaves), fruity (raspberry, pear, peach, melon, etc), and spicy (cloves, nutmeg, cinnamon). At the bottom are the base notes, 'which form the wake of the perfume with the deep and lasting notes: wood and balsam'; these carry hints of cedar, patchouli and moss (wood); and vanilla, heliotrope and tonka bean (balsam). It takes almost twelve hours for a rose to play all its notes, says Delbard. If a rose seems to have no scent, maybe it is tired or cold – or simply not responding to the grower's attempt to market its fragrance.

Delbard has in effect borrowed Septimus Piesse's gamut of smells and expressed it not musically but in colour-coded pyramids. '*J'inventai la couleur des voyelles!*' (I invented the colour of vowels) wrote Rimbaud famously in his poem, 'Alchimie du Verbe', and here comes another Frenchman inventing the colour of smells.

As for the rose in the history of perfumery, its fluctuating popularity reflects changing tastes and developing technologies. Although Aristotle had a proper grasp of the principles of distillation, the ancient world made its perfumes by macerating flowers and spices with oils and fats, never by distilling them with water or steam.

The ancient Greeks were by no means the first to perfume their oils. Already by the thirteenth century BC, Pylos in the south-western Peloponnese had a flourishing industry making rose- and sage-scented oils (see Chapter 1); and the civilizations of the Persians, Medes and Babylonians were renowned for their luxurious unguents. Alexander the Great famously encountered them after he had crushed the Persians at Issus, and his companions led him to defeated King Darius's tent to wash away the stains of battle.

Here, when he beheld the bathing vessels, the water-pots, the pans, and the ointment boxes, all of gold curiously wrought, and smelt the fragrant odours with which the whole place was exquisitely perfumed, and from thence passed into a pavilion of great size and height, where the couches and tables and preparations for an entertainment were perfectly magnificent, he turned to those about him and said, 'This, it seems, is royalty.'[4]

The account comes straight out of Plutarch. Yet however impressed he was by Persian luxury, Alexander reserved Darius's most precious casket for an item of far greater value to him than mere unguents: his copy of Homer's *Iliad*.

The Greeks were nonetheless quick to assimilate the more refined Persian skills and tastes in perfumery, as we know from Theophrastus. Most Greek perfumes used a base of Egyptian or Syrian olive oil pressed from coarse olives, he tells us, but for roses (then worn chiefly by men), sesame oil was considered more receptive because of its higher viscosity. First, the perfumers steeped suitable spices in sweet wine: for rose perfume, the spices were ginger grass, *aspalathos* and sweet flag, and a quantity of salt. 'This treatment is peculiar to [rose] perfume,' noted Theophrastus, 'and involves a great deal of waste, twenty-three gallons of salt being put to eight gallons and a half of perfume.' Because of its high salt content, rose oil was considered an excellent remedy for inflamed ears.

Unlike iris spikenard and sweet marjoram (made from the roots), rose and gillyflower perfumes were made from the flowers; in the case of roses, fresh flowers were used in preference to dried. From Theophrastus we learn, too, that rose was one of the few perfumes given a colour (red, from alkanet), and that all floral perfumes have little vigour. At their peak after two months, they deteriorate after a year.

From the evidence of Pylos, ancient perfumers ran thriving businesses, storing their wares in lead vessels and alabaster phials in north-facing upper rooms to reduce the risk of evaporation. Faced with indecisive buyers, they would dab customers' wrists with rose oil to override all other scents, giving their customers little choice but to buy the proffered rose. Rose was recommended as an additive to lighten the scent of other perfumes, and to impart a sweet fragrance to wine, but not in food, where it was considered too obtrusive. Roses were also used to make perfume powders, and as fresh rose petals to enhance and refresh compound perfumes. It was clearly a special favourite of Theophrastus, who found its fragrance energizing. 'This perfume is also considered to be good against lassitude, because its heat and its lightness make it suitable, and also because it penetrates to the inner passages. Some say that *kypros* is quite as efficacious: for this too has a delicate scent.'

Writing some three and a half centuries after Theophrastus, Pliny the Elder crammed as much information as he could about perfumes and perfume-making into his vastly inclusive *Natural History*, thereby conveying Rome's enthusiasm for unguents in general and the perfume of roses in particular. They made their unguents from oils and sweet-smelling substances, he explained, adding colouring matter such as cinnabar and alkanet, and sometimes salt to aid the oil's retaining properties (but never salt and alkanet together, or so he says, disagreeing here with Theophrastus).

The whole process is brought to life on the walls of Pompeii's House of the Vettii, in a cartoon frieze illustrating the art of perfumery. The 'workers' are winged cupids and psyches, who first press the oil, which they then heat in a cauldron together with aromatics, stirring the pot as they add still more ingredients. The perfumed oil is bottled and put on sale; in the final scene, a young matron seated on a cushion and fanned by a slave smells the product on her bare arm. Giving a frisson to the enterprise is the notion that the Vettii brothers who commissioned the frieze were quite possibly freed slaves who may themselves have stirred the perfume pot in their earlier lives. The brothers certainly became rich enough to paint their cupids at work and at play.[5]

After Rome's fall, the combined effect of Christian asceticism and barbarian austerity cast perfumery into the shadows. The early Christian

Church heartily disapproved of anything to do with smells: burning incense before an image of the Emperor had been a standard test of imperial loyalty, and roses were doubly tainted with pagan idolatry. But just as the western Church gradually transformed the rose into a very Christian image, so it sublimated pagan practices and drew incense into its own rituals.

The next major advance in perfumery – of particular significance for roses – came not from the Christian West but from the empire of the Arabs, which had spread rapidly eastwards and westwards from the Prophet Muhammad's heartland in Arabia. This was the art of distillation, whose application to perfumery is often attributed to the great eleventh-century Persian physician and polymath Ibn Sînâ (Avicenna), but it was already well established more than a century earlier, when a detailed description of distilling apparatus appeared in the work of another Persian physician, the philosopher and alchemist al-Râzî, known to the Latins as Rhazes. He even referred specifically to the *al-anbîk* (an Arabic word that has come to us as 'alembic') as 'that apparatus in which rose-water is made'.

First you put the substance into the gourd-shaped part of the apparatus, explained al-Râzî, then you place the alembic over it, securing the join with rags smeared with marshmallow and glue. After leaving it to dry, you put it in a stove and arrange a cup to receive the resultant liquid, drop by drop.

After that you kindle a fire of the proper intensity under the pot. If it be a humid substance a gentle fire by means of charcoal or some other fuel should be used . . . If properly heated for a long time the substance passes over in the form of water into the receiver. This is called the distillate ('muquattar') no matter what the distilled substance is.[6]

More than 1,000 years later, much the same process persists in the small homestead distilleries of the Middle East such as the one I visited in Qamsar, northern Iran, where the cauldrons were heated with gas (see Chapter 12). The roses used were known locally as *Gol Mohammedi,* and because the product was destined for Mecca, rosewater was added to the initial water before the gas was lit.

Preparing rosewater for the seated Sultan Ghiyath al-Din, from a manuscript on Indian cookery and the preparation of sweetmeats, the Ni'matnama-i Nasir al-Din Shah, *c.1495–1505. In the foreground are ten glass distillery flasks.*

Long celebrated as the country of roses, Persia had developed a perfume industry from the beginning of the ninth century at least. Shiraz with its extensive rose fields was the great Persian centre for making rosewater – an industry so important that the province of Faristan was required to pay a yearly tribute of 30,000 phials of rosewater to the Treasury of Caliph al-Mamun in Baghdad,[7] and rosewater was sent all over the world – to China, India, the Yemen, Egypt, Andalusia and the Maghreb of North Africa.

Roses were still flourishing in and around Shiraz when the German traveller and physician Engelbert Kaempfer visited the region in the 1680s, especially in one of its north-western suburbs. As Kaempfer recorded, 'Even as the roses in Persia are produced in greater abundance and with finer perfume than those in any other country in the world, so also do those of this particular district in the vicinity of Shiraz, excel in profusion and in fragrance those of any other locality in Persia.'

Damascus was a later but no less important centre, here described by the renowned Arab cosmographer and religious leader al-Dimashkî, who died in 1327. Writing of the Nahar Mizzah branch of the River Barada, which runs through Damascus, he explained that its name came from a village known originally as al-Munazzah (the Incomparable) 'because of the healthy air, the pure water, the beautiful pleasure-houses, the delicious fruit, the many flowers and roses and the production of rose-water; the residue of which is thrown on the roads, lanes and alleys of this place like dirt. Thus the smell is incomparable and finer than musk until the roses are overblown.'

Rosewater is especially prized throughout the Muslim and Arab worlds as an expression of hospitality. When the Danish traveller Carsten Niebuhr visited Arabia and the Yemen in the 1760s, he was struck by the way rosewater and perfumes were added to the usual pipes on visits of ceremony. As he wrote after his return (he was, in fact, the sole survivor of the journey), when the visitors were ready to retire, a servant came in to sprinkle the company with rosewater, while another perfumed the visitor's beard, and the wide sleeves of his gown. 'When we first saw the ceremony used . . . we were a good deal surprised to see a servant sit down beside us, and cast water upon our faces.'

Rosewater is not the only product of distillation. Once the part of the rose fragrance that is soluble in water has vaporized and condensed as rosewater, floating on its surface you will find an oily surface layer of rose oil that can be extracted by a process of double-distillation to produce 'attar' or 'otto' of roses. It seems the early Arab and Muslim chemists were less interested in this, as none of their early works describe a separate process to extract the oil, although their distillations will inevitably have produced drops of the oil along with the rosewater, and some of their instructions for making rosewater refer to a more concentrated elixir which presumably contained rose oil.

The Italian Geronimo Rossi of Ravenna usually takes credit for developing the technique to separate rose oil from rosewater (described in a European source dated 1574), but it may also have been developed independently in the Arab world. Rossi himself later described his discovery; and distilled rose oil appears in the price lists of German apothecaries from the early 1600s.

This gives the lie to the charming story – still current – that rose oil was 'discovered' by chance in 1612 at a feast, some say their wedding feast, given by the ambitious, intelligent and supremely beautiful Princess Nur Jahan for her husband, the Mughal Emperor Jahangir, at which the princess filled an entire canal with rosewater. As she walked with the emperor by the edge of the fragrant water – in some versions they are gently rowing – they noticed an oily scum floating on its surface. Once the oil was skimmed off, the whole court recognized it as the most delicate perfume known to the East, and they 'afterwards endeavor'd to imitate that by Art, which was originally the production of Nature'. In his memoirs, Jahangir attributed the invention 'during our reign' to Nur Jahan's mother, claiming that 'if one drop is rubbed on the palm it will perfume a whole room and make it seem more subtly fragrant than if many rosebuds had opened at once. It cheers one up and restores the soul.'[8] This is still not early enough for the Mughals to claim credit for the oil's discovery.

Just as Greek knowledge had inspired the medieval chemists and alchemists of the Arab world, so the Persians' and the Arabs' perfected skills in distillation and perfumery travelled back towards the West by two main routes: through Alexandria and the old Roman provinces of North Africa, then up through Muslim Spain; or through Constantinople, 'the greatest city-port in Christendom', which stood at the crossroads of East and West, teeming with traders from Persia, Russia, Armenia, the Balkans, the Levant, Syria, and the Italian city states of Venice, Amalfi, Naples and Genoa.

The trading connection helps to explain how the Italians became Europe's perfumery kings in the sixteenth and seventeenth centuries. From Italy, a taste for refined perfumes – and the skills to make them –

spread throughout Europe. When the notorious Catherine de' Medici travelled to France to marry Henri II, she took with her a Florentine perfumer named René, who later set up shop on the Pont au Change, where his Italian powders and perfumes became the latest fashion. Catherine is also said to have encouraged the foundation of a French perfume industry at Grasse, close to Nice in the South.

Across the Channel in England, Edward de Vere, Earl of Oxford, sparked a fashion for sweet waters and perfumes at the court of Queen Elizabeth I when he returned from Italy around 1573, bringing with him:

Gloves: sweete bagges, a perfumed leather Jerkin, and other pleasant thinges, and that yeere the Queene had a payre of perfumed Gloves trimmed only with foure Tuftes or Roses, of cullered Silke, the Queene tooke such pleasure in those Gloves, that shee was pictured with those Gloves uppon her hands, and for many yeeres after it was called the Earle of Oxfords perfume.

The English were already making sweet waters and washes, as the early herbals reveal, but the Italians were very much better at it; and from this time onwards, the 'secrets books' of arcane knowledge and household hints were full of recipes for perfuming clothes and masking body smells with rosewater and other concoctions, many of them lifted straight from Italian sources. Washing with water was not yet associated with cleanliness. Europeans of the sixteenth century used friction and perfume to shake off unpleasant odours. 'To cure the goat-like stench of armpits,' wrote the French author of a self-help health guide of 1572, 'it is useful to press and rub the skin with a compound of roses.'

Gradually, as the seventeenth century progressed, the French succeeded in snatching the perfumer's crown from the Italians: now French perfumes and French perfumery manuals became the rage. As the 'French Perfumer' boasted in a tiny book of recipes for powders, wash balls, essences, oils, waxes, pomanders, pastes and sweet waters:

The best Wash-balls were made formerly at *Bolognia* in *Italy*, for the *Bolonais* had found the Secret to prepare and perfume the Soap so well, that no body a long time attempted to find it out; but they have been of late so negligent, and we have applied our selves that way with so good Success, that we have found the way to make them better than they ever did.

By the 1750s, the French court of Louis XV rivalled Ancient Rome in its love of perfumes. Known as '*la cour parfumée*' (the perfumed court), it reputedly demanded the wearing of a different perfume on each day of the week. Tastes in perfumes were changing, too. Gone were the feral

In this portrait of Madame de Pompadour (1758) French rococo artist
François Boucher places King Louis XV's mistress in a woodland setting surrounded
with roses in reference to the perfumed court.

odours of musk and civet, with their undertones of excrement and sex, and in their place reigned the delicate scents of spring flowers: not just the ever-popular rosewater, but waters scented with violets, thyme, lavender and rosemary. The change was signalled by the King's mistress, Madame de Pompadour, who projected herself in the canvases of her favourite court painter, François Boucher, luxuriating in silk and festooned with rococo roses, in her corsage, in her hair, at her feet.

And so roses and light floral perfumes remained popular for more than a century, ceding ground temporarily whenever the leaders of fashion reverted to heavier perfumes with an animal base. Despite her supposed love of roses, the Empress Josephine relished the sensual odours of musk, civet and ambergris. Sixty years after her death, her boudoir at Malmaison still smelt unmistakably of musk, unless that is another myth dreamed up to support Napoleon's battlefield instruction that she was not to wash in anticipation of his homecoming.

After Josephine, floral scents came back into fashion at least until the 1860s, chief among them the rose, while musk was again relegated to the courtesan's chamber, if not the brothel. In a work permeated with roses, Eugene Rimmel hesitated over whether to advise 'the ladies' on their choice of perfume, then had these words to say to the nervous:

Use simple extracts of flowers which can never hurt you, in preference to compounds, which generally contain musk and other ingredients likely to affect the head. Above all, avoid strong, coarse perfumes; and remember, that if a woman's temper may be told from her handwriting, her good taste and good breeding may as easily be ascertained by the perfume she uses

Eugene Rimmel belonged to the old school of perfumery which admired simplicity over complexity, flowers over animals, the fresh and familiar over the sultry and exotic. But tastes were becoming more complex, aided by the chemists' discovery of synthetic fragrances such as coumarin, found naturally in the tonka bean and synthesized from coal tar by the English chemist William Henry Perkin in 1868 (it smells of new-mown hay). The French perfumer Aimé Guerlain used it in 'Jicky' (created in 1889), said to be the oldest perfume still in existence and one of the first truly 'vertical' perfumes, with fresh citrus notes on top;

351

flowers (rose and jasmine) and 'woody' notes (vetiver, orris root and patchouli) in the middle; and base notes that included the synthetic aroma chemicals of coumarin and vanillin. Simple florals were on the way out, just as tastes in horticulture now favoured the outlandish and the strange. Huysmans's anti-hero of *À Rebours* pushed tastes to the limit, preferring monstrous exotics to 'the pretentious, conformist, stupid flowers, like the rose, which belong exclusively in porcelain holders painted by young girls'.

But if you train your nose well, you will still find the unmistakable smell of roses in many 'modern' perfumes, including some of the very best, such as Chanel's No. 5, hailed as 'a masterpiece of modernist sculpture from 1921, one you can wear'. The French food writer and rose lover Sylvie Girard-Lagorce detected the heady fragrance of Bulgarian roses in Dior's Diorissimo, launched in 1956, and more roses wafting in the top notes of Estée Lauder's Private Collection of 1973. She found roses, too, in Cabochard by Grès, Anaïs Anaïs by Cacharel, Caron's Fleurs de Rocaille and Infini, Jean Patou's Joy, Yves Saint Laurent's Y, and Lancôme's Trésor – this last smelling (according to the eccentric biochemist and perfume expert Luca Turin) of powdery rose and vetiver, and from a distance 'the trashiest, most good-humored pink-mohair-sweater-and-bleached-hair thing imaginable'.

If you hanker after a particular rose scent, consult Turin's *Perfumes, the Guide*, written with Tania Sanchez, where the perfumes named after roses are catholic indeed, categorized variously as: turpentine rose, rose liqueur, angry rose, fresh rose, ambery rose, rose chypre, green rose, nostalgic chypre, pale rose, apple mimosa, floral masculine, polite floral, huge rose, brassy peony, fruity rose, syrupy rose, jasmine rose, peachy rose, minty rose, crisp rose, or quite simply 'not rose' but rather 'aldehydic carrot juice'.

For such an ethereal creation as perfume, the methods used to extract the fragrant essence of a rose are remarkably crude, even unpleasant, their grossness mirrored by Patrick Süskind's international bestseller, *Perfume, The Story of a Murderer*. Born into the stink and depravity of eighteenth-century Paris, the dehumanized and desensitized protagonist, Jean-Baptiste Grenouille, would eventually create for himself a superhuman scent from the bodies of dead girls. But first he had to stock up his memory bank of smells: 'The smell of a sweating horse meant just as much to him as the tender green bouquet of a bursting rose-bud, the acrid stench of a bug no less worthy than the aroma arising from a larded veal roast in an aristocrat's kitchen.'

After learning the art of distillation at the house of the perfumer and glover Guiseppe Baldini on Paris's Pont au Change (where Catherine de' Medici's Italian perfumer had set up shop before him), Grenouille travelled south to Grasse, even then at the heart of France's perfume industry, where he learned the much older technique of *enfleurage* (known to the Egyptians, Greeks and Romans), which used oils or fats to capture the smells of natural materials such as flowers. This could be done in two ways: *enfleurage à froid* (absorption), or the hot process known as maceration or *enfleurage à chaud*. In the former (rarely if ever used today), petals were individually embedded on plates layered with

Workers sorting through roses for the Perfumery Bruno Court at Grasse, France's centre of the perfume industry, in the 1910s.

353

animal fat; once the fat had absorbed the fragrance, it was processed to yield a perfumed oil.

Grenouille mastered the hot process of maceration or *enfleurage à chaud,* in use right up until the twentieth century but little practised in modern perfumery because of the damaging effects of heat. Fats such as pork lard and beef tallow were heated in copper cauldrons over a fire or water bath, making 'a creamy soup into which [the journeyman] pitched shovelfuls of fresh blossoms, while Grenouille constantly had to stir it all with a spatula as long as a broom'. Now and then the soup got too thick, and they had to sieve it quickly to remove the 'macerated cadavers', adding fresh blossoms until all the piles had passed through the cauldron of fats. At the end of the day, the refuse was steeped in boiling water and wrung out in a screw-press, to extract every last bit of fragrance. 'The majority of the scent, however, the soul of the sea of blossoms, had remained in the cauldron, trapped and preserved in an unsightly, slowly congealing greyish-white grease.'

After several days of such treatment, the fat would become saturated, unable to absorb any more odours. Then it could be sieved one final time, sealed into jars and sold as perfumed pomades; or its fragrance could be further extracted from the fat by mixing it with pure alcohol to produce a 'concrete essence'. And so the scent of roses passed from the petals to the fat to the alcohol. A final stage remained, as Grenouille discovered: filtering the perfumed alcohol to remove any last traces of oil and then distilling the alcohol over a gentle flame to produce 'the finest oil of the blossom, its polished scent concentrated a hundred times over to a little puddle of *essence absolue'.* No longer sweet, this absolute essence 'was almost painfully intense, pungent and acrid. And yet one single drop, when dissolved in a quart of alcohol, sufficed to revitalize it and resurrect a whole field of flowers.'

Such a messy way of capturing the scent of rose has long been out of favour, its place in perfumery taken by essential oils obtained by distillation ('attar' or 'otto' of roses, known as 'rose essence' in per-fumery), and 'rose absolute', extracted by solvents or carbon dioxide at high pressure. The much-fêted attar or otto of roses came to Europe from Turkey and more particularly from around Kazanlik in modern Bulgaria, a small tract of country on the southern side of the Balkan mountains,

Anne Marie Trechslin's watercolour of 'Kazanlik', the Damask rose used in the Bulgarian perfume industry.

then in the Turkish province of Rumelia. Here, in the fine valley of the Tunja, sheltered by mountains and well watered by streams, Ottoman merchants had introduced towards the end of the seventeenth century an old Damask rose, 'Kazanlik', for the production of rose oil; elsewhere in Turkey it seems the otto industry developed much later.

The word 'attar' comes via Persian from the Arabic '*itr*' meaning essence or scent, thus betraying its roots in Arab chemistry.[9] Although its method of distillation was known to Italian and French perfumers, it was a rare and costly commodity that was slow to enter European commerce. Distilled by villagers and carried south to Turkish ports, the rose oil was shipped to Venice and on to the courts of Europe. By 1850, Kazanlik (whose name in Turkish means literally 'the place of stills') processed 600 tons of rose petals to produce more than one and a half tons of the precious oil a year.

An early British Vice-Consul from Adrianople (now Edirne, across the border in Turkey) painted an unduly rosy picture of the rose harvest: 'at sunrise the plains look like a vast garden full of life and fragrance, with hundreds of Bulgarian boys and girls gathering the flowers into baskets and sacks, the air impregnated with the delicious scent, and the scene enlivened by songs, dancing, and music'. A more down-to-earth account from about the same time talked of the rose workers finding that their fingers were so hardened 'they do not feel the pricking of the thorns, but became covered with a dark resinous substance emanating from the flower stalks'. At the day's end the men would scrape the gum off their fingers, roll it into balls, and smoke it mixed with tobacco in their cigarettes.

Early apparatus to double-distil the precious attar was extremely primitive: small copper stills, connected with a straight tin tube, cooled by passing through a wooden trough fed by a stream of water. A flask at the end of the tube collected the distillate. Flowers and their calyces went straight into the still as soon as they reached the distillery: twenty pounds of flowers to sixteen and a half gallons of water. The apparatus was then sealed with clay or fuller's earth, the furnace lit and the water boiled for an hour or more until it had produced two flasks of distillate, when the petals were thrown away and the hot water in the still used for the next batch of flowers. The distillate from four separate operations (eight flasks in total) was then distilled a second time, producing just a single

*Bulgaria's perfume industry in 1903, showing the distillation of roses
in a factory at Kazanlik and the maceration of petals in oil.*

flaskful, this time collected in a spherical container with a long neck. This last was put to cool and, after a day or so, a yellow layer of otto would have risen through the water to the top of the flask, where it could be skimmed off by a long-handled tin funnel punched with a hole at the bottom to let any remaining water escape. You can still find such primitive stills among the Turkish rose growers of Isparta, and in Bulgaria, but most roses today go to more modern, steam-operated distilleries.

From the 1880s, Turkey and Bulgaria vied with each other for supremacy in the world market for otto of roses. Both were checked by the Great War of 1914–18, when food production took precedence over roses, but a decade or so later, when Maud Grieve was writing her pamphlets on roses and fragrant flowers, Bulgaria had regained her footing as the world's major producer, just ahead of Turkey. France was also steadily developing its rose oil industry, and there were pockets of production in Cyprus (around the village of Milikouri), Germany, Algiers and Morocco. The beautiful Dades valley, south of the Atlas Mountains in Morocco, remains an important centre of production.

In earlier times, attar was produced in the Fayyum oasis, south-west of Cairo, and since the Mughals, India developed a thriving attar industry centred around Ghazipur, north-east of Benares, on the left bank of the Ganges. This has virtually died out and production has moved further west into Uttar Pradesh (especially around Jaunpur), using *R. × damascena* 'Bussorah' or 'Barwana'. Economics, as always, dictates what is produced where, for as Maud Grieve drily remarked, countless millions of rose blossoms fade unused in sun-drenched California, because 'the world's supply of Otto of Roses, one of the most expensive of the volatile oils, is produced in countries in which men and women will sell their time for a fraction of what American labour demands'.

Turkey might now have the edge on Bulgaria in terms of quantity of production, but Bulgarian oil is regarded as finer in quality and therefore commands a higher price: a kilogram of certified organic rose oil from Bulgaria's 2008 harvest currently commands around €7,000. Bulgarian rose otto is pale yellow or slightly olive yellow, and its smell is described by an industry chemist as 'warm, deep-floral, slightly spicy and immensely rich, truly reminiscent of red roses, often with nuances in the spicy and honeylike notes'.

Rose absolute, by contrast, is extracted using a solvent traditionally benzene but now more typically petroleum ether or n-hexane, and there is some interest in using supercritical carbon dioxide. This method is more common in France and Morocco, where the Centifolia – is the main rose used. After early harvesting (when the roses are still sparkling with dewdrops) the flowers are stirred in a vat with the solvent, which draws out the aromatic compounds and other soluble compounds such as colour. Vacuum processing removes the solvent for reuse, leaving a waxy residue known as rose concrete. This is then mixed with alcohol to dissolve the aromatic constituents, and the alcohol is in turn subjected to low-pressure evaporation to produce rose absolute, also known as Rose de mai absolute when Centifolia roses are used. Centifolia rose absolute is an orange-yellow to orange-brown viscous liquid, with a 'rich and sweet, deep-rosy, very tenacious' odour. It is used extensively in medium- to high-priced perfumes, especially those with a floral, chypre or oriental base, and to 'round off the sharp corners or rough notes in synthetic compositions'. Damask roses produce a more reddish liquid (as in Bulgarian rose absolute), used extensively in high-class perfumes. Today, some processes apply supercritical carbon dioxide to turn rose concrete into rose absolute.

When I visited Robert Calkin last summer, he produced from his refrigerator a small flaçon not of rose absolute but of twenty-year-old attar of roses: to my untrained nose, the first sniff brought a smell of childhood sweets, the rose equivalent of the little hard violets that remind me of maiden aunts. With Robert's help, I was able to translate aspects of this smell into notes of honey, bitter almonds (chemically benzaldehyde, used in synthetic almonds), and a faint whiff of dried haystack. Rose absolute is softer, apparently, less pungent, more complete and recognizably 'rosy', retaining the softness that attar of roses has lost to the water.

On my own, I would not have been able to isolate and identify the different elements that make up this essence of rose: the bitter and the sweet, the heavenly and the disreputable, the familiar and the unexpected. Poetry comes closest to containing such duality, and the strange heady odour arising from Robert Calkin's little flaçon of twenty-year old attar of roses made me think of Jo Shapcott's poem 'Rosa sancta', written in answer to one of Rilke's French rose poems (see Chapter 19).

Now you've made
a saint out of me,
Saint Rose, open-handed,
she who smells of God naked.

But, for myself, I've learned
to love the whiff of mildew
Because though not Eve, exactly,
yes, I stink of the Fall.

Through smell, I believe we are getting closer to understanding the mystery of the rose and why this flower above all others retains such a powerful hold on our imagination.

Modern Times

Chapter Seventeen
Rose Mania

Rose mania, which gripped Europe and America in the mid to late nineteenth century, may not have been as sudden or as catastrophic as the tulip fever that flared among the Dutch in the 1630s, but it defined its age just as dramatically. Accumulation, expansion and conspicuous display were the new watchwords, as breeders competed to bring the newest, largest, most spectacular varieties to market, and consumers of all classes sought to acquire the latest breeds.

By the 1880s, rose parties were all the rage in Britain (or so an editorial in the *Gardeners' Chronicle* would have us believe), held 'every day, all day long, and far into the night'. If rose parties at midday were apt to be hot, dusty and exhausting affairs, 'Roses at break of day – a dewy one – are simply divine – so full of beauty, freshness, and fragrance, as to fill and satisfy and soothe our every sense of pleasure'. Roses by moonlight offered even greater pleasures, when they seem 'so different in colour and even form as to appear altogether new and different flowers. The perfume, too, is fuller, richer, sweeter; and perhaps, to enjoy Roses to the full, it would be well at times to meet them in the gloaming or by moonlight alone.'

Written for wealthy garden owners and their head gardeners, the *Gardeners' Chronicle* naturally recorded their readers' more extravagant floral happenings, such as the Covent Garden bookseller Mr Bohn's 'grand Rose fête' at his Twickenham home for between 200 and 300 'nobility and gentry', mostly neighbours, who flocked to admire his roses – 'some thousands in number' – all magnificently in bloom, among them revered varieties such as the flaming 'Géant des Batailles', the more ethereal 'La Reine', the beautiful new 'Paul's Queen Victoria' and a number of prized yellows, such as 'Cloth of Gold' and 'Persian Yellow'. Of equal interest to readers were the 3,000 tea-scented roses that graced the wedding in March 1878 of the future Prime Minister Lord Rosebery, a 'pretty' idea suggested by his bride, Hannah de Rothschild, and achieved by Lord Rosebery's gardener and the many glasshouses at his disposal.

The Americans were even more wildly extravagant. In midwinter New York, 1884, the Vanderbilts threw a party for some 1,000 guests, for whom they had bought 50,000 cut roses, among them the very choicest varieties, including 'Maréchal Niel', 'Général Jacqueminot', and 'Larmarque'. The rose had replaced the camellia of fifty years previously, when the camellia retailed freely at a dollar apiece, while the humble rose went for a tenth of the price. 'Now the rose is queen, and the poor camellia finds none so poor to do her reverence.'

But rose mania – and certainly the mania for breeding new varieties of rose – actually started with the French, and the coterie of amateur and professional rose-growers living in and around Paris at the time of the First Empire. These are the men whose names have already been linked to Empress Josephine, and whose skills and rose passions came to be universally identified with her: men such as Du Pont, Cels, Descemet, Vibert, Vilmorin, and the administrator of Napoleon's parks nurseries and gardens, Le Comte Jean-Baptiste-Louis Lelieur de Ville-sur-Arce, who dedicated his little rose monograph to the Empress in suitably flowery terms.

Redouté's exquisite portraits of their best creations further inflamed passions, and the mania for growing new roses spread like a virus to other French centres, adding new names such as Laffay at Auteil, Calvert and Prévost at Rouen, the Guillots at Lyon, and crucially introducing new Chinese blood into the mix. For while many of the early French rose-breeders were renowned for their European crosses – especially the patriotic Gallicas – men like Jean Laffay immediately identified the precious gifts the Chinese rose might bring: strong clear colours, delicate shapes and repeated flowering throughout the season.

By the 1830s, French success at rose-breeding prompted the now forgotten but then fashionable novelist of upper-class life, Mrs Charles

Gore, to write an English call to arms, *The Rose Fancier's Manual* (based, it should be said, on a French original), designed 'to render *every* amateur a rose grower', and to bring rose creation in England up to the same heights as her success with dahlias. In Mrs Gore's opinion, climate was not the main reason for French pre-eminence, as England's superior soil and horticultural excellence soon made up for the drab English weather. No, the factors underlying French success were partly economic and partly social. Unlike the English, who were engrossed in growing tender exotics, the French were deterred by the high cost of fuel, and therefore devoted their attention almost exclusively to hardy plants. Furthermore, she maintained, as the French retired to their summer seats in May and stayed there until December, they spent all their money on growing plants that would adorn their flower gardens during the summer season. 'They care little for any that cannot be brought to perfection in the open air; and precisely the same motive which promotes the cultivation of the dahlia in England, has brought the rose to greater perfection in France.'

The Americans, too, puzzled over France's undoubted success at breeding roses, concluding that the answer lay in differences of national character. As rose mania crossed the Atlantic, nurseryman S. B. Parsons of Flushing, New York, declared that:

The French are constantly searching for improvements in horticultural science and practice, with an enthusiasm rarely found in the more cold Englishman, whose skill seems less to consist in the creation of new varieties, than in growing perfectly those already known None, indeed, can surpass the English in the art of growing fine plants, but we are chiefly indebted to the French for the finest new varieties of the Rose.

Given his high opinion of French talents, Parsons was all the more regretful that 'so little confidence can be placed in the greater number of French rose growers', apart from a handful of honourable exceptions such as Laffay, Vibert and Verdier. Even these did not escape censure. After a very pleasant visit to Laffay, Parsons was nonetheless 'rather disappointed in finding so little method in the arrangement of his grounds'.

*

While France took the commercial lead in breeding new varieties, England is generally credited with introducing one of the most mysterious of the 'new roses' that was to play its part in siring the repeat-flowering roses of the nineteenth century: the little red Portland rose, cultivated from at least 1783, when it appeared as the 'Portland Crimson Monthly Rose', *Rosa portlandica,* in the catalogue of a London nurseryman and seedsman of City road and Covent Garden, Luker and Smith.[1]

Mystery surrounds both its parentage and its provenance. Redouté included it as an Autumn Damask in the first volume of his magnificent *Les Roses*; his splendid image of the semi-double bright red rose convinced Dr C. C. Hurst that it resulted from the mating of a Chinese rose (probably 'Slater's Crimson China') with a Damask-Gallica cross. Recent DNA testing of 100 'old' cultivated rose varieties appeared to confirm this theory, placing the five Portland roses midway between the European roses (Damasks, Gallicas and Albas) and the later Chinese-European crosses, such as the Hybrid Perpetuals, Teas and Hybrid Teas.

The scientists had, however, taken the lead from Dr Hurst and assumed from the start of their experiments that the Portlands had a China parent, which rose-growers now generally dispute. After many years' acquaintance with Portland roses, Peter Beales believes that while Damasks and Gallicas clearly played a part, no China rose was ever involved. Peter Harkness further elucidates the confusion by suggesting that two different roses each bore the Portland name: an early 'Portlandica' or 'Portland Crimson Monthly Rose', cultivated in Britain from at least 1775, and a later Portland rose – Redouté's 'Rosier de Portland', also known as *R. paestana* – originating perhaps in Italy around 1795, which found its way first to England and then to France.

Harkness also sheds light on how the Portland rose got its name, discounting the usual theories that it was named after either the second or third Duchess of Portland and proposing instead that it was first named after the Portland estate where it was cultivated. The later rose (named 'Le Rosier de Portland' by French grower André Du Pont in or after 1803) may even have honoured the third Duke of Portland, he suggests, for his help in persuading the Board of Admiralty to grant a passport to nurseryman John Kennedy, allowing him to pass safely through the English blockade of French ports during the wars with

Napoleon. A conservative-leaning Whig politician, Portland had joined the cabinet of William Pitt the Younger in 1794 and remained a member until Pitt's death in 1806.

The attribution to the Duke is more plausible than to either of the duchesses, although his mother, the second Duchess of Portland, Margaret Cavendish Bentinck, has a good claim to posthumous recognition. Friend of plantsman Phillip Miller, botanical artist Mary Delany and philosopher Jean-Jacques Rousseau, with whom she went plant-collecting in the Peak District, she amassed an immense natural history collection to rival that of Sir Hans Sloane and died, aged seventy, in 1785. So she will almost certainly have witnessed the first-generation Portlands blooming on her estate, however the rose was named at the time.

And whoever actually 'discovered' the Portland rose, it found its way to France, where Le Comte Lelieur (or strictly speaking his gardener, M. Souchet) bred a seedling at the imperial flower garden of Sèvres in the Parc St Cloud around 1812; it was first named R. 'Lelieur' or 'La Quatre Saisons Lelieur' in his honour, and only later, after Napoleon's downfall, renamed 'Rose du Roi'. Redouté painted it for his third volume of *Les Roses*, where Thory named it *Rosa bifera macrocarpa*. Licur's rose is pricklier than its Portland parent, more obviously double (Thory counts four to five rows of petals compared to the Portland's two or three), and its perfume is said to be 'delicious'. It would go on to become one of the founder ancestors of a new race of Hybrid Perpetuals. Although relatively few Portlands remain in cultivation, they are worth growing for their heady boudoir scent, especially evident in 'Comte de Chambord', 'Jacques Cartier' and both 'Rose de Rescht' and 'Rose du Roi'.

The French brought two more early crosses into circulation. This time they really were chance couplings between Europe and China, and both occurred outside metropolitan France. First came the roses now known as Noisettes, after their nurserymen breeders. These originated at the very beginning of the nineteenth century as a spontaneous hybrid between the Musk rose (*R. moschata*) and a China rose (assumed to be 'Parsons' Pink China') in hot and humid Charleston, South Carolina, in the garden of the wealthy rice planter John Champneys. Champneys first raised the bastard offspring in 1802, a non-remontant climber known as 'Champneys' Pink Cluster'. Perhaps in return for the original gift of the China rose,

Rosa Noisettiana.

Rosier de Philippe Noisette.

P. J. Redouté pinx.

Imprimerie de Remond

Langlois sculp.

The first Noisette rose, bred in Charleston South Carolina by nurseryman Philippe Noisette and sent to the Paris nursery of his brother Louis. From the second volume of Redouté's Les Roses, 1821.

Champneys gave a seedling to his neighbour, the nurseryman Philippe Noisette (Thory called him 'one of the cleverest nurserymen' of the southern states of America), and by the second generation the gene of repeat-flowering had resurfaced. Noisette sent seeds and plants to the Paris nursery of his brother Louis, who propagated it for the French market. Horticulture was clearly in their genes: their father had been head gardener to the Comte de Provence.[2]

This startling new rose – known as 'Blush Noisette' or 'le rosier Philippe Noisette' – caused an immediate stir. Redouté painted it at Noisette's Parisian nursery garden, where it flowered in 1818. By the time his third and final volume of *Les Roses* appeared in 1824, the rose had proved its hardiness, having survived the fierce winter of 1822, and was now destined, in Thory's words, 'to become the long-term ornament of our gardens'. It would also make the fortunes of the Noisettes who, in the possibly exaggerated verdict of Mrs Gore, made so much money that by 1838 they 'no longer continue to raise roses from seed', having passed on that role in Paris to Laffay ('a most enthusiastic and intelligent gardener') and Vibert (the author of 'some valuable treatises on the culture of roses').

Britain's premier rose-grower of the time, Thomas Rivers of Saw-bridgeworth, Hertfordshire, conveys the excitement that greeted the first Noisette. 'Perhaps no new rose was ever so much admired as this,' he wrote in 1837. 'When first introduced, its habit was so peculiar and so unlike any other known variety, that the Parisian amateurs were quite enraptured with it.' Its unmistakable perfume linked it to the well-loved Musk rose, while its free growth, hardiness and large clusters of blooms produced very late in the year were (in the words of another English rose-grower, William Paul) 'indeed recommendations of no common order'. Climbing Noisettes such as the highly scented, blush-white 'Madame Alfred Carrière' continue the group's well-earned popularity.

The second bastard rose arose – again by chance – on the Île Bourbon (now La Réunion), a French island in the Indian Ocean lying to the east of Madagascar. The island's location in the southern hemisphere suggests that both parents were colonial imports: an Autumn Damask and a common China rose, again usually identified as 'Parsons' Pink China' or 'Old Blush'; both roses were commonly grown on the island as hedging (in two separate rows) to enclose plantation land. Of all the tangled stories of its origins, that by English nurseryman Thomas Rivers is the most convincing as he credits his version to one of the participants, M. Bréon, a French botanist who travelled to the Île Bourbon in 1817 to take charge of its botanical garden. He had acquired the new rose seedling from a landowner of Saint-Benoît in the eastern part of the island, Monsieur (Edouard) Perichon, who had discovered the new rose while working on his hedges. Judging it 'very different from the others in its shoots and foliage', Périchon had resolved to plant it in his garden, where it 'flowered the following year; and, as he anticipated, proved to be of quite a new race, and differing much from the [other] two roses, which, at the time, were the only sorts known in the island'.[3]

Bréon then sent seeds of the new rose back to France, to his friend M. Jacques, gardener to the Duc d'Orléans at Neuilly on the outskirts of Paris. At Neuilly, Jacques raised a second generation, painted admiringly by Redouté, who called it *Rosa canina burboniana* or 'Le rosier de l'Ile de Bourbon'; and like the Noisette before it, this new rose quickly captured the imagination of French rose breeders. Cuttings also reached Parisian horticulturist Monsieur Neumann, and his plants were available commercially from 1821, known variously as 'Rose Edouard', 'Rose Neumann' and sometimes 'Rose Dubreuil'; as the rose was a hybrid, the roses produced from Jacques' seeds would not have matched these clones exactly.

Clearly entranced with this new breed – which he described as 'a beautiful semi-double rose, with brilliant rose-coloured flowers, prominent buds, and nearly evergreen foliage' – the patriotic Thomas Rivers used the story to berate 'the lukewarmness of English rose amateurs' who, despite the Bourbon's abundant seeding, made no attempt to improve it by raising new seedlings. Instead, 'this pleasing task has been left to our rose-loving neighbours the French, who have been very industrious, and as a matter of course, have originated some very beautiful and striking varieties'.

Indeed, just twenty years after their first introduction to English markets, Bourbons were hailed as the stars of autumnal roses (none perhaps 'more beautiful, or more deserving the especial notice of the Amateur'); and from just one or two varieties, their numbers had swelled in nursery catalogues to more than 100. Some have returned to favour today, despite their occasional bad behaviour in wet weather and susceptibility to black spot. Particular favourites include the rose-pink 'Louise Odier', and the sublime powdery-pink-blush-white 'Souvenir de la Malmaison', which positively hates the wet. ('This rose, at its best, is the most beautiful of the Bourbons', declared Peter Beales, 'but at its worst can be horrid.')

Of less lasting fame were the Boursault roses, once thought to have descended from a cross between *R. chinensis* and the alpine rose, *R. pendulina,* but their chromosome count now indicates some other parent, possibly the cinnamon rose, *R. majalis.* They take their name from one of the most colourful of the revolutionary rose-growers: Jean-François Boursault, a wandering player in the Midi who came to Paris at the outbreak of revolution, created the Théâtre de Molière, and then threw himself into radical politics but was accused of enriching himself when he took charge of street cleansing in Paris. Whatever his ethics or his politics, Boursault was a passionate horticulturist, creating a splendid garden at his country property to the south-east of Paris at Yerres, and another at his Paris home on the rue Blanche.[4] Roses were his passion, and he is credited with introducing several China roses into France from England, including Thomas Evans's *Rosa multiflora carnea,* and William Kerr's white Banksian rose (see Chapter 11), supplying the bouquets which Redouté painted for *Les Roses.*

The group of roses named after Boursault enjoyed a brief limelight from around 1822. Vibert has a 'Rose Boursault' in his catalogue of 1824, placed among the Hybrid Bengal roses that flower only once, but whether the actor-turned-revolutionary bred the rose himself or simply put his name to it is not known. Sadly, Boursault's celebrated rose collection did not survive him. Returning to his original love of the theatre, Boursault launched a new theatrical venture, which was a commercial disaster. Forced to sell his houses and gardens, he retired to near Versailles and by 1838 his collection of roses had quite 'fallen to decay'.

A French rose-grower of more lasting influence was Alexandre Hardy, who had taken charge of the royal Jardin du Luxembourg in 1817 and soon established himself as the man foreign rosarians most wanted to visit when they passed through Paris. You had to catch him early during the rose season, warned the English nurseryman William Paul, who judged him 'very courteous to foreigners', while Mrs Gore called him 'probably the most scientific rose grower in Europe'. New York nurseryman Samuel Parsons met him too, but as they talked for only a few minutes 'amid the bustle of a horticultural exhibition', Parsons came away none the wiser about his *modus operandi*.

Although Hardy's roses were not for sale, he gladly gave them away to 'respectable applicants', or exchanged them for other plants with eminent nurserymen, by whom they were propagated and dispersed. This is surely how his most famous creation reached the French market: the ever-popular, green-eyed Damask hybrid he named 'Madame Hardy' after his wife (born Marie-Thérèse Pezard), which he entrusted to a neighbour, the widow Péan of the Parisian nursery firm of Sylvain-Péan – the rose which sparked my own interest, and which now grows happily in my garden.

Under Hardy, the Luxembourg's collection of roses developed from modest beginnings to its peak in the 1850s, when it contained more than 1,800 species and varieties, including more than 1,000 old European roses and 500 China and remontant hybrids. Writing in 1848, William Paul described it as 'the most splendid collection in France', its roses well established and flowering profusely during the season. 'It is true they look rather drawn,' he added a little disparagingly, 'but when we consider the proximity to the heart of the city, it is surprising that they flourish so well.'

The English were always making sly digs at the French. A common cause of complaint was the French habit of introducing the same rose under multiple names, or even of supplying old roses under new names – '*and charged at high prices*' (the indignant italics are William Paul's own). A century or so later, the English rosarian E. A. Bunyard was still complaining that foreign nurserymen could not name their roses properly. After a dispute with an Italian nurseryman, he feared they left the man unconvinced, 'but he did not play cricket. Overwhelmed by the odour of garlic, we fled the field.'

William Paul also poked gentle fun at the petty jealousies that divided the 'Cultivateurs de Rosiers' in France. On a visit to the gardens of a noted French grower, in the company of a lesser celebrity, Paul was surprised to find little of interest in the grounds, and his host uncommonly taciturn on the subject of roses, although 'exceedingly polite and talkative on other subjects'. The mystery was resolved when Paul received a letter from the eminent rose-grower telling him, in effect, that if 'you visit my establishment again, which I beg of you to do, pray do not bring any French Rose grower with you, for I cannot shew them my rarities and beauties'.

At the time of his visit to France, William Paul was just a few years into his own experimental rose-breeding, which began in 1843 and which would only slowly bear fruit as he tried to catch up the ground already traversed by the 'clever and industrious' French. The French no less than the English were effectively breeding in the dark: the principles of Mendelian heredity were as yet unknown (see later in this chapter), and plant hybridizers had only their intuition and their powers of observation to guide their choice of which varieties to cross.

Rose-grower William Paul was the most famous nurseryman of the Paul clan, starting out at Cheshunt and moving in 1860 to found his own nursery at Waltham Cross. From The Garden, *1903.*

Paul's first fumbled attempts at rose hybridization involved crossing three flowers of the Tea rose 'Goubault' with the Bourbon Rose 'Souchet', hoping to produce a dark-coloured, tea-scented rose. The experiment was not a success. From the thirty-two seeds produced, only four germinated. Three were 'curious cross-breeds, of no floral value, and having little in common with either parent; and one, in leaf, habit, and flower was very similar to the wild Dog Rose'. The same year, he crossed forty other flowers, but their seed crop was equally indifferent and the results 'nothing worthy of record'.

Paul's observations nonetheless allowed him to continue, recognizing that certain varieties are sterile while others that naturally seed abundantly are often self-fertilized. In June 1846 he crossed nearly 1,000 flowers, producing 444 seed-pods whose seedlings bloomed over the next two years. Two striking new crosses made him especially proud. Desiring a bright, dark climbing rose in contrast to the usual whites and yellows, he crossed the Hybrid Bourbon R. 'Athelin' with the Multiflora Rambler 'Russelliana'. The union produced 'Paul's Vivid', which Paul described much later as 'a bright crimson climbing Rose, of great repute in its day, and even now sought after'. And wishing to create a Moss rose with the 'exquisite tint' of the old Alba rose 'Maiden's Blush', he married the latter to a Moss rose of Hardy's creation, 'Moss du Luxembourg', creating from these two fine parents a blush-coloured Moss he named 'Princess Alice' after Queen Victoria's second daughter.

As Paul himself admits, creating new hybrids was a lengthy and uncertain business, and after a time he stopped keeping proper notes. No record identifies the parents of one his best-loved roses, for instance, 'Paul's Himalayan Musk': the drooping leaves suggest a Musk rose, but just how closely related is it to the real Himalayan Musk, R. brunonii? Other breeders were similarly lax, both in their record-keeping and in their choice of mates. Sometimes they simply did not know which were the parents, as in the case of Thomas Rivers's R. 'George IV'. Twenty years later, he could still recall the joy of its discovery.

One morning in June I was looking over the first bed of roses I had ever raised from seed, and searching for something new among them with all the ardour of youth, when my attention was attracted to a rose in the centre of the bed, not in bloom, but growing with great vigour, its shoots offering a remarkable contrast to the plants by which it was surrounded in their crimson-purple tinge; upon this plant I set my mark, and the following autumn I removed it to a pet situation. It did not bloom in perfection the season after removal, but, when established, it completely eclipsed all the dark roses known, and the plant was so vigorous that it made shoots more than ten feet in length in one season. This plant is still living, and nearly as vigorous as ever.

Without a clear understanding of the principles of heredity, it is remarkable that the rose-breeders of the nineteenth century achieved so much. Paul, Rivers and their European and American counterparts could only guess what might happen when two distinct roses mated, guided by theories that were often wrong, for example that 'hybrids and cross-breeds derive their form and habit from the female, the colours of the flowers from the male, while the constitution may be acquired from either parent'. Even Paul, who made this claim based on the opinion of 'our best observers', admitted that while it often held true, 'the exceptions are so numerous that they cannot, according to my experience, be said to prove the rule'.

Throughout much of the nineteenth century, the French remained in the vanguard of rose creation, responsible for producing the first rose in all the new rose groups (often recognized retrospectively) which whipped up such a frenzy among rose-growers. The English were soon to catch up – and disputed French supremacy in certain groups – but other nations lagged behind, as the American horticulturist H. B. Ellwanger candidly admitted. 'Italy and Germany have accomplished almost nothing in this line,' he wrote in the transatlantic *Century Magazine* of July 1883, 'although the climate of these countries is as favorable for the purpose as that of the other two.' He made the same comment about fruits, claiming that while his native America had produced more high-quality fruits than Italy or Germany, 'her contributions to the list of good roses, though larger than those of Italy and Germany, fall far short of what they should be'.

Among the first of these recognizably different groups were the Hybrid Perpetuals, which emerged in the 1830s, descended from a mix of Portland roses such as Lelieur's 'Rose du Roi', Bourbons, and the Hybrid Chinas, the name given to the early, open-pollinated hybrids between the original Chinas and European roses.[5] They were not in fact 'perpetual' at all, producing at best a second flush of flowers in the autumn; the French name '*hybride remontant*' is generally considered more truthful. Most were vigorous, prickly and blessed with dark green leaves and large, fragrant blooms. They certainly led the field among rose exhibitors for much of the century. Jean Laffay of Auteuil, Paris, and later of Bellevue-Meudon, bred many of the most important early Hybrid Perpetuals, among them 'La Reine' (1842) which dazzled William Paul when he saw it in Paris soon afterwards, pronouncing it 'one of the gems of the season; the colour is pink, with a violet hue, very glossy; the flowers are globular in shape, large, and very sweet'.

Tea roses also emerged in the 1830s, although they reached their peak of popularity later in the century. They owe their name to the French, who were the first to smell tea in *R. indica odorata* (or *odoratissima*), one of the four stud Chinas known variously in English as the 'Sweet-scented China Rose', or 'Hume's Blush China' (see Chapter 11). The French called it '*Odeur de Thé* Rose', while the English praised it as 'at once, the most fragrant and most delicate of its tribe'. Disputing the idea that Tea roses smell of the crushed leaves of the real tea plant, *Thea* (now *Camellia*) *sinensis*, Graham Stuart Thomas likened their fragrance to 'a freshly opened pack of gentle China tea – not the full "tarry" quality, but "slightly tarry"'. In the Teas, you also catch a glimpse of the long petals and new colour ranges that would make their successors, the Hybrid Teas, so popular.

Pink Teas originated from crossing a Bourbon rose with 'Hume's Blush China', while yellow Teas came from crossing 'Parks' Yellow Tea-scented China' (the fourth of the old stud Chinas) with 'Blush Noisette'. The pink Teas came first, among them 'Adam' (actually a rich rosy salmon) in 1833 (some sources say 1835 or 1838), named after its creator, a Rheims florist, rather than the biblical Adam. 'Safrano' was the first of the yellows, bred by Beauregard of France in 1839. Both are still available, as is the gloriously buff-apricot 'Gloire de Dijon', bred by Frenchman Jacotot in 1853. The Reverend (later Dean) Samuel Reynolds Hole, first president of the National Rose Society, loved it so much that he admitted this would be the rose he would grow, if he were allowed only one. Comparing it to what cricketers call an 'all-rounder', he declared that it had everything you could wish for in a rose: 'symmetry, size, endurance, colour (five tints are given to it in the Rose catalogues, buff, yellow, orange, fawn, salmon, and it has them all), and perfume . . . good in every point for wall, arcade, pillar, standard, dwarf – *en masse*, or as a single tree'. It was even easy to grow, indoors and out.

The French so enjoyed their Tea roses that in summer and autumn hundreds of plants were sold in the flower markets of Paris, grown on little stems known as '*mi tiges*'. 'They are brought to market in pots,' Thomas Rivers tells us, 'with their heads partially enveloped in coloured

ROSIER ILE - BOURBON

GLOIRE de DIJON (Jacotot *père & fils.*)

Bred in 1853 by Jacotot of France from an unknown Tea rose and the Bourbon
'Souvenir de la Malmaison', the climbing 'Gloire de Dijon' was the favourite rose of the
proselytizing cleric Samuel Reynolds Hole, later Dean of Rochester.

*Generally recognized as the first Hybrid Tea, 'La France' – bred by Guillot
fils of Lyon in 1867 – marks the division between 'old' and 'new' classes of rose.
From Theodor Nietner's* Die Rose *(Berlin, 1880).*

paper in such an elegant and effective mode, that it is scarcely possible to avoid being tempted to give two or three francs for such a pretty object.'

For all their beauty, however, many Tea roses were devilishly tricky to grow in cooler regions such as Britain, weak in growth and drooping in their flowers. Even under glass, they often failed to look their best. London's Horticultural Society overcame their shortcomings at its Chiswick garden by turning the rose house over to fruit and housing the Tea roses in another wooden structure with glazed sides that opened for ventilation, and a fixed roof. The effect was dramatic, as the *Gardeners' Chronicle* was pleased to report on 14 June 1856:

The other day the house was piled up with gigantic Roses, sweeter than the sweetest of the Eastern world; men were wheeling away barrow loads of fallen petals. Devoniensis seemed to have borrowed the shape and size of a Cabbage, and as to FORTUNE's climbing yellow China, its rich Nankin colour was actually glowing with salmon.

For nearly half a century from about 1840, the Hybrid Perpetuals and the Teas were the dominant garden roses, revered by amateurs and professionals. But each group had its drawbacks – the Perpetuals were too coarse and prone to disease, and the Teas too tender – so rose breeders naturally sought to create a new race that would fuse their good qualities and eliminate their faults. Exactly who got there first is a matter of dispute. The contenders include Lacharme of Lyon, who crossed the Hybrid Perpetual 'Jules Margottin' with the Tea rose 'Safrano' to produce the rose-pink 'Victor Verdier' in 1859; and Wiltshire farmer Henry Bennett for his 'Pedigree Hybrids of the Tea Rose', which, although not launched until 1879, were scientifically bred from known parents and given the first official recognition (by the Horticultural Society of Lyon) as *Hybrides de Thé,* or Hybrid Teas.

But the rose generally honoured as the first Hybrid Tea is the silvery-pink if somewhat inconspicuous 'La France', bred by Jean-Baptiste Guillot (Guillot *fils*) in his Lyon nursery. Free-flowering like the Hybrid Perpetuals, it was upright in growth and altogether less sprawling, holding its fine, high-centred buds on a strong neck. Its date of intro-duction – 1867 – marks the dividing line between 'old' and 'new' roses.

According to the rules of the American Rose Society, a rose is 'old' if its group was introduced prior to 1867, and 'new' in the case of all groups introduced from 1867 onwards. So a Damask or a Hybrid Perpetual introduced today would count as an 'old' rose, in contrast to the Hybrid Teas and all later groups, which are definitely 'new'.

Guillot, like so many of his contemporaries, had bred his rose in the dark. Although you will sometimes see its parents honoured as the Tea rose 'Mme Bravy' and the Hybrid Perpetual 'Mme Victor Verdier', Guillot himself had no idea who they were: in his breeding for that year (1864), the seeds of the different Tea roses were simply mixed together, so it was chance and chance alone that spawned the new race of roses that would soon outstrip all others.

Rose-growers around the world continued to breed new roses in the old and new classes, and to breed new classes altogether. Although scientists estimate that only some ten to twenty species have given their genes to the roses we grow today, the family relationships between roses and between classes are as intricate as Noah's, as the first Chinas mated with the European Gallicas and Damasks to beget the Bourbons, which then crossed and re-crossed with the Portlands, the Chinas and the Hybrid Chinas to produce the Hybrid Perpetuals; and the China Teas came together with the Hybrid Perpetuals to beget the Hybrid Teas, which then crossed on the one hand with the Dwarf Polyanthas or Polyantha Pompons to beget the Hybrid Polyanthas, and on the other with *Rosa wichurana,* the wild Chinese rambler, and again with the Teas to beget the Wichurana Hybrids. Even this complex gene-mapping ignores the bloodlines passing from the Musks and the Chinas to the Noisettes and on to the Reverend Joseph Pemberton's Hybrid Musks, enlivened with a strong dash of Multiflora Rambler and more Hybrid Tea; or Lord Penzance's Hybrid Sweet Briars, which mixed pollen from the Bourbons and the Hybrid Perpetuals with Queen Elizabeth I's emblematic Sweet Briar, *R. rubiginosa;* or the Rugosa Hybrids which joined the rougher, tougher red-hipped species from Japan and western Asia to a whole host of partners from Europe, China and North America. It is a complicated dance that sets the head reeling; and there are many more variations to explore, as shown in the table below, which gives a twenty-first-century view of the old and new cultivars that make up the

Genus Rosa, together with the 150-odd genuine (wild) species roses, and their naturally occurring hybrids. The cultivar groups are subject to constant change, and even now there are moves to split the modern Shrub roses into smaller sections, as they presently form a large and very mixed bunch.

A twenty-first-century view of cultivated roses

OLD GARDEN ROSES

Alba, Ayrshire, Bourbon and Climbing Bourbon, Boursault, Centifolia, Damask, Hybrid Bracteata, Hybrid China and Climbing Hybrid China, Hybrid Eglanteria, Hybrid Foetida, Hybrid Gallica, Hybrid Multiflora, Hybrid Perpetual and Climbing Hybrid Perpetual, Hybrid Sempervirens, Hybrid Setigera, Hybrid Spinosissima, Miscellaneous, Moss and Climbing Moss, Noisette, Portland, Tea and Climbing Tea.

MODERN ROSES

Floribunda and Climbing Floribunda, Grandiflora and Climbing Grandi-flora, Hybrid Kordesii, Hybrid Moyesii, Hybrid Musk, Hybrid Rugosa, Hybrid Wichurana, Hybrid Tea and Climbing Hybrid Tea, Large-flowered Climber, Miniature and Climbing Miniature, Mini-Flora, Polyantha and Climbing Polyantha, Shrub.[6]

All the while, rose frenzy was intensifying on both sides of the Atlantic, and wherever western influence was felt. As rose-breeders responded to public demand by breeding ever bigger, more spectacular blooms, so men such as the Reverend Samuel Reynolds Hole in Britain were feeding public passions by forming rose societies and pressing for the public display of their efforts. Blessed with the good looks of a Victorian Gregory Peck, and convinced that 'He who would have beautiful Roses in his garden must have beautiful Roses *in his heart*', Hole discovered his passion for roses while still a young curate at Caunton in Notting-hamshire, where he would stay as vicar for over forty years until appointed Dean of Rochester in 1887. But church affairs surely occupied him less than roses and his self-appointed mission: to raise the status of his favourite flower by giving it a dedicated Rose Show, while at the same time raising standards of rose cultivation.

Never one to watch his words, the Reverend Hole condemned many formal rose gardens as 'dismal slaughter-houses', and told a wealthy woman that she did not deserve beautiful roses until she loved them more. 'If I am accused of discourtesy to the fair sex,' he added, '(she was not very fair, my reader), I can only plead that I have been far more explicit with the male specimen of pseudo-Rosist.'

Hole tells the story himself of how the first Grand National Rose Show came into being. Aggrieved that the rose had no show of its own, unlike

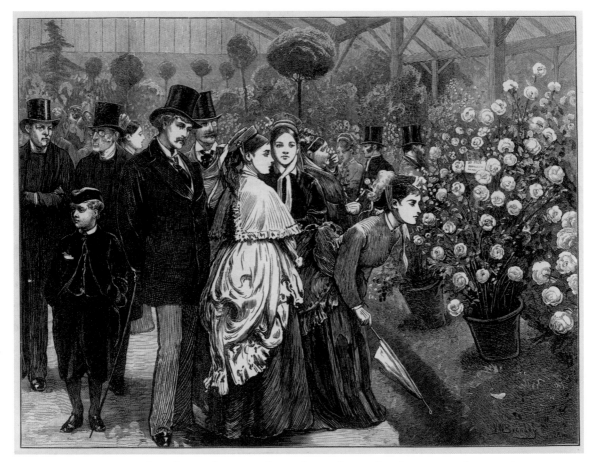

Roses draw the crowds to a rose show at the Royal Horticultural Society's garden at South Kensington, from the Illustrated London News *of 1873.*

the carnation, the tulip, the chrysanthemum and even 'the vulgar hairy Gooseberry', he proposed one in a letter to *The Florist* published in April 1857, suggesting that it should take place near some central station. Met by silence rather than the wild enthusiasm he had expected, Hole then wrote to England's premier rosarians, including Rivers, William Paul and the florist Charles Turner. They gathered at Webb's Hotel in Piccadilly, London, and 'commenced with a proceeding most deeply interesting to every British heart – we unanimously ordered dinner'.

Planning went ahead, nearly £200 was raised in subscriptions, and the first National Rose Show opened its doors at the luxury St James's Hall in July 1858, to immediate acclaim. More than 2,000 people attended at a shilling a time, and among the cup winners was William Paul of the 'glorious Rose-fields' of Cheshunt.

'No words can describe the infinite variety of form, colour, and odour,' enthused the *Gardeners' Chronicle,* nonetheless resorting to its usual gush:

At the sides were crowds of bunches daintily set off by beds of Moss; in the middle rose pyramids, baskets, and bouquets. In one place little solitary blossoms boldly confronted their clustering rivals; in another glass screens guarded some precious gems; and in another great groups of unprotected beauties set at defiance the heated atmosphere of the Hall.

The show transformed itself into an annual event, held the following year at the Hanover Square Rooms, then at Sydenham's Crystal Palace. Hole married the year after that, handing over the reins to the Horticultural Society, which hosted the show at its South Kensington garden until the foundation of the National Rose Society in 1876. The following year, the society recognized Hole's championing of the rose by electing him its president.

More than anyone else in Victorian Britain, Dean Hole was fervid in his efforts to spread word of the rose among his flock. In this, he was outstandingly successful; his plainly titled *A Book About Roses, How to Show and Grow Them* ran to more than fifteen editions in his lifetime, and many more afterwards. For Hole, rose-growing ousted even cleanliness in the pantheon of Christian virtues, and if his prose style strikes a rather florid note today, he admirably laid bare the snobberies that divided rose-lovers along class lines, then as now.

In the very first edition of his rose classic, he describes receiving an invitation from a Nottinghamshire mechanic to judge an exhibition of roses given by working men on Easter Monday, when none of his own roses were yet in bloom. On being courteously assured that this was not a hoax – the roses were growing under glass – he found himself on a raw and gusty Easter Monday taking a train and then a hansom cab to Nottingham's General Cathcart Inn. Here he was met by the landlord and a crowd of exhibitors, some with roses in their buttonholes, others in shirtsleeves, who all welcomed him with outstretched hands 'and seemed amused when, on their apologizing for their soiled appearance, I assured them of my vivid affection for all kinds of floricultural dirt'.

Upstairs, the usual clamouring room was hushed and silent, and the air – 'on other public occasions hot with cooked meats and steaming tumblers, heavy with the smoke and smell of tobacco' – was cool and fragrant from the beautiful roses which completely covered the plain deal table. Clearly humbled by the experience, Hole declared that he had never seen better specimens of cut roses, grown under glass, than those exhibited by these working men.

Their Tea-Roses – Adam, Devoniensis, Madame Willermorz, and Souvenir d'un Ami especially – were shown in their most exquisite beauty; and, coming down to the present time, I do not hesitate to say that the best Maréchal Niel and the best Madame Margottin which I have yet seen, I saw this spring at Nottingham, in the ginger-beer bottles!

After the prizes were awarded, Hole went with some of the exhibitors to inspect their tiny allotments on sunny slopes close to the town, stepping inside their glasshouses where he was mostly unable to stand upright. Here one of his hosts explained that he visited his garden every morning and evening, before and after work, 'and not seldom at noon as well', and another that he found the money for his expensive varieties '*by keeping away from the beershops*'.

So Dean Hole was at least able to tag a Christian moral to his tale: get a man out of the 'dram and beer shops' into the pure fresh air, let him see the marvellous works of God in the garden, 'then build Revealed upon Natural Religion, and hope to see him a Christian'. But his story carried a social message, too, for as he caught the train home from Nottingham, bearing a glorious bouquet of roses with the men's 'best respects to the Missus', the Reverend Hole – by now presumably in a first-class carriage – met with five of his acquaintances who scoffed at his report that a bricklayer had supplied such exquisite blooms. 'Whereupon an expressive sneer of unbelief disfigured each stolid countenance; and a solemn silence ensured, which said, nevertheless, as plainly as though it were shouted, "We don't admire tomfoolery."'

For all his proselytizing zeal, Dean Hole did not succeed in banishing snobbery from the rose garden, nor did the new classes of exhibition roses meet with unanimous adulation. Lone voices regretted the passing of the old roses; and even the rose-grower William Paul admitted that 'one breathes a freer air in company with old friends whose faces, habits, and sentiments are familiar to us'. When talking or writing of new roses, by contrast, he felt 'much as I do when in the company of strangers – that to be at once truthful and polite, we must be guarded'.

The trouble was that in their scramble to meet the public's demand for repeat-flowering roses that would also shine as cut flowers or exhibition blooms, breeders were losing sight of the rose's greatest virtues – toughness and fragrance; and although North American growers were enjoying success with their trailing Wichurana hybrids, and other new classes were beginning to grace the garden, the new century marked a lull in rose breeding. As 'Wild Rose' lamented in the *Gardeners' Chronicle* of 8 September 1900, 'No new Tea seems to have come before us that is likely to be of real value; and I do not think that any one on this side of the Channel has seen anything amongst the new Hybrid Perpetuals worthy of notice. This has been for some years the case so far as French Roses are concerned.'

In fact 'Wild Rose' had missed an important French introduction of 1900: Pernet-Ducher's 'Soleil d'Or', which married the clear yellow of *Rosa foetida* 'Persiana' with the red Hybrid Perpetual 'Antoine Ducher', thereby introducing bright yellow into the Hybrid Teas; virtually all of today's yellow cultivars descend from this original cross.

But France and England were indeed ceding their supremacy in the creation of new roses as rival breeders came to the fore, among them Kordes and Tantau in Germany, Poulsen in Denmark, Lens in Belgium, Pedro Dot in Spain, Lammerts and Warriner in California, the Dicksons and McGredys in Northern Ireland (until the fourth-generation Sam McGredy took his breeding skills to New Zealand in 1972); and by the mid-twentieth century, Japanese breeders such as Seizo Suzuki. The French continued to produce new roses, of course, from breeders such as Delbard, Guillot, Meilland, and more recently Michel Adam; while Britain's rose-breeders now include David Austin, Harkness, Fryer, Cocker and Warner. Canadian-born Keith Zary and American Tom Carruth have joined the ranks of leading rose-breeders so that today rose-breeding is a truly international force, practised by some twenty-five to thirty highly competitive global companies and many smaller breeders.

Rose-breeding often runs in families, as shown by the Kordes dynasty in Germany, which built its success across the generations. Begun by Wilhelm Kordes I in 1887, the Kordes family firm concentrated on roses from the mid-1890s. Of the founder's two sons, Hermann worked at his father's nursery in Elmshorn, Schleswig-Holstein, while Wilhelm II came to England and co-founded a nursery with another German. Still in Britain at the outbreak of the First World War, they were interned on the Isle of Man, where the young Kordes spent his captivity reading everything he could about rose-breeding; this gave him the scientific basis to expand the family business when he joined forces with his brother after the war.

In developing his experimental breeding programme, Kordes took a keen interest in the work of the Austrian monk Gregor Johann Mendel, who had studied natural sciences in Vienna and then (from 1854, for some ten years) conducted a series of remarkable experiments on peas in his cloister garden, as he grappled with the laws of heredity. After Gregor was made Abbot of Brünn, his work on peas lay all but forgotten, until it was rediscovered and experimentally confirmed around 1900, when its relevance to plant breeding became clear.

Armed with a more scientific approach to breeding, Kordes and his brother Hermann established W. Kordes *Söhne* as one of Europe's most successful rose-breeders, growers and retailers, responsible for the hugely popular Hybrid Tea 'Crimson Glory' (1935), and the 'Frühlings' series of Scottish roses, among them 'Frühlingsgold' (1937) and 'Frühlingsmorgen' (1942). Although they had prospered under National Socialism – and by the outbreak of the Second World War were raising more than a million roses every year – the war years naturally deprived them of skilled labour and markets for their roses. But their greenhouses survived the Allied bombings, and Wilhelm and Hermann soldiered on, even breeding new seedlings which were mostly lost to the vicious winter of 1946 to 1947. Since then, the firm's fortunes have risen again, most markedly with their introduction of a new race of climbing roses, the Kordesii hybrids, in the 1950s and 1960s, and the ubiquitous Floribunda, 'Iceberg' (1958). They remain among Germany's leading rose-breeders.

Of all the wartime roses, the one with the greatest appeal is 'Peace', a Hybrid Tea acclaimed as 'perhaps the best known and one of the best loved roses of all times'.[7] Large, faintly scented, with the characteristic high-centred bud and glossy foliage of its class, 'Peace' changes colour according to soil and climate, but is mostly a warm creamy yellow, fringed with pink. I inherited one at the house where I now live in north London. It grows from an old, gnarled stump, producing perfect blooms each year, and must be one of the original plantings. Another in the back garden has lost ground to an unruly hedge but has somehow managed to turn itself into a Climber, scrambling up inside the hedge and flowering at a height of ten feet or so. This rose is clearly a survivor.

'Peace' was in fact conceived before the war at Antibes, on 15 June 1935, when the twenty-three-year-old Francis Meilland pollinated the fifty-five flowers that would eventually produce 'Peace' at the third cross, of the usual muddled parentage. By June 1939, visitors to Antibes showered praise on this glowing rose, and to safeguard its succession Meilland sent bud eyes to Germany, Italy and the United States, where it went to Robert Pyle of the Pennsylvanian firm Conard-Pyle. The rose came out in Europe during the war years under three different names: 'Madame A. Meilland' in France, named after Francis's mother, Claudia; 'Gloria Dei' in Germany; and 'Gioia' in Italy. When the Duke of Windsor saw it growing at Antibes during the last days before the armistice, he was enchanted: 'I have never seen another rose like it. It is certainly the most beautiful rose in the world.'

By a masterful stroke of marketing, Robert Pyle christened the rose 'Peace' and launched it in the United States – with luck and good timing – on 29 April 1945, the date the Soviet Army crossed the Moltke bridge in the battle for Berlin. Shortly afterwards, at the San Francisco conference when forty-nine delegations met to form the United Nations, each head of delegation received a single 'Peace' rose and a card with this message:

This is the 'Peace' rose which was christened at the Pacific Rose Society exhibition in Pasadena on the day Berlin fell. We hope that the 'Peace' rose will influence men's thoughts for everlasting world peace.

Since the US had introduced plant patents in 1930 – in some cases decades before European governments – a healthy share of royalties came back to Meilland in France, enough for him to abandon retailing for breeding, and to lobby for plant-breeders' rights in Europe.

In Britain, the rights to 'Peace' were acquired by the rose world's greatest showman: the flamboyant Harry Wheatcroft, 'champion rose grower and communist', who sported mutton-chop whiskers, wild hair, and a taste in clothes that ran to dog-tooth tweeds, floral shirts and contrary ties. A firm believer in the brotherhood of man, Wheatcroft had had his application to register as a conscientious objector in the First World War refused and he was later court-martialled for disobedience. At the war's end, he thought about entering politics and consulted one of his heroes, the Scottish Socialist James Maxton. 'Stick to rose growing, Harry,' was Maxton's advice. 'You'll bring beauty into the world. Politics is a very dirty business.'

Among the roses he bred himself was the appropriately loud 'Harry Wheatcroft', a flaming vermilion-and-gold Hybrid Tea, which he introduced in 1972 some five years before his death. It was actually an accidental sport, and he is better remembered for his flair in bringing other growers' roses to market, including the coral-red 'Fragrant Cloud' from the German grower Tantau, and the clear pink 'Queen Elizabeth' from Lammerts in the US.

Wheatcroft's heyday was in the 1950s and 1960s, when Hybrid Tea

*Flamboyant rose-grower Harry Wheatcroft wins a gold medal for introducing
the Hybrid Tea rose 'Peace' at the National Rose Society's Westminster show of 1947.
Bred in France before the war by Francis Meilland and christened in America by
Robert Pyle, 'Peace' won fame as the world's favourite rose.*

roses were wildly popular and planted to the exclusion of almost every
other rose (and almost every other garden plant, as perennials were
deemed too much work). The old shrub roses had virtually disappeared
from most nurserymen's lists – not just the Damasks, Gallicas,
Centifolias and Albas known to Shakespeare and Gerard, but also the
early Chinas and the Hybrid Perpetuals, all were cast aside in pursuit of
novelty and fashion.

Over the years, however, others raised their voices in support of the
'lost' breeds, notably Gertrude Jekyll, doyenne of Edwardian gardeners,
and the quietly genteel Edward Ashdown Bunyard, fruit- and rose-
grower, who shot himself on 19 October 1939, depressed by the outbreak
of war and his own impending bankruptcy. Bunyard's *Old Garden Roses*

of 1936 inspired Vita Sackville-West in her choice of roses for Sissing-hurst Castle, a few years after she and her husband Harold Nicolson had bought the romantic ruin in Kent, which they restored and perfected for the rest of their lives. Knowing Bunyard's epicurean tastes, Vita invited him over for lunch and plied him with Indian corn on the cob, woodcock sitting on a *croûton* surrounded by pâté de foie gras arranged in a necklace of truffles, and bottles of Clos Vougeot 1911 and Château Yquem, and when he was 'well-fed and well-wined', took him out to talk roses all afternoon.[6] Long before DNA testing, Bunyard knew his roses well enough to detect common ancestry in the *Rosa gigantea* hybrids and the old Tea and Noisette roses, such as 'Maréchal Niel' and Dean Hole's favourite, 'Gloire de Dijon'.

At Sissinghurst and through her garden writings, Vita championed the old roses at the expense of the new, sometimes with a sharp tang of privilege, as in her introduction to Graham Stuart Thomas's *The Old Shrub Roses* of 1955, when his talk of old roses transported her back to those 'dusky mysterious hours' in an Oriental storehouse as the rugs of Esfahan, Bokhara and Samarkand were rolled out before her (her husband Harold had been attached to the British Legation in Teheran). 'Rich they were, rich as a fig broken open, soft as a ripened peach, freckled as an apricot, coral as a pomegranate, bloomy as a bunch of grapes.' Some of the old roses might well be an acquired taste, she concurred, just as oysters were not to everyone's taste.

I have myself observed with some amusement, a look of dismay coming over the faces of visitors to my own garden where I grow many of the roses dear to my heart and to the heart of Mr. Thomas. 'Surely, surely, that's not a rose as we understand roses?'

No, the rose Vita loved bore little resemblance to the highly coloured Hybrid Teas and Polyanthas and Floribundas of the modern garden. 'It is a far quieter and more subtle thing, but oh let me say how rewarding a taste it is when once acquired.'

Vita Sackville-West died in 1962, having done much to revive interest in the roses she loved so much. While some of the old varieties are lost for ever, many are now widely available from specialist growers, their interests championed by heritage rose societies in Europe, America and elsewhere. Just five years after her death, rose-breeding was revolutionized when the British plant scientist G. P. Hill successfully introduced biotechnology into the process by creating the first test-tube rose – somatic embryos induced in the callus of the climbing Hybrid Tea, 'The Doctor'. One can only imagine Vita's shock had she known that the future of the rose might lie not with gardeners but with scientists and laboratory technicians.

Along with virtually all living organisms, rose cells contain a nucleus in which reside the chromosomes; these contain the vital DNA that defines a plant's unique characteristics, which are passed on to future generations. Organisms that reproduce sexually usually have two sets of chromosomes, one from each parent, and are called diploids. A diploid plant of the genus *Rosa* contains seven pairs of chromosomes; but some roses contain as many as eight sets. Teas, Chinas and Noisettes are typically diploids, while Gallicas, Centifolias and Damasks are commonly tetraploids, having four sets each. Early crosses between the European and Chinese roses often produced triploid roses, which are generally infertile or very low in fertility; this partly explains the difficulties faced by early breeders, before this was known.

Biotechnology allows plant scientists to manipulate ploidy levels, and to create new *in vitro* roses through complex cross-breedings between different species groups and even between genera. Breeders can use this knowledge to develop almost any characteristic they want, although woody shrubs such as roses are very much harder to work with than herbaceous plants; and in Britain at least, genetic manipulation is not allowed on crops or plants that will be grown outside.

For some years now, university-based and other breeding programmes have been developing roses that will flourish in extreme climates. Canada's Agriculture and Agri-Food programme has bred roses tough enough to survive the cold winters of the Canadian prairies, for instance; these are the Parkland roses derived from the native *Rosa arkansana*, and the larger Explorer roses derived from *R. rugosa* or *R. wichurana*. The Iowa State University Research Foundation has bred the free-flowering Buck roses, hardy to USDA zone 5 (in other words, a minimum temperature of

−28.8°C or −20°F) and covering a wide colour spectrum. The University of Minnesota Horticultural Research Center selected the hardiest and healthiest of these as breeding germplasm for its own research programme, designed to create roses that are hardy to USDA zone 4 (a minimum of −34.5°C or −30°F), resistant to black spot, attractive and repeat-blooming. Texas A&M University has gone the other way, using *Rosa wichurana* to create good, disease-resistant roses adapted to the hot, humid regions of the southern United States. Meanwhile, America's KnockOut® Roses, developed by Bill Radler, are winter-hardy and heat-tolerant (although they do not thrive in every climate), disease-resistant, endlessly repeat-flowering and described as 'self-cleaning' (that is, they need no dead-heading). In a market geared towards uniformity, such paragons are already squeezing out the competition.

Other breeding programmes have concentrated more on the aesthetics of the rose. David Austin's English Roses date back to the late 1940s, when he set out to 'combine the beauty of the Old Roses with the practical virtues of Modern Roses'. The first introduced to the market was the soft pink 'Constance Spry' in 1961, in which Graham Stuart Thomas detected the scent of myrrh; this was then back-crossed with other Floribundas and Hybrid Teas to produce repeat-flowering varieties by the end of the decade. Later, Austin crossed his English Roses with Portlands, Bourbons and Hybrid Perpetuals, and then with Rugosas, Wichuranas, Musks and Albas. As Michael Marriott, Austin's technical director, explained to me, in breeding a new rose David Austin looks for well-formed flowers, fine fragrance, attractive growth, good health and resistance to disease, general sturdiness, and an elusive sixth quality – charm; 'good doers' that will also capture the heart.

But the mathematics of rose breeding reveal how stamina and tenacity are as vital in breeders as in their roses. From between 200 and 300 parent roses, some tried and tested, others new to the breeding programme, Austin will make between 150,000 and 160,000 crosses a year, producing up to quarter of a million seedlings. Out of these, he will then select perhaps 10,000 plants with interesting flowers – each plant genetically unique – and these will be budded outside, their numbers gradually whittled down as all their other virtues are tested and explored. At the end of the nine-year cycle, David Austin will

For much of the twentieth century, high-centred Hybrid Tea roses overcame opposition from all other classes. Catalogue from a Cambridgeshire rose-grower.

launch each year between three and six new English Roses, and so the cycle continues.

Other European breeders have followed Austin's example in breeding roses that set out to combine the best of the old with the new, among them Guillot (with the Generosas), Meilland (with the Romanticas), and Poulsen (with the Renaissance roses). Scientists from Cyprus and Greece have joined forces to try to breed the heavenly scent of *Rosa × damascena* into the often scentless Hybrid Teas. And the search continues for the elusive blue rose, long considered impossible without importing genes from another plant, as rose petals have yielded no trace of the true-blue pigment, delphinidin, or its derivatives.

Biotechnology is also raising interest in the cut-flower market – a market increasingly dominated by global economics and factory farming methods. If roses were chickens, their rearing would provoke a public outcry. As with all mass supermarket products, the aim is to produce roses that are low-cost to the consumer and the environment, uniform in appearance, easy to harvest, and long on shelf life. The traditional rose bush resents such mechanization, so breeders are looking at novel varieties that can be grown in small pots and programmed to produce one marketable cut bloom at a time. Increasingly, too, consumers want cut flowers that are fragrant, and as the scent of 'real rose' is difficult to combine with a long vase life, breeders are introducing other scents such as aniseed or lemon.

Although roses are not a food crop, growers are already haunted by the spectre of public disquiet over their genetic sleight of hand. As one British academic suggested at an international symposium held in Antibes, the birthplace of the 'Peace' rose: 'Roses arouse more sentimentality than any other floral crop and public perceptions of genetic manipulation are crucially important.' His warning was clear. The rose is infinitely adaptable and infinitely accommodating to our needs, but by chasing after novelty – plants or blooms that are ever bigger, better, brighter, more docile to our negligent ways – we may lose the very qualities that made us fall in love with the rose in the first place.

Chapter Eighteen
Into the Rose Garden

You will often read that the dedicated rose garden is a creation of Napoleon's Empress Josephine at Malmaison, her home on the outskirts of Paris, where 'she created something never seen before, a pleasure garden devoted entirely to roses'. This is nonsense, I'm afraid, for the simple reason that Josephine never planted a rose garden at Malmaison, choosing instead to scatter roses throughout her estate, especially by the banks of the winding stream, in planting boxes and in her cutting garden, and just occasionally in her great glasshouse. The so-called 'plan' of Josephine's rose garden is an imaginative recon-struction by French landscape architect M. Eugène Touret executed in classic Beaux-Arts style for Malmaison's rebirth as a 'museum of the rose in Josephine's time', some eighty-five years after her death.[1]

Others had in any case planted rose gardens before her. Many were rose enthusiasts and collectors, such as the Dutchman Johan van Hoghelande, the man who introduced Clusius to the Centifolia rose (see Chapter 9), or Landgrave Friedrich II at Kassel, who encouraged his gardener, Daniel August Schwarzkopf, to breed new roses for Kassel's impressive collection. Schwarzkopf's successes included the Gallica 'Perle von Weissenstein' of c.1773, celebrated as Germany's first cultivar. Kassel's roses were planted in an unusually informal 'Rose Bosquet' beneath the Weissenstein rock, consisting of mainly French and Dutch cultivars plus some new roses from the English colonies of North America. Friedrich's successor, Wilhelm IX, took his love of roses further into garden design, demolishing the old castle and using its rubble to create a 'rose island' in his park, newly landscaped in the English style.

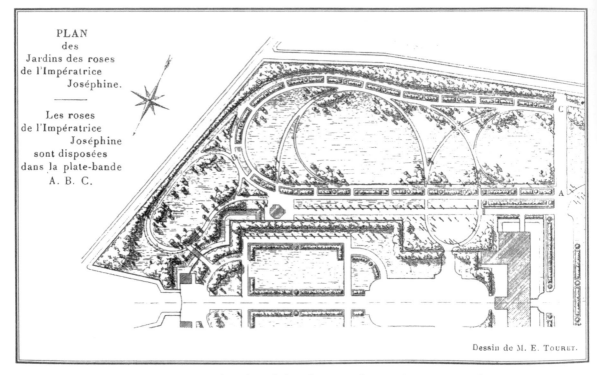

PLAN
des
Jardins des roses
de l'Impératrice
Joséphine.

Les roses
de l'Impératrice
Joséphine
sont disposées
dans la plate-bande
A. B. C.

Dessin de M. E. TOURET.

*Eugene Touret's hypothetical plan of a rose garden at Malmaison appeared in
Jules Gravereaux's book of 1912 on the roses of Empress Josephine.*

Josephine would herself receive roses from Kassel during the temporary interregnum of Napoleon's brother Jerome, who was installed as King of Westphalia.

But the rose garden as we know it owed its inspiration to two forces that came together in the first part of the nineteenth century: on the one hand, the increase in the number of rose varieties available, with all the showy qualities inherited from the new China hybrids; and on the other, a taste for eclectic gardens that developed, in Britain especially, as an antidote to the shaved lawns and artfully constructed Nature of the landscaped park, known throughout Europe as the English Garden except in France, which gave a shared credit to the Chinese for '*le jardin anglo-chinois*'.

One of the pioneers of the nineteenth-century rose garden in Britain was the self-styled 'landscape gardener' Humphry Repton, who inherited the landscaping mantle of Lancelot 'Capability' Brown, but responded to his clients' desires for more Art and obvious refinement in their gardens. People were getting bored, he said, with 'the sameness of gravel walks, in serpentine lines, with broad margins of grass and flowers and shrubs, every where promiscuously mixed and repeated'. They wanted novelty and variety, and Repton was happy to oblige with both.

Repton designed his most famous rose garden late in life for the seventh Earl of Bridgewater at Ashridge in Hertfordshire, a Regency Gothic mansion by the neoclassical architect James Wyatt. At Bridge-water's request, Repton prepared plans for a number of separately themed gardens (fifteen in all) – five in the 'modern style of pleasure ground', and the remaining ten in a variety of styles that mixed up-to-the-minute horticulture with architectural historicism around a broadly medieval theme. These gardens included a holy well, a winter garden, a restored monks' garden, an arboretum of exotic trees, an American garden for magnolias and other ericaceous North American natives, two gardens of raised beds, a grotto, a mount garden – and a rose garden, which Repton called a 'Rosarium' or rosary, centred around a fountain supplied by water from the holy well.

Repton re-drew the rose garden for his last published work, *Fragments on the Theory and Practice of Landscape Gardening,* relying on memory as he did not have to hand the Red Book he had prepared for Bridgewater. In fact his memory produced a more delicate rose garden than the original: in *Fragments,* seventeen beds radiate out from a central water basin and fountain like the petals of a daisy, each filled with large-flowered pink roses, fully double and so low-growing they look like ground-cover roses. The same pink roses are planted outside the surrounding low trellis and appear to clamber up the ornamental arches that ring the garden, interspersed with blush-white flowers of roughly the same size but single and bearing four petals only. At the entrance to the garden is a viewing veranda constructed of French-style trelliswork supporting a canopy of more double pink roses. The whole picture presents a charming if rather formal rose garden which fits well with Repton's other dashes of Regency style, like the hooped 'corbeilles' for flowers that dot many of his lawns.

Humphry Repton's design for a rose garden at Ashridge in Hertfordshire, from his
Red Book of garden plans prepared for the seventh Earl of Bridgewater in 1813.

But Repton's rose garden at Ashridge is entirely hypothetical. As Richard Gorer pointed out in a perceptive article in *Country Life*, when Repton presented Bridgewater with his Red Book of garden plans for Ashridge (in 1813 – the year of Jane Austen's *Pride and Prejudice*), the dwarf Hybrid Tea rose was still forty years away, and very few climbing roses were then available. All belonged to the Synstylae section, bearing clusters of small single flowers, almost all white apart from the pink prairie rose, *R. setigera*, introduced to Britain in 1800, and the pink form of *R. multiflora* ('Carnea'), introduced by Thomas Evans of the East India Company in 1804. Although Repton's ground-hugging pink rose might have been a dwarf Centifolia, such as *Rosa × centifolia* 'De Meaux', this has a very short flowering season in early summer – much earlier than the possible climbers – while the only repeat-flowering pink roses then available would have grown far too tall for the daisy design.

Gorer wonders if it might have been possible to bud large-flowered roses on to more vigorous stock, such as the field or Ayrshire rose, *R. arvensis,* to produce Repton's climbing roses. 'But I have not found any reference to such practice,' he remarks, 'and I am led reluctantly to the conclusion that Repton was not wholly aware of what plants were then available.'

Gorer's view was reinforced by Repton's treatment of his own 'humble Cottage' at Hare Street in Essex, where he obtained permission to extend his garden by twenty-five yards into the high road, and planted rose bushes, climbing roses and a rose pillar to frame his view and block the offending sight of a butcher's shop. The shop would be all too visible during the leafless winter months, of course, and while the paler roses on Repton's pillar may have been Alba roses trained as climbers, the same explanation would not hold for the festooned arches of Ashridge. Like Tudor author Thomas Hill, Humphry Repton does not appear to have known his roses very well.

Given Repton's uncertainties as a plantsman, it is perhaps just as well that Ashridge's rose garden was implemented not by Repton but by the architect James Wyatt's nephew, [Sir] Jeffry Wyatville, who simplified the 'daisy' design to eight segments radiating from a central fountain and enclosed not by arches bearing prophetic roses but by a yew hedge which survives to this day. Despite the disadvantages of a shady site and voracious rabbits, Ashridge's rose garden remains a design classic, its roses twice replanted in the last ten years: first with modern repeat-flowering English Roses by David Austin, and more recently with a collection of repeat-flowering roses, almost all ranging in date from the mid-sixteenth to the mid-nineteenth centuries. These include many of the heavenly-scented Portland roses such as 'Rose de Recht' (also known as 'Rose de Rescht' and *Rosa* 'De Resht'), 'Blanche de Vibert' and

'Jacques Cartier'; the Bourbons 'Louise Odier' and 'Madame Isaac Pereire'; and Hybrid Perpetuals such as 'Reine des Violettes' and 'Ferdinand Pichard'. Around the perimeter are more vigorous old roses, such as the Moss rose 'William Lobb' and modern English Roses, among them the velvety 'Tradescant' and the deep-yellow 'Graham Thomas'. With its emphasis on scented roses which repeat as far as possible, the rose garden at Ashridge proves that is possible to create a formal display without the Hybrid Teas that would soon displace all others in the garden.

The new style of eclectic gardening was also eminently adaptable to the smaller gardens then springing up around industrial centres, attached to villa residences for the prospering middle classes. A host of scribblers arose to meet their needs for instruction in horticulture and taste, at its head in Britain the prolific Scottish garden writer John Claudius Loudon, who is said to have published some sixty million words in his lifetime.

Loudon had the knack of aiming his advice at very specific markets, thereby removing all uncertainties of class and rank. With Loudon, you knew precisely what you could and should do. If you liked flowers and owned a fourth-rate suburban garden (typically where the house formed part of a row or street, and your back garden extended anything from fifty to 300 feet), then according to Loudon you should display eighty different sorts of roses on your trellis, principally chosen from the white and yellow Banksian roses, Boursaults, Noisettes, Multiflora and Indica varieties, plus sixteen or so rose standards spaced ten feet apart, and a further ninety-six choice roses in your fifteen flower beds, along with sixty select deciduous and evergreen shrubs and 350 kinds of choice flowers. The calculation is for a garden of 160 feet in length – Loudon was precise in his mathematics, as he was in everything. By contrast, owners of first-rate gardens, which needed a park, a farm, and between fifty and 100 acres to qualify, might enjoy a dedicated rosarium, together with an ericetum for heathers, an American garden for acid-loving introductions such as magnolias, and a cutting garden – just the sort of compartmentalized estate that Repton had designed for the Earl of Bridgewater.

Before long, the better sorts of gardens were a riot of roses, impelling the *Gardeners' Chronicle* to call for order in their planting: not only should nurserymen weed out less worthy varieties from their catalogues (nurseryman Thomas Rivers had done this already), but garden owners should avoid the cardinal sin of mixing roses that flowered at different times. There was no excuse for having an untidy garden, said the *Chronicle* of 23 March 1850, 'but to have it always faulty, because of an injudicious selection of plants, is too bad'; far better to wait until roses were flowering and then 'to gather them altogether ... into a Rosery of some kind, even if it be of the most simple description'.

It was a solution that would later prove anathema to wild gardener William Robinson, who looked on most rose gardens as an 'ugly pest'. But for much of the nineteenth century, order prevailed and roses were marshalled into separate corners of the garden, preferably as far away from the house as possible, because a rose garden out of season is a 'wilderness to be avoided'. This last advice came from (James) Shirley Hibberd, a working journalist and gardener who took horticulture into the realm of popular culture, and who preached only what he practised. (He was also vegetarian for a time, and believed that teetotalism was a

William Paul's weeping rose – a variation of the popular rose standards he advocated in The Rose Garden *of 1848.*

good idea for those lacking in self-control, but as that did not apply to himself, he felt able to endorse a brand of sherry.)

A true popularizer of do-it-yourself gardening in a leisured age, Hibberd liked roses so much he wrote a practical treatise on their culture, and included the design of his own oval-shaped rose garden in his book for amateur flower gardeners. Despite the scrolls and curlicues in his plan, he recommended the simplest designs, 'for roses are not at all adapted to fill beds that twist like corkscrews, or that are sprinkled over a piece of turf like the holes in a colander'. Ever the practical horticulturist, he was especially good at advising town gardeners how to get the best from their roses. In London's smoky atmosphere, for instance, he could grow his favourite Bourbon, 'Souvenir de la Malmaison' ('finest of all delicately-coloured roses') only under glass; and he helpfully provided a diagram relating the optimum height of roses to the garden's distance from St Paul's Cathedral, explaining that short roses fared best in polluted atmospheres. As with so many of his fellow Victorians, Tea roses were his favourites, but he also admired (and grew) the common Cabbage and Moss roses which opened 'round as a ball, or more like the cheeks of a chubby baby that grows fat because it never cries'.

Hibberd's wife was a semi-invalid for much of her life, and instead of children they cared for a menagerie of animals as they moved house and garden around the suburbs of north London – Pentonville, Tottenham, Stoke Newington, Hornsey, Clissold Park – tending to the local wild-life as well as their own. In *Rustic Adornments for Homes of Taste,* he recommended feeding nightingales two or three worms a day, and 'now and then a spider, though two spiders a day are *quantum suf*'; but such thoughtfulness in his character did not prevent him falling out with his one-time protégé, the irascible Irish gardener and garden writer William Robinson, who emerged towards the end of the Victorian era as the prophet of a more natural style of gardening, and who castigated the rose of modern gardens as 'such an artificial compound, so entirely the result of years of selection and interbreeding, that it will not show itself in full beauty except under the most favourable conditions'.

The two men's ideas on rose gardens were in any case diametrically opposed, and Robinson may well have aimed his barbs at poor Hibberd when he called formal rose gardens 'just as objectionable' as his particular bête noire, formal bedding-out schemes. Roses 'should be everywhere in the garden where they would grow,' thundered Robinson. 'We cannot have too many Roses, or Roses in too many places.' Instead of rose standards (which he described as a 'vexation and a disfigurement', and about the worst investment suburban gardeners could make), Robinson wanted bold masses of roses grouped according to colour and giving a succession of blooms – old favourites such as 'Général Jacqueminot', 'Gloire de Dijon', 'La France', 'Souvenir de la Malmaison', 'Victor Verdier' and the old Moss roses. These should be planted thickly, 'not thinly, like gooseberries', while the climbing varieties should be allowed to 'grace our walls, shade our arcaded walks, festoon our trees, clamber up poles, or spray over the waste spaces'. Even Teas had their place in this rose-filled Eden, sunning themselves on a bank or a warm wall, and Hybrid Perpetuals could (one senses reluctantly) 'occupy the special plots provided for them'.

Robinson's ideas would spill over into the words and plantings of that other great Victorian or, more properly, Edwardian gardener-writer, Gertrude Jekyll, who stamped her personality and her colour schemes on the ample gardens of her age. Jekyll, too, had a passion for roses and firm opinions on how they could be displayed: on pillars, pergolas and iron frames; as rose arches, arbours and rose festoons; as an outer skin to disguise ready-made arbours or summerhouses (you can hear the faint condescension of someone whose breeding and pocket preferred the bespoke); or clambering into shrubs and small trees, in the case of roses with a 'wild way of growth', such as the beautiful milk-white Himalayan musk, *Rosa brunonii*.

'We are growing impatient of the usual Rose garden,' she wrote in *Roses for English Gardens,* describing it as 'generally a sort of target of concentric rings of beds placed upon turf, often with no special aim at connected design with the portions of the garden immediately about it'. To prove her point, she included a photograph of the 'usual rose beds on a lawn. A kind of rose garden that may be much improved upon.' One hopes that the owners never chanced upon this casual slur.

Jekyll's own appreciation of roses, by contrast, was that of an artist-gardener, who relished close contact with her handiwork (she was very short-sighted). On rose pillars, for instance, she ordained that they 'should be so placed that one can go right up to them and see the Roses at eye level and below it and also against the sky, and smell their sweet scent in perfect comfort as they grow'. She was equally determined to banish hyperbole, declaring that 'a Rose garden can never be called gorgeous; the term is quite unfitting'. Even at the height of the rose season, she maintained, 'what is most clearly felt is the lovable charm of Rose beauty, whether of the whole scene, or of some delightful detail or incident or even individual bloom'; gorgeousness belonged to other parts of the garden.

For all Jekyll's love of roses, the examples she included in *Gardens for Small Country Houses* (co-written with the architectural editor of *Country Life,* Lawrence Weaver) are few and generally disappointing, even those by the most respected designers of the age such as Inigo Triggs and Thomas Mawson. And her dream of creating an English rose garden 'embowered in native woodland' proved a poor model at Cliveden in Buckinghamshire, where (Sir) Geoffrey Jellicoe redesigned the woodland rose garden for Lord Astor in 1959, replacing the original Renaissance plan with a fluid reflection of a Paul Klee painting.[2] After struggling for many years, the roses succumbed to shade and competing tree roots, and now the garden has been planted afresh by Isabelle Van Groeningen with more accommodating perennials and grasses.

Far more successful were the generously planted rose gardens created in the *beaux-arts* style for wealthy Americans, such as the railway magnate Henry Edwards Huntington, who had inherited his fortune (and his second wife) from his uncle, Collis Huntington, for whom he ran the Southern Pacific Railroad in San Francisco. When Collis died suddenly in 1900, he left his much younger wife Arabella and his nephew Henry both multimillionaires. The pair eventually married in 1913 and moved into their new house in San Marino, southern California, where seventy gardeners tended the grounds, and Arabella buried her beloved dog Buster in the rose garden. Whenever in residence, she would walk past the eighteenth-century tempietto at 5 p.m. to lay a rose on his grave; her favourite rose was the faintly scented China hybrid, climbing 'Cécile Brunner', also known as the sweetheart rose.[3] The tempietto is still there, encircled by blush-pink Floribundas, 'French Lace' and shielding a statue of 'Love, the Captive of Youth'; but the rose garden itself has undergone several transformations along the way to its present incarnation as a 'collection garden' of more than 1,200 cultivars, grouped chronologically to tell the story of the rose from the Greeks and the Egyptians through to modern times.

Still maintained in close to its original state is the rose garden at Dumbarton Oaks in Washington's gracious Georgetown, a landscape of unfolding compartments created from the 1920s by the American landscape architect Beatrix Farrand for the diplomat Robert Woods Bliss and his art-collector wife Mildred Barnes Bliss. The rose garden is the largest terrace descending eastwards from the Orangery, between the Urn Terrace and the Fountain Terrace, where the ground drops away to the Lovers' Lane Pool. It was the Blisses' favourite part of the garden, and a stone commemorates where their ashes are laid. As they expected

Roses adorn the pergola and outdoor walkway of Herbert Coppell's estate in Pasadena, California, photographed by Frances Benjamin Johnston early in the twentieth century.

to use the garden in winter as well as summer, Farrand gave it large accent plants of clipped box by the entrance steps, at the centre and in the formal rose beds which she edged with dwarf box, *Buxus sempervirens* 'Suffruticosa'. You can see Gertrude Jekyll's influence in her mix of shrub roses and climbing roses in the beds by the retaining wall, where 'Cécile Brunner', 'Gruss an Aachen' and 'Katharina Zeimet' are among the cultivars that remain from the original plant list.

While planning the garden, Farrand advised Mildred to shun most of the pink roses, planting these instead in the cutting garden or among the borders of her vegetable plot. 'But, like you, I see a medley of soft yellows, oranges and orange-salmon colors, blacks and creamy whites, and none of that horrid shade known as "cerise" by the milliners.' Box and yew she thought would bring out the best of the rose colouring, and she also recommended jasmine, honeysuckle, lilies, and 'a general attractive floppy tangle of plants that will make the garden look used and lived in as quickly as possible'.[4]

Today some 900 roses bloom in the well-tended (but not overly controlled) rose garden at Dumbarton Oaks, where the view through the iron gates borrows the surrounding landscape of wooded hills, making you feel as private and secluded as Robert and Mildred Bliss must have felt in the gardens they created and then donated to Harvard University, along with their library and art collection, a gift that uniquely combined their love of Byzantium, pre-Columbian art and landscape history. Pink roses have crept into the rose garden, where the boxwood edging has given way to bluestone for easier maintenance, but otherwise it remains much as Beatrix Farrand had hoped.

Americans took their money and their garden tastes over to Europe, forming expatriate communities around cities such as Paris and Florence, and on the French Riviera where Gertrude Jekyll had earlier remarked on the dearth of roses in the gardens of the English, reasoning that 'Those who care for their gardens do not as a rule come out much before Christmas, and leave at the latest by the middle of May, so that any Rose that does not flower freely during the late autumn or early spring is of little importance, however beautiful it may be.'

The Americans were either bolder gardeners or stayed longer, as roses abounded. At the abandoned convent she bought at Hyères on the

Mediterranean coast, the novelist, socialite and taste-broker Edith Wharton draped roses from the high walls of her terrace, filling another with roses, and contributing the introduction to a guide to *Gardening in Sunny Lands* by an Englishwoman who had spent much time there, Alice Martineau. The secret of gardening in such places, said Wharton, was to recognize that 'in the south, slight differences of soil, of exposure, of the degree of shelter available, seem to count far more than in more equable climes'. Martineau devoted a whole chapter to growing roses, advising southern gardeners to shelter the roses from the mistral, and to prune according to desired flowering times. Among many favourite roses, she singled out the single yellow Banksian rose 'which riots over the gardens of la Mortola', and the beautiful cross produced in the garden of Lord Brougham's villa at Cannes, between a Tea rose and *Rosa gigantea*. 'The pink blossoms, on long swaying branches, are indescribably lovely, and are in full beauty in April.'

Further north, the roses were tamer and the climate less fierce. At her property on the outskirts of Paris, the Pavillon Colombe at Saint-Brice Sous-Forêt, Wharton again sought help with her roses, this time calling on her niece Beatrix Farrand for a rose garden of Floribundas and Hybrid Teas. But perhaps Wharton took her love of cascading roses with her. Twenty-five years after her death, the English garden designer Russell Page wrote in his elegant autobiography, *The Education of a Gardener*, of an affluent American colony in the inter-war years owning châteaux among the woods around Senlis, Rambouillet and Versailles, including one Louis Bromfield, who had 'learnt much of his gardening from Edith Wharton at St Brice, and I think his was the only garden in France where the hybrid musk roses grew – Penelope and Pax and others. They were allowed to grow into large loosely trimmed bushes hanging over the river, loveliest with their clusters of cream and white and rose-pink flowers just as the light began to fade.'

While the English veered increasingly towards naturalism in their rose gardens, and wealthy Americans planted roses on the grand scale, the French took as their starting point the formalism of the great French designers of the seventeenth century, who imposed their masters' will on a subjugated landscape in the form of rigid *allées* marching off towards the horizon, often in goose-foot (*patte d'oie*) formation. After visiting Paris in the 1840s, the American nurseryman Samuel Parsons commented that French gardens had improved since dispensing with the 'Le Nôtre style of style of gardening', but Alexandre Hardy still planted his roses at the Luxembourg in rigidly straight lines, best viewed (said English rose-grower William Paul) from the public promenades raised above the level of the roses. All that softened a monotony of roses was a line of fruit trees planted around the borders to the rectangular plan, and an enclosing fence 'made of light sticks, which are much used in France for similar purposes'.

Rose gardens became especially popular in France around the dawning of the twentieth century, before the First World War brought the frivolities of the *belle époque* to a sudden end. Among the dozens created, two have earned their place among the world's best rose gardens: the Roseraie de L'Haÿ (now the Roseraie du Val-de-Marne), begun by Jules Gravereaux in the 1890s; and the municipal rose garden at the Parc Bagatelle, developed from 1905 by the Commissioner of Gardens for Paris, Jean-Claude Nicolas Forestier.

The son of a cabinet-maker from Vitry-sur-Seine, Jules Gravereaux created his rose garden after retiring (aged just forty-eight) from a highly successful career in retailing, working for the proprietors of the Bon Marché department store. Just as he believed that Empress Josephine had collected every variety then known (see Chapter 10 for his involvement with Malmaison's restoration), so he dreamed of reuniting in his garden the world's entire stock of species and cultivars. To bring order to his ambitions, he turned to the horticulturist and landscape architect Edouard André, whose international design work included public parks and gardens in Luxembourg, the Netherlands (Weldam), Rome (the redesign of the Villa Borghese), Lithuania and England (at Sefton Park, Liverpool). André's solution was to embellish Le Nôtre's stiff geometry of radiating allées with decorative touches, such as trelliswork arbours, vases, statues and stone furniture.

The design worked, and the garden was soon planted with more than 6,000 different varieties of rose, all methodically identified, classified and planted according to type. It would grow even more – up to 8,000 varieties in 1910, by which time Jules Gravereaux was beginning to pass

Jules Gravereaux, who created one of the great French rose gardens at L'Haÿ-les-Roses and helped to enhance Empress Josephine's reputation as a lover of roses.

over responsibility to his son Henri, who reordered the collection into the divisions still mostly current today, laying out the history of the rose like the chapters of a book. Henri continued to oversee the garden after his father's death in 1916, but it slowly succumbed to the weight of its lofty ambitions and after a steady decline, when the Hybrid Teas suffered in particular, it was sold to the Département de la Seine in 1937.[5] When E. A. Bunyard visited in the months before the outbreak of war, he was able to dispel all rumours of the garden's decay: now 'trim neat paths and scrupulously weeded beds show that Paris has not neglected her noble heritage'. (He also visited Malmaison, where he found the gardener devoted all his attention to the modern roses, 'whereas the old Roses were pruned nearly to death, crowded, often without labels and generally struggling against neglect'.)

The other great Parisian rose garden is in the Parc de Bagatelle, at the north-western edge of the Bois de Boulogne, created as a municipal visitor attraction when the city of Paris took over the park which had been landscaped in pre-revolutionary times by the Scottish gardener Thomas Blaikie. Jules Gravereaux supplied more than 1,500 roses, most of which were returned when the state took over the Roseraie de L'Haÿ, and the decision was made to focus on historical roses there and modern roses at Bagatelle. In 1907 Bagatelle's creator, Jean-Claude Forestier, launched the first Concours International de Roses Nouvelles, which continues to this day, and the garden happily accommodates both competitive display

Postcard view of the early 1900s showing the rose garden at the Parc de Bagatelle, Paris, created by J. C. N. Forestier as a municipal visitor attraction and now home to the city's collection of modern roses and an annual competition for new introductions.

and enduring horticultural excellence. On a summer's evening, as shadows lengthen across the formal beds displaying the rose in all its guises (scrambling, rambling, hanging from posts and chains, trimmed into standards or left as bushes), this classic rose garden with its fine orangerie, chinoiserie kiosk and sturdy pergola defies William Robinson's verdict on the dedicated rose garden as an 'ugly pest'.

The rose gardens at Bagatelle, L'Haÿ-les-Roses and elsewhere may have been expressive of national difference, but they were essentially ornamental in character. Other rose gardens took on a more symbolic role, for example the commemorative rose gardens that linked roses with death in the manner of the ancient Greeks and the Romans. In Hackney, east London, the local nurseryman George Loddiges designed a rosarium containing more than 1,000 named varieties of rose for Europe's first non-denominational garden cemetery at Abney Park. Influenced by the 'New World' cemetery at Mount Auburn near Boston, Massachusetts, Abney Park opened in 1840 as a burial ground, free public park and arboretum, set among the landscaped grounds of Fleetwood and Abney houses. The rose theme carried over to the chapel's botanical rose windows, which echo those of Beverley Minster in the East Riding of Yorkshire, ancestral home of Abney Park's prime mover, George Collison.[6] Repton, too, planned to turn his burial place into a rose garden. Some three years before he died, he wrote to the vicar saying he was standing at his chosen burial spot remembering his dream of converting 'a weedy corner into a beautiful Flower Garden, and gathering a barren ear of wild barley I promised it would be a rose'.

At the Peace Palace Park in The Hague, completed in 1913, the Lakeland landscape architect Thomas H. Mawson used not one but two rose gardens to reflect the theme of peace, which he achieved largely by creating a sense of spaciousness and restfulness, and by harmony in design and materials. Mawson had often incorporated separate rose gardens into his commissions for private clients, claiming that no other flower 'provides such a number of varieties with such a wide range of effects nor such an extensive flowering season'. In his plans for the Peace Palace, he brought in the Dutch-born landscape architect Sophia Luyt to design the actual planting, and rose societies donated thousands of roses to the two rose gardens near the pond. Several months after the gardens

In a painting of c.1912 by E. A. Rowe, rose trellises shield the seaside garden of Queen Alexandra and her widowed sister at Hvidöre, Copenhagen, designed by Lakeland landscape architect Thomas Mawson.

opened in 1913, many of the plants and especially the roses were clearly suffering from the sandy soil and poor-quality dune water used for their irrigation. It was an inauspicious beginning for a garden intended to herald the dawning of world peace.

The rose nonetheless continues its reign as flower of choice in many commemorative gardens. 'I have no doubt whatsoever that the rose is the best loved flower in the world,' wrote rose-grower Harry Wheatcroft, 'and a flower that has so many meanings to so many different people. No garden of remembrance is complete without its presence.' Wheatcroft himself was proud of his involvement with two such rose gardens. The first was at Lidice, the Czech village destroyed by the Germans in June 1942 in reprisal for the killing by Czech partisans of Reinhard Heydrich, deputy Reichsprotektor of the Nazi Protectorate of Bohemia and Moravia. All men and boys aged sixteen and over were executed, and women and children were separated and removed to concentration camps. After the war, the 'Lidice Shall Live' committee planned a Garden of Remembrance filled with roses. The original plan had called for some 1,000 roses in total, around a centrepiece consisting of 300 'Peace' roses, but the scheme quickly gathered pace and eventually more than thirty countries donated some 29,000 rose trees. Wheatcroft's nursery alone provided 5,500 roses, including 300 'Peace' roses and more than forty other varieties. As a patriotic nurseryman, Wheatcroft noted that while 7 per cent of the garden's donated roses perished in the first appalling winter of 1955–6, there were no English failures. The garden suffered neglect in the immediate post-Communist era and eventually failed altogether, but in 2001–2 it was rebuilt and replanted, and now some 21,000 rose bushes bloom once more at Lidice.

Wheatcroft's second venture in commemorative rose planting lay closer to home, in the Welsh mining village of Aberfan, where 144 people died (the majority of them children) on 21 October 1966 when a coal tip engulfed a school, some terraced cottages and a farm. Contacted by Nottinghamshire schoolchildren who had raised money to send flowers to remember the children of Aberfan, Wheatcroft persuaded them to send rose trees instead. The council agreed to create a rose garden, to which the Nottinghamshire children donated 200 trees, and Wheatcroft made up the number to 2,000. A sentimental man, Wheatcroft liked to reflect on the lift to the spirits these roses had given, both in Lidice and Aberfan. 'It is really a smile from the products of the earth which stirs the soul of the individual who sees them.'

Honouring the dead is just one of the roles that western rose gardens have assumed. Equally significant is the part roses have played in horticultural imperialism, at once 'taming' a foreign and potentially hostile environment, and keeping alive a memory of home. India was particularly fertile ground for such treatment. Old India-hand Mrs R. Temple-Wright insisted that 'it was the memsahib's duty to lay down a lawn – just as it was her husband's duty to lay down the law', and she behaved in precisely the same imperious manner with roses, briskly advising her compatriots on how to create a garden in India 'in the *quickest,* the least expensive and the simplest way'.

For the memsahib's rose garden, Mrs Temple-Wright recommended that beginners should start with just twenty-four different sorts of roses, all the usual kinds such as 'La France', 'Victor Verdier', 'Edward's Rose', 'Général Jacqueminot', 'Coquette des Blanches', and the yellows 'Gloire de Dijon' and 'Maréchal Niel'. Larger gardens might take three or four of each sort, but one of each was presumably sufficient for smaller gardens. Although India has her own native roses, mostly in the Himalayan regions, Mrs Temple-Wright's recommended varieties all came originally from Europe, sent out at great expense and at the risk of even greater disappointment, as many consignments of plants to India failed altogether. In the 1860s, for instance, you were delighted when more than half your plants survived, as in the case of a Mrs Prinsep, who ordered thirty-six roses of eight different varieties, including Cabbage and Moss roses and the Tea rose 'Aimée Plantier'. Packed in a thick deal box by the Royal Botanic Gardens, Edinburgh, the rooted cuttings were carefully cushioned with dry sphagnum moss and sent by steamer via the Cape of Good Hope to Calcutta and on to Lahore. When the box was opened, fifteen of the roses had died but a satisfying nineteen had survived the journey – enough to merit an honourable mention in the horticultural press.[7] By the end of the century, however, importing roses became less necessary as you could obtain well-rooted cuttings from the gardens at Lucknow and Saharanpur at 2 annas each, or free from friends.

Mrs Temple-Wright's garden would have looked perfectly at home in Bath or Tunbridge Wells: dwarf roses planted either side of a walk, leaving space in front of them for annuals, and a rosary with plenty of room for climbers and ramblers. 'See that your roses get all the sunshine there is,' she advised; 'roses that get only the morning or only the afternoon sun will not bloom perfectly.' She clearly cared more for the well-being of her roses than that of her *malis* (gardeners), recommending that they should be put to the task of clearing every last scrap of grass during May (when temperatures can reach 115 to 120°F), because 'your men will not have anything particular to do in the hot weather'.

A more sympathetic guide to Anglo-Indian gardens is Edith Cuthell, married to a captain based at Lucknow in Uttar Pradesh, who reported in 1905 that the men had decorated the barracks on Christmas Day with 'elaborate greenery, and that pink and white paper roses, so beloved of

Tommy, enshrined our crest and suitable complementary mottoes'. She grew roses as standards around the drive, and as a rose hedge, both of which she pruned (or had her gardeners prune) in the cooler days of October. And she delighted in driving out to Lucknow's Botanical Gardens in November, when the roses 'were coming out in the little set garden, trailing over the *jaffri* work and in the hedges, luxuriant, glowing, a vision of beauty, the real flower of the East, in the cold weather. For a rose cannot stand the tropical sun.'

Alive to the beauty and romance of flowers in their Indian setting, Mrs Cuthell was entranced by the brilliant night-time spectacle of thousands of tiny lamps in the Hosein-a-bad garden, where roses and other shrubs clustered around an ornamental water tank. And she lamented the nightingale's absence 'here, in the plains of India, with the roses all around one, scenting the air and rejoicing the eye with a splendour unknown in other lands'.

But Mrs Cuthell was one of the few memsahibs to voice her appreciation of the Indian landscape; most of her compatriots looked to their gardens to provide a buffer to an alien world. For women like these, Kate Platt of Delhi's Lady Hardinge Medical College and Hospital for Women wrote a guide to staying healthy in the tropics that included advice on gardens.

Most of our favourite old-fashioned flowers grow well in the cold weather, though they may not have quite an English fragrance. Roses, lilies, carnations, pansies, verbenas, phloxes, delphiniums, snapdragons, violets, mignonette, all flourish. With a little trouble and at small expense, one may have a gorgeous display of colour in the garden. The delight of being able to wander right out of one's room in the early morning into an Indian garden is indescribable.

Given the British love of roses – as a shrub and as an emblem – it was only natural that the British architect Edwin Lutyens should plant roses in the gardens to the Viceroy's Palace of New Delhi, the imperial city he planned with Herbert Baker as a garden city rather than a *beaux-arts* capital. Lutyens came to New Delhi in 1912 directly from his work with Raymond Unwin at Hampstead Garden Suburb in north London, and he brought an understanding of how to use roses from his many collaborations with the much older Gertrude Jekyll, whom he knew affectionately as 'Bumps' or 'Mab', the 'mother of all bulbs' (a reference to her figure rather than her green fingers).

Borrowing their structure from Mughal water gardens, Lutyens's viceregal gardens in New Delhi spread westwards from the Rectangular Garden, through the Long Garden with its pergola and rose beds, and on to the Round Pool Garden (also known as the butterfly garden). 'Here the Viceroy would retreat with his wife from a world increasingly alien and uncertain to take afternoon tea and savor the last hour of sun and its magic afterglow. Then a gray haze would steal over the gardens, and on the Ridge, jackals would cry at the moon. The fragrance of roses and mignonettes perfumed the air, and, to Lutyens's delight, the fountains formed lunar rainbows.' Now called Rashtrapati Bhavan, the palace is the official residence of the President of India. Its Mughal gardens are open to the public in February, when everything flowers at once, and parties of schoolchildren are frogmarched at speed around the grounds.

By the time the independence movement gathered force in imperial India, the rose garden 'back home' had sunk into a cliché. 'The English garden, like the English Sunday dinner, is pretty much the same throughout the country,' wrote the arch modernist Christopher Tunnard in the year before the Second World War, quoting the original 'curious gardener', Jason Hill. 'Most gardens consist of rose beds, herbaceous borders, lawn and rockery, and, in all but the very smallest, there is a pergola garlanded with rambler roses.' Tunnard's solution was not to throw out the roses with the Sunday lunch, but to use roses in a garden that was 'rational, economical, restful and comprehensible' – a modern garden, that is, to suit a modern way of living. So although roses did not find their place among the hardy architectural plants included in the second edition of Tunnard's design classic, *Gardens in the Modern Landscape* – plants such as spiky cordylines and Chusan palms, which have become clichés of their own – nor did he ban roses entirely from his modernist Eden. Among the gardens he sketched for his book is a combined rose and tulip garden, where the flowers are planted in separate blocks in well-spaced chequerboard formation next to a zig-zag hedge.

But the cliché proved more enduring than its modernist makeover,

A modernist chequerboard of roses and tulips from Christopher Tunnard's Gardens in the Modern Landscape *of 1938.*

and by the late 1970s, the suburban garden of lawn and roses remained the most popular template for aspiring gardeners – the lawn religiously maintained, the roses conscientiously 'pruned, fed and sprayed', and battle waged (and won) against 'mildew, blackspot, greenfly and thrips'. The choice of roses was in truth a trifle monotonous (salmon and vermilion were especially popular), and the same Hybrid Teas and Floribundas appeared in nearly every street: 'Super Star', 'Piccadilly', 'Fragrant Cloud', 'Wendy Cussons', 'Elizabeth of Glamis', 'Masquerade', 'Orangeade' and 'Iceberg' – the kind of roses visitors missed in Sissinghurst's wilfully aristocratic rose garden. Where space allowed, a well-behaved Climber or Rambler such as the coppery-orange 'Schoolgirl' might be trained to a pergola or fence, but was rarely allowed to clamber up the house.

IDEAL HOME

JULY 1957

TWO SHILLINGS AND THREEPENCE

CONVERSION NUMBER

COTTAGES · BARNS · MEWS · BASEMENTS · GARDENS · MODERNISATION BY DECORATION & FURNISHING

Roses complete the suburban idyll in this magazine cover of 1957.

The template remains in use today, alongside wilder, more luxuriant rose gardens where shrubs and climbers run amuck amid a mixed planting of shrubs, grasses and herbaceous perennials; and alongside gardens that restrain their roses in geometric beds edged with low-growing clipped box, or some other 'tasteful' edging plant.

You will see variations on the wild and the classically tamed in both hemispheres, drawing inspiration from earlier gardener-writers such as Robinson, Jckyll, Farrand, Sackville-West and Russell Page, and to later prophets of the rose. In Australia, for instance, Susan Irvine has written of the two rose gardens she created around Melbourne, the first at Bleak House on the Calder Highway, and later at Gisborne in the Mount Macedon Hills. Beginning with the 'old' roses and familiar crosses, she was astonished to encounter hybrids from Australia's greatest rose breeder, Alister Clark, who bred some 135 roses to suit Australian conditions, often using the cold-susceptible *R. gigantea* as a parent. After Clark's death in 1949, many of his roses were lost, and Irvine set about collecting as many as she could, re-establishing the collection at her second home in a garden inspired by the plantswoman Margery Fish's Somerset home at East Lambrook Manor – this, felt Irvine, was better suited to her 'backdrop of mares and foals grazing on the hill opposite' than a formal English rose garden.

Irvine's Australian rose garden illustrates how the rose has earned its title as the world's favourite flower. Just as its genetic adaptability has turned it into a shrub for all seasons and a shrub for all climes, so the rose finds its placc in whatever sort of garden you desire, whether neat and trim and well behaved, or wild and disorderly and all things in between. By its very versatility, the rose has broken free of its original homelands, when it bloomed wild only in the northern hemisphere, and after travelling westwards from China and Central Asia and later eastwards across the Atlantic it has now triumphantly journeyed south – always adapting itself to local conditions – and shown that it can truly girdle the world.

Chapter Nineteen
The Language of Flowers

By the beginning of the twentieth century, however, you could be
forgiven for thinking that the rose was getting a little tired, and its
symbolism a little tarnished. 'Rose is a rose is a rose is a rose,' declared
Gertrude Stein famously in her poem 'Sacred Emily', which gained the
status of a mantra for modernism, endlessly discussed and endlessly
reinterpreted. It could simply have been nonsense: here is the line in its
original sequence:

> Rose is a rose is a rose is a rose.
> Loveliness extreme.
> Extreme gaiters.
> Loveliness extreme.
> Sweetest ice-cream.

When pressed at a seminar she gave at the University of Chicago, Stein
leaned forward, the better to engage with her questioners, and explained
that in the time of Chaucer and Homer, when language was new, a poet
could 'use the name of a thing and the thing was really there'. But after
hundreds of years had passed, and thousands of poems had been written,
the names had become worn out and stale. 'Yes, I'm no fool,' she added,
'but I think that in that line the rose is red for the first time in English
poetry for a hundred years.'

Given Stein's knack of playing the fool while taking herself all too
seriously, it is hard to know if her explanation is real or not. But her
declaration found its mirror image in the Italian academic and writer

Umberto Eco, who claims to have chosen the title for his novel, *The Name of the Rose* (*Il nome della rosa*), using much the same logic. The title came to him completely by chance, he revealed, after he and his publishers had rejected several others. He liked it 'because the rose is a symbolic figure so rich in meanings that by now it hardly has any meaning left: Dante's mystic rose, and go lovely rose, the Wars of the Roses, rose thou art sick, too many rings around Rosie, a rose by any other name, a rose is a rose is a rose is a rose, the Rosicrucians . . .'

A surprise best-seller of the 1980s, Eco's medieval murder mystery combined theological analysis with literary theory and much game-playing. But you would search in vain for any whiff of roses in the novel's labyrinthine investigations by the Franciscan friar William of Baskerville, assisted by the story's narrator, Benedictine novice Adso of Melk. Roses appear only in the novel's closing line, when an elderly Adso finally puts aside his manuscript, 'I do not know for whom; I no longer know what it is about: *stat rosa pristina nomine, nomina nuda tenemus*'.

The line translates literally as 'The rose of old endures in its name, we hold empty names' – a mystifying comment that might refer to elements in the story, such as Aristotle's lost book on comedy, or to a truly post-modern absence of meaning in a meaningless world. Eco later revealed that he took the quotation from a poem by the twelfth-century monk Bernard of Cluny, on the theme of *ubi sunt*. Slipping the rose into his title seems a deliberate attempt to disorientate the reader, who may stumble across the 'nominalist' reading (that all beautiful things leave only a name behind) right at the end, having made 'God only knows what other choices'. Eco was nonetheless surprised when readers in the United States and Britain drew parallels between his Latin verse and Juliet's declaration (in Shakespeare's *Romeo and Juliet*) that a rose would smell as sweet whatever it was called; for Bernard of Cluny, the opposite held true. All that remains of the real thing 'is precisely this evanescent, powerful, fascinating, magical name'. But in a particularly postmodern twist, the original Bernard was talking not of roses but of Rome, wishing to underscore the impermanence of all things by reminding us that of all Rome's ancient grandeur, only the names remain. Is '*stat rosa*' in fact a mistranscription of '*stat Roma*', as some scholars have suggested, making Eco's chosen title doubly absurd? Or is this just another literary game?

The rose has invariably been freighted with meaning throughout its long history, ever since Sappho planted roses at the shrine of Aphrodite and the Romans gorged on a feast of roses at every possible opportunity. The power of the rose is such that virtually every society where roses are grown has reinvented the rose for its own purposes, and the roses of each succeeding age have talked a subtly different language. Christian roses and Roman roses clearly have little in common, but even roses with a shared heritage may speak in different tongues. Despite their shared imagery of the wounds of Christ as a blood-red rose, the roses of medieval Christianity have an innocence denied to Edith Sitwell's darkly symbolic flower in *The Canticle and the Rose*, rising on its stem from Nagasaki's atomic devastation.

The idea that flowers have a codifiable language of their own dates back to the late eighteenth and early nineteenth centuries, inspired by a combination of Linnaean botany (which classified plants according to their sex lives) and the warm breath of Romanticism fanned by sentimental scientists such as Rousseau and Goethe. First in France, then in Britain and America, the vogue arose for sententious flower books that sought to instruct polite society – ladies especially – in the grammar and vocabulary of this invented language. Aside from its moral purpose, it was also a game and a conceit which claimed pseudo-historical links to the Turkish harem, where 'love letters' were supposedly conveyed by objects bound up in a handkerchief, their meanings deciphered by sound associations rather than any more obvious symbolism.[1]

The template for the genre was *Le Langage des Fleurs* of 1819, written by 'Charlotte de Latour', generally thought to be a pseudonym for Louise Cortambert, mother of the French geographer Eugene Cortambert, although a descendant has denied the attribution. Her book ran to many editions and was widely copied in Britain and America. The first English translation appeared in 1834, dedicated 'by Gracious Permission' to HRH the Duchess of Kent. A fat little book – the perfect gift for a loved one – it opens with a charmingly coloured bouquet of roses, ivy and myrtle, which stand, we are told, for beauty, constant friendship and love respectively.

In her preface, the author claimed historical roots for her material while reassuring readers that she would not 'parade our learning' by

French postcards c.1905, illustrating the language of flowers.

talking of Pliny, or write a 'crabbed treatise' on Egyptian hieroglyphics, or even pen a dissertation on the 'effeminate Chinese' (such casual racism was not then considered offensive). And she took pains to explain the very precise rules of grammar governing this new language, in which it was surely easy to sow confusion, as a flower presented 'in its natural position' was to be understood affirmatively, and when reversed, negatively. 'For instance,' wrote de Latour, 'a rosebud, with its leaves and thorns, indicates *fear* with *hope*; but if reversed it must be construed as saying, "you may neither *fear* nor *hope*." (How, you wonder, might a rosebud be reversed?) Again, divest the same rosebud of its thorns, and it permits the most sanguine hope; deprive it of its petals, and retain the thorns, and the worst fears are to be apprehended.' To make sense of your bouquets, you clearly needed to keep your wits – and Charlotte de Latour's instructions – about you at all times.

After stating her general rules, de Latour arranged her material by the seasons, starting with spring, for which she marshalled an odd variety of plants and sundry meanings, including grass and turf (utility); weeping willow (melancholy); the horse chestnut (luxury); lilac (first stirrings of love); the almond tree (thoughtlessness); and the periwinkle (tender recollections).

Charlotte de Latour's rose appears as the first flower of summer, gathered into a fine bouquet of rose (beauty), violet (modesty) and tulip (declaration of love), which together make up the statement: 'your beauty and modesty have forced from me a declaration of love'. That her rose should signify beauty rather than love is its chief surprise; like all historians of the rose, she traces the flower's enduring fascination back to the Greeks and the Romans, quoting a long poem by Anacreon before setting out the different roses and messages you might wish to send, amplified by a two-way floral dictionary: a rose leaf ('I am not importunate'); a crown of roses ('the recompence [*sic*] of virtue'); the Moss rose (love and voluptuous pleasure); a nosegay of full-blown roses (inviting the great to seize the opportunity of doing good); a white and red rose (ardent love); a rose wreath in a tuft of grass ('everything may be gained by keeping good company'); the Damask rose (grace); the Eglantine (poetry); the Monthly rose (ever fair); a Musk rose (capricious beauty); a rosebud (a young girl); a rose pompone (gentility); a single rose (simplicity); thorns (envy); a white rose (silence); and a white rosebud (a heart ignorant of desire).

Compounding the difficulties of correctly interpreting the grammar of roses, other authors introduced new and sometimes contradictory notions, producing a babel of voices instead of the claimed universal language. Lucy Hooper, for instance, added a Japan rose to indicate that 'beauty is your only attraction'; a May rose for precocity; a dried white rose to say that 'death is preferable to loss of innocence'; and a yellow rose to signify infidelity. And while the language of flowers spilled over into moralizing tales for children and young adults (among them Louisa May Alcott's decidedly sentimental *Flower Fables*), the American author of an etiquette book for young ladies cannot have read Charlotte de Latour on the Moss rose (signifying voluptuous love 'with its pointless thorns, and the soft and green verdure which embosoms its calyx') when he compared young women to the same rose, 'most beautiful in spirit and intellect when they are but half unfolded'.

It was all becoming a little silly; and the French who were the first to introduce the language were also the first to parody it, as in Taxile Delord's delightfully illustrated *Les Fleurs Animées*, which allowed the flowers to talk back. His rose (holding a sceptre of prickly briar stem and worshipped by shiny green beetles) tells an abridged version of her story, thankfully missing many pages of her manuscript or she would have gone on for ever. From her glory days in ancient Greece and Rome, followed by rebirth as Christian symbol and paradisiacal reward for

ROSE

The rose queen from Taxile Delord's irreverent Les Fleurs Animées *of 1847, illustrated by caricaturist J. J. Grandville (Jean Ignace Isidore Gérard).*

425

the followers of Mahomet, the rose had her Second Coming during the days of the Directoire but was now dethroned, said Delord, first by the pale heroine of the Romantics and then by the new woman (he is writing in 1847): '*la femme à reflet, la femme serpent*' (the woman of a thousand facets, the woman-serpent).

Despite such mockery, the language of flowers did not die out immediately, as publishers in France, England and America continued to meet public demand with new editions; and its vocabulary slipped consciously or unconsciously into art, for instance in a portrait of Lillie Langtry by the society portraitist Sir Edward Poynter. Painted the year after she had arrived in London and caught the eye of Edward, Prince of Wales, the portrait shows Lillie holding to her breast the yellow rose of infidelity. And the smaller white rose in her left hand, might that signify the complaisant silence of Edward Langtry towards his wife's adulterous liaison with the Prince?

If the rose eventually lost such precise meanings, it remains for much of the world the classic flower of love, especially red roses and especially on St Valentine's Day, celebrated on the saint's feast of 14 February when some 55 million roses are traded worldwide, and British people (90 per cent of them men) give more than 9 million red roses to their loved ones.[2] Since Chaucer 'invented' St Valentine as the patron saint of mating birds and mortals (see Chapter 6), and since the (mostly French) promoters of courtly love added roses to the celebration, the red rose has become *the* flower to give a lover. Cynics may say the gift lacks inspiration, and that each age gets the rose it deserves. Certainly today's Valentine bouquet is likely to consist of a dozen long-stemmed, perfectly formed red rosebuds, factory-farmed in places where labour is cheap and flown to markets of the developed world in defiance of the environment and common sense.

Yet for all its commercialism and sentimentality, the red rose can still tug the heartstrings when it counts. Several years ago I attended the ruby wedding of the Scottish artist John McLean and his English wife Jan, who had decided to spend her entire retirement lump sum on a party for family and friends. In a musical interlude, the pure coloratura soprano voice of Lorna Anderson cut through the conversations to sing the Robbie Burns classic, 'O my Luve's like a red, red rose, That's newly sprung in

June', unaccompanied at first, then joined by violas and lutes. It said more than any speech about the marriage we were celebrating, and about a love that had lasted and would continue to last 'Till a' the seas gang dry'.

Today's Valentine rose belongs to the flower's sunnier traditions, celebrating love, life and beauty – Venus reborn for modern times – but as Shakespeare warned some 400 years ago, loathsome cankers lurk in sweetest buds. The visionary William Blake saw the cankers with equal clarity, giving us a sick rose on to which you can project all the ills of modern society: venereal disease, prostitution, exploitation, corruption, jealousy, the tangled relations of humankind. Blake's rose is born of experience, not innocence, and even 'My Pretty ROSE TREE' of the same collection turns away from the poet in jealousy, repaying his solicitude with her thorns.

Blake's dark rose then took two different routes into modern consciousness. The first fed into the visions and hallucinations of the symbolists and decadents, who adopted the rose as a moody reminder of immanent death. One of the strangest images in American art is Frederick Stuart Church's *Silence* of the early 1880s, in which a black and withered mummified head sniffs at a rose, uncannily anticipating by just a few years the Egyptologist Flinders Petrie's excavations of the Roman tombs at Hawara and his discovery of real, mummified roses from the second century AD.[3]

Much the same ghostly roses haunt the mournfully sonorous *Poems and Ballads* of English poet Algernon Charles Swinburne, mostly graveyard flowers or roses commemorating dead friends and fellow poets such as Charles Baudelaire. Setting the tone is 'A Forsaken Garden', which he describes as the 'ghost of a garden' fronting the sea, where even 'the weeds that grew green from the graves of its roses / Now lie dead'. But the fabulous rose garden discovered by children in Swinburne's 'A Rosary' would find its way into T. S. Eliot's *Four Quartets*, with its footfalls echoing in the memory,

> Down the passage which we did not take
> Towards the door we never opened
> Into the rose-garden.[4]

William Blake's hand-painted poem 'The Sick Rose' from the original 1794 edition of Songs of Innocence and Experience.

Also emanating from Blake, at least indirectly, is a second strand of tainted, transgressive roses that set out to shock and disturb, sometimes playfully, sometimes more darkly. Virtually synonymous with bourgeois respectability, the rose was a natural target for the Surrealists. Salvador Dali painted a luscious red rose floating serenely above a burnt-brown landscape (*Meditative Rose*), as well as roses bursting out of a woman's head (*Women with Head of Roses* and *Three Young Surrealist Women*), and roses dripping blood from the belly of a naked, ample-breasted woman who swoons against a concrete pillar *(The Bleeding Roses)*. In film, too, roses exert a dream-like potency, as in Jean Cocteau's masterly reworking of Beauty and the Beast, *La Belle et la Bête* of 1946, where 'all the mischief and magic begins when a man picks a rose for his daughter, her sole desire among a sea chest of riches'.[5] Twenty years on, in his fantastical novel *L'Écume des Jours,* Boris Vian turned guns not into ploughshares but into beautiful white roses, blooming uselessly from the end of the steel guns the hero had been hired 'to grow' with his own body heat.

Of all such surrealist encounters with the rose, the most savage was that of the librarian Georges Bataille, who famously fell out with Surrealism's self-appointed high priest André Breton over an essay he wrote for the art review *Documents* on 'The Language of Flowers'. Purporting to examine the exposed sexual parts of flowers, Bataille's essay is fiercely provocative. Naturally, the rose makes several appearances as the plant (along with the humbler spurge) most closely linked to human love – a privilege shared by all flowers, suggests Bataille with more than a nod to Linnaeus, given that procreation is their natural function. The fact that petals become the object of desire rather than the flower's 'useful organs' he brushes aside by stating clinically that 'the object of human love is never an organ, but the person who has the organ'.

Bataille then went on the surrealist offensive, declaring that while flowers and girls might seem at first glance to conform to notions of ideal beauty, most flowers are barely distinguishable from foliage and some are downright hideous. 'Moreover, even the most beautiful flowers are spoiled in their centers by hairy sexual organs. Thus the interior of a rose does not at all correspond to its exterior beauty; if one tears off all of the corolla's petals, all that remains is a rather sordid tuft.'

And that's not all: aside from the 'filth of its organs, the flower is betrayed by the fragility of its corolla'. Unlike leaves, which age honestly, flowers wither 'like old and overly made-up dowagers, and they die ridiculously on stems that seemed to carry them to the clouds'. For Bataille, the philosophers' substitution of natural forms for abstractions was not only strange but absurd; and for anyone still determined to worship the sovereign rose, he threw in a final image of the Marquis de Sade imprisoned among madmen, 'who had the most beautiful roses brought to him only to pluck off their petals and toss them in a ditch filled with liquid manure'.

Bataille's invective against flowers in general and the rose in particular continues to reverberate, and the rose's occasional transgressions appear from time to time when artists and writers are looking to subvert the norms of good behaviour. In 'Slave on the Block', for instance, the American writer Langston Hughes used roses to castigate the 'patronizing Negrophilia' of liberal middle-class white folks. In Hughes's story, a Greenwich Village couple called Anne and Michael Carraway hired the very black and splendidly muscled young nephew of their recently deceased cook, supposedly for household duties but in fact as a fine addition to their collection of primitive Negro art. Much against Anne's will, they are forced to dismiss him when Michael Carraway's scandalized mother discovers the young man shirtless in the library, holding an armful of red roses against his ebony skin.

This intentionally sexualized image prefigures the work of Robert Mapplethorpe, best known for his shots of black men, violent sex – and flowers, despite his insistence that he did not much care for the latter: they needed watering, or dripped on the floor, or slowly died. And because much of his work cannot be seen, his 'perfect' and perfectly disturbing flowers – roses among them – must stand in for the rest. 'Like fig leaves for absent genitalia, they point to the scandal of what is not there.' Who but Mapplethorpe could produce a rose that would slip perfectly into an illustrated edition of *A Season in Hell*, Arthur Rimbaud's splenetic repudiation of western civilization and his own crazed 'alchemy of the verb'? Reproduced in black and white and wreathed in wispy smoke, this rose could only flourish in hell.

And the rose still stands for transgressive sex, even between consenting cowboys. In Annie Proulx's resonant novella *Brokeback Mountain*, Jack Twist is refused another summer tending sheep up the mountain after his boss had spied his antics with fellow cowboy Ennis Del Mar. 'You guys wasn't gettin paid to leave the dogs baby-sit the sheep while you stemmed the rose,' said the foreman, leaning back in his squeaky wooden chair.

Protest and revolt are other 'meanings' in the lexicon of roses that remain fresh through continual reinvention. The white rose Luther used as his emblem (see Chapter 7) re-emerged as the white rose of opposition to Hitler within Germany, while left-leaning labour movements on both sides of the Atlantic have opted for red roses or red carnations as their emblem, sometimes to the confusion of political commentators who cannot always tell their flowers apart.

Celebrating the trend for socialist roses was James Oppenheim's stirring campaign song of 1912, 'Bread and Roses', commemorating the strike of women textile workers in Lawrence, Massachusetts, which ended with the resounding cry:

> . . . Bread and roses! Bread and roses!
> Our lives shall not be sweated from birth until life closes;
> Hearts starve as well as bodies; give us bread, but give us roses.

The French Socialist Party (Parti Socialiste) adopted the red rose late in 1969 when it sought a new sign to mark its break with the French Section of the Workers' International. Illustrator Marc Borret devised the new emblem – a very masculine clenched fist holding a red rose – which crept into use from January 1970.

British New Labour's red rose is blander, less divisive, perfectly in accord with the party's desire to rebrand itself in 1986 under Neil Kinnock's leadership, when Peter Mandelson joined Labour's administration as Director of Communications. Apparently suggested by Kinnock, a keen rose-grower, the 'harmonious' rose replaced the class-laden symbol of the Red Flag, which was thought to narrow the party's appeal. British rose-grower Peter Harkness can vouch for Kinnock's interest in roses. While leader of the party in opposition, Kinnock visited the Harkness stand at the Chelsea Flower Show, where he demonstrated his wide knowledge of roses, especially of a recent Harkness introduction, 'Jacqueline du Pré'. An aide cannily photographed Kinnock against the stand, positioning him next to a Harkness rose called 'Rosy Future'. But roses on their own do not win elections, and Labour had to wait more than a decade before they finally formed a government.

And whatever the logic behind New Labour's rose, the logo is a curious aberration. Neither the rose itself (which looks like a common-or-garden Hybrid Tea) nor its formal representation (a fairly hackneyed stylization) says anything particular about Labour's electoral programme; it could just as equally stand for a local rose-growers' association as a major political party with a social conscience.

Far more successful at conveying meanings are the roses you see in much figurative art of the nineteenth and twentieth centuries. Such attention comes first of all from looking – really looking – at the rose, here described by George Cochran Lambdin, the first American artist to specialize in painting roses. While the rose's beauty was universally acknowledged, few truly understood its charms, which for Lambdin

seem to lie, in greater part, in the fine silky texture of the petals and in their translucency. No other flowers have these in such marked degree, and it is these qualities which make the contrast between the cool, clear rim and the outside of the cup, and its glowing heart. The other charm is that which is most felt when we look down into the depths of the half open bud. It is the charm, which it shares with every beautiful thing which is 'half hidden yet half revealed'.

Lambdin lived in the Philadelphia suburb of Germantown, then a leading American centre of rose cultivation, and it is claimed that he began painting roses to practise his techniques for capturing the flesh tones and 'diaphanous draperies' of another favourite subject of his: young women and girls. But he loved flowers for their own sakes too, and is credited as a founder member of the Germantown Horticultural Society.

Many other artists shared Lambdin's love of roses, and you can 'read' their preoccupations in the flowers they chose, as well as in their chosen styles and techniques. The roses favoured by the Pre-Raphaelites were naturally flowers of the hedgerow or the simplest of garden roses, observed from nature and painted in vivid detail. Think of the dog roses overhanging the brook where Sir John Everett Millais's Ophelia floats to her death. Among her billowing skirts, a pink garden rose drifts with the other flowers she has plucked from her garden, a Centifolia perhaps, echoing Laertes' 'rose of May'. William Morris's earliest commercial wallpaper was also a simple single-petalled rose climbing a trellis.

Even more obviously, the wild briars that encircle the court of the sleeping princess in Sir Edward Burne-Jones's *Briar Rose* paintings mimic the rose in nature, sending out thick and spiny suckers that hold the sequence together. For all the moody theatricality of Burne-Jones's art – and his deliberate avoidance of the moment of awakening – this rose is a thug.

Other Pre-Raphaelites opted for gentler garden roses, including some of the new introductions that fuelled the 'rose mania' years of the mid-nineteenth century. The pink and yellow roses held up to the bride by the bejewelled black boy in Dante Gabriel Rossetti's *The Beloved* look like plump Tea roses – the pinkish-apricot 'Safrano' introduced in

Sleeping knights held fast in Sir Edward Burne-Jones's The Legend of the Briar Rose: The Briar Wood, *completed in 1890 and still displayed in the saloon at Buscot Park, Oxfordshire.*

433

1839, had undertones of sulphurous yellow just like these; the pink 'La France', first of the Hybrid Teas, came in two years after Rossetti began his painting (1865). And if you cast a horticultural eye at John William Waterhouse's St Cecilia slumbering to the accompaniment of angelic strings in a Renaissance flowery mead of oriental poppies and low-growing rose bushes (red and white), you will spot behind Cecilia's chair a pair of standard rose trees bearing rich red blooms, almost certainly Hybrid Teas. (The angel to the left has dirty feet, an unsettling detail.)

These are precisely the sort of rose standards derided by William Robinson as vexatious and disfiguring, an affront to his notion of wild gardening, so it is surprising to discover that Monet planted them in his beloved garden at Giverny. He painted them, too (in *Flowering Garden at Sainte-Adresse*, c.1866, for instance), as did that other Impressionist gardening obsessive, Gustave Caillebotte, who recorded his 'companion' Charlotte Berthier (they never married) admiring them in his garden at Petit-Gennevilliers. Caillebotte also cultivated a rose garden at his family home in Yerres, where he painted a charming pink-flowered rose standard before a boundary wall and the valley landscape beyond.[6]

William Robinson would have infinitely preferred the twilight roses captured by John Singer Sargent in *Carnation, Lily, Lily, Rose,* which he began in 1885 while staying with the American artist Frank Millet in the Cotswold village of Broadway. Two young girls in frilled smocks, daughters of the illustrator Frederick Barnard, play with Chinese lanterns under a canopy of white Aurelian lilies. Around them are pink China roses, iridescent in the twilight, while behind the younger girl a burgundy rose clambers Gertrude Jekyll-style up a pillar. The dark red of the pillar roses matches that of the carnations, which swirl like wildflowers in the long grass.

The apparent naturalism of the scene belies its painstaking execution. Painted at dusk in the short time that filmmakers call 'the magic hour', it is one of the few compositions Sargent ever made outdoors, but the fading light meant that he could paint for only a few minutes each evening. And so he worked in painfully short snatches from September through to November while his friends played tennis (other guests included the novelist Henry James, the poet and critic Edmund Gosse,

Carnation, Lily, Lily, Rose *by John Singer Sargent, painted from life in 1885–6.*

painter Alfred Parsons and the Shakespearean actress Mary Anderson). As the garden had hardly any flowers, he transplanted some from elsewhere, substituting artificial flowers when these died.

'My garden is a morass,' he complained to Robert Louis Stevenson, 'my rose trees black weeds with flowers tied on from a friend's hat.' The girls meanwhile wore woollen vests under their smocks to keep warm. Sargent returned to the painting the following summer, when the Millets

435

had moved to nearby Russell House, and finally completed it that autumn. The title comes from the refrain to a popular song of the 1880s, Joseph Mazzinghi's 'The Wreath', which Sargent and his friends will have sung around the piano in Broadway: 'Have you seen my Flora pass this way? Carnation, Lily, Lily, Rose.'

Some American painters of the nineteenth century were even more particular about identifying the roses they painted. Martin Johnson Heade's Cherokee roses are equal in power to his disturbing portraits of *Magnolia grandiflora* (and far better than his more ordinary garden roses). 'Maréchal Niel' roses were a constant favourite of the American Impressionist Childe Hassam, who is said to have seen reflected in them America's own blending of European and eastern cultures. *The Maréchal Niel Rose* was an alternative title for his *Sonata* painting of 1893, in which a woman hangs her head at a piano, a score of Beethoven's *Appassionata Sonata* open on her knees and her limp exhaustion reflected in the yellow cut rose in a bowl on the piano.

But the most acclaimed nineteenth-century painter of roses was surely the Frenchman Henri Fantin-Latour, who, like the later Mapplethorpe, much preferred his figure studies to his flowers – a verdict not usually shared by the public, who cherish his ability, one much admired by Marcel Proust, to capture his flowers moments before the first petals begin to fall. Each June, after the Paris Salon was over, the artist would retreat to his 'maisonette' in Lower Normandy and its little cottage garden, into which he would wander every morning after breakfast, wearing slippers and an old straw hat, to pick the most richly coloured flowers that had opened overnight. The flowers he loved best were those you might find in the 'old gardens of country priests, growing without too much attention in beds bordered with boxwood'. The latest peonies or chrysanthemums were not to his taste, but 'he made little masterpieces of larkspurs and pinks'.

Mystery surrounds the headily fragrant pink rose named 'Fantin-Latour' in the painter's honour. Although it is usually classed among the Centifolias, its leaves have the dark green smoothness of the China roses, while Peter Beales judged its all-pervading perfume 'rather more Alba-like than Centifolia'. Other authors suggest a Gallica–Hybrid Tea cross, and even a Bourbon.[7] But whatever its parentage, its presence in a garden

The petals are beginning to fall in Henri Fantin-Latour's late nineteenth-century Pink and White Roses, *set against the dark background favoured by Dutch master flower painters of the seventheenth century .*

recalls the stillness of his paintings, and the roses caught at their moment of mature perfection.

Throughout the twentieth century the rose has continued to find its way into works of art, demonstrating its versatility as a motif, and as a reference. Better known perhaps for her calla lilies and cannas, American artist Georgia O'Keeffe included roses among her giant flower paintings, which caused a sensation when they were first shown and stunned viewers by their size, scale, radical palette and undeniable sensuality. Her white roses, by contrast, took the rose into abstraction. O'Keeffe herself explained her intentions in an interview she gave to the *New York Post* in 1946. 'When you take a flower in your hand and really look at it,' she said, cupping her hand and holding it close to her face, 'it's your world for the moment. I want to give that world to someone else.'

And precisely because it comes already laden with meaning, the rose finds favour with artists who are interested as much in ideas as aesthetics. In Anya Gallaccio's *Red on Green,* for instance, the artist assembles for each new installation some 10,000 mass-produced, freshly cut red roses, which she leaves to dry over the course of the exhibition. Whenever the installation goes on show, she first pulls the heads off the stems, then packs them tightly on their bed of greenery laid out in a neat rectangle on the floor. 'So for a couple of days anyway there is this really fantastic surface which is velvety, really seductive and tactile,' she explained. 'Because they're slightly raised off the floor by the layer underneath, they become like the perfect pot-pourri. They dry into perfect rosebuds.'[8]

While Gallaccio uses roses to work through her obsession with time and decay, the German artist Anselm Kiefer turns to the rose to process cataclysmic events and figures from the past. *Let a thousand flowers bloom* (2000) is a colossal work in which a statue of a waving Chairman Mao Zedong is all but obscured by a tangle of dried dead roses, thick and vicious like the barbed wire of no man's land. The title refers to a speech Mao gave in 1957, promising intellectual freedom for all: 'Let a hundred flowers bloom and a hundred schools of thought contend'. Kiefer has multiplied a hundred to a thousand, but revolutionary dreams still wither like the roses, and anyone who dared to criticize Mao's totalitarian rule was swiftly arrested.

One of the most eloquent modern readings of the rose belongs to a series of monumental rose paintings by the American pioneer of abstract expressionism, Cy Twombly. Called simply *The Rose,* the huge paintings each contain three man-size roses in pulsating colours: tangerine, violet, lime green, lemon yellow, crimson, burgundy, a shimmery metallic black, all set against a flat surface of bright turquoise. Paint drips from the roses to form a multicoloured fringe, and as in his earlier rose sequence, *Analysis of the Rose as Sentimental Despair* (1985), the artist has scrawled fragments of verse directly on to the canvas, taking the lines for this latest series from the English translation to *Les Roses,* a cycle of poems written originally in French by the Czech-born Rainer Maria

Rilke. '*Rose, [. . .] flower of all our flowers, inside yourself, petal over petal, do you feel our own palpable pleasures?*' reads the inscription to Twombly's *Rose IV*.

These are unmistakably late works, produced by a fully mature artist who reworks themes obsessively as he stubbornly interrogates his art. While Twombly's earlier roses convey a sense of roses in the making, their red clots emerging like bloodstains through a veil of dripping white paint, these new roses have burst triumphantly into flower. Through them, Twombly projects not just his own reflections on nature, life, death and time – the rose as a memento mori to the fleeting pleasures of life – but centuries of experimentation in using natural objects to convey ideas.

To paint the roses in his studio in Gaeta, Italy, Twombly surrounded himself not with 'real' roses but with images painted by others:

Loosely painted late Renoir flower paintings jostle with eighteenth-century still lifes ripe with abundance; a postcard of a simple photograph of a rose in full bloom sits opposite a late Pierre Bonnard painting, *Nature morte au melon*, 1941, of a yellow melon and a bowl of peaches rendered in swirling, interlocking greens and reds.

The result is both a real rose and a reflection on the rose, thing and thought and whatever else the viewer may bring to the canvas.

Twombly's roses have always been polyglot affairs, borrowing variously from an international gallery of poets, including the Persian Rumi, the Italian Giacomo Leopardi, the Austrian Ingeborg Bachmann, and the Americans T. S. Eliot and Emily Dickinson. For this latest cycle, Rilke is the perfect pan-European choice. Born in 1875 in Prague, then ruled by Austro-Hungary and now the capital of the Czech Republic, he lived variously in Austria, Germany, France and Italy before finally finding refuge in the borrowed Château de Muzot in Switzerland, that 'curious vortex ever at the heart of the European whirlpool'.[9] He wrote mainly in German, but during the years before his death in 1926 in a Swiss sanatorium at the age of just fifty-one, he produced nearly 400 verses in French, including the twenty-seven short poems that make up *Les Roses*.

Roses cast a spell over Rilke from an early age. As a young man he

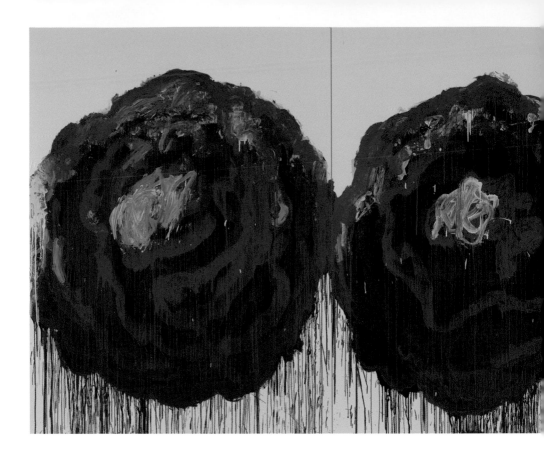

The Rose (IV) *by American artist Cy Twombly, 2008, one of five works inscribed with translated fragments from Rainer Maria Rilke's cycle of French poems,* Les Roses.

recorded in his journal how he had invented a new form of caress: 'placing a rose gently on a closed eye until its coolness can no longer be felt; only the gentle petal will continue to rest on the eyelid like sleep just before dawn'. Progressing beyond the slightly sentimental symbolism of his earlier poems, Rilke's roses developed into the 'bewilderingly beautiful' 'Rose-Bowl' of *New Poems,* in which the inner reality of the flowers unfolds like the transformative process of art. As the German scholar Eliza Marian Butler reminds us, the poet kept a vase of falling roses in his room until the flowers were really dead, then embalmed their petals in books or turned them into pot-pourri.

But it was through his own death that Rilke became forever linked with the rose, an association underscored by the haunting lines he chose for his gravestone in the small mountain cemetery of the Burgkirche at

Raron in Switzerland, surrounded by the snowy Alps of the Valais. He wrote the words in his fiercely particular will, prepared just two months before he died, when he feared madness rather than death:

> Rose, oh reiner Widerspruch, Lust,
> Niemandes Schlaf zu sein unter soviel
> Lidern.
> (Rose, oh pure contradiction, desire
> To be nobody's sleep under so many
> Eyelids.)

After the heady bewitchment of his German roses, and the lighter caresses of his French roses, Rilke seemed able at last to set the rose free.

But the manner of his dying tied him ever more tightly to the rose, for it is said that roses killed him – a myth his chosen epitaph served only to perpetuate.

As romantics tell the story, Rilke died from pricking his finger on a rose thorn while gathering roses for a lover, subsequently contracting blood poisoning from which he never recovered.[10] Although he did indeed prick his left hand on a rose thorn, as he admitted in a letter to his publishers, what really killed Rilke was acute myeloid leukaemia, then largely unrecognized. Doctors (and Rilke himself) considered that the many ailments for which he sought treatment were largely psychological in origin. The verdict on the part played by the rose remains open at best. While it is unlikely that the rose 'killed' Rilke, as some would have it, the incident may have provoked attacks which hastened his decline.

Twombly is not the only artist to respond creatively to Rilke's roses. For a decade or more, the British poet Jo Shapcott engaged in 'tender and taxing' conversations with Rilke's fugitive French lyrics, producing at the end a small collection of poems in which she deftly goes beyond translation and has the roses answer back, turning Rilke's love poem to the rose into one addressed to the long-dead poet. As Shapcott herself explains, her reading of the poems is essentially sexual.

I began to see that in the sequence Rilke's roses were women. And more than that – petal – space – petal – these poems were versions of female genitalia. Once this perception had taken hold I knew I couldn't follow Rilke's pattern of addressing the roses: he speaks to them, tells them what they are like, what makes them up, where their essence is to be found. My roses are given their own voice. They speak. And if you put my poems alongside Rilke's, more often than not you'll find my roses addressing his, saying, in effect: 'It's not like that, it's like this.'

Just one of Rilke's fragments appears in both Twombly and Shapcott: poem number VIII, which Shapcott calls 'Rosa glauca'.

> Overflowing with your dream,
> flower with so many others deep
> inside, wet as one who weeps,
> you lean against the dawn

says Rilke's (male) voice addressing the rose.

> In my dream I could perform
> water acrobatics
> and swam with a troupe:
> we leaned inwards . . .

replies Shapcott's (female) flower, carrying her reflection of the male gaze into the next stanza, to form a perfect rose 'which was, I swear, a dead-ringer for the pattern in your left iris'. And so the teasing, tempting dialogue continues, mimicking the eternal contrariness between men and women.

Rilke's roses, like Shapcott's and Twombly's, are complex, ethereal, ghostly, flirting with abstraction yet stubbornly present – clearly a modern rose for modern times. Umberto Eco gave up far too easily when he declared the rose so overburdened with meanings that it has become virtually meaningless. He should perhaps have followed the example of George Cochran Lambdin and refreshed his vision by looking deep inside a half-opened rosebud to experience the beauty of things 'half hidden yet half revealed'.

Chapter Twenty
Why the Rose?

A s I came to finish this book I made a final journey, to the world's largest rose garden at Sangerhausen in the former East Germany, fearing that in my search for cultural meanings I, too, might be losing sight of the botanical rose. After a short flight from London to Munich and another on to Leipzig, I hired a car and drove westwards across the gently undulating Saxon plain towards the Harz Mountains, the monotony broken by wind farms, sweeping lines of electricity pylons, and the occasional conical spoil heap marking the area's once flourishing mining industries. It seemed an odd landscape for the rose.

Sangerhausen's Europa-Rosarium was nonetheless a revelation. Once I had checked in to my hotel, I walked through the quiet town, its streets and houses planted with climbing roses of every colour, and slipped into the Rosarium by the bottom gate. After a month of rain, the air smelt freshly of rose dew, even from a distance, and I had the sensation of walking into a rose garden that is also a museum, a place where the rose is celebrated calmly and scientifically, but not without grace.

From the handful of wild and cultivated roses known to Theophrastus, Sangerhausen's collection has swollen to include more than 7,800 different forms of cultivated hybrids and 500 wild roses, in a garden of some 75,000 individual rose bushes. Here you will find gathered together in one place around a third of all roses known to the American Rose Society – an astonishing feat for a single garden. To help you digest such variety, the garden is landscaped into separate areas, where rose classes are grouped together with helpful signboards (in German only) setting out their gradual evolution.

Founded by the rose breeder Peter Lambert and two local dignitaries on land provided by the town, the Rosarium opened in 1903 under the benevolent eye of the Kaiserin August Viktoria and the Society of German Friends of the Rose (Verein Deutscher Rosenfreunde). Its brief was to preserve the old rose cultivars that were fast disappearing and to introduce order into the naming of new varieties. Following repeated expansions, it now covers more than 12.5 hectares, the formal planting near the top entrance giving way to a more relaxed landscape style on the slopes leading down towards the town. Such is the power of the rose that the Rosarium survived two world wars and the difficult early years under the German Democratic Republic, when it lost a large part of its library to Moscow and was required to send thousands of rose cuttings as reparations for the war. All efforts to retrieve its valuable old books have so far proved fruitless, although its stock of rose varieties has remained virtually unscathed. Today, the garden itself is funded entirely by the municipality of Sangerhausen, a testament to civic pride. Without the town the rose garden could not survive, but the town is equally unthinkable without its roses.

On my first visit I spent nearly ten hours in the garden, entranced to encounter many historic varieties I had thought long since vanished. Mid-July is not the best time to visit, as the old European roses had finished flowering (the Albas, Centifolias, Damasks and Gallicas of early summer), but here were many of the first China hybrids in bud or bloom, among them the silky pink petals of 'Old Blush' or 'Parsons' Pink', one of the original four stud Chinas; a little 'Champneys' Pink Cluster', the first of the Noisette roses bred by John Champneys of South Carolina; a bed of delicate little Tea roses with mostly French names; a bud of 'La France', the first Hybrid Tea (looking, it must be said, a little sad, and one of the garden's few casualties to black spot); and Pernet-Ducher's 'Soleil d'Or' of 1900, source of the bright yellow in many of today's roses. As Leader Thomas Pawel explained to me, Sangerhausen is a rose collection first and a show garden second; in their aim to collect together as many old roses as possible, they find room for sick roses and for varieties that do not necessarily thrive in Germany's climate. And to demonstrate how few roses – out of so many – have sired the myriad roses of today, one small area is planted with old roses and their

A poster of 1903 celebrating the opening of the Rosarium at Sangerhausen, Germany, now called the Europa-Rosarium and holding the world's largest collection of roses.

parent species, their relationships further explained in a simplified family tree.

Even more revelatory for me were the areas devoted to the garden's 500-odd wild roses (species and their natural hybrids) – an outstanding collection begun in the Rosarium's first decade, when it became home to botanist Dr Dieck's wild roses which had been shown at the Paris Exhibition of 1908. Dotted around the garden are thickets devoted to different botanical groups and geographical areas – wild roses from central Asia, for instance, such as *R. beggeriana,* its small white flowers sharing the musky nutty scent of *R. fedtschenkoana,* one of the Damask parents; or the Cinnamomeae roses from the northern reaches of America, Europe and Asia, including the lovely Arctic rose, *R. acicularis,* with its swelling red hips.

If the wild thickets felt to me like rose heaven, I emerged into the flaming hell of patio roses and the Polyanthas, their popularity assured by long-lasting displays of massed blooms in the brightest of colours, and by their neat and sturdy habits. But spend long enough in the garden and you will be sure to find the roses that suit you best, whether your tastes veer towards the old classics or to more modern classes introduced from 1867 with the first Hybrid Teas. As well as the Miniatures and the Polyanthas, here at Sangerhausen you will find the similarly florid Floribundas, shapely Hybrid Teas and their stately, truss-bearing crosses, the Grandifloras, as well as many hardy modern shrub roses, including Hybrid Kordesii, Moyesii, Musk and Rugosa roses, and the English Roses bred by David Austin. You will also find orchestrated displays of climbing roses and the Scotch roses (*R. spinosissima*), all carefully labelled and explained.

Aided by the garden's extraordinary gene-bank, the Europa-Rosarium is an active partner in the genetic research that is transforming our knowledge of both the history and the future of rose-breeding, and it is a test garden for the tough German programme (ADR or Allgemeine Deutsche Rosenneuheitenprüfung) involved in certificating new roses. With such a wide brief, it is perhaps not surprising that the collection pays less attention to projecting the future. I could find little trace, for instance, of the breeding programmes of US and Canadian universities and research institutes which are attempting to create roses for extreme climatic conditions. But space is limited and they cannot plant everything. The Europa-Rosarium is indeed an extraordinary place, and a pleasure I was glad to have left until last.

As I returned from Sangerhausen, I thought about the question that had intrigued me from the start, one which people often ask when they hear I am writing a history of the rose. 'Why the rose?' they say. 'What is it about the rose that makes it so special?' Why should the rose have accumulated so many meanings, and why is it such a favourite flower to so many?

Part of the answer undoubtedly lies in the way the rose is able to express cultural identities. In the western world and anywhere shaped by contact with the West, the rose has colonized the collective subconscious. The same holds true for much of the Middle East, from pre-Islamic Persia to the present day. The great religions of Christianity and Islam have actively promoted the rose; and although the lotus is seen as the principal flower of eastern religions, the rose plays a small part in Hindu mythology. As the supreme gods Brahma and Vishnu debated which was more beautiful – the lotus or the rose – Brahma, who had never seen a rose, opted for the lotus, but changed his mind when Vishnu showed him a rose. In return, Brahma created Vishnu's wife Lakshmi, the goddess of prosperity, out of 108 large and 1,008 small rose petals, thereby creating a symbol that brought together female beauty, love, innocence and desire.[1]

The rose is just as omnipresent in popular culture. Whether kitsch or high art, its image is always with us, and the flower itself is used to validate any number of products and emotions. When Bob Dylan devoted his 'Theme Time Radio Hour' to flowers, eight of his fourteen chosen artists sang about roses. From the 'bridal pot-pourri' of Bob Wills and his Texas Playboys, belting out 'The New San Antonio Rose', to his final choice, Alain Toussaint and Elvis Costello duetting on 'The Sharpest Thorn', his artists sang variations on the usual floral themes: love going cold (George Jones's 'A Good Year for the Roses'); roses and death (Paul Clayton's collected folk ballad 'The Bonnie Bunch of Roses'); roses and post-punk anger (Kim Shattuck and the Muffs' 'Layin' on a Bed of Roses'); more roses and sentiment (Laura Cantrell's 'When the Roses Bloom Again').

After Geraint Watkins's swelling 'Only a Rose', Dylan paused to give out tips on planting pansies, then muttered fiercely, 'I wasn't gonna play any more rose songs, but how could I not play this one?', slipping in Merle Haggard's song of wine, roses and unrequited love, 'I Threw Away the Rose'. Between songs, Dylan wove a hypnotic narrative of rose lore and rose poetry in his rasping, gravelly voice, taking in the creation of the White House Rose Garden, Gertrude Stein's laconic 'Rose is a rose' and the whole of Robert Frost's short poem, 'The Rose Family'. Other flowers barely showed their faces.[2]

So why do we fall in love with the rose? Why does it haunt the work of painters, poets and songwriters, just as its shadowy forebears haunted the apple trees and smoking altars of Sappho's sacred groves? Why do writers and thinkers of every persuasion continue to use the rose to prove their contrary points, and why do so many gardeners give it pride of place, whether they live in a cottage or a castle?

This book has provided many answers, I hope, but I am particularly struck by two simple facts. The first is that who you are shapes how you see the rose. For the American landscape architect A. J. Downing, the secret of the rose's 'perpetual and undying charm' lay in its being 'a type of *infinity*', without limit to its variety and beauty of form and colour. The co-architect of New York's Central Park – that most democratic of spaces – Downing believed this made the rose 'the symbol and interpreter of the affections of all ranks, classes, and conditions of men'. George Cochran Lambdin saw the rose as only a painter can, savouring the 'fine silky texture of the petals' and noting the contrast 'between the cool, clear rim and the outside of the cup, and its glowing heart'. For the dramatists William Shakespeare and John Fletcher, by contrast, the rose was best because it spoke of human character: 'It is the very emblem of a maid', blushing and modest when courted gently, but shutting itself tight into a bud when rudely wooed.

Just as each person sees the rose differently, so each age and each society projects on to the rose its cherished dreams and aspirations: from the Greeks, to the Romans, to the early Christians and right up to the present day, the rose has reinvented itself. This process can be primarily intellectual, for instance when the pagan rose transmuted into *rosa mystica*. But it can also be physical, as when the Dutch bred the luscious

Centifolia roses worthy of the great Dutch and Flemish masters of the still life. And when roses were beginning to lose their crown to the ncw exotics arriving into Europe from the opening continents of Australia, Africa and South America, men like William Kerr lived (and sometimes died) under foreign skies to bring us new strains of roses from the East. And so the rose was reborn: fresher, brighter, longer lasting, a triumph of science and human ingenuity even if some of the old charms were lost – vigour and scent, especially.

If you want to understand why the rose continues to hold us in thrall, may I suggest that you take a long, deep look inside an opening rose, preferably one of the old shrub roses with their loosely quartered centres. The flower is undeniably sexual. Here is Helkiah Crooke's 'little rose half blowne' of a woman's sex and Jo Shapcott's petal-space-petal of her conversations with Rilke's roses. But here, too, is Dante's metaphor of the Church and Jung's mandala of the unconscious self. Add a smell of sunshine, or a musky hint of cloves. Compare the rose's sturdy prickles with the petals' fragile beauty. Set the white rose next to the red, the golden next to the cream, and then you may see that in our search for metaphor and meaning, the rose is the perfect signifier of love, whether that love is for a man, a woman, an idea, or for the whole of humanity, *caritas* or *amor*. Umberto Eco may believe the rose has so many meanings that it has become virtually meaningless – but when did he last look, really look inside a rose?

And let us not forget the essential geography of the rose: a native of the northern hemisphere, revered in the West but crucially influenced and changed by lands further east, Iran and China especially. Trade, exploration and conquest have shaped the rose just as they have shaped human societies. Without foreign blood – and without the patience and skills of early horticulturists – the rose would still be a simple briar of heaths and hedgerows. And the rose has spread progressively south-wards and truly colonized the world, so that now rose-breeders from the southern hemisphere send us back their best roses.

Roses also come to us laden with stories. I think of the anthropologist Jeremy Swift, who told me of a rose he chanced upon in a sacred mountain of the Gobi desert, where he was talking to nomads, a rose which had somehow survived in this landscape of wild desolation and

Look inside the heart of a rose: detail from Old-fashioned rose, beech mast and clover leaf *(1974) by Rory McEwen. The rose is said to be the Gallica 'Président de Sèze'.*

whose offspring now struggles to survive on a Welsh hillside. I think of a fellow rose enthusiast at a conference to celebrate the life of the rosarian Graham Stuart Thomas, who remembered for me her grandfather's love of roses, which she had clearly inherited. (There must be a gene for such botanical passions.) I think of Peter Kukielski, the curator of the Peggy Rockefeller rose garden at the New York Botanical Garden, who introduced me personally to the roses in his collection. Here in the Bronx he has reserved a corner of his heritage rose bed for roses that hold special meaning for him: Peggy Rockefeller's favourite, a pink Hybrid Rugosa, 'Sarah van Fleet', flanked by two ramblers that commemorate another Peggy (Peggy Martin), a rose-grower from the Mississippi Delta who lost her rose garden and both her parents to Hurricane Katrina. After the waters drained, she found rising from the mud an unnamed rose, which is now marketed as the 'Peggy Martin Survivor Rose'. About their feet Kukielski has planted the yellow-flowered 'Sunny Knockout' rose in memory of his own mother, who told him before she died that whenever he saw yellow roses, it meant she was talking to him. Now the two Peggys are talking to each other, and he joins in whenever he can.

We have our own special roses, it seems, and our reasons for choosing them. David Austin's technical director Michael Marriott named his favourites among the English Roses as 'Harlow Carr', 'Gertrude Jekyll' and 'Lady Hamilton', to which he added the old Alba, 'Königin von Dänemark'; the Multiflora Rambler 'Francis E. Lester', the Shrub rose *R. nutkana* 'Plena' and two species roses, *R. setipoda* and *R. sinowilsonii*. Perfume expert Robert Calkin named as his all-time favourite the Autumn Damask *R.* × *damascena* var. *semperflorens,* also known as 'Quatre Saisons'. Rose-grower Peter Beales gave me ten roses and I suspect could have given me as many more, while Peter Harkness singled out the sweetly scented 'Compassion', the China rose 'Mutabilis', the chamois-yellow Hybrid Musk 'Thisbe', the Hybrid Tea 'Garden Glory' for cutting, and two roses named after his daughters – the Floribunda 'Anne Harkness' and the Hybrid Tea 'Rosemary Harkness'. My own favourites include the Damasks 'Madame Hardy' and 'Kazanlik'; the Portland 'Comte de Chambord', for its heady boudoir scent; and more recently simple Rugosas and Musks and the central Asian parent of the

Damasks, *R. fedtschenkoana.* Favourites change and naming one rose above the rest is somehow beside the point, if it excludes all the rest.

But if you are seeking the greatest rose of all, I believe there is an answer to your quest, one I found in an unexpected source: the biblical Song of Songs, one of the greatest love poems ever written. Set in a fragrant world of fertility and abundance, the Song celebrates the sexual awakening of a young woman and her lover.

'I AM the rose of Sharon, and the lily of the valleys,' sings the girl to her lover in the Authorized King James Version, conjuring up the rose that apothecary Christophe Opoix would one day claim for his home town of Provins. But if you want to know what roses she might have meant, you will quickly discover that there were no roses in biblical Palestine – not the botanical *Rosa* at any rate, not even in the fertile coastal plain of Sharon stretching southwards from Mt Carmel. In Hebrew, the word used is *habasselet.* Unfortunately botanists and biblical scholars cannot agree which flower is meant, and translators have variously given it as tulip, lily, crocus and simply 'wildflower'.[3] Yet 'rose' is the translation that sticks, because of its wide cultural resonance.

The word appears again, in Isaiah 35:1, in a prophetic vision of joyful renaissance: 'The wilderness and the solitary place shall be glad for them; and the desert shall rejoice, and blossom as the rose.' There is even a geographical reference to the 'excellency of Carmel and Sharon', linking this 'rose' to the one in the Song of Songs, but again, the rose we read comes from translation, not from the original.

The roses invoked by the translators of the Authorized Version are nameless and generic. No actual rose can claim the prize. The roses we have planted in Sharon bear witness to the flower's extraordinary potency, which still haunts our collective imagination, forty million years since the first rose bloomed. The ultimate rose is the one we imagine for ourselves.

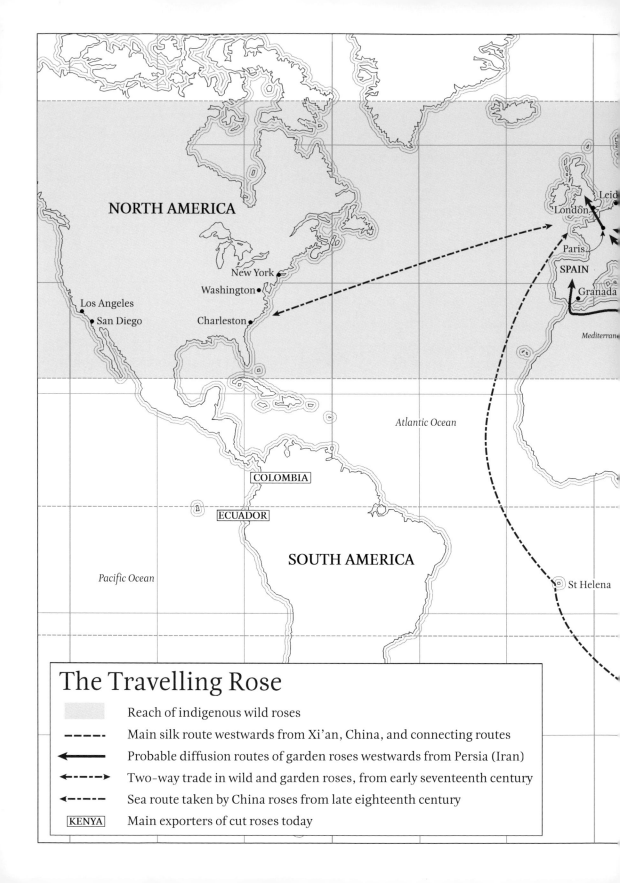

NORTH AMERICA

Leid
London
Paris
SPAIN
Granada

New York
Washington
Los Angeles
San Diego
Charleston

Mediterran

Atlantic Ocean

COLOMBIA

ECUADOR

SOUTH AMERICA

Pacific Ocean

St Helena

The Travelling Rose

Reach of indigenous wild roses

Main silk route westwards from Xi'an, China, and connecting routes

Probable diffusion routes of garden roses westwards from Persia (Iran)

Two-way trade in wild and garden roses, from early seventeenth century

Sea route taken by China roses from late eighteenth century

KENYA   Main exporters of cut roses today

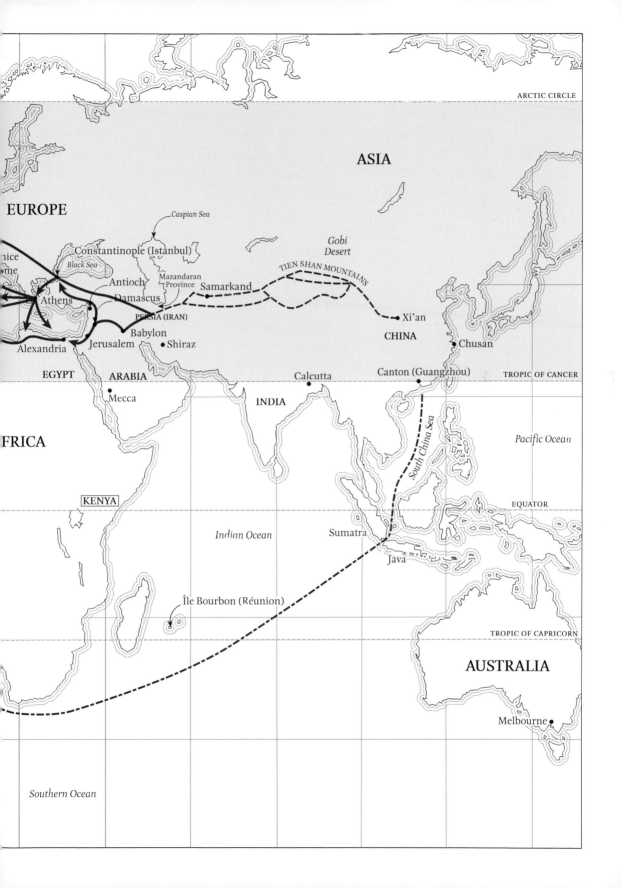

ARCTIC CIRCLE

ASIA

EUROPE

Caspian Sea

Constantinople (Istanbul)

Black Sea

*Gobi
Desert*

nice
me

Antioch

Mazandaran
Province

TIEN SHAN MOUNTAINS

Samarkand

Athens

Damascus

PERSIA (IRAN)

Xi'an

Babylon

CHINA

Chusan

Alexandria

Jerusalem

Shiraz

EGYPT

ARABIA

Calcutta

Canton (Guangzhou)

TROPIC OF CANCER

Mecca

INDIA

FRICA

Pacific Ocean

KENYA

EQUATOR

Indian Ocean

Sumatra

South China Sea

Java

Île Bourbon (Réunion)

TROPIC OF CAPRICORN

AUSTRALIA

Melbourne

Southern Ocean

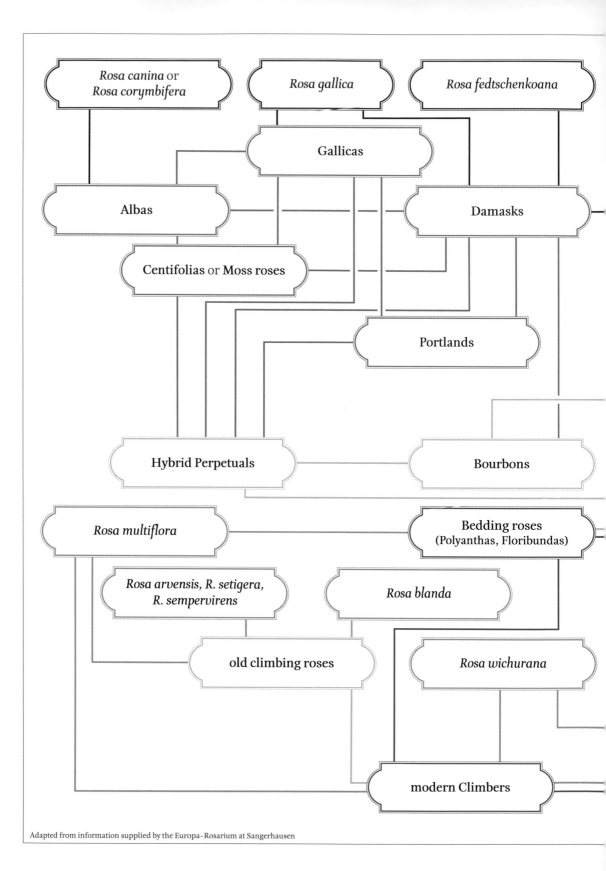

Rosa canina or Rosa corymbifera

Rosa gallica

Rosa fedtschenkoana

Gallicas

Albas

Damasks

Centifolias or Moss roses

Portlands

Hybrid Perpetuals

Bourbons

Rosa multiflora

Bedding roses
(Polyanthas, Floribundas)

Rosa arvensis, R. setigera, R. sempervirens

Rosa blanda

old climbing roses

Rosa wichurana

modern Climbers

Adapted from information supplied by the Europa-Rosarium at Sangerhausen

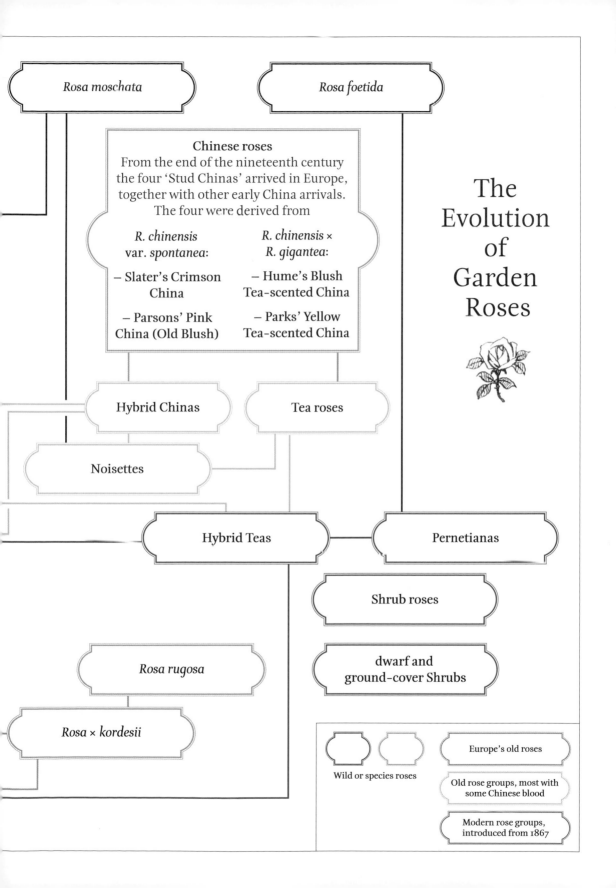

Rosa moschata

Rosa foetida

Chinese roses
From the end of the nineteenth century the four 'Stud Chinas' arrived in Europe, together with other early China arrivals. The four were derived from

R. chinensis var. *spontanea*:
– Slater's Crimson China
– Parsons' Pink China (Old Blush)

R. chinensis × *R. gigantea*:
– Hume's Blush Tea-scented China
– Parks' Yellow Tea-scented China

The
Evolution
of
Garden
Roses

Hybrid Chinas

Tea roses

Noisettes

Hybrid Teas

Pernetianas

Shrub roses

Rosa rugosa

dwarf and ground-cover Shrubs

Rosa × kordesii

Wild or species roses

Europe's old roses

Old rose groups, most with some Chinese blood

Modern rose groups, introduced from 1867

Acknowledgements

This book owes everything to Angus Mackinnon, my editor at Atlantic Books, who suggested it and saw it through to fruition. In the early stages, Dr Mark Nesbitt of the former Centre for Economic Botany at the Royal Botanic Gardens, Kew encouraged me to take the wider view and to accept nothing on trust. Dr Brent Elliott, historian to the Royal Horticultural Society, was a mine of information on all subjects and advised me patiently throughout. Rose-grower Peter Harkness read the manuscript with enormous care and generously shared his great knowledge and love of roses. I am especially indebted to all four.

These libraries and archives provided much of the material in London: Sandra Pearson and her staff in the British Library's Rare Books Reading Room; the British Library's maps and manuscripts collections; the Lindley Library of the Royal Horticultural Society, aided especially by Elizabeth Koper and Elizabeth Gilbert; the library and archives at RBG, Kew; the Wellcome Library; the Botany Library at the Natural History Museum; the library of the Linnean Society of London; and the London Library. In the United States, I enjoyed the superb collections and graceful surroundings of the Huntington Library, San Marino, California (my thanks go to Laura Stalker, Avery Associate Director of the Library); and of Dumbarton Oaks' Rare Books Collection, guided by Linda Lott. Kathryn B. Stack of the Office of Management and Budget eased my way into the White House where Curator William G. Allman introduced me to the White House archives and took me into the Rose Garden, accompanied by Groundskeeper Dale Haney. Anne Bouin welcomed me to the archives at Empress Josephine's Château de Malmaison on the outskirts of Paris, and helpfully guided my reading.

I thank Peter Beales for inspiring my love of old roses and Michael Marriott, Technical Manager of David Austin Roses, for developing my understanding of botanical roses, old and new. I also benefited from the knowledge and passion of the Historic Roses Group, founded by members of the Royal National Rose Society. I am especially grateful to Brigid and Charles Quest Ritson, Milton Nurse and Peter Scott. Of the gardeners and rose growers who introduced me to the dozens of rose gardens I visited in Britain and elsewhere, I want to single out the help I received from Peter Kukielski, Curator of the Peggy Rockefeller Rose Garden at the New York Botanical Garden; Thomas Hawel, Leader of the Europa-Rosarium, Sangerhausen; Clair G. Martin, Shannon Curator of Rose Collections at the Huntington Botanical Gardens; Gail Griffin, Director of Gardens and Grounds at Dumbarton Oaks; and Mick Thompson, Gardens Manager at Ashridge. In Iran, I pay tribute to the good care of Gasht Tour travel agency, Shiraz, and especially Mr Abbas Neyadi-Kazem, and to my travelling companions Chris Potter, Lynn Ritchie and Joan MacIver. After a chance encounter, Mrs Behnaz Tajrishi arranged for us to join a visit to a rose distillation. It was an extraordinary journey.

Individual chapters have benefited from my conversations with experts in their wider fields. I want to thank especially Philippa Campbell for her insights into the symbolic rose; Patrick Spottiswoode of Shakespeare's Globe for roses in Shakespeare; Professor Azim Nanji and Erica Hunningher for the roses of Islam, the Middle East and Iran; Jane Kilpatrick for Chinese roses; and Robert Calkin for sharing his lifelong interest in roses and perfumery. During my Royal Literary Fund Fellowship at Queen Mary, University of London, Professor Julia Boffey helped me with the roses and music of the early Tudor courts, and Professor Catherine Maxwell with roses in Victorian poetry. Similarly at King's College London, Professor Peter Houghton was an expert guide to roses in pharmacology. My thanks, too, to J. B. Jonas for his translations from the Latin of Carolus Clusius and Albertus Magnus, and to Jack Klaff for arranging the translations from the old Dutch of Matthias de l'Obel.

A great many people told me stories, made suggestions or tracked down information for the book. Among these, I want to thank especially Catherine Bailey; Clare Browne, Nicky Humphrey and Emma Luker at the V&A; Phil Baker; Chris Bard; Dr Rachel Blanc; Derek Boshier; Susan Bowden-Pickstock; Julia Buckley at the Herbarium, RBG Kew; Erminia Carillo for roses at Pompeii; Dr Dorian Fuller of the Institute of Archaeology, University College London; Celia Fisher; Ros Franey; Kate Harwood; Robert Irwin; Andrea Jones; Will Kaufman; Jack Klaff; Chaim and Emma Klein; Nikolay Kolev of Alteya Co., Tiffany Loiselle of the Woody Guthrie archives; Michèle Losse, RBG, Kew archives; Toktam Mahmoodi; John and Jan McLean; Robert Mattock; Hermann Moisl; Barbara Mitchell; Chris Petit; Tim Richardson; Martyn Rix; Sue Snell; Ros Southgate; Jeremy Swift; Jill Tovey, Croome Estate archivist; Lucy Waitt, picture researcher at the RHS Lindley Library; Dr Janet Waymark; Dr Stephanie West for the roses of antiquity; Irv Williams, former Superintendent of Grounds at the White House; Lyn Williams; and Richard Williams for roses in music.

For their hospitality in Washington, I thank Bill Ritchie and Andrea Barthello; Ian Birch and Markie Robson-Scott for lending me a place to stay in New York, and Emma Matthews a place to write on the south coast. Rob Petit I thank for his good company, as always.

This book is dedicated to the memory of Pat Kavanagh. Pat was my agent for twenty years during which she gave me the benefit of her cool eye and unwavering support. *The Rose*'s fine production values owe much to her vision. And I am grateful to Caroline Dawnay of United Agents who generously undertook to represent me, despite the contract remaining elsewhere. At Atlantic Books, special thanks go to Sarah Norman who worked tirelessly to turn the manuscript into a work of great elegance and beauty, aided by the tenacity and flair of picture researcher Charlotte Lippmann and the fine jacket designs of Jon Gray.

Finally, to gardeners and rose lovers everywhere: thank you for sharing your knowledge and your enthusiams. *The Rose* is my tribute to you.

Main Sources,
Select Bibliography and Notes

Principal sources are given in the introductions to each chapter, which also serve as a select bibliography. Full references appear online – see www.atlantic-books.co.uk. The numbered endnotes here add additional sources and occasional comments on the text. Within each chapter, a work's full title and publishing details are given at its first listing; subsequent mentions use short titles only.

The most comprehensive introduction to the history of the rose is Gerd Krüssmann, *Roses,* trans. Gerd Krüssmann and Nigel Raban (London, B. T. Batsford, 1982). Mark P. Widrlechner provides an excellent brief overview in 'History and Utilization of *Rosa damascena'*, *Economic Botany*, 35 (1), 1981, pp. 42–58. *The Graham Stuart Thomas Rose Book* (London, John Murray, 1994) is a mine of information, as is Peter Harkness, *The Rose: A Colourful Inheritance* (London, Scriptum Editions with the RHS, 2003).

Throughout this work, my information on individual roses and their histories comes from W. J. Bean, *Trees & Shrubs Hardy in the British Isles,* eighth revised edition (4 vols, London, John Murray, 1980), vol. 4; Roger Phillips and Martyn Rix, *The Ultimate Guide to Roses – A Comprehensive Selection* (London, Macmillan, 2004); Peter Beales, *Classic Roses* (London, Harvill Press, 1997); and Peter Beales et al., *Botanica's Roses: The Encyclopedia of Roses* (Köln, Könemann, c.2005). I also consulted David Austin, *The Rose* (Woodbridge, Garden Art Press, 2009), and Charles and Brigid Quest-Ritson, *The Royal Horticultural Society Encyclopedia of Roses* (London, Dorling Kindersley, 2003). Most rose names follow their listing in the online *RHS Plant Finder.*

To resolve scientific questions, I turned regularly to Andrew V. Roberts (ed.), *Encyclopedia of Rose Science* (Amsterdam, Elsevier Academic Press, 2003) and to the proceedings of international symposia reported in *Acta Horticulturae.*

Chapter One
A Wild Youth

Gerd Krüssmann's *Roses* provided an invaluable starting point (London, B.T. Batsford, 1982. Aside from Krüssmann, my main source on rose fossils was H. F. Becker, 'The Fossil Record of the Genus *Rosa*', *Bulletin of the Torrey Botanical Club*, 1963, vol. 90, pp. 99–110, supplemented by the two works by Guoliang Wang listed below.

Three good articles on Chinese roses are: Guoliang Wang, 'Ancient Chinese Roses', in Andrew V. Roberts (ed.), *Encyclopedia of Rose Science* (3 vols, Amsterdam, Elsevier, 2003), vol. 1, pp. 387–96; Mikinori Ogisu, 'Some Thoughts on the History of China Roses', *The New Plantsman*, vol. 3, part 3, September 1996, pp. 152–7; and Guoliang Wang, 'A Study on the History of Chinese Roses from Ancient Works and Images', *Acta Horticulturae*, no. 751, 'Proceedings of the IV International Symposium on Rose Research and Cultivation', August 2007, pp. 347–56. For a list of wild roses growing in China, see H. Brichet, 'Distribution and Ecology – Continental Asia and Japan', in *Encyclopedia of Rose Science*, vol. 1, pp. 204–10.

I searched for Sumerian, Akkadian and Assyrian roses in Gert D. Groening, 'Gardens as Elements of an Urbanizing World', in J. Janick (ed.), *Acta Horti-culturae*, no. 759, September 2007, pp. 109–23; Stephanie Dalley, 'Ancient Mesopotamian Gardens and the Identi-fication of the Hanging Gardens of Babylon Resolved', *Garden History*, Summer 1993, 21:1, pp. 1–13; Sir Leonard Woolley and P. R. S. Moorey, *Ur of the Chaldees* (London, Herbert Press, 1982), pp. 81–2 and 95–6; Daniel David

Luckenbill, *Ancient Records of Assyria and Babylonia* (2 vols, Chicago, University of Chicago Press, 1926), vol. 1, p. 87, relating to the spoils of Assyrian King Tiglath-Pileser I; and R. Campbell Thompson, *A Dictionary of Assyrian Botany* (London, British Academy, 1949).

For background on the classical world I turned to Simon Hornblower and Antony Spawforth (eds), *The Oxford Classical Dictionary,* third edition (Oxford University Press, 1999), and on the Mycenaean perfume industry: Cynthia W. Shelmerdine, *The Perfume Industry of Mycenaean Pylos* (Göteborg, Paul Åströms Förlag, 1985), especially pp. 23–5 and Chapters 4 and 6. Sir Arthur Evans wrote of his excavations in *The Palace of Minos, A Comparative Account of the Successive States of the Early Cretan Civilization as Illustrated by the Discoveries at Knossos* (4 vols, London, Macmillan and Co., 1928), vol. 2, part 2, pp. 454–9. Arthur O. Tucker identified the flora in 'Identification of the Rose, Sage, Iris, and Lily in the "Blue Bird Fresco" from Knossos, Crete (ca. 1450 B.C.E)', *Economic Botany*, vol. 58, no. 4, Winter 2004, pp. 733–5.

I used these editions of ancient Greek and Roman texts: Herodotus, *The Histories,* trans. Aubrey de Sélincourt, revised John Marincola (London, Penguin Books, 2003); Theophrastus, *Enquiry into Plants, and Minor Works on Odours and Weather Signs,* trans. Sir Arthur Hort (2 vols, London, Heinemann, 1916), and *De Causis Plantarum,* vol. 1, trans. B. Einarson and G. K. K. Link (London, William Heinemann, 1976); Virgil, *Georgics,* trans. Peter Fallon (Oxford University Press, 2006); Pliny the Elder, *The Natural History of Pliny,* trans. John Bostock and H. T. Riley (6 vols, London, Henry G. Bohn, 1855–7), especially vol. 4, pp. 310–14; and Pliny the Younger, *Complete Letters,* trans. P. G. Walsh (Oxford University Press, 2006).

The quotation from Bartholomaeus Anglicus comes from John Trevisa's translation of *On the Properties of Things* (2 vols, Oxford, Clarendon Press, 1975), vol. 2, p. 1029; and Henry Swinburne's remarks on Paestum from *Travels in the Two Sicilies,* second edition (4 vols, London, 1790), vol. 3, p. 195. Count Laszlo de Almásy's view of Herodotus is taken from Michael Ondaatje, *The English Patient* (London, Picador, 1993), pp. 118–19.

1. No roses appear in Ernst F. Weidner, *Der Zug Sargons von Akkad nach Kleinasien* (Leipzig, 1922), p. 69, where the list specifies only 'Feigenbaum, Birnbaum, Weinstock' (fig tree, pear tree, vine). In 'History and Utilization of *Rosa damascena*', *Economic Botany,* 35 (1), 1981, pp. 42–58, Mark P. Widrlechner points out that the Assyrian word for rose has not been adequately identified.

2. The date of the final destruction of the palace at Knossos is disputed – rival claims suggest *c.*1375 BC or even *c.*1200 BC.

3. Another translation by David Grene of *The History: Herodotus* (Chicago, University of Chicago Press, 1987), p. 608, gives 'sixty blossoms' rather than sixty petals, but the original Greek translates as either 'leaf' or 'petal', and the latter is clearly intended.

4. Krüssmann, *Roses,* p. 31, points out that 'burn' may be a mistranslation (elsewhere Theophrastus is translated as saying 'the roses were pruned back each year and consigned to the bonfire'); he further suggests that

the Greeks were unlikely to have lifted their plants each year and that Theophrastus may have been referring to the technique of layering.

Chapter Two
Aphrodite's Flower

Information on the roses of ancient Greece is relatively sparse. I refer to these texts: Homer, *Iliad,* trans. A. T. Murray and revised by William F. Wyatt (2 vols, Cambridge, Mass., Harvard University Press, 1999), vol. 2, p. 507; Hesiod, *Theogony, and Works and Days,* trans. M. L. West (Oxford University Press, 1988), pp. 8–9; Anne Carson, *If Not, Winter, Fragments of Sappho* (London, Virago, 2003), pp. ix–x, 7, 115, 191; *Greek Lyric II, Anacreon, Anacreontea, Choral Lyric from Olympus to Alcman,* trans. David A. Campbell (Cambridge, Mass., Harvard University Press/ The Loeb Classical Library, 1988), pp. 107 and 169; *Greek Lyric Poetry,* trans. M. L. West (Oxford, Clarendon Press, 1993), pp. xvi–xvii; Herodotus, *The Histories,* trans. Aubrey de Sélincourt, revised John Marincola (London, Penguin Books, 2003), pp. 87–8; and Theophrastus, *Enquiry into Plants, and Minor Works on Odours and Weather Signs,* trans. Sir Arthur Hort (2 vols, London, Heinemann, 1916), vol. 2, p. 365. These works are now considered to contain verse by Anacreon's later imitators: *Odes of Anacreon,* trans. Thomas Moore Esq of Middle Temple (London, 1800); and *The Works of Anacreon,* trans. Mr Addison (London, 1735). Peter Harkness challenges many of the myths surrounding Sappho and Greek roses in 'The Muse of Lesvos and the Queen of Flowers', *Historic Rose Journal,* no. 21, Spring 2001, pp. 4–6.

Several of the sources listed for Chapter 1 also provided much useful background here, including Gerd Krüssmann, *Roses* (London, B. T. Batsford, 1982); Simon Hornblower and Antony Spawforth (eds), *The Oxford Classical Dictionary*, third edition (Oxford University Press, 1999); and Cynthia W. Shelmerdine, *The Perfume Industry of Mycenaean Pylos* (Göteborg, Paul Åströms Förlag, 1985). I also turned to Samuel Noah Kramer, *History Begins at Sumer* (Philadelphia, University of Pennsylvania Press, 1981), p. 305 and *passim*; Walter Burkert, *Greek Religion* (Cambridge, Mass., Harvard University Press, 1985); and Nigel Wilson (ed.), *Encyclopedia of Ancient Greece* (New York, Routledge, 2006).

As well as Harkness and Krüssmann, these were helpful on the roses, plants and gardens of ancient Greece: E. S. Forster, 'Trees and Plants in Homer', *The Classical Review*, July 1936, vol. 50, no. 3, pp. 97–104; Maureen Carroll, *Earthly Paradises: Ancient Gardens in History and Archaeology* (London, British Museum Press, 2003) pp. 28–31; Lyn Foxhall, 'Environments and Landscapes of Greek Culture', in Konrad H. Kinzl (ed.), *A Companion to the Classical Greek World* (Malden MA/Oxford, Blackwell, 2006), pp. 245–80; and *The Oxford Classical Dictionary* (1999).

1. Even this date is disputed, and the poem's composition is dated variously from the extreme end of the ninth century to the mid-seventh century BC.
2. *The Poetical Works of Elizabeth Barrett Browning* (London, Smith, Elder & Co, 1897), p. 576.
3. The *arrhephoroi* were two or four girls aged between seven and eleven, chosen to serve Athena. At the rite marking the end of their service, they took covered baskets through an underground passage to the precinct of Aphrodite in the Gardens, where they exchanged their baskets' unknown contents for something equally mysterious. See Hornblower and Spawforth (eds), *The Oxford Classical Dictionary*, p. 175, and the entry on 'Aphrodite', and Burkert, *Greek Religion*, pp. 152–6.
4. See Barbara Seward, *The Symbolic Rose* (New York, Columbia University Press, 1960), p. 19, and Krüssmann, *Roses*, p. 29.
5. Compare with Proverbs 7, verses 17–18: 'I have perfumed my bed with myrrh, aloes, and cinnamon, Come, let us take our fill of love until the morning: let us solace ourselves with loves.'

Chapter Three
Rome's Frenzy

Sources for Roman roses are many and varied. Gerd Krüssmann, *Roses* (London, B. T. Batsford, 1982) usefully provides a chronological account of the rose in Roman literature and its uses in ancient Rome, pp. 32–6. I refer to these editions of Roman texts: Virgil, *Eclogues, Georgics, Aeneid I–VI*, trans. H. Rushton Fairclough and revised G. P. Goold (Cambridge, Mass., Harvard University Press, 1999); *Roman Farm Management, The Treatises of Cato and Varro*, done into English, with notes of modern instances, by a Virginia farmer (New York, Macmillan, 1913); Lucius Junius Moderatus Columella, *On Agriculture*, trans. H. B. Ash, E. S. Forster and E. H. Heffner (3 vols, London, Heinemann, 1941–5); Pliny the Elder,

The Natural History of Pliny, trans. John Bostock and H. T. Riley (6 vols, London, Henry G. Bohn, 1855–7); Pliny the Younger, *Complete Letters,* trans. P. G. Walsh (Oxford University Press, 2006); Apicius, *Cookery and Dining in Imperial Rome,* trans. Joseph Dommers Vehling (New York, Dover Publications, 1977); and Apuleius, *The Transformations of Lucius, Otherwise Known as the Golden Ass,* trans. Robert Graves (Harmondsworth, Penguin, 1950).

These works were helpful on Roman festivals, customs and daily life: *Ovid's Fasti,* trans. Sir James George Frazer (London, Heinemann, 1931); Michele Renee Salzman, *On Roman Time, The Codex-Calendar of 354 and the Rhythms of Urban Life in Late Antiquity* (Berkeley, University of California Press, 1990); J. M. C. Toynbee, *Death and Burial in the Roman World* (London, Thames & Hudson, 1971), pp. 141–53; and on roses and the Syrian army, A. S. Hoey, 'Rosaliae Signorum', *The Harvard Theological Review,* vol. 30, 1937, pp. 15–35; and R. D. Fink, A. S. Hoey and W. F. Snyder, 'The Feriale Duranum', *Yale Classical Studies,* vol. 7, 1940, pp. 115–20.

I was privileged to see several rose burial wreaths excavated by Flinders Petrie and now held in the Herbarium at the Royal Botanic Gardens, Kew. Sir W. M. Flinders Petrie described his excavations at Hawara in *Ten Years' Digging in Egypt (1881–1891)* (London, The Religious Tract Society, c.1923), pp. 93–7 and 103–4, while plant expert Percy E. Newberry looked more closely at the rose wreaths in 'On the Vegetable Remains Discovered in the Cemetery of Hawara' for W. M. Flinders Petrie, *Hawara, Biahmu, and Arsinoe* (London, Field & Tuer, 1889) pp. 46–53. Also useful on the wreaths was

L. Keimer, 'La Rose Égyptienne', *Études d'Égyptologie,* Fascicule V (Cairo, Imprimerie de l'Institut Français d'Archéologie Orientale, 1943); and on roses in Roman Egypt, Naphtali Lewis, *Life in Egypt under Roman Rule* (Oxford, Clarendon Press, 1985).

Two authors stand out for their researches into the flowers of Pompeii and Herculaneum: first, pioneering archaeologist Wilhelmina F. Jashemski, in *The Gardens of Pompeii, Herculaneum and the Villas Destroyed by Vesuvius* (New Rochelle, NY, Caratzas Bros, 1979), and vol. 2, *Appendices* (New Rochelle, NY, Caratzas Bros, 1993); and a work co-edited with Frederick G. Meyer, *The Natural History of Pompeii* (Cambridge University Press, 2002). Of more popular appeal is *Gardens of Pompeii,* trans. Lori-Ann Touchette (Los Angeles, J. Paul Getty Museum, 2001), by Pompeii's chief botanist, Annamaria Ciarallo. See also Annamaria Ciarallo and M. Mariotti Lippi, 'The Garden of "Casa dei Casti Amanti" (Pompeii, Italy)', *Garden History,* vol. 21, no. 1, Summer 1993, pp. 110–16.

For roses in the lives of Cleopatra, Mark Antony and Emperor Heliogabalus, I turned to Michael Grant, *Cleopatra* (London, Phoenix Press, 2000), Martha Brier (ed.), *Plutarch's Lives of Caesar, Brutus and Antony* (New York, Macmillan & Co, 1909), pp. 174–7 and 188; J. Stuart Hay, *The Amazing Emperor Heliogabalus* (London, Macmillan, 1911); and Aelius Lampridius, 'Antoninus Elagabalus', in *Lives of the Later Caesars,* trans. David Magie (London, The Folio Society, 2005).

1. Horace's 'Ode to Pyrrha' is quoted in Barbara K. Gold, 'Mitte sectari, rosa quo locurum sera moretur: Time and Nature in Horace's *Odes*', *Classical*

Philology, vol. 88, Jan–Oct 1993, pp. 16–31, and 'Persian Fopperies', in Mark van Doren (ed.), *An Anthology of World Poetry* (New York, 1928), pp. 349–50.

2. See Wilhemina F. Jashemski, 'The Garden of Hercules at Pompeii: The Discovery of a Commercial Flower Garden', *American Journal of Archaeology*, vol. 83, no. 4 (October 1979), pp. 403–11.

3. In the second century AD, villagers in Roman Egypt wrote a letter about flowers for a family wedding, noting that 'Roses are not yet in full bloom here – in fact they are scarce – and from all the nurseries and all the garland-weavers we could just barely get together the thousand that we sent you with Sarapas, even with picking the ones that ought not to have been picked till tomorrow. We had all the narcissi you wanted, so instead of the two thousand you asked for we sent four thousand.' See Lewis, *Life in Egypt under Roman Rule*, p. 80.

4. Jashemski, in her *Appendices*, pp. 348–58, calls it the House of the Wedding of Alexander, but it appears as the House of the Gold Bracelet in Jashemski and Meyer (eds), *The Natural History of Pompeii*, pp. 158–60.

5. C. E. W. Steel, *Cicero, Rhetoric and Empire* (Oxford University Press, 2001), p. 26.

6. Geraldine Norman, 'Art Market: Victorian Values', *Independent on Sunday*, 6 June 1993.

7. Vern G. Swanson, *Sir Lawrence Alma-Tadema: The Painter of the Victorian Vision of the Ancient World* (London, Ash and Grant, 1977), p. 43. Sold for $20,000 on completion in 1888, the

value of *The Roses of Heliogabalus* had dropped to $260 in 1960.

Chapter Four
Of Travels and Trade

Several strands come together in this chapter. For a fascinating introduction to plant hybridization, see Noel Kingsbury, *Hybrid, The History and Science of Plant Breeding* (Chicago, University of Chicago Press, 2009). Major C. C. Hurst's paper *The Genetics of the Rose*, delivered to the Great International Rose Conference, held in London in July 1928, is reprinted from *The Rose Annual for 1929* (Croydon, 1929). Hurst's work also appears in *The Graham Stuart Thomas Rose Book* (London, John Murray, 1994), pp. 297–340. For contemporary approaches to genetics, see Session Four on Genetic Resources at the Second International Symposium on Roses held at Antibes, France, 20–24 February 1995, reported in *Acta Horticulturae*, no. 424, July 1996. Also key is a paper by M. Martin et al., 'The Domestication Process of the Modern Rose: Genetic Structure and Allelic Composition of the Rose Complex', *Theoretical and Applied Genetics* (2001) 102: 398–404.

For the histories of individual roses and their various classes, as well as works listed at the start of these notes, I consulted T. G. Tutin et al. (eds), *Flora Europaea* vol. 2, *Rosaceae to Umbelliferae* (5 vols, Cambridge University Press, 1968), p. 27; Ellen Willmott, *The Genus Rosa* (2 vols, London, John Murray, 1914), vol. 2, p. 326; Sarah Coles, '*Rosa fedtschenkoana*', *Historic Rose Journal*, no. 7, March 1994, pp. 6–7; Thomas Cairns (ed.), *Modern Roses X* (Shreveport, Louisiana, The American Rose Society, 1993); Catherine

E. Meikle (ed.), *Modern Roses VIII* (Harrisburg, Penn., McFarland Company, 1980); and M.-F. Tarbouriech, 'Management of Genetic Resources in the Genus *Rosa*', in *Acta Horticulturae*, no. 424, July 1996, p. 312.

For the parentage of Damask roses, see Hikaru Iwata, Tsuneo Kato and Susumu Ohno, 'Triparental Origin of Damask Roses', *Gene* 259 (2000), pp. 53–9; and for the techniques involved: Jeff L. Doyle and Jane L. Doyle, 'A rapid DNA isolation procedure for small quantities of fresh leaf tissue', *Phytochemical Bulletin*, vol. 19 (1), Jan–March 1987, pp. 11–15; Maurice Jay, 'The Domestication of the Modern Rose analysed by Biochemical and Molecular Techniques', in the *Historic Rose Journal*, no. 20, Autumn 2000, pp. 24–9; and Judy Rose, 'Rose Fingerprinting', in the *Historic Rose Journal*, no. 21, Spring 2001, pp. 16–20.

To investigate the origins of the rose in Iran, I looked at Charles Joret, *La Rose dans l'Antiquité et au Moyen Age, Histoire, Légendes et Symbolism* (Paris, 1892); Donald Newton Wilber on the Caspian in *Persian Gardens and Garden Pavilions* (Washington DC, Dumbarton Oaks, 1979), p. 55; and Jonas Hanway, *An Historical Account of the British Trade over the Caspian Sea*, second edition (2 vols, London, 1754), part 3, vol. 1, pp. 191–3. Looking more generally at the spread of plants and agriculture from the Middle East and the Islamic world, I consulted Daniel Zohary and Maria Hopf, *Domestication of Plants in the Old World*, third edition (Oxford University Press, 2000), pp. 248–9; Andrew M. Watson, *Agricultural Innovation in the Early Islamic World, The Diffusion of Crops and Farming Techniques 700–1100* (Cambridge University Press, 1983), pp. 82, 87, 95,

117–19, 183; D. Fairchild Ruggles, *Gardens, Landscape, and Vision in the Palaces of Islamic Spain* (University Park, PA, Pennsylvania State University Press, 2000), pp. 3 and 17–18; and these works by John H. Harvey: 'Gardening Books and Plant Lists of Moorish Spain', *Garden History*, vol. 3, no. 2 (Spring 1975), pp. 10–21; and 'The Book of Abu 'L-Khayr', *Garden History*, 1993, 21:1, pp. 118–20. For the travels of Alexander the Great, I am indebted to Robin Lane Fox, *The Search for Alexander* (London, Allen Lane, 1980) – see pp. 286, 313, 349 and *passim*.

These works give a western view of the crusades: Robert Lee Wolff and Harry W. Hazard, *A History of the Crusades*, vol. 2, *The Later Crusades 1189–1311* (Madison, Milwaukee, University of Wisconsin Press, 1969), pp. 463–4 and 469–70; Ernest Barker, 'The Crusades', in Sir Thomas Arnold and Alfred Guillaume (eds), *The Legacy of Islam* (Oxford, Clarendon Press, 1931), pp. 54–5, 60–62 and 76; Danielle Régnier-Bohler (ed.), *Croisades et Pèlerinages: Récits, Chroniques et Voyages en Terre Sainte, XIIe-XVIe siècle* (Paris, Robert Laffont, 1997), pp. 928–30 and 935; and Bernard J. Ficarra, 'Disease to Death during the Crusades', in Manfred Waserman and Samuel S. Kottck (eds), *Health and Disease in the Holy Land* (Lewiston, New York, Edwin Mellen Press, c.1996), p. 135. The inimitable Christophe Opoix set out his fanciful Thibaut-Provins connection in *Histoire et Description de Provins* (Provins, 1823), pp. 445–52. An earlier reference to Opoix's story can be found in M. l'Abbé Rozier, *Cours Complet d'Agriculture* (12 vols, Paris, 1781–1805), vol. 8, p. 624; and see François Joyaux, *La Rose, Une Passion Française, 1778–1914* (Brussels, Editions Complexe, 2001), p. 24.

On Marco Polo and his plants, I read
E. Bretschneider, *History of European
Botanical Discoveries in China* (London,
1898), pp. 1–5, who takes his observations
from Colonel Henry Yule (ed.), *The Book of
Ser Marco Polo, the Venetian,* second revised
edition (London, John Murray, 1875); and
Laurence Bergreen, *Marco Polo, From
Venice to Xanadu* (New York, Alfred A.
Knopf, 2007). Since this chapter was
written, Robert Mattock has published an
intriguing summary of his researches
on 'Silk Route Hybrids', in the *Historic
Rose Journal,* no. 38, Autumn 2009,
pp. 10–18.

1. Guoliang Wang, 'A Study on the
   History of Chinese Roses from
   Ancient Works and Images',
   Acta Horticulturae, no. 751,
   pp. 347–56.
2. Joret, *La Rose,* pp. 13–14, author's
   translation. Krüssmann further
   points out that garden roses were
   known in Persia from the twelfth
   millennium BC.
3. *Le Livre de l'Agriculture d'Ibn-al-
   Awwam,* trans. J.-J. Clément-Mullet
   (2 vols, Paris, 1864), pp. 281–3;
   and see Joret, *La Rose,*
   pp. 145–6.
4. See www.la-seine-et-
   marne.com/histoire/provins-
   rose.html. The 61-volume
   Dictionnaire des Sciences Naturelles of
   1827 also cast doubt on the story,
   arguing that far from returning with
   Thibaut from Syria, this rose was
   already known in antiquity, and was
   probably the same rose praised by
   Homer in the *Iliad.* See F. G. Levraut
   (ed.), *Dictionnaire des Sciences
   Naturelles* (Strasbourg, 1816–45),
   vol. 46, p. 274.

Chapter Five
The Virgin's Bower

Four sources have helped to shape this
chapter. Jack Goody, *The Culture of Flowers*
(Cambridge University Press, 1993)
relates flowers to the main world
religions, and in Chapters 2, 3 and 5
traces the gradual shift from pagan to
Christian roses. Much of the detail of rose
lore and rose writings comes from Eithne
Wilkins, *The Rose-Garden Game, The
Symbolic Background to the European
Prayer-beads* (London, Victor Gollancz,
1969). The late John Harvey's *Mediaeval
Gardens* (London, B. T. Batsford, 1981)
remains unbeaten on the plants and
gardens of the period; and for an
intriguing blend of art history and
gardens I turned to Marilyn Stokstad and
Jerry Stannard, *Gardens of the Middle Ages*
(Lawrence, Spencer Museum of Art and
University of Kansas, 1983).

Also useful is semiotician Beverly
Seaton's perceptive article on radical
shifts in thinking about flowers, 'Towards
a Historical Semiotics of Literary Flower
Personification', in *Poetics Today,* vol. 10,
no. 4, Winter 1989, pp. 679–701; and you
will find much unexpected detail in Lisa
Cucciniello, 'Rose to Rosary: The Flower
of Venus in Catholicism', in Frankie
Hutton (ed.), *Rose Lore, Essays in Cultural
History and Semiotics* (Lanham, Lexington
Books, 2008), pp. 63–91. For more
Christian rose imagery, see Douglas Gray,
'The Five Wounds of Our Lord', in *Notes &
Queries,* vol. 208, Jan–Dec 1963 (London,
Oxford University Press, 1963), pp. 50ff.,
82ff., 127ff. and 163 ff.

St Cecilia's story is taken from Jacobus
de Voragine, *The Golden Legend: Selections,*
trans. Christopher Stace, introduced by
Richard Hamer (London, Penguin Books,

1998), and St Dorothy's from David Farmer, *The Oxford Dictionary of Saints,* fifth edition (Oxford University Press, 2003). For other contemporary voices, I consulted these works: Tertullian in *The Ante-Nicene Fathers, Translations of the Writings of the Fathers down to A.D. 325,* vol. 3, ed. Alexander Roberts and James Donaldson (Grand Rapids, Eerdmans, 1870, American reprint of Edinburgh edition), pp. 95–6, 102 and 703; Augustine, *The City of God Against the Pagans,* ed. and trans. R. W. Dyson (Cambridge University Press, 1998), p. 1128; Samuel J. Eales (ed.), *Cantica Canticorum, Eighty-Six Sermons on the Song of Solomon by Saint Bernard* (London, 1895), pp. 287–91; John Lydgate, *Lydgate's Minor Poems, The Two Nightingale Poems (AD 1446),* ed. Otto Glauning (London, Early English Text Society, 1900), p. 20, and Lydgate's 'A midsummer rose', in John Burrow (ed.), *English Verse 1300–1500* (London, Longman, 1977), pp. 280–88; H.R. Loyn and John Percival (eds), *The Reign of Charlemagne, Documents on Carolingian Government and Administration* (London, Edward Arnold, 1975), pp. 64–7; Alcuin, 'Farewell to his Cell', in Frederick Brittain, *The Penguin Book of Latin Verse* (Harmondsworth, Penguin, 1962), pp. 137–8; and Walahfrid Strabo, *Hortulus,* trans. Raef Payne, commentary by Wilfrid Blunt (Pittsburgh, Pennsylvania, Hunt Botanical Library, 1966).

On Dante, I quote from Dante Alighieri, *The Divine Comedy,* trans. by Charles S. Singleton, vol. 3, *Paradiso, 1: Italian text and translation* (Princeton, NJ, Princeton University Press, Bollingen Series LXXX, 1975), pp. 343, 347 and 379. See also Bernard, Abbot of Clairvaux, *The Steps of Humility,* trans. George Bosworth Burch (Cambridge, Mass., Harvard University Press, 1940), pp. 77–81 and 245–6; and Barbara Seward, *The Symbolic Rose* (New York, Columbia University Press, 1960), p. 36. The two illustrated editions of Dante are *Dante's Divine Comedy . . . with illustrations by Gustave Doré* (London, Arcturus, c.2006) and Albert S. Roe, *Blake's Illustrations to the Divine Comedy* (Princeton, NJ, Princeton University Press, 1953), pp. 193–6 and plate 99.

1. Marilyn Stokstad, *Medieval Art* (New York, Harper & Row, 1986), pp. 391–2.

2. Quoted in Goody and taken from Henry Phillips, *Flora Historica: Or the Three Seasons of the British Parterre,* second revised edition (2 vols, London, E. Lloyd and Son, 1829), vol. 1, p. xxvi.

3. *The Bible,* Isaiah 28: 1–5. And see the Apocrypha's Book of Wisdom on the wickedness of wearing rose garlands: Wisdom 2: 8, *The Apocrypha* (Cambridge University Press, 1895).

4. According to other authorities, St Cecilia was martyred in Sicily between 176 and 180 under Emperor Marcus Aurelius, and some sources see her as legendary.

5. Quoted in Goody, *The Culture of Flowers,* p. 90, who takes it from Agnes Lambert's helpfully detailed 'The ceremonial use of flowers: a sequel', in *The Nineteenth Century, A Monthly Review,* vol. 7, Jan–June 1880 (London, Kegan Paul), pp. 808–27. For more on Venantius and the roses of medieval Christianity, see Anthony Lyman-Dixon, 'Radegund's Roses', *Historic Gardens Review,* no. 21, May 2009, pp. 31–3.

6. Eliza Allen Starr, *Patron Saints* (1871, republished 2003 by Kessinger Publishing, Whitefish, Montana), p. 100.

7. *The Golden Legend or Lives of the Saints as Englished by William Caxton*, ed. F. S. Ellis,(London, J. M. Dent, The Temple Classics Series, 1900), vol. 4, p. 238. For the many different names of the rose see Wilkins, and Anne Winston-Allen, *Stories of the Rose, The Making of the Rosary in the Middle Ages* (University Park, PA, Pennsylvania State University Press, 1942), p. 88.

Chapter Six
Sex and Sorcery

All my English translations of the *Roman de la Rose* come from Guillaume de Lorris and Jean de Meun, *The Romance of the Rose*, third edition, trans. Charles Dahlberg (Princeton, NJ, Princeton University Press, 1995). One of the best introductions to current scholarship on the *Roman* is Kevin Brownlee and Sylvia Huot (eds), *Rethinking The Romance of the Rose, Text, Image, Reception* (Philadelphia, University of Pennsylvania Press, 1992). For different readings of the *Roman* (not all of them convincing), I consulted C. S. Lewis, *The Allegory of Love, A Study in Medieval Tradition* (Oxford, Clarendon Press, 1936); Denis de Rougemont, *Passion and Society*, trans. Montgomery Belgion, second edition (London, Faber and Faber, 1956); John V. Fleming, *The Roman de la Rose: A Study in Allegory and Iconography* (Princeton, NJ, Princeton University Press, 1969); Susan Stakel, *False Roses, Structures of Duality and Deceit in Jean de Meun's* Roman de la Rose (Saratoga, Anma Libri, 1991); and Alan Gunn, *The Mirror of Love* (Lubbock, Texas Tech Press, 1952).

More generally on love (courtly and otherwise) and contemporary love poetry, I read Paul F. Watson, *The Garden of Love in Tuscan Art of the Early Renaissance* (Philadelphia, Art Alliance Press, 1979); Mary Frances Wack, *Lovesickness in the Middle Ages, the* Viaticum *and its Commentaries* (Philadelphia, University of Pennsylvania Press, 1990); Peter L. Allen, *The Art of Love, Amatory Fiction from Ovid to the* Romance of the Rose (Philadelphia, University of Pennsylvania Press, 1992); and Peter Dronke, *Medieval Latin and the Rise of the European Love-Lyric* (2 vols, Oxford, Clarendon Press, 1968).

On landscape and gardens as a setting for the *Roman* and poetry generally, I found these particularly helpful: Derek Pearsall and Elizabeth Salter, *Landscapes and Seasons of the Medieval World* (London, Paul Elek, 1973); Derek Pearsall, 'Gardens as Symbol and Setting in Late Medieval Poetry', in Elisabeth B. MacDougall (ed.), *Medieval Gardens, Dumbarton Oaks Colloquium on the History of Landscape Architecture IX* (Washington DC, Dumbarton Oaks Research Library and Collection, 1986), pp. 235–51; A. Bartlett Giamatti, *The Earthly Paradise and the Renaissance Epic* (Princeton, NJ, Princeton University Press, 1966); Jerry Stannard, 'Medieval gardens and their plants', in Marilyn Stokstad and Jerry Stannard, *Gardens of the Middle Ages* (Lawrence, Spencer Museum of Art/University of Kansas, 1983); and Teresa McLean, *Medieval English Gardens* (London, Collins, 1981).

For Chaucer, I turned to Geoffrey Chaucer, *The Riverside Chaucer*, gen. ed. Larry D. Benson, third edition (Boston, Mass., Houghton Mifflin, c.1987), supplemented by Laura L. Howes, *Chaucer's Gardens and the Language of*

Convention (Gainesville Tallahassee, University Press of Florida, 1997). For the St Valentine's connection, see Jack B. Oruch, 'St. Valentine, Chaucer, and Spring in February', in *Speculum* 56.3 (1981), pp. 534–65; and Alban Butler, *Butler's Lives of the Saints, February,* revised by Paul Burns (Tunbridge Wells, Burns & Oates, 1998), pp. 148–50. On Christine de Pizan and the 'Quarrel of the Rose', these were particularly helpful: Thelma S. Fenster and Mary Carpenter Erler, *Poems of Cupid, God of Love* (Leiden, E. J. Brill, 1990); Joseph L. Baird & John R. Kane, *La Querelle de la Rose: Letters and Documents* (Chapel Hill, North Carolina Studies in the Romance Languages and Literature, no. 199, 1978); and Alice Kemp-Welch, *Of Six Mediaeval Women, To which is added a Note on Mediaeval Gardens* (London, Macmillan, 1913).

A good sourcebook on sexual imagery is Gordon Williams, *A Dictionary of Sexual Language and Imagery in Shakespearean and Stuart Literature* (3 vols, London, The Arthouse Press, 1994), which led me to Helkiah Crooke, Nicholas Culpeper and many others. Also useful was Eric Partridge, *A Dictionary of Slang and Unconventional English,* second edition (London, George Routledge & Sons, 1938). Barbara Seward in *The Symbolic Rose* (New York, Columbia University Press, 1969) took me on a wild goose chase through Freud; but for a reliable guide to roses in Jung (and elsewhere), see Philippa Campbell, 'Rose is a rose is a rose', in *Harvest 2009,* no. 1, pp. 21–31, published by the C. G. Jung Analytical Psychology Club, London. Among *The Collected Works of C. G. Jung,* I consulted volumes 12 (*Psychology and Alchemy*), 14 (*Mysterium Coniunctionis*), and 16 (*The Practice of Psychotherapy*).

All Shakespearean quotations are taken from the Arden edition; and see the chapter 'Lewd Interpreters', in Stanley Wells, *Looking for Sex in Shakespeare* (Cambridge University Press, 2004), pp. 10–37.

I know of no English translation of the whole of Albertus Magnus's *De vegetabilibus* of c.1260. For my translation I am indebted to J. B. Jonas. John Harvey includes Albertus's chapter on pleasure gardens in *Mediaeval Gardens* (London, B. T. Batsford, 1981), p. 6; and Jerry Stannard discusses his plants (including roses) in 'Identification of the Plants Described by Albertus Magnus, *De Vegetabilibus*', in *Res Publica Litterarum, Studies in the Classical Tradition,* vol. 2, 1979 (University of Kansas), pp. 281–318. Sources for the roses and rose gardens of medieval Europe include Claire Noble (ed.), 'Norwich Cathedral Priory Gardeners' Accounts, 1329–1530', in *Farming and Gardening in Late Medieval Norfolk* (Norfolk Record Society, vol. 61 for 1997), pp. 14 and 79-80; Stephanie R. Hovland, 'The Gardens of Later Medieval London', *The London Gardener,* vol. 12, 2006–7, pp. 37–53; McLean, *English Medieval Gardens,* pp. 73–4; and Howes, *Chaucer's Gardens,* p. 24. The old man's advice to his young wife is taken from *The Goodman of Paris, A Treatise on Moral and Domestic Economy by a Citizen of Paris c.1393,* trans. Eileen Power (Woodbridge, Boydell Press, 2006), pp. 2, 133–4 and 198–9.

1. Luke 2: 23; and see J. Huizinga's *The Waning of the Middle Ages* (Harmondsworth, Penguin Books, 1968), pp. 113–15.
2. Williams, *A Dictionary of Sexual Language,* see entries for bud, flower,

garland, rose, velvet; in *A Dictionary of Slang and Unconventional English*, Partridge relates the rose as a euphemism for pissing to women only. And see Gamini Salgado, *The Elizabethan Underworld*, revised edition (Stroud, Alan Sutton Publishing, 1995), p. 44, who suggests that 'the many "Rose Alleys" in old English towns nearly always had less to do with fragrant flowers than with the habit of "plucking a rose" – an Elizabethan euphemism for making water'.

3. Robert Herrick, 'To the Virgins, to Make Much of Time', in W. Carew Hazlitt (ed.), *Hesperides, The Poems and Other Remains of Robert Herrick* (2 vols, London, John Russell Smith, 1869), vol. 1. pp. 87–8.

4. Helkiah Crooke, *Mikrokosmographica, A Description of the Body of Man* (London, 1615), p. 223 – but pages wrongly numbered, actually p. 235.

5. Nicholas Culpeper, *A Directory for Midwives or, A Guide for Women in their Conception, Bearing, and Suckling their Children* (London, 1651), p. 30.

6. *The New English Valentine Writer, or The High Road to Love; For Both Sexes* (London, 14 February 1784), pp. 54–5.

7. See Sigmund Freud, *The Interpretation of Dreams* and *On Dreams*, vols 4 and 5 of *The Complete Psychological Works of Sigmund Freud*, trans. and ed. James Strachey (London, Hogarth Press, 1953) – see vol. 4, p. 319; and vol. 5, pp. 347–8 and p. 652.

8. C. G. Jung, *Mysterium Coniuncionis*, vol. 14 of *The Collected Works of C. G. Jung*, trans. R. F. C. Hull, second edition (London, Routledge & Kegan Paul, 1970), pp. 305–7. Jung goes on to say that 'The rose-garden is a

"garden enclosed", and like the rose, a soubriquet of Mary, the parallel of the "locked" prima materia'; and he draws attention to the duality of the rose and of the ecclesiastical figure of the 'mother-beloved'.

9. This, at least, is the view put forward by Pierre-Yves Badel in 'Alchemical Readings of the *Romance of the Rose*', Brownlee and Huot (eds), *Rethinking the Romance of the Rose*, pp. 262–85.

10. For the Latin text, see Alberti Magni, *De vegetabilibus Libri VII*, ed. Ernst Meyer and Karl Jessen (Berlin, Reimer, 1867), Book 6, tract. I, cap. XXXII, pp. 445–8. Stannard (in 'Identification of the plants described by Albertus Magnus') tentatively identifies *Rosa alba* and *R. arvensis*, and proposes *R. foetida* for Albertus's stinking rose.

Chapter Seven
Secrets of the Rosy Cross

For the Rosicrucian story and much background detail, I am indebted to Frances A. Yates, *The Rosicrucian Enlightenment* (London, Routledge & Kegan Paul, 1972), supplemented by Christopher McIntosh's *The Rosicrucians: The History, Mythology, and Rituals of an Esoteric Order* (San Francisco, Weiser Books, 1998). See also Ralph White (ed.), *The Rosicrucian Enlightenment Revisited* (Hudson, NY, Lindisfarne Books, 1999).

Jorge Luis Borges's story 'Tlön, Uqbar, Orbis Tertius' appears in *Collected Fictions*, trans. Andrew Hurley (London, Allen Lane/The Penguin Press, 1999), pp. 68–81. Borges's reference to Andreae can be found in Thomas De Quincey, 'Historico-Critical Inquiry into the Origins of the Rosicrucians and the Free-masons', in

David Masson (ed.), *The Collected Writings of Thomas De Quincey* (14 vols, Edinburgh, Adam and Charles Black, 1890), vol. 13, *Tales and Prose Phantasies*, p. 405. Classical references to roses and silence are elusive, but see Simon Hornblower and Antony Spawforth (eds), *The Oxford Classical Dictionary*, third edition (Oxford University Press, 1996), pp. 728–9. Henry Peacham's rose of secrecy comes from 'The Truth of Our Times' (1638), in *The Complete Gentleman, The Truth of Our Times, and The Art of Living in London*, ed. Virgil B. Hettzel (Ithaca, Cornell University Press for the Folger Shakespeare Library, 1962), pp. 230–31.

Martin Luther's emblematic rose is taken from *Luther's Works*, vol. 49, Letters II, ed. and trans. Gottfried G. Krodel (Philadelphia, Fortress Press, 1972), pp. 356–9, and see Arthur Edward Waite, *The Brotherhood of the Rosy Cross* (London, William Rider & Son, 1924), pp. 639–41. More rose emblems appear in Adam McLean (ed.), *The Rosicrucian Emblems of Daniel Cramer*, trans. Fiona Tait (Edinburgh, Magnum Opus Hermetic Sourceworks n. 4, 1980), emblems 31, 51 and 105; and Robert Fludd, *Sophiae cum Moria Certamen* (including *Summum Bonum* by Joachim Frizius) (Frankfurt, 1629).

For the publishing history of the Rosicrucian manifestos, see Yates, *The Rosicrucian Enlightenment*, pp. 235–8, and her translations of the two manifestos, pp. 238–60; and Johann Valentin Andreae, *The Chymical Wedding of Christian Rosenkreutz*, trans. Edward Foxcroft (London, Minerva Books, n.d.). Parisian Gabriel Naude captures the French furore in *Instruction à la France sur la Vérité de l'Histoire des Frères de la Roze-Croix* (Paris, 1623), pp. 25–8.

On German roses, see Dr Clemens Alexander Wimmer, 'A Rose at Goethe's – Research on *Rosa x francofurtana* at Goethe's Garden-House in Weimar', trans. Marita Protte and Daphne Filberti, in the *Quarterly Rose Letter* of the Heritage Roses Group, May 2004. Glenn Alexander Magee discusses Goethe's alchemical experiments in *Hegel and the Hermetic Tradition* (Ithaca, Cornell University Press, 2001), pp. 57 and 57–61; see also Alice Raphael, *Goethe and the Philosophers' Stone* (London, Routledge & Kegan Paul, 1965), p. 227, and Adam McLean, *A Commentary on Goethe's Fairy Tale* (Edinburgh, Magnum Opus Hermetic Sourceworks no. 14, c.1982), p.58. Kassel's roses appear in Salomon Pinhas, *Rosen-Sammlung zu Wilhelmshöhe, Nach der Natur Gemalt von Salomon Pinhas, Kurfürstlich Hessische Hof-Miniaturmaler 1815*, trans. Margaret Marks (Regensburg, Schnell und Steiner, 2001), pp. 9–30.

For Yeats's involvement in Rosicrucianism I have followed Richard Ellmann, *Yeats, The Man and the Masks* (London, Faber and Faber, 1961), especially pp. 89–101; and for the historical background, Christopher McIntosh, *The Rosicrucians*, and his admirably succinct chapter 'The Rosicrucian Legacy', in White (ed.), *The Rosicrucian Enlightenment Revisited*. For the symbolism of the rose in Yeats's work, see Richard Ellmann, *The Identity of Yeats* (London, Macmillan & Co., 1954), especially pp. 62–76; and Barbara Seward, *The Symbolic Rose* (New York, Columbia University Press, 1960), pp. 88–117. Among editions of Yeats's work I consulted W. B. Yeats, *The Secret Rose*, with illustrations by J. B. Yeats (London, Lawrence & Bullen, 1897); *The Wind Among the Reeds* (London, Elkin

Mathews, second edition 1899); *Autobiographies* (London, Macmillan, 1955), p. 254; and 'Rosa Alchemica', in *The Secret Rose and Rosa Alchemica* (Doylestown, Pa, Wildside Press, n.d.), pp. 153–97.

1. See entry 7a for 'rose' in *The Oxford English Dictionary,* second edition, vol. 14 (Oxford, Clarendon Press, 1989), p. 104, but the *OED*'s source is wrong: Dymock's letter to Vaughan appears in *Letters and Papers Foreign and Domestic of the Reign of Henry VIII,* vol. 21.1, 1546, entry 935 of 26 May 1546. Dymock's further correspondence is recorded at http://www.british-history.ac.uk/report.aspx?compid=80857. Date accessed: 30 July 2009. Entry 1062, John Dymock to the Privy Council.

2. De Caus recorded his designs for the unfinished garden in Salomon de Caus, *Hortus Palatinus* (Frankfurt, Johann Theodor de Bry, 1620), dedicated to the Elector Palatine.

3. Yates, *The Rosicrucian Enlightenment,* pp. 113–17, and Descartes' autobiographical comments in his *Discours de la Méthode* (Leiden, 1637), p. 12.

4. Elias Ashmole tells the story of John Dee's visit with Sir Edward Kelley to Bohemia and Germany in *Theatrum Chemicum Britannicum* (London, 1652), pp. 480–3. The claim that Bacon was wearing Rosicrucian shoes in the frontispiece to his *Historia Regni Henrici Septimi* (Frankfurt, 1642) appears in Manly P. Hall, *An Encyclopedic Outline of Masonic, Hermetic, Qabbalistic and Rosicrucian Symbolical Philosophy* (Los Angeles, Philosophical Research Society, 1988), p. 94.

Chapter Eight
Elizabeth's Briar

My principal source on the roses of Shakespeare's day is John Gerard, *The Herball or Generall Historie of Plantes* (London, 1597), pp. 1077–89, occasionally expanded and corrected by Thomas Johnson in 1633; it is illuminating to compare Gerard's original with the garden roses in John Parkinson's *Paradisi in Sole, Paradisus Terrestris* (London, 1629), pp. 412–21, and in his later herbal *Theatrum Botanicum* (London, 1640), pp. 1016–21. Except where indicated, the details of Gerard's life come from: Mary Edmond, 'John Gerard, Herbalist', *The Genealogists' Magazine,* vol. 14, no. 5, March 1963, pp. 137–45; Robert H. Jeffers, *The Friends of John Gerard (1545–1612), Surgeon and Botanist* (Falls Village, Connecticut, Herb Grower Press, 1967); and B. D. Jackson, *A Catalogue of Plants Cultivated in the Garden of John Gerard, in the years 1596–1599* (London, 1876). Gerard's two plant catalogues share the same title: John Gerard, *Catalogus arborum, fruticum, ac plantarum tam indigenarum, quam exoticarum . . . in horto Johannis Gerardi Civis & Chirugi Londinensis nascentium* (London, 1596) and (London, 1599).

For consistency, my quotations from Shakespeare all come from the Arden editions, including sonnets 35 and 54, which are taken from Katherine Duncan-Jones (ed.), *Shakespeare's Sonnets* (London, The Arden Shakespeare, 1997), pp. 35–6 and 54–5. For Shakespeare's life, I was inspired by Charles Nicholl, *The Lodger, Shakespeare on Silver Street* (London, Allen Lane, 2007), especially Chapters 5 and 6 about the lodging house and its neighbourhood. I also enjoyed

Peter Ackroyd, *Shakespeare, The Biography* (London, Vintage, 2006), and James S. Shapiro, *1599: A Year in the Life of William Shakespeare* (London, Faber and Faber, 2005). On plants in Shakespeare, I learned much from Henry N. Ellacombe, *The Plant-Lore & Garden-craft of Shakespeare,* second edition (London, 1884); Mats Rydén, *Shakespearean Plant Names, Identifications and Interpretations* (Stockholm, Almqvist & Wiksell International, 1978), pp. 14–17; and Katherine Duncan-Jones's unravelling of the corn rose mystery, 'Deep-Dyed Canker Blooms: Botanical Reference in Shakespeare's Sonnet 54', *The Review of English Studies,* vol. 46, no. 184 (November 1995), pp. 521–5. Eleanour Sinclair Rohde writes on Shakespearean flora, Elizabethan gardens and herbals with obvious enjoyment; her most relevant works are *The Old English Herbals* (London, Minerva Press, 1972), first published 1922, pp. 98–119; and *Shakespeare's Wild Flowers, Fairy Lore, Gardens, Herbs, Gatherers of Simples and Bee Lore* (London, Medici Society, 1935).

Among the many gardening books consulted I found Alicia Amherst's *A History of Gardening in England* (London, 1895) illuminating and enjoyable, although she does not always locate her sources. Roy Strong's *The Renaissance Garden in England* (London, Thames & Hudson, 1979) remains a classic, as do his writings on the portraiture and pageantry of Elizabeth's court. Charles Estienne's *Maison Rustique, or, The Countrey Farme,* trans. Richard Surflet (London, 1616) is helpful on contemporary gardening practice (the original French edition was much earlier); and the RHS Lindley Library in London has an unpublished Masters thesis by Margaret E. Marston on

The History of Plant Propagation in England to 1850, submitted to the University of Nottingham in 1953. Blanche Henrey is my authority on gardening books – here the first volume of *British Botanical and Horticultural Literature Before 1800* (London, Oxford University Press, 1975). *The Garden Book of Sir Thomas Hanmer Bart* (London, Gerald Howe, 1933) provides a wealth of detail on garden flowers of the mid-seventeenth century.

To feel my way into Elizabethan London, I read Liza Picard, *Elizabeth's London* (London, Weidenfeld & Nicolson, 2003); Louis B. Wright, *Middle-Class Culture in Elizabethan England* (Ithaca, Cornell University Press, 1958); Thomas Dekker, *The Wonderful Year 1603,* ed. A. L. Rowse (London, Folio Press, 1989); and consulted several editions of John Stow's *A Survey of London. The A–Z of Elizabethan London* (London, Topographical Society, 1979) by Adrian Prockter and Robert Taylor was helpful in plotting Shakespeare's walk from Silver Street to Holborn.

To piece together the story of the Tudor rose, I turned to *Hall's Chronicle; containing the History of England, during the reign of Henry the Fourth and the succeeding monarchs, to the end of the reign of Henry the Eighth* (London, 1809), collated with the editions of 1548 and 1550, ed. Sir Henry Ellis; William Camden, *Remains Concerning Britain,* ed. R. D. Dunn (Toronto, University of Toronto Press, 1984); C. W. Scott-Giles, *Shakespeare's Heraldry* (London, J. M. Dent, 1950); 'Badges, Their History and Variety', in *The National Magazine,* vol. VI, January to June 1855, pp. 48–52; W. J. Petchey, *Armorial Bearings of the Sovereigns of England,* second edition (London, Bedford Square Press, 1977); and the second revised edition of Christophe Opoix, *Histoire et Description de Provins* (Provins, 1846). Gerd Krüssmann's *Roses* (London, B. T. Batsford, 1982), pp. 43–4, provided other interesting leads. My guide to Tudor lyrics, including those written by Henry VIII, was John Stevens, *Music & Poetry in the Early Tudor Court* (Cambridge University Press, 1979).

A number of works helped to identify individual roses. Krüssmann compares the roses named and grown by the early botanists in *Roses*, pp. 48–54; and François Joyaux discusses European roses introduced before 1800 in the *Encyclopedia of Rose Science* (3 vols, Amsterdam, Elsevier, 2003), vol. 1, pp. 395–402. Also useful were: Gisele de la Roche and Gordon D. Rowley, *Commentaries to Les Roses by P. J. Redouté, A Contribution to the History of the Genus Rosa* (Antwerp, De Schutter, 1978); and W. J. Bean, *Trees & Shrubs Hardy in The British Isles*, eighth edition revised (London, John Murray, 1980), vol. 4. Graham Stuart Thomas unravels 'The Mystery of the Musk Rose' in *The Graham Stuart Thomas Rose Book* (London, John Murray, 1994), pp. 220–24; and Peter Harkness further illuminates the field rose, *Rosa arvensis*, in *The Rose, A Colourful Inheritance* (London, Scriptum Editions/Royal Horticultural Society, 2003), pp. 40, 43, 72–3. The online notes to this work (see www.atlantic-books.co.uk) provide many more detailed references.

Louis B. Wright first alerted me to Thomas Hill's wide publishing career; my view of him conflicts with that of Richard Mabey, who edited *The Gardener's Labyrinth* (Oxford, University Press, 1987) and declared the text full of 'the kind of knacks and wrinkles that nuture green-fingeredness'. For an interesting account

of Hill's life, see Francis R. Johnson, 'Thomas Hill: An Elizabethan Huxley', *The Huntington Library Quarterly,* vol. 7, no. 4, August 1944, pp. 329–51. Although later editions of Hill's work contain some fine words about roses, all quotations here are from the first edition, as the closest to Hill's intentions: Didymous Mountain (Thomas Hill), *The Gardeners Labyrinth* (London, 1577), pp. 22–3. Rebecca Bushnell introduced me to the rich literature of 'secrets' books in *Green Desire, Imagining Early Modern English Gardens* (Ithaca, Cornell University Press, 2003), and I looked especially at these works: Thomas Hill, *The Most Pleasaunte Arte of the Interpretacion of Dreams* (London, 1576) and *A Briefe and Pleasaunt Treatise, Intituled: Naturall and Artificiall Conclusions* (London, 1586); and Hugh Platt or Plat, *The Jewell House of Art and Nature* (London, 1594) and *Delightes for Ladies* (London, 1602).

1. Liza Picard in *Elizabeth's London*, p. 80, says Gerard's garden 'was probably where Furnival Street is now, halfway between Fetter Lane and Shoe Lane, on land that had been owned by the Abbot of Malmesbury up to Henry's dissolution of the monasteries and then became the property of Lord Burghley'.

2. Antiquarian William Camden suggests that the white rose was first introduced by John of Gaunt's brother, Edmund Langley (*Remains Concerning Britain*, p. 180); Scott-Giles says it was originally a badge of the Mortimer Earls of York and may have been chosen by Richard Plantagenet (later third Duke of York) to signify his claim to the throne through his Mortimer descent

(*Shakespeare's Heraldry*, pp. 136–7). As the latter points out (p. 129), the Yorkist King Edward IV had used an irradiated white *rose en soleil*.

3. See, for example, Susan Doran (ed.), *Elizabeth, The Exhibition at the National Maritime Museum* (London, Chatto & Windus with the NMM, 2003). Objects included gold coins of Henry VIII and his Queens inscribed: 'HENRIC VIII RVTILANS ROSA SINE SPINA' – a dazzling rose without thorns, p. 12.

4. A. H. Bullen (ed.), *The works of George Peele* (2 vols, London, 1888), vol. 2, pp. 304–14.

5. Thomas Hesketh, perhaps, who often sent Gerard plants from Lancashire and the north of England, see Amherst, *A History of Gardening*, p. 165.

6. James I: Volume 9: August–October, 1604, *Calendar of State Papers Domestic: James I, 1603–1610* (1857), pp. 140–63. URL: http://www. british-history.ac.uk/report.aspx? compid=14994. Date accessed: 09 April 2008. Gerard held the lease for a short time only, surrendering it in 1605 to Robert Cecil, who in turn surrendered it back to the Queen in June 1611.

7. For the story of both these striped roses, see de la Roche and Rowley, *Commentaries to Les Roses*, pp. 172–4; François Joyaux, *La Rose de France, Rosa Gallica et sa Descendance* (Paris, Imprimerie Nationale, 1998), pp. 19–20, and *Encyclopedia of Rose Science*, vol. 1, pp. 397–8; *The Garden Book of Sir Thomas Hanmer Bart*, p. 112. Peter Harkness credits Henry Andrews with popularizing the 'Fair Rosamund' legend – see

Harkness, *A Colourful Inheritance*, p. 160.

8. According to Marston, *The History of Plant Propagation*, p. 21, it was common practice in the seventeenth century to bud roses low down and then to layer the shoot that developed from the bud, in order to obtain roses on their own roots. The same technique was used for multiplying a new variety, but Hill tells us nothing of this.

Chapter Nine
Dutch Masters

This chapter began for me with Clusius's description of the Centifolia rose in *Rariorum Plantarum Historia* (Antwerp, 1601), pp. 113–14, its importance confirmed by the rose's earlier appearance in Matthias de L'Obel's *Kruydtboeck* (Antwerp, 1581), part 2, p. 241.

The details of Clusius's life come from Florence Hopper, 'Clusius' World: The Meeting of Science and Art', in L. Tjon Sie Fat and E. de Jong (eds), *The Authentic Garden, A Symposium on Gardens* (Leiden, Clusius Foundation, 1991), pp. 13–36; Florike Egmond et al. (eds), *Carolus Clusius, Towards a Cultural History of a Renaissance Naturalist* (Amsterdam, Royal Netherlands Academy of Arts and Sciences, 2007); and Harold J. Cook, *Matters of Exchange, Commerce, Medicine, and Science in the Dutch Golden Age* (New Haven, Yale University Press, 2007), especially Chapter 3, 'Reformations Tempered', pp. 82–132. A 1594 inventory of Leiden's plants appears in Dr F. W. T. Hunger, *Charles de l'Escluse (Carolus Clusius), Nederlandsch Kruidkundige, 1526–1609* (2 vols, 'S-Gravenhage, Martinus Nijhoff, 1927), vol. 1, pp. 223, 232–3.

For information on Jacques de Gheyn II, I turned to Claudia Swan's fascinating *Art, Science, and Witchcraft in Early Modern Holland, Jacques de Gheyn II (1565–1629)* (Cambridge University Press, 2005); de Gheyn's early biographer, Karel van Mander, *The Lives of the Illustrious Netherlandish and German Painters, from the first edition of the Schilder-boeck (1603–1604)*, trans. Michael Hoyle et al. (Doornspijk, Davaco, 1994), pp. 433–8; and reproductions of de Gheyn's flower album in *Le Héraut du Dix-Septième Siècle, Dessins et Gravures de Jacques de Gheyn II and III de la Fondation Custodia Collection Frits Lugt* (Paris, Institut Néerlandais, 1985).

Among the many books I consulted on Dutch and Flemish art, and floral portraits, these were especially helpful: Marie-Louise Hairs, *The Flemish Flower Painters in the XVIIth Century*, trans. Eva Grzelak (Brussels, Lefebvre & Gillet, n.d.); Paul Taylor, *Dutch Flower Painting, 1600–1720* (New Haven, Yale University Press, 1995); *Pick of the Bunch from the Fitzwilliam Museum* (London, John Mitchell & Son, 1993); Celia Fisher, *Flowers and Fruit* (London, The National Gallery, 1998); Frank Lewis, *A Dictionary of Dutch & Flemish Flower, Fruit, and Still Life Painters, 15th to 19th century* (Leigh-on-Sea, F. Lewis, 1973); Peter Mitchell, *European Flower Painters* (London, Adam and Charles Black, 1983); Chapter 6 of Sam Segal, *A Prosperous Past, The Sumptuous Still Life in the Netherlands 1600–1700* (The Hague, SDU Publishers, 1989); Bob Haak, *The Golden Age, Dutch Painters of the Seventeenth Century*, trans. and ed. Elizabeth Willems-Treeman (London, Thames & Hudson, 1984); and Svetlana Alpers, *The Art of Describing, Dutch Art in the Seventeenth Century*

(Chicago, University of Chicago Press, 1984). These works had a more botanical focus: M. Jacobs, 'Revolutions in Plant Description', in J. C. Arends et al. (eds), *Liber Gratulatorius in Honorem H. C. D. De Wit* (Wageningen, H. Veenman & Zonen BV, 1980), pp. 167–8; and Wilfrid Blunt and William T. Stearn, *The Art of Botanical Illustration*, revised edition (Woodbridge, Antique Collectors' Club, 1994). The online notes make clear my debts to all these authors.

Simon Schama offers an excellent introduction to Dutch life in *The Embarrassment of Riches, An Interpretation of Dutch Culture in the Golden Age* (London, Collins, 1987); and see also volumes 2 (*Cities and Cultural Exchange in Europe, 1400–1700*) and 4 (*Forging European Identities*) of Robert Muchembled and William Monter (eds), *Cultural Exchange in Early Modern Europe* (4 vols, Cambridge University Press, 2006–7).

For a history of Centifolia roses, see Gisele de la Roche and Gordon Rowley in *Commentaries to Les Roses by P. J. Redouté, A Contribution to the History of the Genus Rosa* (Antwerp, De Schutter, 1978), pp. 184–202; the story of the large Dutch Centifolias appears on pp. 188–9. I also consulted W. J. Bean, *Trees & Shrubs Hardy in The British Isles*, eighth edition revised (London, John Murray, 1980), vol. 4; F. Joyaux, 'History of Roses in Cultivation/European (Pre-1800)', in Andrew V. Roberts (ed.), *Encyclopedia of Rose Science* (3 vols, Amsterdam, Elsevier, 2003), vol. 1, p. 397; and these scientific papers: M. Martin et al., 'The Domestication Process of the Modern Rose: Genetic Structure and Allelic Composition of the Rose Complex', *Theoretical and Applied Genetics*, vol. 102, 2001, pp. 398–404; 'The work of

Dr C. C. Hurst', in *The Graham Stuart Thomas Rose Book* (London, John Murray, 1994), p. 306; and Hikaru Iwata et al., 'Triparental Origin of Damask Roses', *Gene*, vol. 259, 2000, pp. 53–9.

1. Quoted in Egmond et al., *Carolus Clusius*, p. 39, and see also Florike Egmond, 'A European Community of Scholars: Exchange and Friendship among Early Modern Natural Historians', in Anthony Molho et al. (eds), *Finding Europe, Discourses on Margins, Communities, Images ca. 13th – ca. 18th Centuries* (New York, Berghahn Books, 2007), pp. 174–5. The Garet family came originally from Antwerp.

2. See www.essentialvermeer.com, 'Economics and Dutch Painting', consulted 29 October 2009; and Michael North, *Art and Commerce in the Dutch Golden Age* (New Haven, Yale University Press, 1997), pp. 74–8.

3. Peter Paul Rubens, *Correspondance de Rubens,* ed. Charles Ruelens and Max Rooses (6 vols, Antwerp, 1887–1909), vol. 2, pp. 119–22, letter of 1 November 1617. For an explanation of technical terms, see Taylor, *Dutch Flower Painting*, Chapter 3.

4. Peter Mundy, *The Travels of Peter Mundy in Europe and Asia 1608–1667,* vol. 4, *Travels in Europe 1639–47,* ed. Lieut. Col. Sir Richard Carnac Temple (London, Hakluyt Society, 1925), second series, no.55, pp. 70–71.

5. Jennifer Potter, *Strange Blooms, The Curious Lives and Adventures of the John Tradescants* (London, Atlantic Books, 2006), pp. 12–13.

6. Bunyard, *Old Garden Roses*, pp. 37–40. Bunyard dates its appearance to between 1583 (when Rembert Dodoens's herbal failed to include a Centifolia) and 1589 (when Clusius received the rose from Johan van Hoghelande), thus overlooking the entry in Matthias de L'Obel's *Kruydtboeck.* See also Bean, *Trees & Shrubs*, pp. 67–8. Bean tells us that the Swiss botanist Jean Bauhin saw it in flower at Pforzheim in Germany in July 1595 and was told that it was bought at great price in 'the city of Delphi' – a story Bean treats with caution, as Delphi had long since crumbled into ruins. Might Bauhin have been told that the rose came not from Delphi but from Delft?

Chapter Ten
Memories of Malmaison

Much that is written on Empress Josephine is simply fanciful. The French author and rosarian who has delved into the archives is François Joyaux – see especially *Les Roses de l'Impératrice, La Rosomanie au Temps de Joséphine* (Brussels, Editions Complexe, 2005). I trust and respect his facts even if I do not always share his interpretations. Two works made me question the Josephine myth: André Leroy, *Les Roses de Redouté et de Joséphine* (Paris, Sceaux, 1950), and *Vues du Château et du Parc de Malmaison* (Paris, Perrin, 2003) by Bernard Chevallier, Director of the Musée Nationale des Châteaux de Malmaison et Bois-Préau.

For contemporary accounts of Malmaison's gardens, I turned to: Alexandre de Laborde, *Description des Nouveaux Jardins de la France et de ses Anciens Châteaux* (Paris, 1808); Seth William Stevenson, *Journal of a Tour Through Parts of France, Flanders, and*

Holland (Norwich, 1817), pp. 84–9; and the Caledonian Horticultural Society's *Journal of a Horticultural Tour Through Some Parts of Flanders, Holland and the North of France, in the Autumn of 1817* (Edinburgh, 1823), pp. 396–405. The handsome volumes Josephine commissioned on her rare plants (but not her roses) are: E. P. Ventenat, *Jardin de la Malmaison* (Paris, 1803); and Aimé Bonpland, *Description des Plantes Rares Cultivées à Malmaison et à Navarre* (Paris, 1813). For a contemporary English view of French rose gardens, see John Claudius Loudon, *An Encyclopaedia of Gardening* (London, 1822), p. 1224; and William Paul, *The Rose Garden* (London, 1848). And for a twenty-first-century perspective, see H. Walter Lack, *Jardin de la Malmaison, Empress Josephine's Garden* (Munich, Prestel, 2004); Marina Heilmeyer adds an essay on 'Malmaison Today', pp. 307–19.

As well as H. Walter Lack's 'botanical' reading of Josephine's life, and works by Bernard Chevallier, my sources on Josephine herself included her letters, edited by Bernard Chevallier et al., *Impératrice Joséphine, Correspondance, 1782–1814* (Paris, Payot, 1996); and her bored lady-in-waiting, Mme G. Ducrest, *Mémoires sur l'Impératrice Joséphine, ses Contemporains, la Cour de Navarre et de la Malmaison* (3 vols, Paris, 1828–9), vol. 1, pp. 310–11. For a thorough appraisal of Josephine's interest in natural history, see Christian Jouanin and Jérémie Benoit, *L'Impératrice Joséphine et les Sciences Naturelles* (Paris, RMN, 1997), which I consulted in the archives at Malmaison; and for her interest in Australian exotica, see Jill Duchess of Hamilton, *Napoleon, the Empress and the Artist* (East Roseville, NSW, Kangaroo Press, 1999). The one possible rose in Malmaison's inventory

made after Josephine's death appears in Serge Grandjean (ed.), *Inventaire Après Décès de l'Impératrice Joséphine à Malmaison* (Paris, 1964), p. 278.

For information on nurserymen Lee and Kennedy, a good source is E. J. Willson, *James Lee and the Vineyard Nursery Hammersmith* (London, Hammersmith Local History Group, 1961). The archives at the Royal Botanic Gardens, Kew, hold the nursery's 1808 rose list: Record Book 1793–1809, ff. 259 and 404–6, 'A list of Roses sold by Lee & Kennedy, Nursery & Seedsmen, Hammersmith'.

I traced the growing French interest in roses – and the gathering Josephine myth – through these authors: M. Lelieur, *De la Culture du Rosier avec Quelques Vues sur d'autres Arbres et Arbustes* (Paris, 1811); Auguste de Pronville, *Nomenclature Raisonée des Espèces, Variétés et Sous-variétés du Genre Rosier* (Paris, 1818); C.-A. Thory, *Rosa Candolleana* (Paris, Hérissant Le Doux, 1819); J.-P. Vibert, *Observations sur la Nomenclature et le Classement des Roses, Suivies du Catalogue de Celles Cultivées* (Paris, 1820); J.-P. Vibert, *Essai sur les Roses* (Paris, 1824); and Jean Louis Auguste Loiseleur Deslongchamps, *La Rose, Son Histoire, Sa Culture, Sa Poésie* (Paris, 1844).

Redouté's rose portraits are exquisite and worth trying to see in the original: Claude Antoine Thory, *Les Roses, par P. J. Redouté . . . avec le texte par C. A. Thory* (3 vols, Paris, 1817–24). My main source for Redouté's life (and his roses) was Gisele de la Roche and Gordon D. Rowley, *Commentaries to Les Roses by P. J. Redouté, A Contribution to the History of the Genus Rosa* (Antwerp, De Schutter, 1978), supplemented by Marianne Roland Michel, *The Floral Art of Pierre-Joseph*

Redouté (London, Frances Lincoln, 2002), pp. 13–25.

On roses coming back to Malmaison, see Jules Gravereaux, *La Malmaison: Les Roses de l'Impératrice Joséphine* (Paris, Éditions d'Art et de Littérature, 1912); and Jean Ajalbert, *Dix Années à Malmaison (1907–17)* (Paris, Flammarion, 1920). Full references and sources appear online.

1. The Scottish contingent nonetheless judged Malmaison's collection of Cape heathers 'insignificant, when compared with several collections both in England and Scotland'. *Journal of a Horticultural Tour*, p. 405.

2. The visitor was the Comte de la Garde-Chambonas, quoted in Chevallier and Pincemaille, *L'Impératrice Joséphine, Correspondance*, p. 266 (author's translation). Egyptian Damietta (Damiata or Domyat) is a Mediterranean port city at the mouth of the Nile. Joyaux, in *Les Roses de l'Impératrice* (p. 158), suggests that the rose may have been similar to the nineteenth-century 'Rose d'Alexandrie', and has probably died out.

3. *Thomas Jefferson's Garden Book 1766–1824* (Philadelphia, The American Philosophical Society, 1985), p. vii.

4. Quoted in Charles Léger, *Redouté et son Temps* (Paris, Éditions de la Galerie Charpentier, 1945), p. 52.

5. See her bills in the Croome archive at Worcester Record Office, such as bill number 496 of 5 June 1797.

6. For an excellent annotated list of Malmaison's known roses, see Joyaux, *Les Roses de l'Impératrice*, pp. 155–61.

7. *The Gentleman's Magazine: and Historical Chronicle,* July–December 1811, vol. 81, p. 479, under 'Domestic Occurrences' for 14 November; and for Kennedy's 1802 visit, see Jouanin and Benoit, *L'Impératrice Joséphine et les Science Naturelles,* p. 23. William Paul tells the story of Kennedy's passport in *The Rose Garden,* p. 13.

8. Salomon Pinhas, *Rosen-Sammlung zu Wilhelmshöhe,* trans. Margaret Marks (Regensburg, Schnell & Steiner, 2001), p. 24.

9. The catalogue is included in Thory, *Rosa Candolleana,* pp. 13–19, and Joyaux, *Les Roses de l'Impératrice,* p. 162. Gallicas and Gallica hybrids form the largest group (sixty in total), followed by Centifolias (thirty). Chinese roses include *Rosa sempervirens undulata* 'de Chine', *R. sempervirens bracteata* 'Macartney', and *R. sempervirens Sinica trifolia.*

10. Vibert, *Observations,* p. 11, and for his father's catalogue, see Jean Descemet, *Catalogue d'Arbres, Arbrisseaux, Arbustes, Plantes, Oignons de Fleurs, Graines de Fleurs et Potagères* (Paris, 1782), pp. 16–17. The Dutch had many more roses at this time: see, for instance, the Grand Catalogue . . . de Voorhelm & Schneevoogt, au Grand Jardin Fleuriste à Harlem en Hollande of 1788, pp. 47–8, which lists some 110 roses. For more on Descemet, see François Joyaux, *Descemet: Premier Rosiériste Français (1761–1839)* (Paris, Connaissance et Mémoire, 2005).

Chapter Eleven
Chinese Whispers

This chapter is based on archival material and contemporary writings about early China roses, supplemented where necessary by modern works. Readers wishing to follow up original and other sources should consult the online notes; see www.atlantic-books.co.uk.

Two essential early works are by a physician of the Russian legation at Peking (Beijing): Emil Bretschneider, *Early European Researches into the Flora of China* (Shanghai, 1881), and *History of European Botanical Discoveries in China* (2 vols, London, 1898). For a full account of the introduction of traditional Chinese plants to Britain, drawing on many new and original sources, see Jane Kilpatrick, *Gifts from the Gardens of China* (London, Frances Lincoln, 2007); also of general interest is Alice M. Coats, *The Quest for Plants, A History of the Horticultural Explorers* (London, Studio Vista, 1969), pp. 87–142. For my botanical authorities on Chinese roses, I turned to W. J. Bean, *Trees & Shrubs Hardy in the British Isles,* eighth edition (4 vols, London, John Murray, 1980), vol. 4; and Roger Phillips and Martyn Rix, *The Ultimate Guide to Roses, A Comprehensive Selection* (London, Macmillan, 2004).

Petiver's Chusan rose appears in James Petiver, *Gazophylacii Naturae & Artis. Decas Quarta* (London, 1702), p. 56, and his Chinese paintings in *Musei Petiveriani,* 'An Abstract of what Collections I have received the last Twelve Months' (London, 1695–1703), p. 44. Contemporary accounts by travellers, diplomats and botanists give a sense of how it felt to travel into China. These were particularly helpful: Peter Osbeck, *A Voyage to China and the East Indies,* trans. from German by John Reinhold Forster (2 vols, London, 1771); Sir George Staunton Bt, *An Authentic Account of an Embassy from the King of Great Britain to the Emperor of China* (2 vols, London, 1797); John Barrow,

Travels in China (London, 1804); Clarke Abel, *Narrative of a Journey in the Interior of China . . . in the Years 1816 and 1817* (London, 1818); John Francis Davis (late his Majesty's Chief Superintendent in China), *The Chinese: A General Description of the Empire of China and its Inhabitants* (2 vols, London, Charles Knight & Co, 1836); and for a more recent and Chinese perspective on the political and commercial background, Fa-ti Fan, 'Science in a Chinese Entrepôt, British Naturalists and their Chinese Associates in Old Canton', *Osiris,* 2003, second series, vol.18, *Science and the City,* pp. 60–78. The later plant hunters wrote frequently and well about their travels – see Robert Fortune, *Three Years' Wanderings in the Northern Provinces of China* (London, John Murray, 1847); Ernest Henry Wilson, *A Naturalist in Western China* (2 vols, London, Methuen & Co., 1913); and most recently Roger Phillips and Martyn Rix, *The Quest for the Rose* (London, BBC Books, 1993), pp. 41–59. The early European sighting of the strange new China rose is taken from *Memoirs of the Baroness d'Oberkirch, Countess de Montbrison* (3 vols, London, 1852), vol. 2, pp.118–19.

The story of William Kerr's plant hunting in China comes mostly from special collections: British Museum (Natural History), *Sir Joseph Banks (1743–1820): Correspondence Transcribed by Dawson Turner* (generally known as the 'Dawson Turner Correspondence'), especially vols 14 and 18; Royal Botanic Gardens, Kew, Kew Record Book 1793–1809 (ff. 255–6), Kew Record Book 1804–1826 (ff. 1, 3, 12, 22, 24, 26, 45–6, 52, 55, 72–5), and Goods Inwards 1809–18 (ff. 73, 148–53); Sir Joseph Banks's 'Hints on the Subject of Gardening' at the Linnean

Society of London, MS 115; correspond-
ence with and about William Kerr in the
British Library manuscripts collection
(Additional MS 33,981, ff. 138–9v, 181,
227–8, 234–5, 248–9, and Additional MS
33, 982, ff. 75–80 and 230–32); and the
Royal Horticultural Society's watercolours
of Chinese roses executed by Chinese
artists under the supervision of John
Reeves, held at the RHS Lindley Library in
London. More generally on Banks I turned
to Neil Chambers (ed.), *The Letters of Sir
Joseph Banks: A Selection 1768–1820*
(London, Imperial College Press, c.2000),
and Harold B. Carter, *Sir Joseph Banks
1743–1820* (London, British Museum
[Natural History], 1988).

Tracking the chronological
introduction of Chinese roses – and
identifying them botanically – is
exasperating, as few authorities agree.
Among many other works, I consulted
Carl Linnaeus, *Species Plantarum*, a
facsimile of the first edition 1753 (2 vols,
London, Ray Society, 1957), vol. 1, p. 492;
Philip Miller, *The Gardeners Dictionary*,
seventh edition (London, 1759); John Hill,
Hortus Kewensis (London, 1768), p. 454;
Nicolai Jacquin, *Observationum
Botanicarum, Pars I–III* (Vienna, 1764–8),
part 3, p. 7 and plate 55; William Aiton's
Hortus Kewensis (London, 1789) and the
later revision by his son, William
Townsend Aiton (London, 1810); John
Lindley, *Rosarum Monographia; Or a
Botanical History of Roses* (London, 1820);
H. C. Andrews, *Roses: Or a Monograph of
the Genus Rosa* (2 vols, London, 1805–28),
vol. 2; and Claude Antoine Thory, *Les
Roses, par P. J. Redouté* (3 vols, Paris, 1817–
24). These I cross-referred where
necessary to *Curtis's Botanical Magazine*
and other contemporary journals, and to
the *Transactions* of the Horticultural

Society of London. Gerd Krüssmann
provides a useful chronological list of
introductions in *Roses* (London,
B. T. Batsford, 1982), pp. 80–81.
Dr C. C. Hurst's work on China roses and
the four stud Chinas appears in Graham
Stuart Thomas, *The Graham Stuart Thomas
Rose Book* (London, John Murray, 1994),
pp. 308–12; and Ann P. Wylie discusses it
in her Masters Memorial Lecture of 1954,
'The History of Garden Roses, Part I',
reprinted in the *Journal of the Royal
Horticultural Society*, vol. 79, no. 12,
December 1954, pp. 555–71.

Aside from those already listed, these
works are also helpful on Chinese roses:
Guoliang Wang, 'A Study on the History of
Chinese roses from Ancient Works and
Images', *Acta Horticulturae*, no. 751,
August 2007, pp. 347–56; 'Ancient
Chinese Roses', in *The Encyclopedia of Rose
Science* (3 vols, Amsterdam, Elsevier
Academic Press, 2003), vol. 1, pp. 387–
94; H. Brichet on the distribution and
ecology of wild Chinese roses from the
same source, vol. 1, pp. 204–12; Mikinori
Ogisu, 'Some Thoughts on the History of
China Roses', *The New Plantsman*, vol. 3,
September 1996, pp. 152–7; and Hazel Le
Rougetel, *A Heritage of Roses* (London,
Unwin Hyman, 1988). Without resolving
the contradictions, Brent C. Dickerson
has helpfully gathered together historical
references to rose classes including the
Chinas and to individual cultivars in *The
Old Rose Advisor* (Portland, Oregon, Timer
Press, 1992); and he offers a much richer
and more complicated account of early
China imports in *The Old Rose Informant*
(San Jose, Authors Choice Press, 2000) –
see pp. 466–78, 'The First Eighteen
Chinas'. Elfrida Chappell and Peggy
Nicholl recount the Bermudan rediscovery
of old China roses in *Old Garden Roses in*

Bermuda (The Bermuda Rose Society, 1984), pp. 9, 14, 18 and 26. Tuppy Cooper and Lee Davidson (eds) update the story in *Roses in Bermuda* (1994) – not seen. Charles Quest-Ritson writes of Chinese Climbers in *The Climbing Roses of the World* (Portland, Oregon, Timber Press, 2003).

1. Michel de Montaigne, *The Complete Works of Michael de Montaigne,* ed. William Hazlitt (London, J. Templeman, 1842), pp. 561–2. Bretschneider, in *Early European Researches,* says (p. 3): 'It does not seem, that any botanical collection was sent from China to Europe by Jesuit missionaries previous to the middle of the 18th century.' But see Peter Davidson, 'The Jesuit Garden', in John W. O'Malley et al., *The Jesuits II: Cultures, Sciences, and the Arts, 1540–1773* (Toronto, University of Toronto Press, 2006), p. 87.

2. Many accounts of early introductions are either vague or contradictory. For instance, among the rather unbotanical list of fifteen different roses in the sixth French edition of Louis Liger, *La Nouvelle Maison Rustique* (2 vols, Paris, 1749), vol. 2, p. 357, is a puzzling 'Rose de Sienne ou de la Chine'. There is also a monthly rose ('Rose de tous les mois') said to flower seven or eight times a year with the aid of 'small ordinary attentions', but no mention of Chinese origin. Liger also writes of an annual 'Rose d'Inde' (vol. 2, p. 332), which could be raised from seed each year.

3. Linnean Society, MS 115, 'Hints on the Subject of Gardening by Sir Joseph Banks 1792'.

4. 'Observations on Chinese Scenery, Plants, and Gardening, made on a Visit to the City of Canton and its Environs, in the Years 1793 and 1794; being an Extract from the Journal of Mr. James Main, sent thither by the late Gilbert Slater, Esq. of Layton, Essex, to collect the Double Camellias, &c', *The Gardener's Magazine* (London, 1827), pp. 135–40. There were other flower markets around Canton, but these were out of westerners' reach. See Fan, 'Science in a Chinese Entrepôt', p. 73.

5. Roxburgh's *Hortus Bengalensis* of 1814 credits Kerr with the introduction of three roses to the Hon. East India Company's Botanic Garden at Calcutta: *R. inermis* (Pa-mo-li) and *R. microphylla* (Hai-tong-hang), both from China; and *R. procumbens.* Calcutta was also growing *R. triphylla* (Cha-te-qui-fa), *R. chinensis, R. indica* and *R. semperflorens,* plus five other varieties described as coming from Europe, India, Bhutan, Nepal and Asia. W. Roxburgh, *Hortus Bengalensis* (Serampore, 1814), p. 38.

6. William Curtis, *The Botanical Magazine; or, Flower-Garden Displayed,* vol. 8, 1794, no. 284. Slater's famous garden of exotics was to the east of London.

7. For more about Hume and Wormleybury, see Kate Harwood, 'A Hertfordshire Garden in the Eighteenth Century', *Herts Past and Present,* third series, no. 2, Autumn 2003, pp. 12–16.

8. RHS Lindley Library, Drawings Collection, John Reeves S2, ff. 36, 37, 32 and 44. The Chinese names given by Reeves and Kerr are as follows: Slater's Crimson (Reeves, Tsuy Yong Fee; a possible match for Kerr's

Soi-yang fei); Hume's Old Blush (Reeves, To Me Muey Qui; Kerr Mui Quai); Parsons' Pink/Monthly Blush (Reeves, Yuet Qui; Kerr, Yeut-qai-faa). Kerr's plant names appear in Royal Botanic Gardens, Kew, Kew Record Book 1793–1809, fol. 1, plants from China on board the *Henry Addington,* received at Kew in August 1804.

Chapter Twelve
The Prophet's Rose

This chapter results from a very personal encounter with the rose in Middle Eastern cultures, especially Iran, and the part it has played in Islamic – and pre-Islamic – life. My principal guide to the rose in Islamic thought is Professor Annemarie Schimmel, whose works include 'The Celestial Garden in Islam', in Elisabeth B. Macdougall and Richard Ettinghausen (eds), *The Islamic Garden* (Washington DC, Dumbarton Oaks, 1976); *And Muhammad is His Messenger – The Veneration of the Prophet in Islamic Piety* (Chapel Hill, University of North Carolina Press, 1985); and *A Two-Colored Brocade, The Imagery of Persian Poetry* (Chapel Hill, University of North Carolina Press, 1992). I used the online edition of Brill's *Encylopaedia of Islam* for context, supplemented by its online *Encyclopaedia of the Qur'ān.*

On gardens and garden roses, I turned first to Penelope Hobhouse, *Gardens of Persia* (London, Cassell Illustrated, c.2003), and to a paper on 'Islamic Gardens' given to me by Professor Azim Nanji. I also found these helpful: John Brookes, *Gardens of Paradise, The History and Design of the Great Islamic Gardens* (London, Weidenfeld & Nicolson, 1987); Emma Clark, *The Art of the Islamic Garden*

(Marlborough, Wilts, Crowood Press, 2004); D. Fairchild Ruggles, *Gardens, Landscape, and Vision in the Palaces of Islamic Spain* (University Park PA, Pennsylvania State University Press, 2000); Vita Sackville-West, 'Persian Gardens', in A. J. Arberry (ed.), *The Legacy of Persia* (Oxford, Clarendon Press, 1953); Andrew M. Watson, *Agricultural Innovation in the Early Islamic World: The Diffusion of Crops and Farming Techniques, 700–1100* (Cambridge University Press, 1983), p. 93, and pp. 117–19; James L. Westcoat Jr and Joachim Wolschke-Bulmahn (eds), *Mughal Gardens, Sources, Places, Representations, and Prospects* (Washington DC, Dumbarton Oaks, 1996); and Donald Newton Wilber, *Persian Gardens and Garden Pavilions* (Washington DC, Dumbarton Oaks, 1979). The best source on historical roses is John Harvey; apart from his articles listed in the sources for Chapter 4, I consulted 'Garden Plants of Moorish Spain: A Fresh Look', *Garden History,* vol. 20, no. 1 (Spring 1992). The Sumerian paradise-land comes from Samuel Noah Kramer, *History Begins at Sumer: Thirty-Nine Firsts in Man's Recorded History,* third revised edition (Philadelphia, University of Pennsylvania Press, 1981), p. 143.

All Edward FitzGerald's translations from the *Rubáiyát of Omar Khayyám* are taken from an undated edition illustrated by Anthony Rado, which belonged to my mother. The (uncredited) publisher is Edgar Backus of Leicester. Godfrey W. Mathews describes FitzGerald's grave in *A Visit to the Shrine of our English Omar* (Liverpool, E. A. Bryant, privately printed, 1929); my own visit took place on 18 June 2007. My sources for Babur include *The Baburnama, Memoirs of Babur, Prince and Emperor,* trans. and ed. Wheeler M.

Thackston (Washington DC, Freer Gallery of Art & others, 1996), pp. 250 and 359–60; and for the rose names of his daughters, Annemarie Schimmel, *The Empire of the Great Mughals,* trans. Corinne Attwood (London, Reaktion, 2004), pp. 144–5.

On travels throughout the region, I started with Vita Sackville-West's *Passenger to Teheran,* with a new introduction by Nigel Nicolson (Heathfield, Cockbird Press, 1990), and Robert Byron's travel classic, *The Road to Oxiana* (London, Pimlico, 2004, first published Macmillan 1937). I then worked backwards, consulting these among other works: Sir Robert Ker Porter, *Travels in Georgia, Persia, Armenia, Ancient Babylonia etc During the Years 1817, 1818, 1819, and 1820* (2 vols, London, 1821); *Sir John Chardin's Travels in Persia,* trans. Edmund Lloyd (London, 1720); Ronald W. Ferrier, *A Journey to Persia, Jean Chardin's Portrait of a Seventeenth-century Empire* (London, I. B. Tauris, 1996); and Thomas Herbert's revised and enlarged *Some Yeares Travels into Africa & Asia the Great* (London, 1638).

My main guides to roses and nightingales in Persian literature and mystic thought are Annemarie Schimmel, 'The Celestial Garden', and William L. Hanaway Jr, 'Paradise on Earth: The Terrestrial Garden in Persian Literature', both in MacDougall and Ettinghausen (eds), *The Islamic Garden;* and Schimmel, *A Two-Colored Brocade,* pp. 169–81. Among many works consulted, I quote from these works of poetry: Hafez, *The Hafez Poems of Gertrude Bell,* introduced by E. Denison Ross (Bethesda, Maryland, Ibex Publishers, c.2007), p. 115; Michael C. Hillmann, *A Lonely Woman, Forugh Farrokhzad and her Poetry* (Washington, Mage Publishers/Three Continents Press,

1987), p. 14; and Mahmud Kianush (ed. and trans.), *Modern Persian Poetry* (Ware, Rockingham Press, 1996), pp. 153–4. I end with a quotation from T. E. Lawrence, *Seven Pillars of Wisdom* (Harmondsworth, Penguin, 1962 edition), p. 3.

1. Iram was a legendary garden in the Qur'an that was so richly adorned it merited destruction for daring to challenge the Almighty.

2. Dr M. I. H. Farooqi, *Plants of the Qur'an,* fifth revised edition (Lucknow, Sidrah Publishers, 2000), p. 204.

3. Etymologically, gardens and paradise are closely linked. The Arabic word for garden, *jannah,* is used in the Qur'an for paradise, the reward of the hereafter. English 'paradise' (Greek *paradeisos*) comes from the old Persian *paridaiza,* meaning walled enclosure.

4. Stuart apothecary John Parkinson used this story in a jibe aimed at Muslims and pagans (notwith-standing the place of the rose in Christian iconography): 'The miserably infatuated Turkes will not suffer a Rose leafe to lye upon the ground, or any to tread on them in honour of their Mahomet, from whose sweat they are perswaded the Rose sprang up; somewhat like unto the old Pagans, who held the Rose which formerly was white to become red from the blood of *Venus,* falling thereon from her foote hurt by a thorne as shee ran among the bushes to helpe her *Adonis.*' John Parkinson, *Theatrum Botanicum* (London, 1640), p. 1021.

5. Harvey, 'Garden Plants of Moorish Spain', p. 71, quoting the third

edition (1825) of Loudon's *An Encyclopaedia of Gardening*, Book 1, ix, 290, p. 63. Loudon confuses the century and gives the author's name as 'Ebn-Alwan'.

6. See Wolfhart Heinrichs, 'Rose versus Narcissus', in G. J. Reinink and H. L. J. Vanstiphout (eds), *Dispute Poems and Dialogues in the Ancient and Mediaeval Near East* (Leuven, Department Oriëntalstiek, 1991), pp. 183–6; and W. Heinrichs, 'Ward', *The Encyclopaedia of Islam*.

7. See Nasser D. Khalili et al., *Lacquer of the Islamic Lands* (London, Nour Foundation with Azimuth and Oxford University Press, 1996), and especially the eighteenth-century pen box from Esfahan, pp. 58–9.

Chapter Thirteen
American Beauties

These general works on American horticulture, commerce and roses-in-art helped to shape the chapter: Ulysses P. Hedrick, *A History of Horticulture in America to 1860* (New York, Oxford University Press, 1950); Chauncey M. Depew (ed.), *One Hundred Years of American Commerce, 1795–1895* (2 vols, New York, D. O. Haynes, 1895); 'American Horticulture', vol. 1, pp. 248–56; and especially Bruce Weber, *American Beauty, The Rose in American Art, 1800–1920* (New York, Berry-Hill Galleries, 1997). For an interesting discussion of gardening and moral improvement, see Tamara Plakins Thornton, in Massachusetts Horticultural Society and Walter T. Punch (ed.), *Keeping Eden, A History of Gardening in America* (Boston, Little Brown, 1992), pp. 189–203. Hazel Le Rougetel, *A Heritage of Roses* (London,

Unwin Hyman, 1988), also provided many useful leads: see especially pp. 17–25.

For the text of President Reagan's declaration of the rose as the USA's national floral emblem (signed in the White House Rose Garden on 7 October 1986), see Proclamation 5574, filed with the office of Federal Register, 21 November 1986 (Pub.L.99-449, Oct 7, 1986, 100 Stat.1128). Thomas Jefferson's roses appear in Edwin Morris Betts (ed.), *Thomas Jefferson's Garden Book 1766-1824* (Philadelphia, American Philosophical Society, 1944), vol. 22, pp. v–x, 5, 23, 159, 167, 280, 291 and 634–5; and his indoor roses in Margaret Bayard Smith, *Forty Years of Washington Society* (London, T. Fisher Unwin, 1906), p. 385.

Among much early settler literature, I consulted Captain John Smith, *The Generall Historie of Virginia, New-England and the Summer Isles* (London, 1624); William Strachey, *The Historie of Travell into Virginia Britania* (1612), ed. Louis B. Wright and Virginia Freund (London, Hakluyt Society, second series, no. 103, 1953); Alexander Young, *Chronicles of the Pilgrim Fathers of the Colony of Plymouth, from 1602 to 1625* (Boston, 1841) and *Chronicles of the First Planters of the Colony of Massachusetts Bay from 1630 to 1636* (Boston, 1846); John Josselyn, *New-Englands Rarities Discovered: in Birds, Beasts, Fishes, Serpents, and Plants of that Country* (London, 1672); Daniel Denton, *A Brief Description of New-York: Formerly Called New-Netherlands* (London, 1670); Edward Winslow, *Good Newes from New-England* (London, 1624); and Albert Cook Myers (ed.), *Narratives of Early Pennsylvania, West New Jersey and Delaware, 1630–1707* (New York, Charles Scribner's Sons, 1912).

For the Bartram and Collinson connection, see Edmund Berkeley and Dorothy Smith Berkeley (eds), *The Correspondence of John Bartram 1734–1777* (Gainesville, University Press of Florida, 1992), especially pp. 84, 116–17, 397 and 423. Andrea Wulf writes well about their collaboration in *The Brother Gardeners: Botany, Empire and the Birth of an Obsession* (London, William Heinemann, 2008).

My version of the history of the Cherokee rose comes from Georgia's State History Guide, http://www.shgresources. com/ga/symbols/birdflower/, which does at least recognize that the flower is native to China. For details of its 'discoverer's' life I consulted Henry Savage Jnr and Elizabeth Savage, *André and François André Michaux* (Charlottesville, University Press of Virginia, 1986). Michaux's American roses appear in Andreas Michaux, *Flora Boreali-Americana* (2 vols, Paris, 1803), vol. 1, pp. 295–6.

On Castilian roses and the role of California's Spanish missions, I turned to J. N. Bowman, 'The Rose of Castile', *Western Folklore,* vol. 6, no. 3 (July, 1947), pp. 204–10; *Cultivating Pasadena, From Roses to Redevelopment,* Automobile Club of Southern California, The Labyrinth Project (Annenberg Center for Communication, University of Southern California, 2005); Guadalupe Vallejo, 'Ranch and Mission Days in Alta California – Part II', *New Century Magazine,* December 1890, vol. 41, no. 2, pp. 189–92; and photographic material in the Huntington Library. I quote from Helen Hunt Jackson, *Ramona, A Story* (Boston, Roberts Bros, 1884) pp. 19–20; and Charles F. Lummis, *The Home of Ramona: Photographs of Camulos* (Los Angeles, 1888).

The three rival American rose manuals written in the 1840s are: Robert Buist, *The Rose Manual* (Philadelphia, 1844); William Robert Prince, *Prince's Manual of Roses* (New York, 1846); and S. B. Parsons, *The Rose: its History, Poetry, Culture, and Classification* (New York, Wiley & Putnam, 1847). Mrs Frederick Love Keays's charming *Old Roses* (New York, Macmillan & Co., 1935) gives an inter-war view, while among contemporary works on American roses, I turned to Stephen Scanniello and Tania Bayard, *Roses of America* (New York, Henry Holt, 1990); Clair G. Martin, *100 Old Roses for the American Garden* (New York, Workman Publishing, 1999); and the entertaining and perceptive *In Search of Lost Roses* by Thomas Christopher (New York, Avon Books, 1989). Both Martin and Christopher track the progress of pioneer roses, as does Roy. E. Shepherd, *History of the Rose* (New York, Macmillan, 1954), pp. 186–9, and see Jen Carlson, *Wagon Trains Lead to Roses in December* (Drain, Oregon, 1959). Brent C. Dickerson's *The Old Rose Advisor* (Portland, Oregon, Timber Press, 1992) provides fascinating detail on individual roses.

Among the Huntington Library's fine collection of nurserymen's catalogues I consulted Hovey & Co.'s *A Descriptive Catalogue of Roses* for 1845 and 1846; Waban Conservatories, *Catalogue of New, Rare, and Beautiful Roses and Plants,* (Boston, Spring 1875); and D. M. Dewey, *The nurseryman's specimen book of American horticulture and floriculture, fruits, flowers, ornamental trees, shrubs, roses, &c.* (Rochester, New York, 1872). The mawkish roses appear in *Christmas Roses and New Year's Gift, A present for Young People* (Boston, Philips, Sampson & Company, 1848), 'Christmas Roses', pp. 21–9. My sources on Pasadena's Tournament of Roses include *Cultivating Pasadena*, p. 16; Joyce Y. Pinnery, *A Pasadena Chronology* (Pasadena Public Library/City of Pasadena, 1978); Book Club of California, *Treasures of California Collections: The Pasadena Tournament of Roses, New Year's Day 1893, as described by Hamlin Garland* (San Francisco, 1956); and Kevin Starr, *Inventing the Dream: California through the Progressive Era* (New York, Oxford University Press, 1985), p. 103.

On the White House Rose Garden, as well as secondary sources in the White House archives, I consulted William Seale, *The White House: The History of an American Idea* (Washington DC, American Institute of Architects Press, 1992) and Rachel Lambert Mellon, 'President Kennedy's Rose Garden', *White House History*, vol. 1, 1983, pp. 5–11. My 2008 list of roses planted in the White House Rose Garden came from Irv Williams, retired horticulturist of the White House.

1. Josselyn on rose remedies, *New-Englands Rarities Discovered*, and see Michael Wassegijig Price, 'Wild Roses and Native Americans', in Frankie Hutton (ed.), *Rose Lore, Essays in Cultural History and Semiotics* (Lanham, Lexington Books, 2008), pp. 9–18.

2. John Parkinson, *Theatrum Botanicum* (London, 1640), p. 1017. Tradescant's roses come from Jennifer Potter, *Strange Blooms, The Curious Lives and Adventures of the John Tradescants* (London, Atlantic Books, 2006), p. 304.

3. See Peter Harkness, 'Ancestry & Kinship of the Rose', Royal National Rose Society, *Rose Annual 2005*, pp. 72–3, summarizing research on the spread of the Cherokee rose. Gerd Krüssmann discusses the Cherokee rose in *Roses*, trans. Gerd Krüssmann and Nigel Raban (Portland, Oregon, B. T. Batsford, 1982), p. 46; and see Leonardi Plukenetii, *Amaltheum Botanicum*, vol. 4 of *Opera*, second edition (London, 1769 – original edition 1705), p. 185. See also Edward P. Vining, *An Inglorious Columbus* (New York, D. Appleton & Co., 1885); and C. G. Leland, *Fusang or The Discovery of America by Chinese Buddhist Priests in the Fifth Century* (London, 1875). China expert Dr E. Bretschneider (see sources listed for Chapter 11) denounced Hoei-shin as a 'lying Buddhist priest' and a 'consummate humbug'.

4. Huntington Library, San Marino, California, photograph album: *Reminders of a Sojourn in California, February 1908 to May 1909.*

5. On 'Harison's Yellow', some say it was his father, Richard, who made the cross: see Christopher, *In Search of Lost Roses*, p. 15. This rose is often (wrongly) linked to the 'Yellow Rose of Texas'.

6. *New York Times*, 23 May 1879, p. 5, 'Flowers for the Poorest'; and for Jacob A. Riis's letter, 'Flowers for the Poor. To the Editor of the *New York Times*', 24 June 1888, p. 12. See also David M. Lubin, *Picturing a Nation, Art & Social Change in Nineteenth-Century America* (New Haven, Yale University Press, 1994), p. 216.

7. Much of the material on the Rose Garden is from the White House archives, including the Note on 'Use of the term "Rose Garden"', MCN, 13 December 2005, Office of the Curator of the White House, quoting an

article by Lillian Porter Say, 'Through the White House Fence', in the *Christian Science Monitor* of 19 December 1942. Historical images of the Rose Garden appear on http://www.whitehousemuseum.org /grounds/rose-garden.htm.

Chapter Fourteen
A Cure for Divers Ills

I quote from two English translations of Dioscorides: Pedanius Dioscorides, *Dioscorides de Materia Medica . . .* new indexed version in Modern English by T. A. Osbaldeston and R. P. A. Wood (Johannesburg, IBIDIS, 2000); and John Goodyer's charming seventeenth-century rendition in Robert T. Gunther, *The Greek Herbal of Dioscorides,* facsimile of the 1934 edition (London, Hafner Publishing, 1968). A good source on Dioscorides' life and work is John M. Riddle, *Dioscorides on Pharmacy and Medicine* (Austin, University of Texas Press, 1985); and on his and other illustrated herbals, Minta Collins, *Medieval Herbals, The Illustrative Tradition* (London, British Library, 2000).

On the general history of medicine, I turned to Fielding H. Garrison, *An Introduction to the History of Medicine,* fourth edition (Philadelphia, W. B. Saunders Company, 1929); E. T. Withington, *Medical History* (London, 1894); and Andrew Wear, *Knowledge and Practice in English Medicine, 1550–1680* (Cambridge University Press, 2000). These three authors write well on Galen and the theory of humours, as does Minta Collins, and Benjamin Woolley in *The Herbalist, Nicholas Culpeper and the Fight for Medical Freedom* (London, HarperCollins, 2004), pp. 42–4. My source on the 'Rosa Medicinae' was

H. P. Cholmeley, *John of Gaddesden and the Rosa Medicinae* (Oxford, Clarendon Press, 1912); some scholars believe that John of Gaddesden was Chaucer's model for his Doctor of Physick.

For a good discussion of the Juliana Anicia Codex, see Collins, *Medieval Herbals,* pp. 39–50; and Leslie Brubaker, 'The Vienna Dioskorides and Anicia Juliana', and John Scarborough, 'Herbs of the Field and Herbs of the Garden in Byzantine Medicinal Pharmacy', in Anthony Littlewood et al. (eds), *Byzantine Garden Culture* (Washington, Dumbarton Oaks Research Library and Collection, 2002). The Codex resurfaces in *The Turkish Letters of Ogier Ghiselin de Busbecq,* trans. Edward Seymour Forster (Oxford, Clarendon Press, 1927), p. 243; and as a reduced-size facsimile in Otto Mazal, *Der Wiener Dioskurides* (Graz, Akademische Druck-u. Verlaganstalt, 1998).

For insights into Prophetic, Islamic and pre-Islamic medicine, see Ibn Qayyim al-Jawziyya, trans. Penelope Johnstone, *Medicine of the Prophet* (Cambridge, Islamic Texts Society, 1998); Minta Collins on the illustrated Arabic herbals in *Medieval Herbals,* pp. 115–39; and S. Zillurrahman, 'Arab Medicine During the Ages', trans. from Urdu by Dr M. N. Mathur in *Studies in the History of Medicine & Science,* vol. 14, nos 1–2, new series (1995–6), pp. 1–39. I also consulted many helpful entries in the online *Encyclopaedia of Islam,* edited by P. J. Bearman et al. (Brill, 2009), including those by A. M. Goichon on 'Ibn Sina', Penelope C. Johnstone on 'Ward', and F. Sanagustin on 'Ma' al-Ward'.

A classic study of herbals is Agnes Arber, *Herbals, Their Origin and Evolution, A Chapter in the History of Botany 1470–1670,* third edition, introduced and

annotated by William T. Stearn
(Cambridge University Press, 1986),
supplemented by Minta Collins on
Medieval Herbals and her introduction to
the British Library's *A Medieval Herbal, A
Facsimile of British Library Egerton MS 747*
[the *Tractatus de herbis*] (London, British
Library, 2003). Blanche Henrey remains a
trusted authority on herbals and other
early gardening books in *British Botanical
and Horticultural Literature before 1800*
(3 vols, London, Oxford University Press,
1975).

I track the rose through the herbals
and early plant writings of William
Turner, looking at: *Libellus de re herbaria
novus* (London, 1538); *The names of herbes
in Greke, Latin, Englishe, Duche and Frenche
wyth the commune names that Herbaries and
Apotecaries use* (London, 1548); *A New
Herball* (London, 1551); and *The Seconde
parte of William Turners Herball* (Collen,
1562). I also quote from *A New Herball by
William Turner, Parts II and III,* edited by
George T. L. Chapman, Frank McCombie
and Anne Wesencraft (Cambridge
University Press, 1995), and found useful
background in Whitney R. D. Jones,
*William Turner, Tudor Naturalist, Physician
and Divine* (London, Routledge, 1988).

Among others, I consulted these
herbals: F. G. Meyer et al., *The Great
Herbal of Leonhart Fuchs, De historia
stirpium commentarii insignes, 1542* (2 vols,
Stanford, CA, Stanford University Press,
1999); Printer Richard Banckes's herbal of
1525, printed in London; *The Grete Herball*
(London, 1526); William Langham, *The
Garden of Health* (London, 1578); and John
Gerard, *The Herball or Generall Historie of
Plantes* (London, 1597).

1. Reported online: http://www.whats
newinpharma.com/Pharma/Articles.

aspx/24572, accessed 19 November
2008. See also *Nursing in Practice,* 22
September 2008. Both these sources
report on announcements made at
the OARSI (Osteoarthritis Research
Society International) World
Congress of Osteoarthritis held in
Rome, 18–21 September 2008. And
see sources listed for Chapter 15.

2. See Riddle, *Dioscorides on Pharmacy
and Medicine,* p. 11. Even in
Dioscorides' time, there were
different schools of medicine; the
closest agreement was on humours,
but this was not total. Dioscorides did
not accept that there were only four
humours, and largely ignored the
matter.

3. 'Bill of Medicines Furnished for the
Use of Edward I. 34 and 35 Edw. I.,
1306–7', Miscellaneous records in
the Queen's Remembrancer's Office,
communicated by the Rev. Charles H.
Hartshorne, in *The Archaeological
Journal,* vol. 14, 1857, pp. 267–71.
Hartshorne takes his information on
pomegranates from William
Langham's *The Garden of Health.* For
the trade in imported rosewater, see
Robert S. Lopez and Irving W.
Raymond, *Medieval Trade in the
Mediterranean World* (London, Oxford
University Press, 1955), pp. 108–9.

Chapter Fifteen
The Housewife's Friend

Works by John Gerard and John Parkinson
provide the chapter's starting point:
Gerard's original *Herball* of 1597 and the
revised edition of 1633, edited by Thomas
Johnson; and Parkinson's *Paradisi in Sole
Paradisus Terrestris* (London, 1629) and
Theatrum Botanicum (London, 1640).

Several other works listed in the sources for Chapter 14 were also of use, including William Langham, *The Garden of Health* (London, 1578) and Agnes Arber, *Herbals, Their Origin and Evolution*, third edition (Cambridge University Press, 1986).

Among the many published works on home remedies consulted, John Partridge's *The Treasurie of Commodious Conceites* (London, 1584) was particularly useful, later issued as *The Treasurie of Hidden Secrets, Commonly called, The good-huswives Closet of provision, for the health of her Houshold* (London, 1637). I used the fifth edition of Gervase Markham, *The English House-wife* (London, 1637), which differs little from the first edition of 1612/1613, and I also consulted W. M.'s *The Queens Closet Opened, Incomparable Secrets in Physick, Chyrurgery, Preserving and Candying, &c* (London 1659), and Thomas Raynald's *The Birth of Man-kinde; Otherwise Named, The Womans Booke* (London, 1634).

For the different approaches of William Coles and Nicolas Culpeper, I read William Coles's *The Art of Simpling* (London, 1656) and *Adam in Eden: or, Natures Paradise* (London, 1657), and these works by Culpeper: *The English Physitian Enlarged,* second edition (London, 1653), and several editions of the physicians' bible, including the third edition, *A Physical Directory; Or a Translation of the Dispensatory Made by the Colledg of Physitians of London* (London, 1651) and the fourth, *Pharmacopœia Londinensis: Or the London Dispensatory* (London, 1653). Benjamin Woolley provides an excellent introduction to the man and his methods in *The Herbalist, Nicholas Culpeper and the Fight for Medical Freedom* (London, HarperCollins, 2004).

John Evelyn's radical plan for sweet-smelling plantations around London appeared in *Fumifugium, or The Inconvenience of the Aer and Smoak of London Dissipated* (London, 1661), pp. 24–5; my reading of it was guided by Joel Schwartz, 'Environmental Pollution and Human Health: An Epidemiological Perspective', in C. Richard Cothern and N. Phillip Ross (eds), *Environmental Statistics, Assessment & Forecasting* (Lewis Publishers, 1994); and Mark Jenner, 'The Politics of London Air, John Evelyn's *Fumifugium* and the Restoration', in *Historical Journal*, 1995, vol. 38, no. 3, pp. 535–51.

To track the rose in home remedies from the seventeenth and eighteenth centuries I read the seventh edition of Robert Boyle, *Medicinal Experiments; Or, A Collection of Choice and Safe Remedies* (London, 1731); John Wesley, *Primitive Physick: Or, An Easy and Natural Method of Curing Most Diseases* (London, 1747); William Buchan, *Domestic Medicine; or, the Family Physician* (Edinburgh, 1769); and Anna Baines and Jean Imray (eds), *Elizabeth Serrell of Wells Her Recipes & Remedies, An Eighteenth Century Kitchen Commonplace Book* (Wells, Keepsake Press, 1986). Roses have already disappeared from the last two.

For the nineteenth century, two works were especially helpful: *A New Medico-statistical Almanac for 1852 . . . to which is annexed a complete translation of the Pharmacopœia Londinensis of 1851* (London, 1852); and the reprint of a work first published in the 1870s: Frederick A. Flückiger and Daniel Hanbury, *Pharmacographia, A History of the Principal Drugs of Vegetable Origin Met with in Great Britain and British India* (Dehra Dun, India, International Book Distributors, 1986).

The long entry on roses in Maud

Grieve's *A Modern Herbal,* ed. Mrs C. F. Leyel (Harmondsworth, Penguin Books, 1978, first published 1931) looks back over the history of the rose in medicine and brings its story into the twentieth century. For current uses, I consulted Michael Wassegijig Price, 'Wild Roses and Native Americans', in Frankie Hutton (ed.,) *Rose Lore, Essays in Cultural History and Semiotics* (Lanham, Lexington Books, 2008); Sezai Ercisli and Muharrem Güleryüz, 'Rose hip utilization in Turkey', *Proceedings of the First International Rose Hip Conference Acta Horticulturae* 690, September 2005, pp. 77–81; David E. Allen & Gabrielle Hatfield, *Medicinal Plants in Folk Tradition, An Ethnobotany of Britain and Ireland* (Portland, Timber Press, 2004); Richard Mabey, *Flora Britannica* (London, Sinclair-Stevenson, 1996); and *Herbal Drugs and Phytopharmaceuticals on a Scientific Basis,* second edition (Stuttgart, Medfarm, 2001), which quotes the very negative monograph on rose hips from the German Commission E (B. Anz. no. 164, 1 September 1990). Much more positive evidence is presented in Inci Çinar and A. Sinan Çolakoglu, 'Potential Health Benefits of Rose Hip Products', *Acta Horticulturae* 690, September 2005, pp. 253–7, although roses in any form are absent from Marilyn Barrett (ed.), *The Handbook of Clinically Tested Herbal Remedies* (2 vols, Binghamton NY, Haworth Press, 2004). Looking for the rose in Chinese medicine, I consulted *Herbal Pharmacology in the People's Republic of China, A Trip Report of the American Herbal Pharmacology Delegation* (Washington DC, National Academy of Sciences, 1975) and found one listing for rose hips, but roses were not listed in other sources consulted, including

Richard Hyatt, *Chinese Herbal Medicine, Ancient Art and Modern Science* (London, Wildwood House, 1978).

Among works on alternative remedies, I read Non Shaw, *Bach Flower Remedies, A Step-by-Step Guide* (London, Element, 2002); Dan Kenner and Yves Requena, *Botanical Medicine, A European Professional Perspective* (Brookline, Mass., Paradigm, 2001); and Monika Joshi, 'The Tradition of the Rose in East Indian Culture and Ayurvedic Medicine', in Hutton (ed.), *Rose Lore,* pp. 53–62.

1. See *Adam in Eden*, p. 40. Coles may have lifted this description of roses in the sickroom from his arch rival, Nicholas Culpeper, who wrote in his slightly earlier *The English Physitian Enlarged* (1653 edition, p. 317): 'Red rose Water is of wel known, and familiar use in al occasions (and better then Damask Rose Water) being Cooling and Cordial, freshing quickning the weak & faint spirits, used either in meats, or broths, to wash the Temples, to smel to at the Nose, or to smel the sweet vapors therof out of a perfuming pot, or cast on a hot Fire-shovel.'

2. See Woolley, *The Herbalist,* pp. 174–6: Culpeper used the 'decumbiture' method of prognosis, casting a horoscope to determine the position of the planets at the time the illness arose. For diagnosis and treatment, he relied more obviously on medical principles, such as close examination of the patient and studying the signs of disease.

3. Boyle sets out his sorry tale of ailments in the preface to *Medicinal Experiments,* explaining that he was born the 'thirteenth or fourteenth'

child of a mother who was aged forty-two or forty-three when she died of consumption.

4. Allen and Hatfield, *Medicinal Plants in Folk Tradition,* p. 151. There was also a Highlands poultice of 'wood leaves of roses', which the authors think might be common figwort, and Irish remedies calling for 'briars' without specifying whether they were brambles or wild roses. 'In Donegal, however, the juice of a plant expressly named as *ros* has been a cough cure.'

5. Rose products do not appear to feature significantly in traditional Chinese medicine, although the dried hips of *Rosa laevigata* were listed among 248 plant and animal drugs in *The Atlas of Commonly Used Chinese Traditional Drugs* by the Revolutionary Committee of the Institute of Materia Medica, Chinese Academy of Medical Sciences, Peking (1970) – see *Herbal Pharmacology in the People's Republic of China,* p. 206. The dried hips were apparently used to treat premature ejaculation (decocted alone or boiled with sugar and taken orally); and combined with other ingredients to treat urinary conditions such as enuresis and polyuria, and diarrhoea.

6. See 'A Systematic Review on the *Rosa canina* Effect and Efficacy Profiles', *Phythotherapy Research,* vol. 22, issue 6, pp. 725–33.

Chapter Sixteen
Heaven's Scent

On smell generally, I found two works especially thought-provoking: Richard Palmer, 'In Bad Odor: Smell and its Significance in Medicine from Antiquity to the Seventeenth Century', in

W. F. Bynum and Roy Porter (eds), *Medicine and the Five Senses* (Cambridge University Press, 1993), pp. 61–8; and Alain Corbin, *The Foul and the Fragrant, Odor and the French Social Imagination* (*Le Miasme et la Jonquille*) (Leamington Spa, Berg Publishers, 1986). Other general works consulted included Constance Classen et al., *Aroma, The Cultural History of Smell* (London, Routledge, 1994); and Diane Akerman, *A Natural History of the Senses* (London, Chapmans, 1990). Among philosophical and neurological approaches to smell, these proved useful: I. Kant, *Anthropology from a Pragmatic Point of View,* trans. V. L. Dowdell (Carbondale and Edwardsville, Southern Illinois University Press, 1978), §22 p. 46; B. S. Eastwood, 'Galen on the elements of olfactory sensation', in *Rheinisches Museum für Philologie,* vol. 124, 1981, pp. 268–89; Gregorius Reisch, *Margarita Philosophica* (Basileae, 1583), Book 10, tract 2, ch. 17, 'Quid olfactus'; Donald A. Wilson and Richard J. Stevenson, *Learning to Smell, Olfactory Perception from Neurobiology to Behavior* (Baltimore, John Hopkins University Press, 2006), pp. 12–13; and Joris-Karl Huysmans' novel *Against Nature* [*À Rebours*], trans. Margaret Mauldon (Oxford University Press, 1998). *National Geographic* reported the results of its smell survey in vol. 172, October 1987, pp. 514–25.

My guide to the smell of roses is Robert Calkin, 'The Fragrance of Old Roses', in the *Historic Roses Journal,* no. 7, Spring 1999, pp. 2–7. These works relating specifically to roses are also of great interest: L. Langlès, *Recherches sur la Découverte de l'Essence de Rose* (Paris, 1804); Dr R. Blondel, *Les Produits Odorants des Rosiers* (Paris, 1889); and J. Ch. Sawer, *Rhodologia, A Discourse on Roses and the*

Odour of Rose (Brighton, W. J. Smith, 1894). Sawer's aim in his slim but fascinating book was 'to interest persons located in some of our Colonies where the climate, etc., is suitable to the development of the rose'. Sir Francis Bacon writes of the smell of roses in 'Of Gardens, XLVI', in *The Essayes or Counsels, Civill and Morall,* ed. Michael Kiernan (Oxford, Clarendon Press, 1985), pp. 139–45; and Mrs M. Grieve provides a useful early twentieth-century view in *Roses and Pot Pourri,* assisted by Miss Ella Oswald (Chalfont St Peter, 1927). Henri Delbard describes his smell pyramid in *A Passion for Roses, The Notebooks of Henri Delbard,* trans. Edward Lucie-Smith et al. (London, Thames & Hudson, 1996), pp. 4–5.

On perfumery from historical to modern times, I relied especially on: Theophrastus, 'Concerning Odours', in *Theophrastus, Enquiry into Plants and Minor Works on Odours and Weather Signs,* trans. Sir Arthur Hort (2 vols, London, Heinemann, 1916), vol. 2, pp. 323–89; Eugene Rimmel, *The Book of Perfumes* (London, Chapman & Hall, 1865); Friedrich A. Flückiger and Daniel Hanbury, *Pharmacographia, A History of the Principal Drugs of Vegetable Origin* (originally published London 1874); Charles H. Piesse, *Piesse's Art of Perfumery and the Methods of Obtaining the Odours of Plants,* fifth edition (London, Piesse and Lubin, 1891); Mrs M. Grieve assisted by Miss Ella Oswald, *Fragrant Flowers. Perfumery in Ancient and Modern Times* (Chalfont St Peter, 1926); Frances Kennett, *History of Perfume* (London, Harrap, 1975); Mark P. Widrlechner, 'History and Utilization of *Rosa damascena*', *Economic Botany,* 35(1), 1981, pp. 42–58; and most of all Paul Jellinek,

The Psychological Basis of Perfumery, ed. and trans. J. Stephan Jellinek (London, Blackie Academic & Professional, 1997).

These three works added a historical French perspective: H. de Monteux, *Conservation de Santé et Prolongation de la Vie* (Paris, 1572), p. 265, quoted in Georges Vigarello, *Concepts of Cleanliness, Changing Attitudes in France Since the Middle Ages,* trans. Jean Birrell (Cambridge University Press, 1988), p. 17; *The French Perfumer* (London, 1696), p.11, translated from Simon Barbe, *Le Parfumeur françois* (Lyon, 1693); and Colin Jones, *Madame de Pompadour, Images of a Mistress* (London, National Gallery, 2002). For the perfume industries of Iran, Turkey and India, I consulted these works: M. Haghighi et al., 'Research and Current Profile of Iranian Production of Damask Rose', *Acta Horticulturae* 769, International Symposium of Asian Plants with Unique Horticultural Potential, pp. 449–53; Berrin Torolsan and Patricia Jellicoe, 'The Essential Rose', in *Cornucopia,* vol. 1, issue 2, 1992, pp. 76–80; and B. P. Pal, *The Rose in India* (New Delhi, Indian Council of Agricultural Research, revised edition 1972), pp. 190–93.

To investigate the chemistry of perfumes, I turned to R. J. Forbes, *Short History of the Art of Distillation* (Leiden, E. J. Brill, 1948); Steffen Arctander, *Perfume and Flavor Materials of Natural Origin* (Elizabeth, NJ, 1961); Charles Sell (ed.), *The Chemistry of Fragrances,* second edition (Cambridge, Royal Society of Chemistry, 2006); Dr Maria Lis-Balchin, *The Chemistry & Bioactivity of Essential Oils* (East Horsley, Amberwood Publishing, 1995), p. 90; and H. Schulz, 'Fragrance and Pigments: Odiferous Substances and Pigments', *Encyclopedia of Rose Science* (3 vols, Amsterdam, Elsevier, 2003), vol. 1, pp. 231–3. Much well-researched information on how perfume was made historically appears in Patrick Süskind's bestselling novel, *Perfume, The Story of a Murderer,* trans. John E. Woods (Harmondsworth, Penguin Books, 1987), while for today's rose perfumes I consulted Sylvie Girard-Lagorce, *The Book of Roses,* trans. Josephine Bacon (Paris, Flammarion, 2000) and the refreshingly outspoken Luca Turin and Tania Sanchez, *Perfumes, The Guide* (London, Profile Books, 2008). Jo Shapcott's poem 'Rosa sancta' is taken from *Tender Taxes, Versions of Rilke's French Poems* (London, Faber and Faber, 2001), p. 67.

1. Gertrude Jekyll and Edward Mawley, *Roses for English Gardens* (London, Country Life, 1902), p. 12. Jekyll's bad smells appear in *Wood and Garden* (Woodbridge, Suffolk, Antique Collectors' Club, 1981 reprint from 1899 edition), p. 315.

2. Smelt close at hand, *R. arvensis* is intensely pungent, containing a high proportion of aldehydes, which are widely used in perfumery, while *R. moschata* is a combination of clove (eugenol) and soft rose (phenylethyl alcohol).

3. See Calkin, *The Fragrance of Old Garden Roses* (Historic Roses Group, undated). Calkin's analysis roughly agrees with that provided by Jellinek for essence absolute of rose obtained by solvent extraction (*The Psycho-logical Basis of Perfumery,* p. 53). Results will depend on how the oil is obtained: rose oil obtained by steam distillation contains very little phenylethyl alcohol (typically 1–3 per cent), but between 7 and 25 per cent of stearoptene.

4. *Plutarch's Lives, The Translation called Dryden's,* revised A. H. Clough (5 vols, Boston, Little, Brown and Co., 1864), vol. 4, p. 184.

5. See Lauren Hackworth Petersen, *The Freedman in Roman Art and Art History* (New York, Cambridge University Press, 2006), pp. 5–6. Of course, art does not necessarily mimic life.

6. Forbes (*Short History of the Art of Distillation,* p. 35) attributes the invention of distillation to Muslim chemists, but the Brill online edition of the *Encyclopaedia of Islam* traces the description of an alembic back to alchemical Greek literature and the work of Zisimus of Panoplis (third to fourth century AD), whose writings were known to the Muslims. See P. Carusi, 'Alembic', *Encyclopaedia of Islam, Three,* ed. Gudrun Krämer et al., (Brill, 2009), Brill Online, con-sulted British Library, 13 January 2009.

7. Son of Harun al-Rashid and Islam's great patron of philosophy and science, al-Mamun became caliph in 812 and died in 833. This confirms that al-Râzî was not the first to have applied distillation to perfumery.

8. Wheeler M. Thackston (ed. and trans.), *The Jahangirnama, Memoirs of Jahangir, Emperor of India* (New York, Oxford University Press, 1999), p. 163. Monika Joshi tells a version of this story (and discusses rose oil in India) in 'The Tradition of the Rose in East Indian Culture and Ayurvedic Medicine', in Frankie Hutton (ed.), *Rose Lore, Essays in Cultural History and Semiotics* (Lanham, Lexington Books, 2008), pp. 53–62.

9. The related Hindi word *itr* describes a product made by absorbing rose flower distillate in oil of sandalwood.

Chapter Seventeen
Rose Mania

The literature on rose breeding from the nineteenth century onwards is extensive. Among nineteenth-century works, I consulted Thomas Rivers Jr, *The Rose Amateur's Guide* (London, 1837); Mrs Gore, *The Rose Fancier's Manual* (London, Henry Colburn, 1838); S. B. Parsons, *The Rose: Its History, Poetry, Culture, and Classification* (New York, Wiley & Putnam, 1847); and William Paul, *The Rose Garden,* facsimile of 1848 edition (New York, Earl M. Coleman, 1978). For a twentieth-century perspective I turned to E. A. Bunyard, *Old Garden Roses* (London, Country Life, 1936); Ann P. Wylie, 'Masters Memorial Lecture, 1954, The History of Garden Roses, Part I', in *Journal of the Royal Horticultural Society,* vol. 79, no. 12, December 1954 (two further parts followed in 1955); Gerd Krüssmann, *Roses* (London, B. T. Batsford, 1982); Graham Stuart Thomas, *The Graham Stuart Thomas Rose Book* (London, John Murray, 1994); and many invaluable works by Peter Harkness, among them *The Rose: A Colourful Inheritance* (London, Scriptum Editions with the Royal Horticultural Society, 2003); 'Repeat-flowering Old Roses, Part I', *Historic Rose Journal,* no. 22, Autumn 2001, pp. 19–22; and 'Ancestry and Kinship of the Rose', *The Rose Annual 2005* (St Albans, Royal National Rose Society, 2005), pp. 60–63. Michael Marriott brings the story up to date in 'History of Roses in Cultivation/Modern (Post-1800)', in Andrew V. Roberts (ed.), *Encyclopedia of Rose Science* (3 vols, Amsterdam, Elsevier, 2003), vol. 1, pp. 402–9.

The contemporary gardening press gives an idea of how roses are perceived, individually and collectively: for the UK, *The Gardeners' Chronicle* was especially helpful. My American sources include Bruce Weber, *American Beauty, The Rose in American Art, 1800–1920* (New York, Berry-Hill Galleries, 1997), p. 22; Alfred Henderson, 'American Horticulture', in Chauncey M. Depew (ed.), *One Hundred Years of American Commerce, 1795–1895* (2 vols, New York, D. O. Haynes & Co, 1895), vol. 1, p. 252; and H. B. Ellwanger, 'Old and New Roses', *Century Magazine,* vol. 26, no. 3 (new series, vol. iv), July 1883, pp. 350–58. For French works, see the sources listed for Chapter 10. For the history of individual roses and groups, I consulted Gisele de la Roche and Gordon D. Rowley, *Commentaries to Les Roses by P. J. Redouté* (Antwerp, De Schutter, 1978); W. J. Bean, *Trees & Shrubs Hardy in the British Isles,* eighth edition (4 vols, London, John Murray, 1980), vol. 4; Peter Beales, *Classic Roses* (London, Harvill Press, 1985); Brent C. Dickerson's *The Old Rose Advisor* (Portland, Oregon, Timber Press, 1992); Roger Phillips and Martyn Rix, *The Ultimate Guide to Roses, A Comprehensive Selection* (London, Macmillan, 2004); and David Austin, *The Rose* (Woodbridge, Garden Art Press, 2008).

On the men and women who breed roses: François Joyaux offers an excellent introduction to French rose-growers in *La Rose, Une Passion Française, Histoire de la Rose en France, 1778–1914* (Brussels, Editions Complexe, c.2001). Jack Harkness adds much biographical detail in *The Makers of Heavenly Roses* (London, Souvenir Press, 1985). William Paul describes his early efforts at rose breeding in 'On the improvement of plants, by selection, hybridising, and cross-breeding, having special reference to the Hollyhock and the Rose', *Contributions to*

Horticultural Literature (Waltham Cross, William Paul & Son, 1892), pp. 436–55. My information on Kordes comes from Charles Quest-Ritson, 'The House of Kordes', *Historic Rose Journal,* no. 25, Spring 2003, pp. 2–7. Dean Samuel Reynolds Hole and Harry Wheatcroft tell their own stories: Hole in *A Book About Roses* (Edinburgh, William Blackwood & Sons, 1869, and many subsequent editions); and Wheatcroft in *The Root of the Matter* (London, Golden Eagle, 1974). Bill Radler writes of his Knockout® Roses in Pat Shanley and Peter Kukielski (eds), *The Sustainable Rose Garden, Exploring 21st Century Environmental Rose Gardening* (New York, Manhattan Rose Society, 2008), pp. 57–66, and David Austin of his English Roses in *The Rose,* pp. 116–21. Krüssmann's *Roses* gives brief notes on the main roses introduced by some leading hybridizers, pp. 152–63, and for today, Tommy Cairns lists a total of 195 rose breeders worldwide in *Modern Roses XI* (San Diego, Academic Press, 2000).

The online notes (see www.atlantic-books.co.uk) locate my sources more precisely and indicate the scientific papers consulted for the latest advances in rose-breeding technology. When in doubt, I turned to Andrew V. Roberts (ed.), *Encyclopedia of Rose Science* (3 vols, Amsterdam, Elsevier, 2003); and to the proceedings of successive international symposia reported in *Acta Horticulturae.*

1. *A Catalogue of Trees, Shrubs, Green-house Plants, Seeds, and Bulbous Roots* sold by Luker & Smith, London (1783), p. 16. Bean says the Portland was in cultivation from 1775, known as the 'Scarlet Four Seasons' and *Rosa paestana.* Phillips and Rix (*The Ultimate Guide to Roses,* p. 76) say the name was in use from about 1775, although the original Portland rose, 'Portlandica', was first recorded as a Portland rose in 1782. See the online notes, and Harkness, 'Repeat-flowering Old Roses, Part I' pp. 19–22 and 'Ancestry and Kinship of the Rose', pp. 60–63.

2. For the story of the Noisette roses, see de la Roche and Rowley, *Commentaries to Les Roses,* p. 318; Thory, *Les Roses,* vol. 2, pp. 77–8, and vol. 3, p. 104; and Joyaux, *La Rose,* pp. 89–90. Joyaux suggests that Philippe Noisette first gave a hybrid seedling to Champneys, who returned the favour with one of its offspring. Beales, *Classic Roses,* p. 15, specifies that Philippe sent Louis seeds and plants. Rivers writes of the Noisette in *The Rose Amateur's Guide,* p. 80, and Paul in *The Rose Garden,* p. 151.

3. See Victor F. Lewis, *The Romance of the Rose* (Lewis, 2009), pp. 6–9, based on an unpublished paper by Peter Harkness.

4. English rosarian Ellen Willmott named a M. Cugnot as the probable originator of the Boursault rose, also suggesting that 'some professional Rose-grower' may have obtained the rose from M. Boursault's garden, using his name to increase its cachet. She located Boursault's garden in today's Chausée d'Antin. Ellen Willmott, *The Genus Rosa* (2 vols, London, John Murray, 1910–14), vol. 2, pp. 302–3.

5. Credit for the first Hybrid China usually goes to Mr Charles Brown of Slough in 1815. Known as 'Brown's Superb Blush', his rose resulted from a cross between Hume's Blush China and a Gallica.

6. Tommy Cairns (ed.), *Modern Roses XI, The World Encyclopeadia of Roses* (San Diego, Academic Press, 2000).

7. The probable seed parent of 'Peace' was an unnamed seedling resulting from a cross between two other unnamed seedlings whose own parents involved crosses between 'George Dickson' and 'Souvenir de Claudius Pernet', and 'Joanna Hill' and 'Charles P. Kilham'. The direct pollen parent was 'Margaret McGredy'.

8. Vita's letter to her husband on 20 January 1937 is quoted by Edward Wilson, 'The Brogdale Lecture 2006, Edward Bunyard, F.L.S., 1878–1939', in *The Linnean,* vol. 23, no. 4, October 2007, pp. 21–35.

Chapter Eighteen
Into the Rose Garden

My trawl through successive writings on rose gardens began with Humphry Repton's *Fragments on the Theory and Practice of Landscape Gardening* (London, 1816), assisted by his son J. Adey Repton. Michael Thompson's *Proposals for the Rosary at Ashridge* (Ashridge 1977) and Richard Gorer's *Country Life* article of 11 March 1982, 'The Puzzle of Repton's Roses', provided insights into Repton's rose garden at Ashridge, as did Stephen Daniels more generally in *Humphry Repton, Landscape Gardening and the Geography of Georgian England* (New Haven, Yale University Press, 1999). My source on Kassel's roses was Margot Lutze and Horst Becker, *Rosen-Sammlung zu Wilhelmshöhe* (Regensburg, Snell & Steiner, 2001), pp. 13–25; and see the fascinating article by Harald Enders on 'Early rose breeding in Germany' for

the website set up by New Zealand rose enthusiast Jocelen Janon (http://www.rosarosam.com/ articles/harald_enders/early_germany_0 2.htm).

I then turned to these writers to investigate the nineteenth century's rapid proliferation of rose gardens: John Claudius Loudon, *The Suburban Gardener and Villa Companion* (London, 1838); S. B. Parsons, *The Rose, its History, Poetry, Culture and Classification* (New York, Wiley & Putnam, 1847); William Paul, *The Rose Garden* (London, 1848); Shirley Hibberd, *The Amateur's Flower Garden* (London, 1871) and *The Rose Book, A Practical Treatise on the Culture of the Rose* (London, Groombridge & Sons, 1864); and William Robinson, *The English Flower Garden* (London, John Murray, 1883). For wider introductions to these last two writers, see Anne Wilkinson, 'The Preternatural Gardener: The Life of James Shirley Hibberd (1825–90)', in *Garden History,* vol. 26, no. 1, Summer 1998, pp. 153–75; and Richard Bisgrove, *William Robinson, The Wild Gardener* (London, Frances Lincoln, 2008).

Thomas Mawson's *The Art and Craft of Garden Making* (London, B. T. Batsford, 1900) takes the rose garden into the twentieth century; it ran to five editions, the last completed in 1926 with the aid of his son, E. Prentice Mawson. Edwardian rose gardens are further celebrated in two of Gertrude Jekyll's collaborative works: *Roses for English Gardens,* with Edward Mawley (London, Country Life, 1902); and *Gardens for Small Country Houses* (London, Country Life, 1912), with Lawrence Weaver. Jules Gravereaux provides an excellent listing of early twentieth-century French rose plantings in *Les Roses Cultivées à L'Haÿ en 1902*

(Paris, 1902). For the modernist rose garden, I consulted Christopher Tunnard's classic *Gardens in the Modern Landscape* (London, Architectural Press, 1938) and his second revised edition of 1948. The 1970s suburban cliché of a rose-and-lawn garden comes from Anne Scott-James and Osbert Lancaster, *The Pleasure Garden* (Harmondsworth, Penguin Books, 1979).

For cemetery rose gardens, I began with George Collison, *Cemetery Interment: Containing a Concise History of the Modes of Interment Practised by the Ancients* (London, 1840). I also looked at Edward W. Leewin, '"The Arts of Peace": Thomas H. Mawson's Gardens at the Peace Palace, The Hague', *Garden History*, vol. 28, no. 2, Winter 2000, pp. 262–76; and Harry Wheatcroft's involvement with commemorative rose gardens for Lidice and Aberfan, which he describes in his cheerfully self-publicizing autobiography, *The Root of the Matter* (London, Golden Eagle, 1974).

These works were useful on rose gardens in British India: Caroline and Charles Carlton, 'Gardens of the Raj', in *History Today*, vol. 46, no. 7, July 1996, pp. 22–8; Mrs Temple-Wright, *Flowers and Gardens in India, A Manual for Beginners,* fourth edition (Calcutta, Thacker, Spink & Co, 1913); Edith Cuthell, *My Garden in the City of Gardens, A Memory with Illustrations* (London, John Lane/The Bodley Head, 1905); Kate Platt, *The Home and Health in India and the Tropical Colonies* (London, Ballière, Tindall & Cox, 1923); and Robert Grant Irving, *Indian Summer, Lutyens, Baker and Imperial Delhi* (New Haven, Yale University Press, 1981).

Visits to the archives at Dumbarton Oaks in Washington DC and the Huntington Library in San Marino, California, provided useful material on the rose gardens there, supplemented by Diane Kostial McGuire (ed.), *Beatrix Farrand's Plant Book for Dumbarton Oaks* (Washington, Dumbarton Oaks, 1980). Expatriate American gardens feature in several works, including Katie Campbell, *Paradise of Exiles, The Anglo-American Gardens of Florence* (London, Frances Lincoln, 2009); May Brawley Hill, *On Foreign Soil: American Gardeners Abroad* (New York, Harry N. Abrams, 2005); Mrs Philip (Alice) Martineau, *Gardening in Sunny Lands, The Riviera, California, Australia* (London, Richard Cobden-Sanderson, 1924), introduced by Edith Wharton; and Russell Page, *The Education of a Gardener* (London, Harvill Press, 1995, first edition 1962). Susan Irvine has written several books on Australian rose gardens; I turned especially to *Susan Irvine's Rose Gardens* (South Melbourne, Hyland House, 1997).

1. The plan appears in J. Gravereaux, *La Malmaison, Les Roses de L'Impératrice Joséphine* (Paris, Editions d'Art et de Littérature, 1912), p. 42.
2. Geoffrey Jellicoe, *The Studies of a Landscape Designer over 80 Years,* vol. 3, *Studies in Landscape Design* (Woodbridge, Garden Art Press, 1996), p. 3.
3. 'A Day in Henry Huntington's House', manuscript supplied by the Huntington Library, California.
4. Dumbarton Oaks Research Collection, letter from Beatrix Farrand to Mrs Robert Woods Bliss, 7 July 1922.
5. In 1968, management passed to the Département du Val-de-Marne. Today it has 3,177 varieties, including

182 species. See http://www.rose raieduvaldemarne.com. Gravereaux lists his original plantings in *Les Roses Cultivées à L'Haÿ en 1902* (Paris, 1902). For Bunyard's visit, see Edward A. Bunyard, 'Rose hunting in 1939', *New Flora and Silva*, vol. 12, November 1939, pp. 11–17.

6. The term 'rose window' applies to circular windows that radiate like the spokes of a wheel. It may derive originally not from *rosa* but from the old French 'roué' meaning 'wheel', in use from the thirteenth century. The rising cult of the Virgin and the emergence of High Gothic in architecture turned the wheel into a many-petalled rose.

7. See report by Dr Cleghorn to the Botanical Society, Edinburgh, in *Gardeners' Chronicle*, 18 June 1864, p. 583.

Chapter Nineteen
The Language of Flowers

Art galleries and their online collections inspired much of this chapter, guided initially by Andrew Moore and Christopher Garibaldi, *Flower Power, The Meaning of Flowers in Art* (London, Philip Wilson Publishers, 2003), and Bruce Weber, *American Beauty, The Rose in American Art, 1800–1920* (New York, Berry-Hill Galleries, 1997).

Gertrude Stein's poem 'Sacred Emily' is published in *Geography and Plays* (Boston, Four Seas Co., 1922). For a discussion of its relevance, see Thornton Wilder's introduction to Gertrude Stein, *Four in America* (New Haven, Yale University Press, 1947), pp. v–vi, and Philippa Campbell, 'Rose is a Rose is a Rose', *Harvest*, 2009, number 1. Umberto

Eco discusses his choice of title for *The Name of the Rose* in *Reflections on the Name of the Rose,* trans. William Weaver (London, Secker & Warburg, 1985), and see also Ronald E. Pepin, 'Adso's Closing Line in *The Name of the Rose*', *American Notes and Queries,* vol. XXIV, nos 9 and 10, May–June 1986, pp. 151–2.

American academic Beverly Seaton is an excellent guide to the literal and literary language of flowers in 'French Flower Books of the Early Nineteenth Century', *Nineteenth Century French Studies,* vol. 11, nos 1 and 2, 1982–3, pp. 60–71, and in her extended *The Language of Flowers, A History* (Charlottesville, University Press of Virginia, 1995). Of the flower books themselves, I read Charlotte de Latour, *The Language of Flowers* (London, Saunders & Otley, 1834), and several of her imitators, including Lucy Hooper, *The Ladies' Hand-book of the Language of Flowers* (London, 1844). Taxile Delord offers a welcome antidote in *Les Fleurs Animées,* drawings by J. J. Grandville (Paris, 1847).

Among nineteenth- and twentieth-century poets, I looked for roses in William Blake, *Poems and Prophecies* (London, Everyman's Library, reissued David Campbell Publishers Ltd, 1991), and Edith Sitwell, *The Canticle and the Rose, Selected Poems 1920–47* (London, Macmillan, 1949). Catherine Maxwell's article on roses in Swinburne led me to T. S. Eliot's rose garden: see Maxwell, 'Eliot's Four Quartets and Swinburne's A Rosary', in *The Explicator,* Winter, 1994, vol. 52, no. 2, pp. 101–4. I end with the rose poems of Rilke and Jo Shapcott; see Rainer Maria Rilke, *The Complete French Poems,* trans. A. Poulin, Jr (Saint Paul, Minnesota, Graywolf Press, 2002), 'Les

Roses', pp. 1–21, and Jo Shapcott, *Tender Taxes* (London, Faber and Faber, 2001). My guides to Rilke included E. M. Butler, *Rainer Maria Rilke* (Cambridge University Press, 1941), whose exposition of Rilke's rose poems is exemplary; George C. Schoolfield, *Rilke's Last Year* (Lawrence, University of Kansas Libraries, 1966); and the judicious biography of Ralph Freedman, *Life of a Poet: Rainer Maria Rilke* (New York, Farrar, Straus & Giroux, 1996).

After Blake, I tracked transgressive roses through the surrealists and especially Georges Bataille's essay on 'The Language of Flowers', in *Visions of Excess: Selected Writings, 1927–1939*, ed. Allan Stoekl, trans. Stoekl et al., in *Theory and History of Literature*, vol. 14 (Manchester University Press, 1985), pp. 10–14. For a fascinating entrée into the territory, see Christopher Looby, 'Flowers of Manhood: Race, Sex and Floriculture from Thomas Wentworth to Robert Mapplethorpe', in *Criticism* (Wayne State University Press), vol. 37, no. 1, Winter 1995, pp. 109–56. Mapplethorpe's roses appear in *Pistils* (London, Jonathan Cape, 1996), *Flowers* (Boston, Bulfinch Press/Little, Brown & Co., 1990), and Arthur Rimbaud, *A Season in Hell,* trans. Paul Schmidt, photographs by Robert Mapplethorpe (Boston, Little, Brown & Co., *c.*1997). Langston Hughes's story 'Slave on the Block' is from *The Ways of White Folks* (London, George Allen & Unwin, 1934), pp. 19–31; and Annie Proulx's 'Brokeback Mountain' from *Close Range, Wyoming Stories* (London, Fourth Estate, 1999), p. 299.

On socialist roses, I consulted Jane Thompson, *Bread and Roses, Arts, Culture and Lifelong Learning* (Leicester, National Institute of Adult Continuing Education, 2002); Bob Franklin, *Packaging Politics,*

Political Communications in Britain's Media Democracy (London, Edward Arnold, 1994), pp. 132–3; and John Bartle, 'Market Analogies, The Marketing of Labour and the Origins of New Labour', in Nicholas J. O'Shaughnessy and Stephan C. M. Henneberg (eds), *The Idea of Political Marketing* (Westport, Connecticut, Praeger, 2002), p. 53. For more on the French Parti Socialiste's red rose, see http://www.lours.org, 'le poing et la rose'.

Finally, these are some of the works I consulted on artists and their roses: Judith Bumpus, *Impressionist Gardens* (Oxford, Phaidon, 1990); Pierre Wittmer, *Caillebotte and his Garden at Yerres* (New York, Harry N. Abrams, 1991); Frances Spalding, *Magnificent Dreams, Burne-Jones and the Late Victorians* (Oxford, Phaidon, 1978); Jacques-Émile Blanche, *Propos de Peintre* (3 vols, Paris, 1919–28), especially the introduction by Marcel Proust and vol. 1, pp. 41–8, on Fantin-Latour; Theodore E. Stebbins Jr, *The Life and Works of Martin Johnson Heade* (New Haven, Yale University Press, 1975); Nicholas Callaway (ed.), *Georgia O'Keeffe, One Hundred Flowers* (Oxford, Phaidon, 1987); and Nicholas Alfrey et al. (eds), *Art of the Garden, The Garden in British Art, 1800 to the Present Day* (London, Tate Publishing, 2004). As well as visiting Twombly's rose paintings several times, I read Nicholas Cullinan, 'Between Roses and Shadows', in Nicholas Serota (ed.), *Cy Twombly, Cycles and Seasons* (London, Tate Publishing, 2008); Richard Leeman, *Cy Twombly, A Monograph* (London, Thames & Hudson, 2005); Jackie Wullschlager, 'Last-chance timeless beauty', *Financial Times,* 12 February 2009; and Cy Twombly, *Blooming, A Scattering of Blossoms and Other Things* (Paris, Editions Gallimard, 2007).

1. Lady Mary Wortley Montagu wrote about the practice in letters circulated to friends and later published as *The Turkish Embassy Letters* (London, Virago, 1994).

2. Flowers & Plants Association/TNS Sofres: figures from Valentine's Day 2008.

3. See David B. Dearinger (ed.), *Paintings and Sculpture in the Collection of the National Academy of Design* (New York, Hudson Hills Press, 2004), vol. 1, pp. 104–5. Church exhibited a watercolour of *Silence* in 1880, and produced a related etching. The oil painting is dated 1884.

4. T. S. Eliot, 'Burnt Norton', *Four Quartets* (London, Faber and Faber, 1959), p. 13. Swinburne's roses are from Algernon Charles Swinburne, *Poems and Ballads, Second Series* (London, Chatto & Windus, 1878), pp. 27–31. See Catherine Maxwell's article listed under the main sources for this chapter. Questioned about his rose symbolism, Eliot replied: 'There are really three roses in the set of poems; the sensuous rose, the socio-political Rose (always appearing with a capital letter) and the spiritual rose: and the three have got in some way to be identified as one.' Maxwell is here quoting Eliot in Helen Gardner, *The Composition of Four Quartets* (London, Faber and Faber, 1978), p. 137.

5. Diane Ackerman, *A Natural History of the Senses* (London, Chapmans, 1990), p. 34.

6. Gustave Caillebotte, *Roses, Garden at Petit-Gennevilliers, c.1886*, and *Landscape near Yerres, c.1877*. The family of rose-grower Jean-François Boursault had owned a property at Yerres, just across the river from the Caillebotte family home.

7. Charles Quest-Ritson traces its first appearance to Edward Bunyard's rose list of 1938–9 in 'The mystery of "Fantin Latour"', *Historic Rose Journal*, no. 38, Autumn 2009, pp. 2–4.

8. Sebastian Smee, 'A dying art', *Daily Telegraph*, 1 June 2004. For details of *Red on Green*'s touring history, see http://collection.britishcouncil.org; and Alfrey et al. (eds), *Art of the Garden*, pp. 182–3.

9. Orville Schell, 'In Switzerland, Wild Roses and an Elegy', *New York Times*, 1 January 1989.

10. Edmond Jaloux identified the lover as the young Egyptian beauty, Mme Eloui Bey; see Jaloux, *La Dernière Amitié de Rainer Maria Rilke* (Paris, Robert Laffont, 1949), pp. 149–53. From her photograph, she looks uncannily like Nefertiti recast as a 1920s starlet.

Chapter Twenty
Why the Rose?

My information on the Europa-Rosarium at Sangerhausen comes from a visit in July 2009 and subsequent correspondence with its Leader, Thomas Pawel. For the Rosarium's history, see *100 Jahre Rosarium Sangerhausen* (Sangerhausen, Rosenstadt Sangerhausen, 2003); and Hella Brumme, 'The Europa-Rosarium at Sangerhausen', in Tommy Cairns (ed.), *Modern Roses XI, The World Encyclopedia of Roses* (San Diego, Academic Press, 2000), pp. xxiii–xxiv. For an example of the Rosarium's contribution to research, see A. V. Roberts et al., 'DNA Amounts of Roses (*Rosa* L.) and Their Use in

Attributing Ploidy Levels', *Plant Cell Reports,* 2009, 28: pp. 61–71.

This chapter draws on many of the sources listed throughout the book; see also J. Ole Becker et al., 'Roses and Emotive Appeal: "If Zeus Chose us a King of the Flowers . . . "', *Acta Horticulturae,* no. 751, August 2007, p. 360; and Monika Joshi, 'The Tradition of the Rose in East Indian Culture and Ayurvedic Medicine', in Frankie Hutton (ed.), *Rose Lore, Essays in cultural history and semiotics* (Lanham, Lexington Books, 2008), pp. 53–62. Andrew Jackson Downing's democratic rose comes from *Rural Essays* (New York, 1853) pp. 25–7; and the rose of dramatists John Fletcher and William Shakespeare from Lois Potter (ed.), *The Two Noble Kinsmen* (The Arden Shakespeare, Third Series, 1997), Act 2, Scene 2. My reading of biblical roses is guided by Ariel Bloch, and poet Chana Bloch, *The Song of Songs* (Berkeley, University of California Press, 1998).

1. When writer Salman Rushdie married his fourth wife, Padma Lakshmi, in Manhattan in April 2004, the floor was strewn with rose petals – *New York Times,* 25 April 2004.

2. In Britain, Bob Dylan's 'Theme Time Radio Hour' on flowers was broadcast in January 2008. For rose songs in Indian movie songs, see Joshi, 'The Tradition of the Rose in East Indian Culture', p. 60. Among the many rose songs Dylan ignored are 'The Yellow Rose of Texas', Janis Joplin's 'Rose', Françoise Hardy's 'Mon Amie la Rose', Joan Baez's 'Barbara Allen', 'Budding Roses' by Dylan's early hero Woody Guthrie, and the instrumental 'My Wild Irish Rose' by Keith Jarrett.

3. See Bloch, *The Song of Songs,* pp. 148–9. The King James Bible usually translates the Hebrew '*shoshannah*' as lily rather than rose (its more usual assumed meaning); other translations include 'lotus', 'hyacinth' and 'lily'. The botanical identity of both '*habasselet*' and '*shoshannah*' is unknown, however.

Index

NOTE: all species roses are listed under '*Rosa*' and all cultivars under 'Rose'; some old rose names are included; page numbers to the illustrations are shown in *italics*.

507